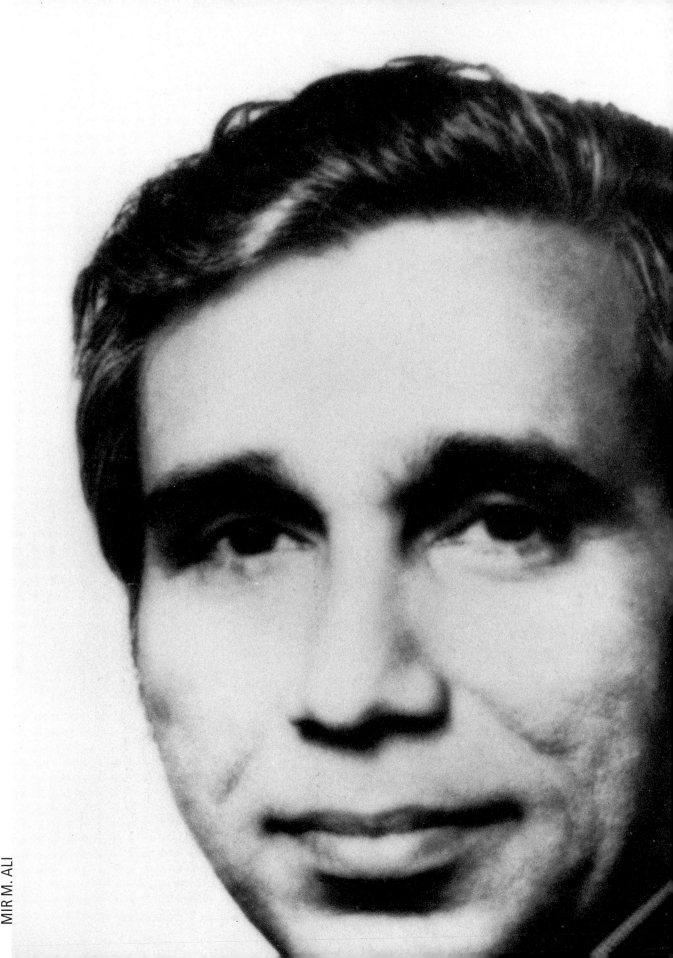

ART OF THE SKYSCRAPER
THE GENIUS OF FAZLUR KHAN
MIR M. ALI

Rizzoli
NEW YORK

Mir M. Ali

ART OF THE SKYSCRAPER

THE GENIUS OF FAZLUR KHAN

First published in the
United States of America in 2001 by
Rizzoli International Publications, Inc.
300 Park Avenue South,
New York, NY 10010

ISBN: 0847823709
LCCN: 2001089820

Designed by Tracey Shiffman
with Eileen Nakada

Distributed by St. Martin's Press
Printed and bound in Singapore

Endpapers: from Kenny Project, Roof
Plan (p. 67)

Page 1:
Fazlur Rahman Khan (1929-1982)
[Courtesy: Skidmore, Owings and Merrill;
photograph by National Photo Serrvice]

This page:
Detail from drawing of
Onterie Center (p. 103)
and detail from photograph of
John Hancock Building
under construction (p. 115)

CONTENTS

Preface 6

Chapter 1 The Man at the Top 8

Chapter 2 University of Illinois 20

Chapter 3 Setting the Stage 28

Chapter 4 Strength by Design 38

Chapter 5 Exploration and Innovation 52

Chapter 6 Adventures in Design and Accolades 84

Chapter 7 The Tower of Strength 106

Chapter 8 A Tube of Tubes 122

Chapter 9 The Gateway to Mecca 136

Chapter 10 The Supreme Integrator 150

Chapter 11 A Votary of Structural Art 162

Chapter 12 The Tall Building Council and Other Affiliations 172

Chapter 13 A Lover of Humanity 180

Chapter 14 Journey to the Eternal World 194

Chapter 15 The Khan Chair and More Recognition 202

Chapter 16 The Spirit Lives On 211

Epilogue 225   References/Bibliography 228   Bibliography of Articles and Papers Authored or Co-authored by Fazlur R. Khan (1954-1982) 230
Brief Chronology 232   Major Projects 232   Honors/Awards/Recognition 233   Student Thesis Projects Supervised at IIT 234
Professional Registration 234   Acknowledgements 235   Postscript 236   Index 238

PREFACE

Fazlur Rahman Khan left behind a legacy of **tall** building design through work spanning a quarter century. His buildings and structures stand in many **of the** major cities of the world. His stature as an innovator in structural engineering is acknowledged internationally. Yet even a cursory assessment will reveal Khan was far more than a gifted structural engineer who devised improved solutions to structural problems—he was a philosopher, a thinker and a prolific writer. He had a keen interest in people, in the arts, and in music and literature. He loved life and lived every moment of it—whether for work, rest, or play. In design, he believed in logic, truth, objectivity, and rationality. He practiced collaboration. He was disciplined, but not reluctant to explore non-traditional ideas. He rejected arbitrariness and obscurity of structural concepts. Khan is the innovator of the tubular principle, a revolutionary concept in tall building design.

Despite outstanding achievements during his rather short life—including the monumental structures that have been described and illustrated in professional magazines and newspapers—no biography or monograph treating his work as a whole has been published. (One book, titled *Technique and Aesthetics in the Design of Tall Buildings*, attends to the proceedings of the Fazlur Rahman Khan Memorial Session—sponsored by the Committee on Aesthetics in Design of the American Society of Civil Engineers [ASCE] during their Annual Fall Meeting in Houston, Texas, in 1983. The book was published by the Institute for the Study of the High-Rise Habitat at Lehigh University in 1986. It records descriptions by colleagues of Khan and his work.)

This book was written with two main objectives: first, to provide a biography of a life worth studying; and second, to describe his projects and accomplishments. I knew Khan personally and worked in a team he led on a project at Skidmore, Owings and Merrill (SOM). My combined academic and professional backgrounds in structural engineering and architecture were helpful for critiquing his projects and appreciating his design philosophy. For me, this book has been a joy to write, not simply because I have been privileged to be in the company of one of the world's greatest structural engineers, but also because his closest associates and friends went out of their way to help me in this endeavor. I had the benefit of knowing and interviewing many who were directly associated with Khan.

The early chapters prepare the reader for Khan's contributions in research, education and professional practice. The book opens with a discussion of his early childhood, youth, education, marriage and his sudden death in Saudi Arabia in 1982. Then it focuses on his post-graduate education at the University of Illinois at Urbana-Champaign, during 1952-55; it also addresses the development of tall buildings in Chicago, starting from the late nineteenth century, and includes a consideration of the circumstances that were to lead Khan to take the leadership in tall building design. Following this, his quest for innovative structural systems and for achieving an optimum clarity of engineering is described.

His innovations resulting in new building forms and systems were facilitated by his research in the SOM's office, where he worked on many major projects. As an educator, he supervised student projects at the Illinois Institute of Technology (IIT), Chicago. His contribution to the classification of tall building structures, considering the effects of scale, is also discussed.

Khan's professional reputation was based on his successful design of noteworthy buildings with unique characteristics. Case studies of his significant high-rise and low-rise building projects show that he had mastery of both types, in both steel and concrete. Instead of following a strictly chronological order, I discuss his concrete and steel high-rise buildings, in separate groups, first; followed by the composite buildings; the low-rise structures; and his two last projects, One Magnificent Mile and the Onterie Center. His most significant projects of large size, such as the John Hancock Center, the Sears Tower, and the Haj Terminal, deserve special treatment; these are individually presented in separate chapters.

Chicago's John Hancock Center and Sears Tower are two of Khan's best known projects. Hancock gained Khan instant international recognition. The complexities of the design process and the need for collaboration between engineers and architects are reviewed. Applications of innovative design, materials and technology that culminated in the Sears Tower are covered, as well. Considerations of urban and social implications of a massive building are emphasized. For both Hancock and Sears, the integration of structural analysis and design, of architectural function and of aesthetics, is explained.

Khan's design concepts for the Haj Terminal project in Jeddah, Saudi Arabia, the largest fabric roof structure in the world, are then reviewed. It comprises tents that reflect the Arab culture and contribute to the spirituality of the annual haj event. It demonstrates Khan's ingenuity and abiltiy to work not only on tall buildings but also on large-scale "permanent" tent structure using a fabric roof.

Khan, a structural engineer by training, grew into a complete designer and a master builder, integrating aesthetics, construction, technology, and the building services systems. With him, it was important to synthesize engineering and architecture through a clear design logic, as was characteristic of such leaders as William LeBaron Jenney, John Wellborn Root, Pier Luigi Nervi. It is indeed helpful here to relate Khan's career to such giants of engineering and architecture.

He also had a prominent role in the shaping of professional organizations. With the Council on Tall Buildings and Urban Habitat (CTBUH), he collaborated to formulate its major policies. Since he was actively involved in this organization from its inception until his death, the book provides an overview of the Council. His other major professional affiliations are also presented.

Changing pace, the humanistic side of Khan as a philosopher-engineer is described. His love for many cultures and his interest in people are portrayed. His deep concern for the United States, the world at large, and his own roots in Bangladesh demonstrate the depth of his feelings.

Khan's untimely death and the circumstances surrounding it are described. Recognition granted posthumously, especially focusing on the establishment of the Fazlur Rahman Khan Chair at Lehigh University, are presented. Finally, the book makes an assessment of the impact that Khan has made on the design and construction industries, as well as on society at large. His legacy is immeasurable.

His major projects, publications, awards and honors, affiliations and his student projects at IIT are listed at the end of the book.

Khan once stated he did not wish to be known as Fazlur Khan; he preferred to be called by his full name, Fazlur Rahman Khan. The Arabic meaning of the name is lost when the middle name is dropped. In essence, I have respected this in the book; however, I have yielded frequently, rather reluctantly, because he is known internationally as Fazlur Khan.

Finally, Khan's success was not solely due to his own genius and acumen, but also to the support and collaboration of his colleagues and associates. The enormous success of his projects was possible because of team work and collaboration with his fellow architects and engineers—that was part of Khan's genius. The contributions by others are credited whenever possible. This is a book about Khan, though, and I naturally tried to focus on *his* life and works.

Mir M. Ali

chapter 1

THE MAN AT THE TOP

"Fazlur Khan is a leader among the world's designers of great buildings. In this new era of the skyscraper, in this time of concern for human safety, comfort, and convenience in high-rise homes and offices, he is a philosophical leader of thought."

—*Engineering News-Record* (*ENR*, 1972)*

Fazlur Khan has been referred to variously as the "Einstein of Structural Engineering," as "philosophical engineer," as "gentle giant." *Engineering News-Record* identified him as "master builder" and "thought leader." The *Hindustan Times* described him as "a towering personality." But perhaps most fitting is the appellation given Khan by *Newsweek* magazine—the "man at the top."

The present-day skyscraper is the story of Fazlur Rahman Khan—a modest, thoughtful and fast-moving engineer's engineer, whose zest for exploration and invention was matched by his belief that there is always a better way to design a building. He rejuvenated tall building design from the conventional rigid frame system to the tubular system by imagining the true response of buildings in three-dimensional space (Khan, 1974a; 1974b). He was simply looking for the logical solution to the problem of developing a structural system that would cost the least but perform the best.

Prior to 1965, the design of structural systems for skyscrapers was done in a conventional way by fastening together beams and columns to create a stiff structural grid for resisting wind forces. Khan was the first person to question this and to tackle the entire issue of structural systems for tall buildings. He devised a whole range of systems: shear wall-frame interaction systems; framed tubes (including bundled tube and tube-in-tube); braced tube; mixed steel-concrete systems; and superframes. Out of all these innovations, he is most well known for his tubular design, which, in its basic skeletal form, uses a building's closely spaced perimeter columns for wind resistance.

What might have been the source of Khan's idea of utilizing a tubular form for tall buildings? Coming from a tropical country he would have been familiar with tall bamboos, which are hollow and tubular, with nodes at intervals. How about a tall building that will be tubular in form like the bamboo—the floors acting as diaphragms thought of as analogous to its nodes? Is it possible that he might have taken lessons from the solid tubular form of silos and grain elevators visible from highways in rural Illinois? We may never know. But there is much that we do know. One plausible explanation that Khan himself offered is that he got this idea almost accidentally and applied it on the DeWitt-Chestnut Apartments in Chicago—a 43-story reinforced concrete building completed in 1965. Khan (1974b) wrote in this regard:

*
This citation and those listed throughout the entirety of this book refer to papers detailed in the References/Bibliography section (pp 228-229).

It was almost accidental that in 1961 the author, working together with his architectural partner, Bruce Graham, stumbled on the idea of a hollow thin walled tube with punched holes as the basic exterior of buildings. Refinement of this first idea of punched hole hollow tube led to the framed tube concept, which was first used on the 43-story DeWitt-Chestnut Apartment building. . . . The basic tube concept was further extended both for concrete and steel, and finally for bearing wall construction leading to a number of new structural systems.

The columns in DeWitt-Chestnut were spaced only at 5 ft. 6 in. (1.7m) on center so that large window openings could be created, eliminating the need for intermittent mullions. Khan's engineering analysis revealed that this was a very efficient three-dimensional structural system, highly resistant against lateral loading.

Joseph Colaco, a close associate of Khan on the John Hancock Center project during the 1960s, and now the President of CBM Engineers in Houston, Texas, agrees that Khan hit upon the tube concept—which he applied to DeWitt-Chestnut—not by design but merely by accident. On the other hand, Hal Iyengar, also a close associate of Khan since 1960, and a former partner of Skidmore, Owings and Merrill (SOM), who worked with him on many projects (including the John Hancock Center and the Sears Tower), has a slightly different viewpoint. He suggests Khan found it by trial and error as the outcome of a natural evolutionary process. He argues that, Khan realized, while exploring efficient structural systems, that to reduce a tall building's lateral sway the perimeter columns should be closely spaced; as well, that the spandrels should be made deeper, until they interfere with architectural function and aesthetics, to create a system resembling an enclosure consisting of pierced-walls. This logically led to the frame tube concept. For the Dewitt-Chestnut Apartment building, without any core, but with closely-spaced perimeter columns, he found that the three-dimensional response of the structure to wind forces contributed to a much larger component of the total sway compared to the shear racking component of frames paralleling the direction of wind. The building designed on this premise was found to be quite stiff. Thus he focused on the exterior facade and concentrated on defining the relationship between the exterior structure and the architectural facade. Both Colaco's and Iyengar's observations point to the fact that the idea of a tube was first seriously investigated and implemented when Khan was working on the Dewitt-Chestnut Apartment building. Even by Khan's own admission he hit upon it not by pure chance but "almost" by accident, implying both Iyengar's and Colaco's viewpoints—that is, partly by accident and partly through exploration.

The tubular concept was explained by Khan (1967) when he wrote:

In a frame structure the total lateral drift due to wind load is caused by three primary factors: bending moments in the girders, contributing about 65 percent of the total deflection; bending moments in the columns, contributing about 15 percent; and axial stresses in the columns due to overturning moments (column shortening effect), which contribute about 20 percent of the total drift. The first two factors represent the frame action, which can be manipulated. The third factor is based on statics and cannot be altered. By simulating an infinitely rigid diaphragm between the columns, the frame-action can be eliminated, in which case the resulting structure will be left with only 20 percent of its original drift. This can be achieved by developing structural systems that act like rigid boxes or tubes composed of the exterior columns.

He carried the framed tube concept further when he designed the John Hancock Center, a diagonally braced tube building; and, for the Sears Tower, he bundled nine tube modules, creating an efficient, rigid structure. As the direct result of his extraordinary work, Khan's name is permanently associated with the tubular design of tall buildings.

▲ ▼

Some notables who can be compared with Fazlur Khan are Pier Luigi Nervi, Robert Maillart, Felix Candela, Heinz Isler, to name a few; and lately, Peter Rice and Santiago Calatrava. All of them have a common link, which is: the desire to connect structural engineering to architecture. They all believe in harmony between structural form and aesthetics. They all recognize that simplicity and logic bring forth, from buildings, elegance, discipline, and placid expression. For Khan, structural logic was all-important to architecture.

Both Nervi and Maillart deeply influenced Khan's thinking in regard to connecting structure and aesthetics—but perhaps even more so than these was the influence on Khan of Mies van der Rohe. His building projects epitomize a structuralist approach to architecture. His writings also bear this out. In *Two Glass Skyscrapers*, Mies wrote (Johnson, 1978):

> Skyscrapers reveal their bold structural patterns during construction. Only then does the gigantic steel web seem impressive. When the outer walls are put in place, the structural system, which is the basis of all artistic design, is hidden by a chaos of meaningless and trivial forms. . . . Instead of trying to solve the new problems with old forms, we should develop the new forms from the very nature of the new problems.
>
> We can use the new structural principles most clearly when we use glass in place of the outer walls, which is feasible today since in a skeleton building these outer walls do not actually carry weight. The use of glass imposes new solutions.

In a 1950 address at the Illinois Institute of Technology (IIT) in Chicago, Mies further rhapsodized (Johnson, 1978):

> Technology is rooted in the past.
> It dominates the present and tends
>   into the future.
> . . . . . .
> Technology is far more than a method,
> it is a world in itself.

As a method it is superior in almost every respect.
But only where it is left to itself as in
gigantic structures of engineering, there
technology reveals its true nature.
…   …
Wherever technology reaches its real fulfillment,
it transcends into architecture.
It is true that architecture depends on facts,
but its real field of activity is in the realm
of significance.
I hope you will understand that architecture
has nothing to do with the invention of forms.
…   …
Architecture depends on its time.
It is the crystallization of its inner structure,
the slow unfolding of its form.
That is the reason why technology and architecture
are so closely related.
Our real hope is that they grow together,
that someday the one be the expression of
the other.

▲ ▼

Khan's ascent to the stature of being a leader in tall building design is rather surprising to many. It is significant to note that when Khan left Bangladesh (then East Pakistan) in 1952 for higher studies in the United States, he had seen nothing that could be called high-rise, nor even mid-rise. Yet, coming from such a background, he revolutionized the design of tall buildings and became internationally known for his skill in engineering design and architecture. People of his own family and those closely associated with him acknowledge that despite his professional stature and fame, he remained humble. Although he eventually became a reputed American structural engineer, he never forgot his roots and remained a true Bangladeshi at heart.

Fazlur R. Khan was born on April 3, 1929 in Dhaka, Bangladesh (Bengal of then British India). His father, Abdur Rahman Khan was from the district of Faridpur in Bengal. He was a brilliant mathematician, a well-known scholar, author, and educator. He held a high position in the government as an administrator in the department of education. At one time, he became the Principal of Teachers' Training College in Dhaka; and later the Principal of Jagannath College also in Dhaka. Subsequently, he was named Rector of Jagannath College where he was instrumental in completing the construction of a two-story science building and launching the Bachelor of Science degree program. In recognition of his service and achievement, the college administration honored him by naming one of its student dormitories after him. In further acknowledgment, he was granted the title of *Khan Bahadur* (honorable hero) by the British government for his contributions to public education.

Apart from translating the Qur'an and the Traditions of Prophet Muhammad in Bengali, Abdur Rahman Khan wrote a number of books—such as: *A Rational Arithmatic*; *Principles and Methods of Teaching*; *The Haj Journey* (in Bengali); *My Life* (in Bengali), a book of essays; and a textbook on algebra. His books engineering was also according to his father's wishes. He wanted to study either physics, a subject that he liked because of its mystical aspects and esoteric nature, or engineering. His father suggested that engineering would be a better choice because it demanded strict discipline and rigor. Of course, at that time, the practical engineering challenges facing the newly independent nations of India and Pakistan overshadowed the challenges of a classical scientific subject like physics. Moreover, Fazlur Khan, like his father, was a born mathematician—but with a flair for practical and mechanical tasks. Thus engineering became his natural choice, and he never expressed any regrets about this decision.

He began his engineering education in 1946, and graduated—from Bengal Engineering College in Shibpur, a suburb of Calcutta, India—in 1950, with the highest ranking in his undergraduate civil engineering class. His Bachelor of Science in Engineering degree was, however, awarded by the University of Dacca (now called University of Dhaka), East Pakistan, after he moved to the new country of Pakistan, carved out of India in 1947. The Bengal Engineering College was established in the nineteenth century, and its civil engineering program is one of the oldest in Asia.

M. Mujbur Rahman, Chief Engineer (retired) of Bangladesh Steel and Engineering Corporation was a classmate and close friend of Khan at Presidency College in Calcutta and Bengal Engineering College. Rahman recalled Khan's depth of observation during his student life. Rahman recounted the following incident: "While we were eating together in the dining room of Heaton House European Hostel, Fazlu instructed the bearer to change my plate. I asked him why he did so. He said, 'there is a hairline crack in your plate where bacteria may grow'. Because of such precision of Khan's observation, the expression 'perfect like the Taj Mahal, correct like Khan' went around about him in student circles." Rahman further reminisced about Khan's study habits. "Most of the students studied till late night but Fazlu would take a long time in the shower singing songs, and he went to sleep early. I asked him how he managed it. He replied, 'I carefully listen to teachers in class, then look up the same thing in the book, then think about it and sleep'. I learned that a genius is both born and built."

Following his graduation, Khan's professional life started in August, 1950, with the position of Assistant Engineer with the Design Division, Communications and Buildings (C&B) Department, Government of East Pakistan—where he worked on the design of reinforced concrete bridges and buildings. In May 1951, he was offered a teaching position at the Ahsanullah Engineering College, a college affiliated with the University of Dacca. He stayed there until 1952, when he was awarded a Fulbright Scholarship for graduate studies at the University of Illinois at Urbana-Champaign. During the next three years there he earned enough credits for two Master of Science degrees—one in structural engineering and the other in theoretical and applied mechanics—leading, finally, to a doctorate in structural engineering in 1955.

Upon completing the doctoral degree program, Khan joined SOM in Chicago. It so happened that while he was considering several offers from top engineering firms across the country, he came across a friend on the street in Chicago who worked at SOM. During his conversation with this friend, he came to know that SOM was involved in a few interesting projects and had some openings. That prompted him to go to the SOM office immediately. As he recalled later, he simply walked off the street on impulse and requested an interview. After about five minutes, he was hired, and to his surprise, given total responsibility for the design of seven highway and railroad bridges ordered by the U.S. Air Force Academy (Civil Engineering, 1980). Khan was startled by this offer, and he immediately accepted. "Without such opportunities," he said, "life doesn't move. You have to grab them." Thus he began his long and productive association with SOM.

After working as a structural engineer for two years Khan returned to his home country in 1957 to accept the position of Director of the country's Building Research Center, but at the last moment the offer was withdrawn because of some "political deal going on." He started doing consulting work after his return to Dhaka. Soon he was offered an attractive position as executive engineer with the Karachi Development Authority in Pakistan. He worked there as a technical advisor to the chief engineer's office but felt he was too involved in routine administrative work. He sensed that he could not apply his technical abilities there as he would like to. Having only status without the expected professional challenge made him return to SOM in 1960, after a brief correspondence with his former employer.

The same year, during his tenure in Karachi Development Authority, he married Liselotte Anna Olga Turba of Vienna, Austria—an artist with a degree in biology. Liselotte, who lived in the United States, was divorced with a son, Martin, from her previous marriage; and she was a Christian—a potential difficulty, as she might not be accepted readily by Khan's family, who were conservative and Muslim. Khan knew this and went to see his father to present his case for approval. Even though he was very close to his father, he was hesitant to propose it himself, not being sure how his father might react. He asked his cousin, Zeaul Huq, to speak to his father on his behalf. When Khan was waiting outside, Huq entered his father's room and disclosed to him Khan's plan to marry Liselotte. On hearing this, Khan's father, a deeply religious man, uttered the following words: "Marriages are made in the heaven." The following year the Khans had a daughter—Yasmin—who later followed in the footsteps of her father and became a structural engineer.

Khan's family wanted him to return home after completing his doctoral studies, and settle there. This wish was not fulfilled; nevertheless, Abdur Rhaman Khan eventually accepted Fazlur's absence from home, when he became aware of his son's tremendous success abroad.

▲ ▼

"This is your beginning and my end.
    The flow (of life) continues mixing both of us"
                    —Opening verse of a Tagore song

This Bengali lyric by poet Rabindranath Tagore, carved on a gravestone in Chicago's Graceland Cemetery, is a fitting epitaph for Fazlur Rahman Khan. It was a favorite of Khan's, and he used to sing it often. His friend Prabhas Nag sang it during the eulogies before Khan's burial on April 2, 1982.

Khan died on March 27 in Jeddah, Saudi Arabia, while on an around-the-world business trip. Present for his burial, I vividly remember the occasion. His body, shrouded in white wrapping cloth, was placed in an open coffin—following Islamic tradition. It was a cloudy day with a light drizzle. We offered our prayers and paid last respects to him; his body was lowered into the grave and covered with earth. People who gathered there began to disperse. As I was leaving, a middle-aged woman whom I did not know started a conversation with me about Khan. She sighed deeply and said, "Today we put down a great man."

The whole day I reflected on the fact that our lives are full of uncertainty. When I had visited with Khan before he left on his overseas trip, I had not the slightest idea that it would be the last time I would see him alive. Here was a man who had revolutionized the design of high-rise buildings, who knew so well how to ingeniously put together the structural elements of a tall building for achieving optimum strength and stiffness so it could stand up against the enormous natural forces of gravity and wind. His accomplishments in structural design in only 25 years are almost unparalleled by any account. Yet, he could not withstand the brutal clutches of death that snatched away his vitality and spirit so abruptly, without notice, at a premature age of 52—when he was responding to the call of duty. If such is the fate of a man who was sent to earth with a clear mission of serving society, of contributing to human civilization, where does the average man or woman stand in the grand scheme of things?

At the funeral home, at the cemetery, and at the offices of SOM where he was a partner, I saw the sad faces of his friends, relatives, colleagues, and well-wishers. These faces told me how he was loved and admired for his modest and gentle nature. From my brief contacts with him, from 1980 to 1982, I witnessed this and learned that he had malice toward none.

Curiously enough, a strange and mystic sense of immortality seems to surround Khan through the monumental structures that he designed and that now stand tall in Chicago and in other cities looking up to the Heavens, announcing the glory of his spirit, transcending the unrelenting passage of time.

∎

Left: House of Fazlur R. Khan's father at Aga Masih Lane,
Dhaka, Bangladesh, where Khan was born and raised as a child
[Courtesy: Asif Iqbal]

Family picture of Fazlur Khan with his father, brothers, and sister.
Standing: Mahbubur R. Khan (left); Fazlur R. Khan (right).
Sitting: Abdur R. Khan (center); Masuda Khan (left); Zillur R. Khan (right) (circa 1947)
[Courtesy: Faizur R. Khan]

17

Abdur Rahman Khan, father of Fazlur Khan (1963)
[Courtesy: Faizur Rahman Khan]

Liselotte Khan with daughter Yasmin (circa 1962)
[Courtesy: Faizur Rahman Khan]

Fazlur Khan with Chester Siess (circa 1958) at 402 West Nevada, Urbana
[Courtesy: Chester P. Siess]

chapter 2

UNIVERSITY OF ILLINOIS

"It is not always easy to pin-point the most important reason for my occasional successes in innovations . . . I have come to realize that the three years I spent at the University of Illinois first under the advisorship of Thomas Shedd, but more significantly under the research environment and advisorship of Chester Siess have indeed been the most significant and responsible factors in shaping my attitudes and approach to structural design."

—Fazlur R. Khan (1981)

Fazlur R. Khan went to the University of Illinois at Urbana-Champaign in 1952 to pursue graduate studies in structural engineering. He was attracted to this institution because of its reputation worldwide in the field of engineering. This reputation was due to the names of renowned people like Hardy Cross, Thomas Shedd, N. M. Newmark, and Ralph Peck. The Civil Engineering Department of this university had received worldwide recognition not just because of the reputation of these engineering faculty members and others like Talbot, Richart, Wilson, and Westergaard, but also because of the graduates it produced and the pioneering work done at the Structural Engineering Research Laboratory in both reinforced concrete and structural steel. Between the two world wars, it became the main center of reinforced concrete research. When I was an undergraduate engineering student at the Ahsanullah Engineering College (affiliated with University of Dhaka, and later upgraded to East Pakistan University of Engineering and Technology in 1962) during 1960-64, I had already heard of the University of Illinois primarily through the names of Hardy Cross for his moment distribution and column analogy methods; Ralph Peck for his well-known textbook on foundation design, co-authored with Hanson and Thornburn; Thomas Shedd for his textbook on structural analysis co-authored with Vawter; and N. M. Newmark for his international fame at that time. Also, an excellent textbook on structural analysis by C. K. Wang of the Department of Architecture at this university was well known to undergraduate students of civil engineering.

Khan departed for Urbana-Champaign from Dhaka, an old city in the heart of Bangladesh (formerly East Pakistan). He had studied engineering at Bengal Engineering College in Calcutta, India, and moved to Dhaka after the creation of East Pakistan, the eastern region carved out of former Bengal, a province of British India (India and Pakistan became independent from the British rule in August, 1947). He taught at the local engineering college in Dhaka for two years and could not, perhaps, ever adjust to the reality of a divided Bengal, and by extension a divided India, as is apparent from his feelings for and association with Indians and Pakistanis alike in later days.

In the early 1950s, Dhaka (whose ancient name was Jahangirnagar, named after Mughal Indian Emperor Jahangir) was just an old historical city with ancient building structures and was

20

often referred to as a "city of mosques." Most were brick buildings built primarily for residences, and also for some offices and institutions. High-rise construction was totally absent. Calcutta was a larger and more populous city then; there was hardly any building in Dhaka that could even be called mid-rise. Dhaka had a population of less than half a million. Noticeable changes in the population pattern began in the early and mid-1950s, when large-scale migration to Dhaka from other towns and rural areas took place. Multiple three-story, walk-up housing complexes were built in Azimpur and Motijheel areas to meet the urgent housing needs. But there were no buildings over three stories at that time. It is with this background that Khan left Dhaka in 1952.

I can relate to this well from my own experience. When I left Dhaka for Canada in September, 1970, it still belonged to East Pakistan. By that time the city had grown considerably. The population had surged to about 2.5 million and several buildings were built as tall as 10-stories. The foundation of the 27-story Eastern Federal Union Insurance building on DIT Avenue had been laid and its construction just had started. Because of the ensuing civil war with Pakistan, the construction was interrupted and only completed in the mid-1970s after Bangladesh became independent. Upon arriving in Canada, I was struck by the several majestic tall buildings in Montreal and Toronto—particularly the Toronto-Dominion Bank designed by Mies van der Rohe. It was at the University of Waterloo, where I studied in the early 1970s, that I first heard about Khan. His name was being repeatedly mentioned in various professional magazines of engineering and architecture.

It is not known how Khan got his admission to the University of Illinois, since it was extremely competitive for foreigners—particularly for those coming from a new country like Pakistan. But it can be guessed that he was accepted because of his top academic record and that the Bengal Engineering College was well known by then. Moreover, this university, like many other research universities, would admit a large number of foreign students in those days—a tradition that still continues. It is almost certain, however, that Khan chose the University of Illinois for its great reputation in civil engineering. Although Khan came from a relatively underdeveloped country at that time, he had already developed a worldwide vision because of his familiarity with the West and other parts of the world through reading—especially from books on philosophy and psychology.

Because of Khan's ambitious nature and his determination to excel, he had a burning desire to work with someone with a good reputation. He lucked out when Professor Thomas Shedd agreed to be his advisor. Shedd advised him to take the types of courses that would enable him to view structural engineering from multiple perspectives and help him gain adroitness in structural analysis and design. Khan took courses on structural theory and steel design with Shedd in addition to others in concrete design and foundations. Shedd was a man of practical interests and would often discuss the evolution of the codes of practices. He also emphasized the need for structural engineers to thoroughly learn the principles of mechanics. Khan took courses with Ralph Peck, who taught the otherwise mysterious subject of soil mechanics in a lucid and interesting way, giving his instruction a practical orientation. He was deeply influenced by Peck, which helped him develop a keen interest in foundation design, and he later came up with innovative foundation design concepts for some of his major buildings.

Under the guidance of Shedd, Khan also became convinced that to be a good structural engineer a thorough grounding in theoretical and applied mechanics would be essential. The mystic nature of the unseen, but surely existent, forces in structures and the stresses in materials can be appreciated and the associated complexity may be grasped only through an in-depth under-standing of the mechanics of the structure and its material behav-ior. Only through such visualization of immanent forces flowing through a structure can a structural engineer have a feel for the complex and intricate structural response to loads and anticipate possible problems that the structure may be vulnerable to. Khan took two important courses with James Smith, who taught by looking at real-life problems of material behavior in great detail.

Khan took his concrete courses with Chester Siess. Even though Siess was experienced in teaching for only four years at that time, Khan noticed that he always encouraged critical think-ing. He observed the amazing and unique capability of Siess to "bring to light the normal and the special aspects of behavior of reinforced and prestressed concrete under different conditions of loading." About his experience of Siess's teaching method and how he was influenced by it, Khan (1981) wrote:

> To me this aspect of his teaching proved to be much more important and fundamental than cramming the theoretical formulas used in design or analysis. He (Siess) taught the sub-ject of reinforced concrete, not primarily with a series of so many equations and formulas, but through the critical evalua-tion of research, both theoretical and experimental, which formed the foundation for those equations and formulas. By the time I had taken most of his courses over a period of two years, I think I had begun to develop my own critical approach to the key aspects of reinforced and prestressed con-crete behavior, and in fact of all structures, vis-a-vis, the elas-tic, plastic, and ultimate strength, creep, shrinkage and temperature effects. Come to think of it, the awareness of the interrelation of these characteristics has indeed been the foun-dation of my own contributions to structural innovations.

Khan did extremely well in his preliminary examination. "His performance in the prelim was unmatchably superb" said Chester Siess. It is clear that Khan's contact with Shedd, Peck, Siess, and others at the University of Illinois had a tremendous influence on him for his forthcoming professional life. Because his interest was to do research on prestressed concrete, Shedd suggested that he should seek Siess to be his advisor for the research program. Siess agreed. Narbey Khachaturian, another professor in the Civil Engineering Department, acted as co-advisor and research director. The title of Khan's thesis was *Analytical Study of Relations among the Various Design Criteria for Rectangular Prestressed Concrete Beams.* The thesis commit-tee was comprised of C. P. Siess, N. Khachaturian, R. B. Peck, T. C. Shedd, and J. O. Smith. Siess was in charge of the thesis.

I had an opportunity to meet Chester Siess for the first time on December 18, 1997, at his retirement home in a suburb of

Champaign. I already knew his name as an authority on concrete structures. Siess fondly remembered Khan as one of his brightest students who was a "gentleman" and an "engineering genius." He recalled that Faz and Lisl came to his daughter's wedding. He pointed his finger to a collage of artwork by Lisl Khan hanging on his living room wall, which was signed by her and dated 1968.

Chester Siess thus became the next person with whom Khan worked closely after Shedd. He adapted quickly to the academic and research environment created by Siess and availed himself of the unique opportunity to develop himself as an avid researcher. He began looking at research in a broader perspective than the thing in itself and realized that such an outlook helped him to face and delve into any challenge with a certain positive approach due to his trained and observant mindset. He was impressed by the experimental research environment of the civil engineering department and the culture surrounding it. He felt that such an environment offered the students a real world feeling for engineering materials, which could pave the way for conceiving new structural systems and to innovatively design traditional structural components. Khan's research did not involve experimental work, yet by being part of the lab environment, he was greatly influenced by it and was fully convinced of its importance in real-life situations.

When Khan discussed his research possibilities with Siess, he was given the choice of any topic that he felt comfortable with within the realm of his interest in prestressed concrete and analytical work. It is not clear why he was particularly interested in prestressed concrete. But it seems Khan was probably impressed by the novelty and innovative nature of this combination of concrete and steel—a concept that was still very new, and by the ingenuity of Eugene Freyssinet—who was still active. In fact, Freyssinet's first major prestressed concrete bridge spanning 180 ft. (55m) over Marne River in France, the Luzancy Bridge, was built earlier in 1946. Freyssinet demonstrated how the tensile stresses in a concrete beam could be eliminated and, in fact, its tensile zone could be put into compression by using high strength cables or strands stretched in tension through a hole along the entire length of the beam and anchored at each end. A designer can skillfully manipulate the bending behavior of the beam with the use of prestressing technique in concrete and overcome its weakness in tension. Of course, Freyssinet got the idea of prestressed concrete in the early 20th century, but he seriously began to develop his concepts on prestressing in 1921, when he completed the 64-meter-span, two-hinged arch railroad bridge over the Sambre, known as the Candelier Bridge (Billington, 1983). Although reinforced concrete was well established at that time, prestressed concrete was viewed as revolutionary because of the simplicity of the underlying concept and the practical benefits of prestressing to minimize cracking in concrete, and thereby resulting in lightweight structures. Also, its potential for bridges, parking garages, and other long-span structures was recognized. Khan could, perhaps, envision its future possibilities, and appreciate the technical genius of Freyssinet.

Khan proposed the development of an optimum design method for prestressed concrete structures to Chester Siess, who asked him a few incisive questions and accepted the proposal. One day when Khan and a few others were discussing certain aspects of his approach to optimization in the presence of Siess, his logic and the way he developed a new set of equations for optimization were questioned by someone in the group who asked Khan why he was not deriving his equations following the methods used by Freyssinet or Magnel. Siess responded to this on behalf of Khan by saying that the problem with reading too many books may be that one is not able to think independently. He wanted Khan to keep on thinking independently and not follow someone else's approach to the same problem. This remark by Siess left a lasting impression on Khan's mind.

In his doctoral thesis, Khan, in his way of original thinking, observed that there was a need to establish practical relationships among the significant variables in the design of prestressed concrete beams. In a design office, the typical trend is to design for multiple criteria that demand considerably more intuition and skill on the part of the designer of prestressed concrete structures than is required in the design of reinforced concrete structures. Thus the designer must have recourse to detailed formulas relating the various criteria or must adopt a trial and error procedure. Khan developed four optimum design criteria and derived optimum design expressions for each criterion in terms of dimensionless quantities involving the dead and live load moments, the concrete and steel stresses at different stages of loading, and the gross steel percentage (Khan, 1955). He further established relationships among the allowable concrete and steel stresses and the minimum factors of safety against cracking and failure. He also presented these relationships in a graphical form for clear understanding. If allowable stresses and other relevant data are given for design, the charts could be used to determine directly the probable minimum margins of safety against cracking and failure. He presented a total of 43 figures in his thesis out of which a large number of charts were for different design criteria and for different conditions and stages of loading. These charts were the harbinger of many future design aids developed by others for prestressed concrete design. He also carried out in his thesis a critical study of five code specifications for prestressed concrete that were prevailing at that time.

Based on analytical studies, Khan concluded that definite interrelationships existed among the different variables and the safety factors against cracking and failure. He also found that the design expressions and the factors of safety were very sensitive to the loss factor defined as the ratio of stress in steel reinforcement after all losses have occurred to that at transfer of prestress. This ratio should be predicted with maximum possible accuracy. He further concluded that specifications for the design of prestressed concrete structures could be simplified by eliminating redundant or incompatible requirements.

Khan got enough course credit by taking courses in both civil engineering and theoretical and applied mechanics simultaneously to get two Master's degrees in two years. He completed his Ph.D. thesis in the very short time of one year after that. When Siess was asked about how Khan managed to get three graduate degrees in three years and how the Civil Engineering Department allowed that to happen, he replied, "Faz was unusually brilliant and we could make an exception for someone like him."

Khan maintained contact with the University of Illinois even after he was well established professionally at SOM. He would occasionally use the lab facilities of the University for testing his innovative structural systems. For example, in the early 1960s when he was working on the 38-story reinforced concrete Brunswick Building in Chicago, an early project, he faced the challenge of designing a transfer perimeter girder at the second floor level that would carry the closely spaced perimeter columns (see Chapter 6). The large widely spaced columns at the ground level would carry the loads from the transfer girder. The extremely high loads that were transferred downward to this girder demanded a deep and massive solid concrete section. Khan contacted Siess at the University of Illinois where he was supervising a research program in deep beams. His concern was about shear in the girder on such an unusually large and deep girder carrying unusually heavy loads applied under different load conditions. A 1:12 scale model of the two-span girder was tested. The test program defined the failure mode and demonstrated that the girder could carry about 25 percent more than the theoretical load capacity. Thus Khan was satisfied with his design and thought it to be efficient for the building.

Siess felt that Khan had the uncanny ability to anticipate problems in his design. Until he was convinced that all such problems had been fully addressed and resolved he would postpone completion of his design. Siess quipped to me: "I tried another exactly same model of the deep beam without any web reinforcing in it but didn't tell Faz about it. This model beam carried the same load as the other one." When asked why he did that, he replied that in such a deep beam the arching action controls the behavior and web reinforcing is not really needed for structural strength. He just wanted to verify that. Siess added, "I didn't tell Faz because I don't recommend unreinforced concrete for anything. The web reinforcing should have been used anyway."

Khan had some precast prestressed concrete bridge girders load-tested at the University of Illinois. When he was working on the John Hancock Center in Chicago, he wanted a joint test for the building at the University of Illinois. This was done in 1965 in collaboration with Professor William Munse. When I asked Munse about the purpose of this test, he replied "the test specimen was a slice of the big spliced joints along the diagonal braces that we tested to find the tensile strength of bolted splice connections."

Several years later, in 1975, Khan was invited by the Department of Architecture of the University of Illinois at Urbana-Champaign to give a special seminar on "Historical developments of High-Rise Building Design and Construction," which was recorded on a videotape. It is an excellent 90-minute presentation outlining the history of tall buildings and their evolution influenced by many factors such as urbanization, population growth, industrialization, and technological advancement. It is a good educational aid for instructors in architecture and structural engineering. Khan also gave a number of seminars at the Civil Engineering Department of the University. I had met and spoken with Siess on a few occasions to talk about Khan. He was one of the people who deeply influenced Khan's career and professionalism. When I first called him to talk with him about Khan, he invited me to his residence the very same day. When we met, he was fully prepared and while he was narrating several incidents—related to Khan—he gave me the ACI publication SP-72, which was intended to be a tribute to Siess on his retirement containing a collection of papers that were presented in "Three Sessions to Celebrate C. P. Siess' Contributions to Research, Education, and Practice," at a special event held on November 1, 1979 in Washington, D.C. This publication contains a paper by Khan (1981) that gives the reader a rare glimpse into his student life at the University of Illinois.

One incident that Khan mentioned in this paper and that Siess personally related to me was about Joseph Colaco. Khan was in the midst of designing the 100-story John Hancock Center in Chicago, and attempting to develop an appropriate design philosophy for this innovative steel structure. He was looking for a top-notch structural engineer with a Master's degree to join his team. When Khan called Siess at the University, Colaco was sitting in front of Siess in his office. At that time Colaco was in the final stage of his Ph.D. degree program. Siess suggested Colaco, whom he considered an outstanding student. He was full of admiration for him and told Khan that he would be an asset for his team. Since Siess was a specialist in concrete, Khan guessed and suggested to him that Colaco must be doing his research in concrete and "made the great mistake" of expressing his reservations about Colaco's ability and suitability for getting involved in such a large structural steel building project. Siess didn't hesitate a second to answer by asking Khan what his research subject was when he did his doctoral work. This was a rude awakening for Khan and he recalled an earlier encounter that he had with Siess many years back. He reminded himself once again that in the final analysis, research is not "the thing in itself, but the process of sharpening a person's critical thinking, strengthening the tenacity to search for an answer and indeed broadening one's approach to new problems." Khan immediately accepted Siess's suggestion and was able to convince Colaco to join his group. Joe Colaco worked with Khan at SOM for several years and is now a successful innovative structural engineer in his own right. Colaco himself also narrated this story to me at a later date.

During our conversation Siess also described a few other projects, including the foundation design of the John Hancock Center in Chicago and One Shell Plaza in Houston, that Khan had consulted with him about. He explained some of these projects in vivid detail with specific information on the various dimensions and other factual data.

Khan was also supervised in his research by his co-advisor Narbey Khachaturian, who narrated to me how he met Khan on the first day of his arrival at the campus as a graduate student from Bangladesh. Khachaturian was then a very young faculty member and did not yet have the full standing to supervise Ph.D. students. At that time, in the 1950s, graduate faculty members were classified in three categories: limited standing, that is, those who could teach 400-level advanced courses; Master's standing, those who could teach all courses and supervise Master's students; and full standing, those who could also supervise doctoral students. Only a few senior professors had the full standing status who could supervise Ph.D. students as advisors.

Khachaturian, although he was not the chief advisor, was constantly involved with Khan's thesis direction and research progress and attended all the meetings related to his dissertation. He recalled that Khan developed some equations representing the optimization criteria for prestressed concrete design before and after the loss of prestress as part of his research. Khan was, according to him, "a man of aspirations" who would always like to improve the status quo, the common attribute of all innovators. He always worked on his research totally independently like the students at "European universities" and presented his ideas in the meetings more as a matter of consultation and informing his superiors of what he was doing rather than seeking a direction from them. Khachaturian even went so far as to say that he himself was inspired to carry out his own future work in prestressed concrete after observing Khan's passion for it. Subsequently, he published a monograph on prestressed concrete design in which he extended and updated many of the ideas and design charts that Khan developed earlier in his doctoral thesis. According to him, Khan liked to "play with ideas of optimization" in different ways but always searched for truth. Unlike many other students, Khan did not want to get too involved in mathematical analysis and other esoteric approaches—although he was good at it— but rather he would like to develop in a pragmatic way efficient structural design solutions that would offer economy, performance, and elegance of the structure. Khachaturian told me further that he had been in touch with Khan during his SOM days, and he believed that Khan was one of the best structural engineers in America. He felt that Khan was at ease with the architectural culture and respected aesthetic values in buildings, which, in turn, gained him the respect of architects. Khachaturian also observed that Khan was an intuitive builder and if he (Khachaturian) designed a building, he would certainly like to run it by Khan who could give valuable insight by just looking at the design without ploughing through the calculations.

When Khachaturian was asked what else he thought of Khan as a person, he replied that he worked with Khan once regarding the development of some new concepts and criteria for fire prevention in buildings, and discovered that Khan was a "profound thinker." According to him, Khan had no particular pet topic. "He (Khan) was a universal man, a man who would look at all aspects—social, architectural, aesthetic, you name it—the entire universe. Khan was also a very good and perceptive listener. He could grasp very quickly what you would tell him. He had that unusual mental ability."

A program at a university is as good as its faculty and students make it. Faculty members are the precious resources of a university. Undoubtedly, the University of Illinois had a great impact on Khan's professional life, as acknowledged by Khan himself. But then the University of Illinois has produced thousands of fine engineers. Some people are born as movers and shakers, with a mission in life. He was one of these uncommon men who came to this earth to revolutionize tall building design and appeared in the sky of the building profession as a shooting star, or perhaps a comet, for a short time.

chapter 3

SETTING THE STAGE

"The idea of architecture coming out of the structure is a very old one, and it has persisted throughout architectural history. Perhaps the grandest period of the structure being so intertwined with the architecture that they are inseparable, is the Gothic. Of course, there are other ideas about architecture, and there was an equally great period in the Renaissance where great artists did buildings. That is another way to approach building, but our approach, and we think it appropriate for today, is the structural one."

—Myron Goldsmith (1986)

When Fazlur Rahman Khan joined the renowned Chicago architectural firm SOM in 1955 after completing his education at the University of Illinois, America was undergoing a major urban reform following the end of World War II. Buildings were experiencing a major transformation, evolving into a new form and architectural vocabulary. Even though Chicago had been the birthplace of high-rise buildings with the contributions and design innovations of such architects and engineers as William Le Baron Jenney, Louis Sullivan, John Wellborn Root, and Daniel Burnham into late nineteenth and early twentieth centuries, New York City took the initiative in high-rise construction starting with 1920. Following World War II, however, that leadership returned to Chicago.

Khan's appearance on the Chicago scene as a prominent figure in the 1960s and 1970s can be logically viewed in a historical context. Anyone familiar with the history of building construction knows that many advancements in building practices originated from Chicago. Randall (1949) listed these practices as: balloon construction of frame buildings, fireproof

**28
28**

construction, the rational proportioning of the areas of isolated footings, the use of steel grillages to secure shallow footings, the Chicago caisson, the evolution of skeleton construction and wind bracing, and the development of reinforced concrete construction. Randall wrote, "great credit must be given to the outstanding engineers and architects whose vision, ingenuity, and inventions led to the development of present-day building construction." He further observed, "Except for occasional comparatively dormant periods of economic depression, the city has served as a large-scale research and testing laboratory; the detailed history of its buildings represents a continuous and successful battle for improved construction upon soil that has presented difficult problems" (Randall, 1949).

Jenney, a visionary engineer, commonly referred to as the "father of the skyscraper," is considered the founder of the "First Chicago School." A civil engineer by training, he practiced architecture in Chicago. His engineering background, like Khan's, influenced his design. Root, another leader of the First Chicago School, demonstrated that visual design of a building could be made effective in conjunction with its structural expression. Louis Sullivan, sometimes referred to as the "prophet of tall buildings," is acclaimed by architectural historians primarily because of his all-encompassing architectural background. Jenney's tall buildings, however, preceded those by Sullivan.

Although greatly influenced by European architectural schemes and theory, the tall building as a type blossomed fully in two American cities—Chicago and New York. The skyscraper continues to remain the preeminently American building type, even though it has become more universal now. Skyscrapers are now found in all continents, and particularly in Asia.

Several factors led to the growth and development of high-rise buildings in Chicago in the late 19th century. These included the increase in value of urban space, a strong economy, and the appearance on the scene of a few gifted engineers and architects (Newhouse, 1992). After the Great Chicago Fire of October 9, 1871 destroyed some 18,000 buildings valued at $192 million there was an immediate need to rebuild much of the downtown with buildings of more permanent construction. Most multi-story buildings of that time were of masonry following old historical models. The principles of metal framing and its architectural expression were not yet fully known, although the invention of the Bessemer process in 1855 had made steel-framed buildings possible. The need for more urban space and the destruction resulting from the devastating fire created an urgent demand for new and superior structural solutions for high-rise commercial buildings. The use of the skeletal metal frame brought significant change to the construction industry with the development of such buildings in the wake of the catastrophe. The fire, disastrous as it was, provided both impetus and space, which contributed to Chicago's becoming the birthplace of modern skyscrapers (Bennett, 1995).

Following the fire, there was rapid growth and economic prosperity in the city of Chicago. As a result, there was a rapid growth in population. In the year of the fire, the city's population was 300,000. In the decade that followed, it rose to 500,000. By 1890 it had grown to 1.1 million and by 1900, it reached 1.7 million. This unprecedented growth of the city's inhabitants was paralleled in the construction of new and larger buildings. An important development around this time that offered an added impetus to the construction industry was the World's Fair in Chicago, initially known as the World's Columbian Exposition. It was conceived from a national desire to commemorate the four-hundredth anniversary of the discovery of America by Columbus. Originally scheduled for the year 1892, it actually opened in 1893. The World's Fair was a huge undertaking, propped up by a popular enthusiasm. Architects and builders took their roles of pre-eminence, and the leading figures in architecture and engineering, such as Daniel H. Burnham (Chief of Construction for the project), William Holabird, Louis H. Sullivan, John W. Root, Charles A. Coolidge, Corydon T. Purdy, and others, created its adequacy and splendor. It stirred the imagination of the masses and invited them to consider the future possibilities of the beauty of architecture. By the turn of the century, skeleton construction, development of structural steel, and caissons were accepted practice, and reinforced concrete was on its way to acceptance by the building profession. By then the materials and methods of construction had been devised, and engineers and architects were well prepared to meet the demands for high-rise construction. Industrial society demanded the concentration of many citizens in a small area to conduct its business enterprise efficiently. This resulted in increased land values in the business district, and a demand for taller buildings (Hoyt, 1933). To date, no other city in the United States has had such a stimulus to improved building construction, in conjunction with industrial wealth sufficient to finance immediate rebuilding hand-in-hand with technological innovations.

Four skyscraper ages may be broadly identified in the evolution of tall buildings (CTBUH, 1995). The first skyscraper age is characterized by the advances in structural engineering and the expression of the steel frame in the building elevation. The architects and engineers of this era involved in tall building design formed what has come to be known as the First Chicago School.

The invention of the first passenger elevator in 1878 made the construction of high-rise buildings become practical. The first Leiter Building of 1879, designed by Jenney, marked the beginning of the skeletal form with a glass and structure facade (Billington, 1983). Jenney's next major work was the 10-story Home Insurance Building of 1885, a Chicago landmark considered the world's first skyscraper (demolished in 1931). It incorporated a steel-and-iron structural system that was revolutionary in that it demonstrated how the structure could determine the form. Jenney thus created a load-carrying structural metal frame in which the building did not rely on masonry walls to carry the vertical loads. Such characteristic features were the forerunners of high-rise structures yet to come. His third building is the second Leiter Building of 1891, where the facade is so clearly structural that it opened up unprecedented forms and styles for future skyscrapers. Also, in 1891, John Wellborn Root, an engineer practicing as an architect, designed the Monadnock Building—a 16-story masonry building in Chicago and the world's tallest building at that time. To this day, it is a powerful brick structure and one of Chicago's historical landmarks. Both Jenney and Root espoused an ideal calling for plain structures that are utilitarian, economical and free from ornamentation; together, they are the principal proponents of the First Chicago

School—which empirically found that structure was usually unsatisfying as the principal visual element in design (Bilington, 1983). Although Louis Sullivan, known for his dictum "form must follow function," was not an engineer, his design for the Carson Pirie Scott building in the center of Chicago's Loop, is a powerful expression of a steel-framed structure. During the same period, some high-rises were also built in New York. Some notable examples are: the World Building of 1890 (destroyed in 1955), 309-ft. (94-m) high; Manhattan Life of 1894 (destroyed in 1930), 346-ft. (105-m) high; Park Row of 1899, 386-ft. (117-m) high; and the Singer Building of 1908 (destroyed in 1968), 612-ft. (186-m) high. However, the skeletal frame construction developed in Chicago (the "Chicago Skeleton") dominated the design philosophy of high-rises during this skyscraper age.

The second skyscraper age sought aesthetic solutions through the use of historical models. The 1920s brought economic prosperity, giving rise to a flurry of building construction activities in America. Architects and engineers of the first Chicago school legitimized the building of tall structures. The new generation of architects began employing style and ornamentation from ancient monuments of Greece to Italian Renaissance. Privately financed, corporate-owned skyscrapers became a symbol of pride for New York, the nerve center of business and financial activities. An extreme illustration of skyline experimentation was the Chrysler Building of 1930. The building had incorporated a vivid Art Deco style and dominated New York's skyline. The Empire State Building of 1931 was an immensely skillful masterpiece and at 102 stories became the tallest; very quickly, it came to symbolize New York City. A number of other noteworthy buildings were built in the 1930s. Tall building design was now in the hands of architects rather than engineers. The Great Depression and World War II, however, saw a sharp decline in tall building construction; it continued until the 1950s. Finally, when Chicago once again assumed the initiative, tall building design was returned to the hands of engineers and structuralist architects.

The third skyscraper age was ushered in by the European school most notably practiced by Walter Gropius, Mies van der Rohe, and Le Corbusier; it is often loosely united under the rubric of the International Style. The architectural movement came to be known as Modernism. Immediately before World War II, when air-conditioning and fluorescent lights were not yet in place, the need for natural light and ventilation largely dictated the form of high-rise buildings. Grouping office spaces around hallways would provide optimum daylight and air, but would restrict the width of the building to around 60 ft. (18 m). This required closely-spaced columns. Previously, buildings had heavy masonry facades giving the building stability and an appearance of massiveness, but concealing the actual structure. Following World War II, when the construction of tall buildings resumed in Chicago around 1950, Art Deco was fast disappearing from the scene, to be replaced by the International Style characterized by a more forthright expression of the structure.

The German architect, Ludwig Mies van der Rohe, emigrated to Chicago in 1938 to head the Department of Architecture at IIT; he taught there until his retirement in 1958. Mies held the conviction that the source of his architecture was technology. He demonstrated his ideas of structural architecture in his 860 Lake

Shore Drive Apartment Building. Those ideas were further corroborated by his proposed convention hall for Chicago, a huge freestanding building 700 ft. (212 m) on the side, and topped by a grid of long-span trusses. In refining curtain-wall construction—whose glazed envelopes carried none of the building's weight—he most clearly revealed the structure. He determinedly eschewed old structural forms, choosing instead to accept the new forms that were integral to the very nature of the new challenges of his time. It seems no coincidence that some of the most spectacular tall buildings after World War II were designed by Chicago firms.

Influenced by Miesian structuralism, Myron Goldsmith, a structural engineer-architect, a partner of SOM, and a professor of architecture at IIT, had been working on projects in the 1950s featuring the structure of buildings. In his Master's Thesis of 1953, Goldsmith, under the supervision of Mies van der Rohe, explored the "scale effect" on tall buildings and their aesthetic expression (Blaser, 1987). He worked on a number of new structural types in both steel and concrete for tall buildings. Three tall buildings in steel, each of 60 stories in height, were investigated by providing three different arrangements of diagonal bracing on the perimeter walls. Interior columns were eliminated leaving the floors with clear spans. Both vertical and lateral loads were carried on the stiffened perimeter walls. No detailed structural analysis was, however, carried out and Goldsmith was not yet aware of the tubular principle.

Goldsmith also thoroughly examined the structure of an 80-story concrete office building in which dead and live loads were carried to the foundation by a superframe in which eight columns forming three 180-by-140 ft. (54 x 42m) bays, supported six horizontal platforms spaced fifteen stories apart. Seven floors were hung below and seven were supported above the platform, leaving the floor in the middle free of columns. These study projects were intended to appraise the effects of scale on buildings in terms of stiffness against deformations, as well as to examine the potential of such structures for exhibiting new modes of architectural expression. Goldsmith continued his work as a faculty member at IIT through Master's Thesis projects of his students.

The International Style had been a reaction to the Beaux-Arts eclecticism and historically based architectural models (CTBUH, 1995). Its leaders rejected ornamentation and decor as well as historical reference in building architecture and accepted instead a structural and rational representation of building form. The Miesian model of building expression came to be widely accepted by architects in Chicago during the 1950s and 1960s. The most dominant theme of Mies' work was that clarity of structure was at its core. This led to the formation of what is known as the "Second Chicago School" for which Goldsmith was one of the major contributors (CTBUH, 1995; Blaser, 1987) and of which Fazlur Khan assumed a leadership role. Khan introduced innovative ideas in tall building design along the path charted by Mies and Goldsmith with the active collaboration and partnership of SOM architects, notably Bruce Graham. He was not only influenced by Mies in his thinking that architecture *is* structure, but also he was part of the zeitgeist of the 1960s as represented by other engineers like Frei Otto, Buckminster Fuller, and to some extent Alexander Calder and Kenneth Snelson. Otto and Fuller became known for the membrane structures and the geodesic dome, respectively, whereas Calder for his kinetic and Snelson for tensegrity structures. Khan was thus a child of the holistic spirit of Modernism and constructive art prevailing during that era.

There were other factors as well. Alfred Swenson and Pao-Chi Chang have discussed the issue of market economy as it relates to tall buildings (CTBUH, 1995). According to them, and in a nutshell, the diversity and complexity of the marketplace demand constant variation in skyscraper appearance. Moreover, market economy created the architects as we know them today. Up until the end of the Gothic period, the professionals who executed buildings were often known as "master builders." The word "architect" is derived from the Greek word *architekton*, which essentially means "master builder." The master builders were skilled both in the design and the technology of construction, based on trial and error of the structural entity in the absence of any well-established laws of structural mechanics. However, the design professional, set apart from the builder, gradually reintroduced non-essential forms to buildings. The architect became a harbinger of novel forms, stimulated by the interplay of many minds in the marketplace (CTBUH, 1995). The pursuit of arbitrary and fashionable forms persisted until finally, after World War II, the second Chicago school emerged, a notable outgrowth of the ideas of Jenney, Root, and Mies. Although a few architects remained diehards, there was an obvious need for a new master builder with a new spirit and vision, who could provide a comprehensive style for tall buildings. Fazlur Khan, in responding to this clarion call, became the long-awaited *avant garde* high-rise designer.

Equipped academically in structural theory and mechanics at the University of Illinois, and gifted with keen insights, Khan had no difficulty in developing his cutting-edge techniques of structural analysis and design. He also utilized structural model testing, a tool he enlarged upon after observing such at the college laboratory. He stated later that such tests gave students an intuitive understanding of structures. Although Khan's own doctoral research was theoretical in nature, the lab tests in school were to serve him throughout his professional career. He carried them further with model testing whenever he encountered difficult structural problems or as he investigated new or innovative structural systems.

When Khan first joined SOM in August of 1955, his major assignment was to design the structure for the 2,000-man dining hall at the U.S. Naval Training Center at Great Lakes. (Although he was initially given the responsibility of designing seven bridges for the U.S. Air Force Academy when he was hired, his first major project that he completed was this dining hall. The bridge project was re-assigned to him later.) He had the advantage of being the only engineer in the office with knowledge of prestressed concrete. While his graduate research work had centered on this very subject, he did not yet have professional experience to take charge of such a major project. However, Andrew J. Brown, the mature and experienced Chief Engineer at SOM, recognized the hidden talents of this young engineer. He took Khan under his wing and, to Khan's surprise, gave him complete responsibility for the structure. Khan proved himself worthy of such trust, not only by designing the structure but coordinating with the architects to develop an innovative and efficient system that was aesthetically exciting.

The latitude given Khan, and the autonomous nature of the firm's management style gave Khan the freedom he needed to exercise his judgement and to build his self-confidence. The proximity of his alma mater at Urbana-Champaign also permitted him to maintain contact with his academic mentors, and to carry out experimental investigations there for some of his projects. He recognized the limitations, however: unlike automobiles and aircraft for which full-scale models can be tested, the scale of tall buildings prevents their being duplicated in laboratories. Only portions or models of a building may be tested. A tall building, in its totality, can be put to a comprehensive test only after it is built and the loads are the natural ones—gravity and lateral forces—for which it has been designed. The structure of the building, then, had to be designed to respond to every combination of these forces. Failures could occur, however, if there were errors in assumptions and calculations. Such profound responsibilities weighed heavily on Khan.

Another important point is that although the curtain-wall construction of structure and glass was popular in the 1950s, it had a few drawbacks. Without masonry cladding, these buildings were less stiff compared to their predecessors, and thus needed overly rigid frames to carry the building's weight, its live loads and the lateral wind loads. As buildings got taller, massive columns and internal wind bracing were required, which took up valuable floor space. It was clear by the end of the 1950s that, as a result of the booming economy and the ensuing growth of cities, plus the need for more urban space at high elevations in crowded downtown areas, new structural solutions for high-rise construction became all the more urgent. Khan responded to the challenge. It became the primary motivating force for his quest for structural forms from the very nature of the new challenges facing the architectural and engineering communities of that era.

Meanwhile, during this time Khan demonstrated his engineering discernment when he resolved the complex beam-column connection problem of the Inland Steel Building (1958) in Chicago. Architect Bruce Graham (a former SOM partner) invited him to work on this steel connection detail of unique nature (see Chapter 6). Graham was impressed by Khan's performance and immediately recognized him as a talented engineer.

The time was also right for Khan. The advent of computers, in conjunction with a boom in the construction industry—particularly for commercial office space—following the Great Depression in the U.S. and World War II giving rise to rapid urbanization in the 1960s, facilitated the development of more sophisticated and economical structural forms and systems. Gone were the days when structural engineers relied on the moment distribution method and other classical methods of structural analysis for highly indeterminate complex building frameworks. With such simplistic analyses, they had to make many simplifying assumptions about the structural model, but their simple, reduced analytical models sacrificed the accuracy of structural response to loads. In the absence of more precise methods of analysis and to "err on the safe side," they inevitably over-designed structures. Even though a tall building is a three-dimensional structure, they analyzed it as individual plane frames, assuming a series of rigid frames in each direction for lateral wind forces. Wind bracing was typically placed at the core of the building, and in steel structures, wind bracing was provided in the form of X-bracing, K-bracing, or other diagonals.

After Khan returned from Pakistan in 1960 and began again to practice at SOM, computers were in the budding stage of development and their inherent capabilities were unfolding rapidly. In the early 1960s, the computer began to be utilized as a remarkable tool. It provided the means to analyze complex structural systems, as well as to investigate alternate systems and concepts more precisely and efficiently than ever. Khan was then able to begin his search for structural logic in architecture. He relied heavily on computers to develop and refine his revolutionary tubular principles further for tall buildings.

It is significant to make an observation here that while a concrete tubular building is easier to conceptualize (because of its physical resemblance to concrete core walls with holes), a steel tubular concept extrapolated from the concrete pierced-wall model, is not as simple to either comprehend or implement. Khan was, however, able to rise to this challenge within a few years of his design of DeWitt-Chestnut Apartments—a concrete tubular building. For steel tubes, he used X-bracing on exterior walls first by imitating the wind braces in the form of vertical shear trusses that were employed in the core of the building. Subsequently he used the same idea of closely spaced columns and deep spandrels for framed tube steel buildings similar to framed-tube concrete buildings.

Khan's contact with IIT since 1962 in a teaching capacity, while working simultaneously at SOM, gave him additional opportunity to experiment with innovative systems in a theoretical manner and in an architectural environment through student theses. When Khan joined SOM, the firm was already involved in some important projects that emphasized the structure. Since its founding in 1936, SOM had completed numerous projects involving structural challenges. Louis Skidmore and Nathaniel Owings established the original office in Chicago and the New York office was opened just a year later. In 1938, Skidmore and Owings were joined by John Merrill, an engineer, giving the firm its full name that it has today. Merrill's involvement set the precedent for the full integration of architecture and engineering disciplines that has characterized their work. From its early days, SOM has been involved in major commercial projects that influenced urban and suburban development throughout the United States. The firm subsequently set up offices in other cities and took on international projects.

All these seemingly unrelated conditions found a common ground within the fertile mind of Khan; he could project himself to a loftier plane of intellect and create higher altitudes of the built environment with an unprecedented speed. The phenomenon of Khan conformed to the legacy of the great designers of the nineteenth century who sought optimal forms and least weight structures and who conquered space through construction. He was fortunate to have been involved in the search for optimum structural systems by the engineers and architects in the 1960s. Very soon he was recognized as a rising star in the sky of tall building design. It was only a matter of time until he would develop more innovative structural systems and earn for himself professional recognition, respect from his peers, and a worldwide reputation. He was instrumental in changing the skyline of major U.S. cities, particularly Chicago.

Finally, there is the fourth skyscraper age that occupied the latter part of Khan's career. Beginning in the mid-1970s, it is perhaps the most prolific of the four skyscraper ages. Dramatically altering the American skyline, it has had far reaching consequences in other parts of the world as well. Unlike Modernism that sought structural clarity, the oft-called Post-Modern movement is pluralistic and includes many architectural styles, including Late Modernism. In essence, Post-Modern does not ascribe to any single philosophy or unique stylistic notion. It is a stylistic revolt against "glass box" architecture. Post-Modern architecture is eclectic and is "a portmanteau concept covering several approaches to architecture which have evolved from Modernism," (Jencks, 1988). In a way, it recalls the second skyscraper age and is characterized by ornamental detail, polychromatic color schemes, arbitrary forms, sculptural imagery, and monumental expression.

Needless to say, Khan had a profound distaste for Post-Modern architecture. He vehemently spoke against it until his last days. His principal reason for disdaining such architecture was that the building's natural strength was subordinated by it; such architecture to him lacked a transcendental value because it was based on impulsive whim rather than scientific rationalism and represented a waste of the society's limited natural resources.

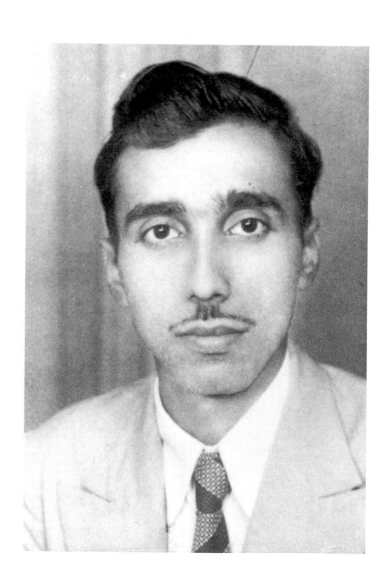

chapter 4

STRENGTH BY DESIGN

"A good structural organism worked out passionately in detail and in general appearance is essential to good architecture."

—Pier Luigi Nervi (1957)

"When thinking design, I put myself in the place of a whole building, feeling every part. In my mind I visualize the stresses and twisting a building undergoes."

—Fazlur R. Khan (*ENR,* 1972)

The debate over whether architecture is primarily art focusing on aesthetics and architectural function or a combination of art and science encompassing structure, engineering, and technology, has been going on for a long time. One thing, however, is clear. If the building has long spans, is tall or slender, or is subjected to extreme loads, the nature of the structural system has a predominant influence on the architectural design solution. Renowned architects such as Nervi, Mies, and lately Calatrava have always realized this. Nervi believed in the inherent aesthetic outcome of a good structural solution for buildings, just as Maillart did for bridges. So, too, with Mies van der Rohe, Myron Goldsmith, and others. Currently, Calatrava is drawing international attention for his many innovative structures.

Shortly after joining SOM, and as the previous chapter shows, Fazlur Khan realized that he was a participant in the process of design that evolved out of the architectural tradition created by many great names in the fields of both engineering and architecture. SOM was already firmly established and well known internationally. He discovered that its prevailing environment of autonomy well suited his aspirations for innovation and inquiry in structural engineering. Despite his inherent philosophical nature, he was a realist at heart when dealing with buildings. He had already demonstrated at the University of Illinois that he was an original and independent thinker. He was quick to realize that SOM was, after all, primarily an architecture firm, and that he would have to deal frequently with architects. Therefore, a spirit of collaboration rather than confrontation should be developed and exercised if he wanted to succeed in this environment.

38
38

He was fortunate to have Andrew Brown as his boss. Brown observed the passion and enthusiasm in Khan and, as noted before, offered him total responsibility to design the structure for the dining hall at the U.S. Naval Training Center at Great Lakes. He was persuasive enough to convince Brown and the client to include full-scale model load tests as part of the contract documents.

Of course, the extent of model testing was somewhat undermined by the advent of computers in the 1960s. Once it became possible to develop realistic computer analysis models for complex structures, the need for expensive and time-consuming model tests in laboratories decreased and became confined to academic research. Khan was quick to orient himself and adapt to this new reality of computers. Recalled Chester Siess, "Once when I was at SOM's office in Chicago, Khan demonstrated to me how, with the use of the computer, he could change design parameters and investigate different column types." At any rate, Khan had to fully satisfy himself by validating his design in some way to avoid any future structural problems. Although he accepted this reality of computer analysis of structures, he never believed that intuitive understanding and simple manual checks by calculations and model testing should ever be replaced by electronic computation.

Another of Khan's early projects at SOM was the design of seven bridges for the U.S. Air Force Academy in Colorado Springs (Khan, 1981). On this project, he worked closely with SOM's architectural design partner, Walter Netsch. He tried out a number of schemes involving steel, reinforced concrete and prestressed concrete for these bridges, five of which were for the highway crossing of the valleys, and two for overpasses for the Atchison, Topeka, and Santa Fe Railroad. He worked independently on these bridges and was able to convince his group that precast post-tensioned girder system would be ideal solution for them. The highway bridges of lengths varying from 360 ft. (108m) to 600 ft. (180m) had single-span lengths of 120 ft. (36m). The post-tensioned girder was designed to have a "tear drop cross-section" and the same cross section was used for the two overpasses for the railroad with two single spans of 72 ft. (21.6m). Khan convinced the Air Force to have a full-scale test of the 120-ft. (36-m) girder loaded to failure. His rationale was that such major prestressed concrete bridges, particularly for railroads, were not very common and it would be important to simulate their behavior in the laboratory. By such validation of his design concepts, Khan developed the confidence to design major structures and to learn more about the behavior of structures by load-test programs.

Upon his return from Pakistan in 1960, Khan worked on a few other projects; some major ones of this time (1960-64) are the 60" Solar Telescope, Kitt Park, Arizona; Container Corporation of America's Corrugator Plant, Carol Stream, Illinois; and Business Man's Assurance Tower, Kansas City, Missouri. It was during this period that Khan had also become engaged in the design of the 43-story reinforced concrete DeWitt-Chestnut Apartments Building in Chicago and the 38-story reinforced concrete Brunswick Building, also in Chicago. During this time, he had been working on various concepts in collaboration with Bruce Graham and Myron Goldsmith, which included the tubular concept. His breakthrough paper on shear wall-frame interaction (Khan and Sbarounis, 1964) opened up new possibilities for designing economical and efficient high-rise buildings employing a combination of conventional rigid frames and shear walls. The paper demonstrated that the stiffness of tall buildings can be drastically increased by this scheme of structural design. While he was working on his major building projects in the early 1960s, he realized the importance of the effect of a tall building's size in the selection of structural systems. This realization, as we noted before, came from his association with Myron Goldsmith, who, under Mies van der Rohe, wrote a Master's thesis in 1953 at IIT proposing an 86-story reinforced concrete superframe (Blaser, 1987). Moreover, a number of student research projects there, where Khan acted as an adviser together with Goldsmith and David Sharpe, further consolidated Khan's understanding of the very important effects of scale on the structural system of tall buildings. One of the appropriate systems for tall building structures that he had identified was the tubular system, evolving from this notion of the influence of scale on the form of tall buildings.

In the past, most high-rise buildings were commonly designed as conventional rigid frames, and when they became inefficient for greater heights, wind bracing in the form of vertical trusses was added to stiffen the building against wind-induced lateral sway. For other buildings, lateral loads would be totally carried by wind bracing or shear walls. The concept of shear wall-frame interaction was not yet fully established. The development and use of the tubular concept by Khan was thus a major leap forward in tall building design beyond the combined action of shear wall-frame interaction. Why did Khan think about such a concept? The answer perhaps lies in Khan's academic background in optimization and his interest in classifying buildings according to their heights similar to the Aristotlian approach of the classification of things. He realized that, as buildings became taller, there is a "premium for height" due to lateral loads, and the demand on the structural system dramatically increased (see Fig. 1). If a building had carried only gravity loads, no additional structural cost would be needed for carrying wind loads. For a building which is low enough, so that wind load is of no major concern, gravity loads will dictate the structural design. However, the quantity of material required will increase due to the effect of wind load as the building exceeds a certain height. Khan understood this problem well and attempted to minimize the premium by developing different structural systems for different building heights (see Chapter 5).

Architects know the importance of scale well. For structures, the concept of scale is really an age-old one. Aristotle thought about scale of things and emphasized that beauty of an object is a matter of size, proportion, and order. Galileo Galilei (1564–1642) proclaimed that the size of organism or artifact has a decisive influence on its structure and function and validated his theory by making accurate observations on both animate and inanimate structures. He suggested that it was impossible to build "ships, palaces or temples of enormous size in such a way that their oars, yardbeams, iron-bolts and in short all their parts can hold together; nor can nature produce trees of extraordinary size because their branches would break down under their own weight" (Blaser, 1987). He realized that if an animal's size is

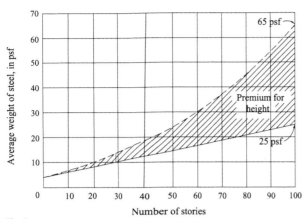

Fig. 1

magnified several times and its bone structure is increased proportionately, it would crumble under its own weight unless the bones are stronger and harder.

We can infer that as we scale up any structural system, the load will eventually be greater than the strength of the structure in a relative sense. Buildings can be made large by using stronger materials and using different shapes. Khan recognized that the strength of a building comes from its design. Strength of material for tall buildings is but one consideration. Other factors are the size, shape and arrangement of the main supporting parts, such as girders and columns. No buildings can be made that will look like the Empire State Building or the Sears Tower but will be as high as the Mount Everest or even a high mountain. As the bones of a giant must be thick and strong, a building of mountainous size must be either almost solid and shaped like a mountain or built with members of stronger materials arranged in a certain fashion. Otherwise, at some enormous height it will crumble under its own weight even if it is shielded under "a hypothetical glass dome" to eliminate any lateral wind forces. Although a logarithmically tapered form of a building could be built to a theoretically infinite height to carry its own weight, it will be impractical from the viewpoints of wind-load resistance, architectural function, stability, and constructability.

When a building's dimensions abruptly change, structural engineers must ask themselves: "how will the behavior of the structural system change?" When the scale changes—whether large or small—they must view the system in a totally different light and look for things that are less obvious in their normal scale of experience. Because of their large size, planes are shaped more like large whales in the ocean rather than like bees, which can fly but are small in size. The aerodynamic effect of a large whale swimming in water is more akin to a large plane flying in the air. A plane made in the shape of a bee or fly may not even be able to fly because of the problem of its scale. Examples of the scale effect indeed abound in the Nature.

Another important concept in structural design is the so-called balanced or fully stressed design, where each part of the structure is equally stressed to the fullest strength of the materials. This notion of logical design was conceived by Oliver Wendell Holmes in his poem: *The Deacon's Masterpiece, or, the Wonderful "One-Hoss Shay": A Logical Story*. Although in this ideal structure all its parts are fully stressed under load, the failure takes place all at once without advanced warning. In building structures, however, different safety levels are usually specified by codes for different member types precluding any abrupt global failure of the structure. Moreover, it is not ideally possible to realize such a logical structure, although attempts to approach this optimum condition to make best use of materials would certainly make sense as our natural resources become more and more scarce. At one time when buildings were designed by hand calculations, it was impractical to achieve optimum design because of the extent of crudeness in engineering assumptions and idealizations involved. Designers in those days would play extra-safe by overdesigning. The degree of accuracy and refinement available today with the use of computers has naturally resulted in more economical structures; but then as structural elements have become lighter and highly stressed, they are also more prone to failure, reducing any room for errors. Khan was conscious of this fact.

An important requirement of tall building design is to maintain stability against lateral loads. As wind-load effects increase geometrically with height, the forces generated in the structure, unless counteracted by adequate design, will cause a tall building to deflect and vibrate excessively, overturn, slide at the base, twist as a whole, or undergo major damage to its beams, columns, and other elements. Therefore, the key to structural design is to avoid these occurrences and, at the same time, to have a least-weight building structure. The goal of such structural design process is minimum cost, or more subtly, the minimum strain energy expended in the structure to resist externally applied loads.

In a way, everything that exists belongs to a universal energy field. Objects in nature have been designed in such a way that minimum energy is expended when some work is done by them. For a structural framework, minimum strain energy will mean minimum expenditure of energy to resist loads. The key to accomplish this is to distribute the forces and deformations as evenly possible throughout the structures, that is, create a uniform energy field through a synergistic combination of the members by selectively choosing the configuration, connectivity, material quality, size, and shape of members. Such an energy field will consequently provide a force flow in the structure through load sharing that is natural to its form and will follow to the shortest load path. It is this optimum load path in buildings that Khan sought to find while investigating innovative structural systems for economy and adequate performance.

To best understand and appreciate structural behavior, Khan believed that he had to have "structural empathy" in which he would immerse himself in the mystical world of stresses and strains within the materials of a structure. Liselotte recounted that Khan had often felt he was himself the building when he worked on a building project (*Khan Tributes*, 1982). Khan also revealed this feeling during an *ENR* interview (*ENR*, 1972). He thus approached buildings in two major ways in thought and practice: mystical and scientific. His firm belief that building design is both a science and an art helped him in combining the two polarities of emotional mysticism and scientific rationalism into a single whole.

When Khan designed the DeWitt-Chestnut Apartments building of 1965 using the framed-tube concept, all steel tall buildings during that era, including the Empire State Building, employed the rigid-frame system in conjunction with additional wind bracing. Lateral loads were resisted by the rigid frames through the moment connections at beam-column joints, augmented in stiffness by vertical shear trusses located within the service core of the building or by other types of wind braces. For concrete buildings, rigid-frame construction was the prevailing practice. Core walls or other types of shear walls were employed to carry lateral forces in some cases. Most concrete buildings then were less than about 20 stories in height. Other concepts that were used included the use of belt and outrigger trusses and engagement of the perimeter columns in resisting lateral loads that could increase the structure's stiffness by about 30% (Khan, 1974b). The 47-story Place Victoria of 1964 in Montreal was the first reinforced concrete building to employ the outrigger principle (Schueller, 1990).

The design of the Empire State Building was accomplished by manual calculations and by making simplifying assumptions and idealizations. As a result, it was overdesigned with excessive consumption of structural steel. The building is thus needlessly too strong. Computers were not available then and the idea of three-dimensional analysis was prohibitive even though it could be conceived. The tubular principles introduced by Khan changed all that. They pushed the state-of-the-art dramatically and signalled the advent of a new era for tall building design. Several new major tall buildings like the John Hancock Center, Amoco Building, and Sears Tower (all in Chicago), and the World Trade Center in New York employed tubular system during the next few years following the construction of the DeWitt-Chestnut Building.

Leslie Robertson, who designed the structure of the World Trade Center in New York in the 1960s, is another remarkable contributor to tubular design. Both towers are tube systems in steel measuring 208 ft. (63m) in plan, and 1,350 ft. (409m) and 1,356 ft. (411m) in height. 14-in. (355-mm) square box columns in the facade are spaced at only 3 ft. 4 in. (1m). Tubular structural systems are so efficient that the quantity of material consumed could be as low as that used in conventional rigid frame buildings half the size.

Robertson wrote about the framed tube idea thus: "in 1962 . . . perhaps for the first time, the concept of the tube was employed in a high-rise building (the design of the World Trade Center completed in 1972). Later, in 1963, a tubular concept in reinforced concrete was developed for the 43-story DeWitt Chestnut Apartments" (ASCE, 1972). This, of course, raises some question about the origin of the tube idea. Jonathan Tucker (1985), however, predated the development of the tube concept to 1961 when he wrote, ". . . skyscraper engineers have shifted the bracing and support required to resist lateral loads from the core of the building to the perimeter. This revolutionary idea was introduced in the early 1960s by several designers, particularly the late Fazlur R. Khan, a structural engineer with the Chicago architectural firm of Skidmore, Owings and Merrill (SOM) . . . the first application of the tubular concept was the framed (or Vierendeel) tube, developed by SOM in 1961." Tucker's statement agrees with that of Khan (1974b) who also assigned the date of conception of the "idea of a hollow thin tube" to the year 1961 (see Chapter 1). Robertson summarized the matter to me this way: "It is not important who conceived the idea of tube first. Tube buildings existed even before the 1960s, but they were not recognized as tubes that could respond to lateral loads in three dimensions. When computers became available in the 1960s, engineers were able to analyze complex structures, and that really facilitated the development of the tube concept. Naturally, time was right then for our ideas on structural systems for tall buildings to culminate in tubular design. Faz and I independently thought of this idea." It is noteworthy that tube-like cooling towers and silos existed well before the 1960s, although they were not identified as such. Unquestionably, Chicago's DeWitt-Chestnut Apartments building is the first known structure that was designed and built as a tube. Also, it is generally recognized that Khan had developed the basic mechanics as well as formulated the mathematical model of tubular behavior and published it (Khan, 1974a).

Curiously enough, Galileo knew that if hollow tubes and solid rods are both made from the same weight of a material, the hollow tube is stronger. The strength of bone comes mainly from its inner structure. It is built up from thousands of compactly arranged tube-shaped units, each called a Haversian system, named after English physician Clopton Havers (1650-1701). This leads to the idea that if columns are placed as a ring similar to the way that the Haversian systems are arranged in bone, the design is much stronger for vertical loads. Khan demonstrated that such a tubular system is also stronger and stiffer for lateral loads.

Tubular design assumes that the perimeter configuration of a building responds to lateral loads as a hollow tube cantilevering out from the ground. Since a solid wall around the building is impractical, window openings are punched into the wall to give the appearance of a perforated tube losing, of course, the ideal solid tubular behavior. In effect, the solid core wall, if placed in the building perimeter with holes pierced in it for windows, will act like a framed tube. The equivalent hollow tube system in its simplest form consists of closely spaced exterior columns tied to deep perimeter or spandrel girders at each floor level. Such an arrangement is called a framed tube, a name assigned to it by Khan himself. Khan (1974a) later made the following observation on framed tube systems:

> From the point of view of construction economy, the framed tube compares favorably with the normal shear wall type construction of medium-rise buildings, but provides a distinct economical advantage for taller buildings. Moreover, the closely spaced column system has the additional advantage of also being the window wall system, thus replacing the vertical mullions for the support of the glass windows. In some recent buildings the elimination of the traditional curtain wall with its metallic mullions was in itself the justification for choosing this structural system.

When the exterior column and girder system carries all or most of the lateral loads, expensive core trusses or shear walls can be eliminated. Fewer widely spaced "gravity" columns are needed in the interior of the building to carry floor loads. Because of the absence of core bracing and of a large number of heavy interior columns, the net leasable area for such a building increases. However, views from the interior of the building to outside are somewhat limited by the presence of the large number of perimeter columns, particularly at the main entry level. The maximum spacing of perimeter or tube columns recommended by Khan is 15 ft. (4.5m); the closer the columns are spaced and the deeper the spandrel girders are made, the better the tubular behavior becomes. Buildings in excess of 30 to 40 stories are suitable candidates for tubular systems. Of course, it is the slenderness ratio (also called aspect ratio), defined as the ratio of the height of the building to its smaller width at the base, rather than the number of stories or the height of the building, that truly determines the structural efficiency of a tall building. The Sears

Tower has a slenderness ratio of 6.5, its height being 1,454 ft. (440m). A 2,500-ft. (757m) high building with a similar slenderness ratio would require a 385 ft. (117m) base, and a modified tubular system similar to that for Sears could be at least theoretically conceivable. But, building sites large enough to accommodate such a massive building with such a large width are difficult to find in downtown cores of cities (unless it is widened or flared at the base like the Eiffel Tower to create openness in the middle, or employs a bridge system linking tubular shafts) and will invariably be restricted by zoning regulations and other land-use constraints. It is obvious that to accomplish a typical 2,500-ft.-tall (757m) skyscraper, structural designers will be compelled to aim for a slenderness ratio ranging from 10 to 12, or even more, which may, of course, render the building sensitive to motion sickness.

Although volumes of materials about the mechanics of tube buildings are available in the literature, (Khan, 1974; Schueller, 1977; Taranath, 1997), we will briefly discuss here some of the relevant basic concepts expounded by Khan.

The framed tube is the basic form for tubular buildings. Assuming that the lateral loads are entirely carried by closely-spaced perimeter columns that are rigidly held together, that is, moment-connected with deep spandrel beams, the building as a whole responds to lateral loads in a three-dimensional manner. The stiff floor system acts as a series of rigid diaphragms and distributes the lateral load to various elements of the tube structure. Looking at one facade of the building at any one story, the beam-column system forms a rectangular grid and resembles a vierendeel. If the tube would behave ideally, then, Khan argued that the exterior walls would act as a single unit and the tube would respond to lateral loads in entirely cantilever bending, and the columns would behave like fibers in a beam and would therefore be in axial tension or compression. For elastic behavior of such an ideal tube, the stress distribution would be linear. However, the actual behavior deviates from this ideal condition. The web frames of the tube parallel to lateral loads behave as rigid frames, that is, the beams and columns bend and shear racking occurs in these frames resulting in a nonlinear axial stress distribution in the columns (Fig. 2). As shown in this figure, the columns in the flange frames perpendicular to the lateral load, on the other hand, should experience a uniform stress distribution under an ideal tubular condition; but, because of the flexibility of these frames, this uniformity is lost and again a nonlinear stress distribution prevails. In simple terms, this means that the basic assumption for beam behavior that plane sections remain plane after bending is no longer valid, that is, the bending stresses are no longer linearly related to the distance from the neutral axis of the section. As shown in Fig. 2, the stresses at the corners of the tube thereby increase whereas those at the centers of both flange and web frames decrease. This phenomenon, as Khan referred to it, is known as shear lag because it is caused by the shear racking behavior of the web frames due to the lack of their shear stiffness. Because of the flexibility of the spandrel girders as a result of the practical constraint on the girder depth and column spacing, the high stresses in the web frames cannot be transferred adequately to the flange frames, giving rise to this

45

Fig. 2

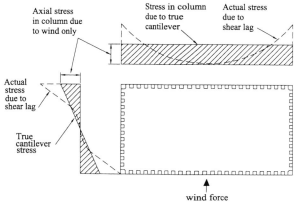

Axial stress in column due to wind only

Stress in column due to true cantilever

Actual stress due to shear lag

Actual stress due to shear lag

True cantilever stress

wind force

phenomenon. Since shear lag alters the tubular characteristics of high-rise structures critically, it plays a crucial role in design. It follows then that the greater the shear lag in a tube building, the less will be the tubular response of the structure to lateral loads. The principal goal of tubular design is therefore to minimize this effect in the system.

The overall deflection of a tube building consists of two components that are caused by cantilever action and frame racking. The larger the cantilever behavior and the smaller the frame racking, the better is the tubular response of the structure and lesser is the shear lag effect. An efficient framed tube should have much more cantilever deflection than that due to frame racking, and hence minimum bending of columns. As a rule of thumb, Khan suggested that an 80 percent cantilever deflection would indicate a very efficient tubular system. A cantilever deflection less than about 50 percent will, on the other hand, indicate an inefficient tubular structure.

In a framed tube, the overturning under lateral load is resisted by the tube form causing compression on the leeward and tension on the windward columns of the flange frames, while the shear from the lateral load is resisted by the bending of the beams and the columns belonging to the web frames. Khan (1974a) suggested that for a very preliminary estimate of the overall resistance, as well as deflection of the building, the tube configuration could be reduced to two equivalent channels resisting the entire overturning moment on the building (Fig. 3). With this simplification and using some approximate rules, an analysis using a computer program will give conservative values of shear and moment in the members. To achieve a realistic design of framed tubes of any proportion and height within the practical range, Khan developed influence curves, which could be used directly as design aids for preliminary design. He defined the important structural properties for tubular action such as bending stiffness of beams and columns, shear stiffness of beams, and axial stiffness of columns (Khan, 1974a). From this, he defined the stiffness ratio, stiffness factor, and an aspect ratio as the primary controlling parameters for the framed tube structure. He then proceeded to represent a 10-story three-dimensional framed tube with an "equivalent plane-frame model" (Fig. 4). By conducting extensive computer analyses of this simplified model, he developed sets of influence curves for various stiffness ratios, stiffness factors, and aspect ratios. He argued that a given framed tube with any number of stories could be converted to a hypothetical 10-story framed tube by using a reduction modeling technique and then analyzed by making use of the influence curves. A reasonable prediction of the complex tubular behavior of the prototype structure thus became possible. He further demonstrated how the lateral sway of the actual structure could be estimated by duly considering the total behavior of the framed tube (Khan, 1974a).

As we can see, Khan dealt with the mechanics of framed tubes by way of defining the behavioral parameters and developed the design aids to facilitate calculations in the design office. At that time, three-dimensional analysis of framed tube structures was prohibitive from a computational point-of-view because of the low speed of computers, primitive as they were, and their memory limitations. This necessitated the use

Fig. 3: Framed Tube Plan

Fig. 4: Substituting an Equivalent Plane Frame for the Framed Tube

46

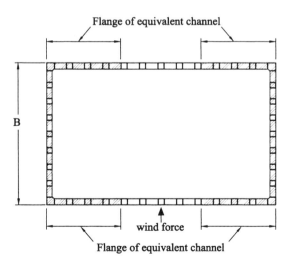

Fig. 3

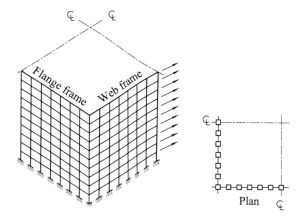

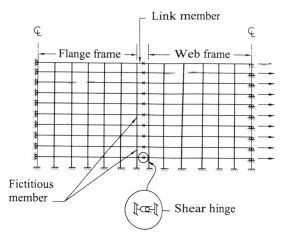

Fig. 4

47

of his design aids. Now, however, they are rarely used because high-speed computers with large memory capability can efficiently analyze modest- to large-size building structures in three dimensions. Of course, similar reduced analytical models based on "lumping" techniques were subsequently developed at SOM to economize on these computer runs. Although these design aids by Khan are no longer in common usage, they are still important and appealing to a design engineer who wants to obtain a good grasp of the mechanics of tubular behavior. Moreover, for many situations, these influence curves can still be used for preliminary sizing of members needed before rigorous computer analyses.

As the building becomes taller, the shear lag effect is magnified. The tubular structure thus loses its efficiency as only a small portion of the total lateral drift is caused by cantilever action and the major portion of the deflection is due to shear racking or frame action. The addition of diagonal bracing members to the exterior frames greatly overcomes this problem by making these frames very stiff in their own planes (like walls). Consequently, the behavior of the tube as a whole approaches ideal tube action, since the shear is now resisted by the diagonals. This structure is known as a braced tube or trussed tube. Not only do the diagonals resist lateral loads but they also act as inclined columns carrying gravity loads. Tensile forces introduced in these members due to lateral loads cannot usually overcome the compression forces induced by gravity loads. A major advantage of this is that columns can be more widely spaced as compared with the framed tube system, yet they can be made to act together as a tube in presence of the diagonals. A major problem may be the difficulty of developing window wall details due to the presence of joints between the diagonals and the columns. Architecturally, the diagonals not only create obstruction in the windows at various floor levels but they also change dramatically the aesthetic expression of the building.

Khan used the braced tube system for the John Hancock Center in Chicago in the mid-1960s (see Chapter 7). Some other major buildings with trusses in the exterior facade are the CitiCorp Center in New York, designed by structural engineer William J. Le Messurier and the Bank of China Building in Hong Kong designed by structural engineer Leslie Robertson. The Onterie Center in Chicago, the last building designed by Khan, is a braced tube building in concrete (see Chapter 6).

The stiffness of a framed tube can also be substantially augmented, as noted before, by using the core to resist part of the lateral load. The floor diaphragm connecting the core and the outer tube transfer the lateral forces to both systems. The core itself could be made up of a solid tube, a braced tube, or a framed tube with closely spaced columns. (It is possible to introduce more than one tube inside the exterior tube.) Such a system is called a *tube-in-tube*, a term coined by Khan himself. The Brunswick Building in Chicago (not originally intended and designed so) and One Shell Plaza in Houston, both designed by Khan, are examples (see Chapter 6).

Another important extension of the tube principle is the bundled tube (also called cellular tube or modular tube). This is where Khan pushed his imagination of structural logic beyond his original frame tube concept. From an engineering viewpoint, the bundled tube concept is an extension of the facade tubular system stiffened with interior frames in both directions resulting in a configuration of cellular tubes. Khan observed that if the perimeter of a tubular building became too large, a simple Vierendeel structural facade is not enough to minimize shear lag; the structure no longer behaves efficiently as a single tube in resisting lateral forces. Together with Bruce Graham, he resolved this problem by laying out the interior columns in square or rectangular modules or cells, adding strength and stiffness to the structure. These cellular tubes, when continuously connected to each other, are forced to act together as an assemblage due to the presence of an overall floor diaphragm encompassing them. The interior rows of columns and girders act as webs of a huge cantilever beam sticking out of the ground, thereby reducing shear lag effect. Khan used this concept for the Sears Tower (see Chapter 8). A bundled tube building in concrete is One Magnificent Mile in Chicago (see Chapter 6).

Since the bundled tube assemblage is obtained from the modular arrangement of tubes, it is possible to achieve different building configurations both in plan and in elevation by simply terminating a tube at any height. This offers great flexibility to architects for developing the building form. This diversity leads to free-form massing in which a building of any shape and form, regular or irregular, can be developed by laying up the basic tube modules that could be of variable shapes according to the designer's wishes as long as such a form does not undercut the basic tubular principle. The possibilities of form are, in this sense, almost limitless; something like the toy buildings built by children. This advantage of the bundled tube accommodates any building footprint where site constraints are present and gives the architect the freedom and flexibility to develop exciting, rather than monotonous, unbroken building facades. Khan (1974b) suggested that for large buildings of extreme height, similar to the framed tubes bundled together, trussed tubes could also be bundled "to optimize the total structural system." This system has a great potential provided the diagonals could be accommodated in the building's structural and architectural planning.

Khan thus showed that several variations of tubular forms were possible. Subsequently, working along this line, others demonstrated that a building could have partial tubular behavior on all sides or full tubular behavior in one direction and partial tubular behavior in the other direction. Rigid frames or shear trusses added to the interior of a tubular building at vantage locations are also viable options to augment the structure's stiffness. In fact, during the late 1970s and early 1980s, prior to his death, Khan was investigating several new possibilities of tube action.

Another significant modification of the tubular concept by Khan was the development of the composite tube. In this system, the perimeter steel frame is stiffened by cast-in-place concrete punched wall, that is, by large concrete columns and deep spandrel girders. Concrete is poured around the closely spaced light steel columns. Speedy erection of the steel frame is achieved by employing light steel columns around the facade.

Interior columns and floor framing are similar to typical steel system for tubular buildings. This system combines the fast erection of steel construction with fireproofing, added stiffness, and moldability of the concrete framework for window wall. Employment of interior steel columns for carrying floor loads eliminates the need for large concrete columns thereby providing much needed floor space in the building while having the stiff concrete tube facade. The system is thus a happy marriage of steel and concrete that complement the properties of each other by deriving their benefits and eliminating their drawbacks (see Chapters 5 and 6). Composite systems were used by Khan for the 20-story Control Data Center in Houston, 36-story Gateway III Office Building in Chicago and the 52-story One Shell Square Building in New Orleans.

It is apparent that the tubular framework is a logical system in which the natural flow of forces is allowed to take place in a three-dimensional structural space. This is consistent with Khan's repeated proclamation that "a building's natural strength should be expressed" (Newhouse, 1992). The richness of Khan's career became apparent from the early 1960s when he developed the tubular design concept for the DeWitt-Chestnut Apartments. It continued into the late 1960s and 1970s. This will be demonstrated in the next five chapters dealing with his research and practice experience.

▲ ▼

How well did Khan's tubular building type integrate with the architectural models of the 1960s and onward? In the 1950s and 1960s, the International Style and modernism in architectural expression encouraged buildings of rectangular prismatic forms. Such forms fitted well into the tubular paradigm. The 1960s represented the high point of modernism, and it is then when Khan conceived the tubular notion and applied it. Even with a few creeping stylistic changes in the building's tops and bases later, the deployment of the structural logic of tubes conceived by Khan was not excluded. Due to a surge in emerging aesthetic fashions like post-modernism and neo-rationalism, however, buildings of irregular and arbitrary forms began to appear on the scene. While post-modernists did not abide by any regulated forms, the neo-rationalists, however, believed that the discipline of architecture was a self-propelled field albeit abiding by a rigorous and coherent system governed by rules. The neo-rationalists attempted to transcend the authority of the post-modernists and to rescue architecture from being the instrument of their arbitrary self-expression, but fell short of being rationalists in the strict sense in seeking the absolute, objective truth. As a result, in the late 1970s and 1980s, new non-prismatic, sculptural, and curvilinear forms were introduced to tall building design by architects who got bored with the Modern architectural style. These irregular shapes challenged the inherent efficiency of Khan's tubular systems, because drastic modification of the tubular facade to express the architectural envelope created weakness in the tubular action by disrupting the frame racking component of tube behavior and rendering the cantilever action somewhat erratic and unpredictable.

In the late 1980s and early 1990s, the trend had continued. It has been a formidable challenge for architects and engineers to develop structural forms that are rational and at the same time could cater to the needs of the new trends in architecture (Ali, 1990). However, "by the 1990s, enthusiasm for postmodernism seemed to be evolving into an eclecticism in which many now seem inclined to disavow allegiance to any single style or philosophy. Indeed, the very notion of 'style' has fallen into disfavor in many circles" (Boyer and Mitgang, 1996). The fusion of form and function is a continual evolving process.

Regarding this departure of architects from modernism, and the beginning of more drastic forms in the 1980s, Goldberger (1989) observed:

> By 1980, one thing was clear: the box, the rationalist dream of the International Style, was making more and more architects uncomfortable. Not only was it no longer the clean and exhilarating structure that would serve as a clarion call to a new age, but it was not even able to hold out much promise of practicality. It was generally inefficient from the standpoint of energy, and it was not as marketable from the viewpoint of real estate operators either.

Khan had an unshakable faith in the fact that a realistic architectural expression directly depends upon an efficient structural form in which optimal strength is achieved by design. Khan wrote a short paper on structural logic just before he left for overseas and only a few days before his death. He wrote it for his opening address at the Architecture Club of Chicago to which he had been elected as president—indeed a rare honor for a structural engineer. Many of the members of the club were proponents of postmodernism. Although he could not present it to the club members due to his untimely death, it was, however, published later in the club journal (Khan, 1982a). He expressed deep concern about the plight of structural logic and lamented in this paper,

> Today it seems the pendulum has swung back again towards architecture that is unrelated to technology and does not consciously represent the logic of structure. Nostalgia for the thirties and even earlier times has hit a large segment of the architectural profession; in many cases facade making has become the predominant occupation.

Khan criticized both the engineer and the architect when he said:

> It is apparent that postmodernism in architecture is very much the result of the architect's lack of interest in the realities of materials and structural possibilities: the logic of structure has become irrelevant once again. This attitude in architecture suits many engineers because of their overspecialization in engineering schools which treat the solution of the problem as the ultimate goal, and not the critical development of the problem itself . . . any structure can be made to work with many engineers gladly willing to play with their computers and come up with the answers to hold up the building.

The paper concluded, however, with a glimmer of hope:

> But logic and reasoning are strong elements of human existence, always important when man must transcend into the next level of refinement. There are already some signs of that happening in architecture. New structural systems and forms are beginning to appear once again and with them new architectural forms and aesthetics. The pendulum of structural logic in architecture continues to swing.

Khan always believed that a building's architectural expression should emanate from the elegance and simplicity of the structural form that is natural to it. These two aspects of a building should be blended in design, in Mies's words "the one be the expression of the other." Unlike the common practice of the architect pre-conceiving the form, Bruce Graham was cooperative with Khan in defining the form based on structural reasoning. This explains why the many buildings designed by them through collaboration are replete with structural expression exhibiting honestly the natural strength of the buildings. It is therefore not surprising that one of the greatest builders of our time, who had left his mark on the architecture of tall buildings, is not an architect but an engineer. The architecture of his tall buildings originated and evolved out of the strict discipline of engineering and structural logic that Graham fully understood and appreciated.

Khan's quest for structural logic did not end with tubular design. He was instrumental in developing another structural concept, the "superframe," for tall buildings. Superframes are very large boxes, each of the boxes about eight to twelve stories high, stacked over one another. Each box comprises large beams and columns that are internally reinforced with lattices or extensive trusswork. Although the superframe concept was not entirely new, Khan applied and extended the concept to its logical limit by considering the lateral-load effects in a different way. We will revisit this topic in some detail later when the latest innovations during Khan's career are discussed.

chapter **5**   # EXPLORATION AND INNOVATION

" *Technology*, from its root meaning of *techne logos*, can be taken to mean 'knowledge gained in the making', through craft, the process of creation, and production. This is the common definition of *tacit knowledge*, that is, knowledge learned through tactile and empirical experience. In this view, design and technology are intimately connected through a unified conception of architecture derived from knowledge of construction, context, and environmental resources."

—Donald Watson (1997)

Technology, as we can see today, is ubiquitous and no one can avoid contact with it in today's society. Using the term "technology" broadly for all applied sciences and engineering, it can be defined as the means by which material things are produced by using the knowledge of physical sciences and mathematics for the welfare of mankind. Architects generally realize that technology is part of architecture. It is a fact that design conception and technical knowledge are interdependent and go hand in hand during the design process (Herbert, 1999). But some fail to appreciate that. Thus, in many academic settings, technical knowledge is not made part of design inquiry.

A remarkable contribution of Fazlur Khan to the building profession was his untiring endeavor to unite architecture and engineering. His research experience at the University of Illinois, his exposure to the architectural/engineering environment at SOM, and his opportunity to teach in the Department of Architecture at IIT, helped in molding his future career path and his personality as a visionary and an innovator. At SOM, in the 1960s and 1970s, he had been involved in a number of major building projects. He quickly realized that with increasing heights of buildings, the status quo of the structural system was no longer acceptable and that the form of the building must be generated from sound engineering principles rather than merely from architectural function and aesthetics. In other words, Louis Sullivan's architectural tenet that "form must follow function" could be reworded as: "function should follow form." A good example of this is the airplane, where the form is determined from rational engineering principles and the function adapts to the form. Force flow in a structural system is determined by the

52
52

53
53
53

form and the tenet then becomes: "form controls the forces . . . this means that function follows form and not the reverse" (Billington, 1983). This is particularly true for tall buildings and complex structural forms, and where the loads are of great magnitude. Khan strongly felt that there was a real need for innovative approaches to tall building design that could respond to the technical and economic needs of society, and could bridge some of the divisive gaps between the artistic and scientific aspects of architecture.

Khan was aware of the limitations of building research. A number of factors had been hindering the progress of research on buildings. Unlike engineering, architectural research is far behind. Architecture is considered a professional discipline that demands creativity, a good sense of aesthetics, and good visual and graphic capabilities. Architects are generally viewed as private practitioners who have professional training from architectural schools. A significant obstacle to promoting research in architectural schools in America is the lack of funding organizations for architectural research and the absence of Doctor of Philosophy programs in most schools. Thus, research in architecture has often been limited to architectural history and behavioral and environmental areas. Even some of these architectural historians are not truly architects, but rather more allied with art historians. Similarly, those engaged in behavioral and environmental research are rarely considered as true architects but are treated as specialists allied with other behavioral and environmental disciplines. The architectural faculty dealing primarily with design studio instruction are either avid theoreticians or professionally oriented practitioners and they emphasize architectural philosophy or creativity in their treatment of the subject. Only a handful of architectural theoreticians engage in true architectural research of esoteric nature. Structural and other technological innovations for buildings as well as construction practice are generally thought to be the responsibility of the engineers.

Most engineering schools generally emphasize research in a rather generic way and are more interested in solid mechanics and applied mathematics rather than design, practice, and technological innovations. If readers look up some recent technical papers in a structural engineering journal, they will know what I mean. Professor Ralph Peck (1997) observed this lingering trend in an article in *Civil Engineering*. Another problem with many engineering professors is that they do not have the opportunity of designing large buildings or structures, although they may be retained occasionally as consultants to give advice. Practicing structural engineers who design buildings on the other hand do not often have the incentive, resources, or time to carry out research and are satisfied with the necessary design improvements to make the structure economicals and buildable. Such improvement or optimization of structural systems is undertaken not for the sake of advancement of knowledge, but rather to be competitive and to realize the objectives of a project within a fixed budget and within a fixed deadline. This is the paradox of building research that Khan once pointed out to me during a conversation in his office.

By associating himself with IIT from 1962 onward, Khan had the distinct advantage of collaborating with architectural students and faculty there, and through his supervision of many student research projects he could conceive new structural systems or validate his intuitive concepts about a potential new system. He used many of these systems for actual building projects at SOM.

Khan's thesis was that a skyscraper, by its very nature and composition, is a complex building type in which a multi-disciplinary design approach is absolutely necessary. Most design firms specializing in tall buildings cannot individually sustain the burden of research activities. The fact that the practicing profession cannot undertake serious research in the architecture of tall buildings, even though there is a clear need for it, underlines the importance of collaboration and interaction between the industry and academia. Thus it becomes apparent why there was no significant progress in the development of new structural systems for multi-story buildings for a long time beyond the conventional rigid-frame concept. Khan had the uncommon ability of not only bridging the gaps between architecture and engineering but also linking the two worlds of academia and practice. This was possible because of his wide-horizon vision and universalist outlook. Very few people in this world are endowed with this rare quality.

Khan left his unforgettable mark on the architectural and engineering professions by his much publicized tubular design concept for high-rise buildings. He recognized in the early 1960s that the rigid frame system that dominated high-rise building construction till then was not necessarily the best structural system as the buildings got taller. Although he recognized that the tubular system that represents an optimum configuration in which the building responds to lateral loads as a whole in three dimensions, he could also sense that between the basic rigid frame and the ultimate tube systems there exists a range of structural systems for various building heights. As we saw in Chapter 4, the building's scale manifests itself through the "premium for height"—a concept that Khan frequently elaborated upon. This concept told him that as the number of stories in a building increases, the total structural material consumption increases drastically. The floor framing system usually carries almost the same gravity loads, although the girders along the column lines will be progressively heavier towards the base of the building to carry progressively larger lateral forces. The column sizes increase progressively towards the base due to the accumulated increase in gravity loads. However, the columns need to be even heavier towards the base to resist lateral loads. The net result is that as the building becomes taller there is a greater demand on the girders and columns to carry lateral forces. What really creates this condition is the fact that the total lateral deflection due to shear racking and cantilever action is greatly magnified and hence the stiffness demand of the building increases dramatically with height. This calls for a structural system that goes well beyond the simple rigid frame concept. Based on his investigations, Khan argued that as the height increases beyond 10 stories, the lateral drift starts controlling the design, the stiffness rather than strength becomes the dominating factor, and the premium for height increases rapidly with the number of stories (Khan, 1972a).

Khan reasoned that the essence of the solution to a problem stemmed from the nature of the problem itself. The structural

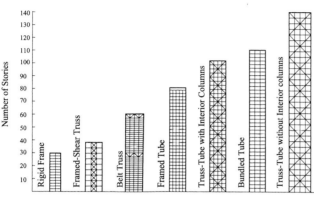

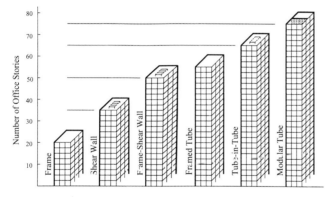

Fig. 5
Fig. 6

system naturally grows out of its justification for its state of being. As Khan might say: seek out what that is and what the structure wants to be and the solution will follow. As a creative designer he did not begin with a preconceived notion of what the building form should be like but rather he searched for the truth, seeking out the solution that is most natural to the problem. If the problem is placed in its proper perspective, the structural system will logically grow out of the creative solutions to the problem. Khan argued that since most of the premium for height of a tall building designed by conventional methods is caused by wind or other lateral load considerations—if systems could be found which automatically kept the wind-load stresses below the allowable 33% overstress permitted by the code, then such a system would not have to pay the premium for height (Khan, 1974b). From this line of reasoning, he then proposed a hierarchy of structural systems for office buildings of ordinary proportions and forms that are appropriate for certain heights (Khan, 1969, 1972c; 1973). Khan initially proposed a diagram of structural systems relating to heights of buildings in 1969. He presented six systems at this time ranging from braced frame to trussed tube (Khan, 1969). Later, he upgraded this diagram with modified structural systems (Khan, 1972c; 1973). He developed these schemes for both steel and concrete buildings (Schueller, 1977; CTBUH, 1995). Feasible structural systems for high-rise buildings, he noted, are rigid frames, shear walls, frame-shear wall interaction, belt trusses, and the various other types of tubular systems (Figs. 5 and 6). Of course, this menu of structural systems for various heights was proposed by Khan more as a guideline and should be treated only as a rule of thumb. It should be remembered that each system has a wide range of height applications depending on other design and service criteria related to variables such as: building shape, height-to-width ratio, architectural functions, exterior loading conditions, building stability, the environment, site constraints, to name a few. For every condition, however, there is always an optimum structural system, although it may not necessarily match one of those proposed by Khan's scheme due to the predominant influence of other factors on the building form.

The type of structural system clearly depends on its height or span changes. This was intuitively known before and was suggested for buildings by Myron Goldsmith in the early 1950s (Blaser, 1987). Goldsmith, an engineer-architect, and a creative thinker certainly inspired Khan in this regard. Khan, however, developed and applied the principle to practical structures. Ideas are not sufficient if not actually realized with applications. The idea of a flying machine existed and the principles of physics and aerodynamics were known before the airplane was invented. But the Wright brothers actually were able to fly for the first time in the airplane that they designed and built. They are given credit and remembered for that.

The menu of structural systems proposed by Khan was based on intensive research and aided by computer simulations. It is the greatest single contribution by him to tall building technology. It acted as a powerful catalyst in the rapid development and use of these systems for buildings constructed in the 1970s and 1980s and that continue to be built today. It also paved the way for more innovative as well as hybrid systems. Availability of computers has made possible the use of complex structural systems that have been generated from Khan's basic systems either by simple modification or by some ingenious combinations. The analysis and design of this new breed of structures have now become more sophisticated. But in this evolution of structural form, a basic fact remains: the structural system must be determined on the basis of its efficiency in terms of material consumption. Although Khan was an ardent believer in using computers for structural analysis, he despised blind dependence on computers. His advice was: "use computers, but always check your results by simple manual calculations and see if the numbers make sense."

Returning to the discussion on the great surge of technology and economic boom that resulted in a second wave of development in Chicago following World War II, suddenly the skyline changed not only in Chicago with the construction of the John Hancock Center and the Sears Tower but also in other cities like New York, Houston, and New Orleans. The Empire State Building in New York was for a long time a symbol of height limit. The World Trade Center broke that 1250-ft. (379-m) record and exceeded the scale of the built environment in the surrounding area. Prior to this new group of tall buildings, multi-story buildings had been relatively short and wide. A wider building was cheaper and stiffer. An extreme example is the 20-story Merchandise Mart building in Chicago that occupies a full block. This was so because a large floor area was required and at that time buildings taller than 20 stories were not practical. Such short and wide buildings repeated from one block to the next created what Khan called "city canyons" where sunlight did not reach street level except for a few hours at a time (Khan, 1972a).

Khan's special interest was to mitigate this condition by providing setbacks and plazas at lower levels and designing tall and slender buildings that would possess inherent strength, vitality, proportion, and elegance. Like Jenney, Mies, Nervi, and Goldsmith, he believed that a good structural system could have a desirable expression in its architectural form. In a framed structural system, no artificial facade should be present that will cover the natural expression of the building's inherent strength. He promoted the idea that the loads should be allowed to flow naturally and let the form of the building arise in its own way, even mathematically, without being subjected to arbitrariness. On many occasions, this could result in great architectural possibilities.

His propensity for innovative designs exploring different structural concepts was coupled with his theoretical understanding of the mechanics of the structure. These theoretical developments were reported in his many publications. His research and innovations can be classified in many ways. In broad terms, they are: the formalization of the shear wall-frame interaction concept, preparation of a structural system menu based on height variation, development of the tubular concept and its modifications, composite construction, computer applications, integration of structure with architectural design

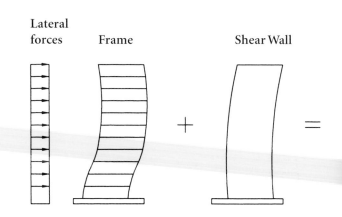

and the building's surroundings, introduction of structural art in tall building design, and forecasting new structural systems and building types.

The biggest challenge for Khan was to develop structural systems for buildings that would be tall and slender, yet not involve a large premium for height. This would demand structural efficiency and a deep understanding of the scale effect. The interaction of shear walls and frames in buildings had been understood and known for some time (Fig. 7). In simple terms, the frames and shear walls would tend to sway independently under lateral load in their own shear mode and cantilever mode, respectively, except that a rigid floor diaphragm would force them to deflect equally to maintain compatibility of deformations (Fig. 8). The building's deformation profile depends upon the relative rigidities of the frames and shear walls that make up the lateral load resisting system.

Khan recognized that the distribution of lateral loads to the shear walls and frames is rather complex and depends on the relative stiffness properties of each frame and shear wall along the entire height of the building. For complex structures, the relative stiffnesses may vary irregularly along the building height and the assumption of rigid diaphragm action becomes questionable where abrupt changes in stiffness and irregular distribution of shear occur. Moreover, the support conditions at the base of the building influence the stiffness of the shear walls and frames. Architectural configuration and other functional requirements often demand buildings of irregular layout both in plan and elevation making structural design more challenging.

Keeping all these factors in mind, Khan published his work in a 1964 paper on frame-shear wall interaction (Khan and Sbarounis, 1964). This paper was "a milestone" in the development of innovative structural systems that enhanced the efficiency and cost-effectiveness of high-rise buildings in both concrete and steel (Fintel, 1982). It demonstrated that the rigidity of high-rise buildings could drastically be enhanced without increasing the cost by introducing shear walls or shear trusses. The method presented in this paper was suitable for easy and practical design office application. Using the early versions of computers, Khan developed several practical design charts based on mathematical solutions for the interaction forces and by employing a forced convergence procedure. These design aids have been used for numerous high-rise buildings and were in use in engineering design offices even after the advent of high-speed computers in the 1970s.

Although the charts developed by Khan are no longer used because of the clear advantage of using efficient computers and the availability of improved modeling and analytical techniques today, the significance of these charts still remains valid for preliminary design during the conceptual stage of structural system selection. In the frame-shear wall interaction system, it is a known fact that the shear wall contributes the least stiffness in the top region to the overall system. Thus the shear wall is pulled back by the frame in the upper portion of the building and pushed forward in the lower portion (see Fig. 7). Hence the lateral shear is mostly carried by the frame in the top region. Even though Khan understood this well, for the sake of maintaining structural continuity, however, he was against dropping

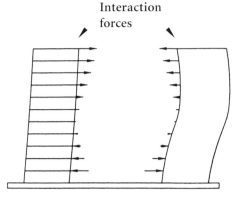

Interaction forces

Fig. 7

57

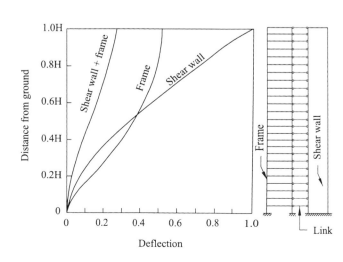

Fig. 8

Distance from ground

1.0H
0.8H
0.6H
0.4H
0.2H
0

Shear wall + frame
Frame
Shear wall

0   0.2   0.4   0.6   0.8   1.0

Deflection

Frame
Shear wall
Link

off the shear wall completely near the top beyond the point where it becomes less effective.

The inherent limitations of moment-resisting frames led Khan to explore other systems for taller buildings that included frame-shear wall combinations, trussed tubes, framed tubes, and other structural systems. Investigative studies were conducted by graduate students at IIT under the supervision of Myron Goldsmith, Fazlur Khan, and David Sharpe. Khan identified the heights for which various structural systems were efficient and economical and recognized a range of structural systems with reasonable slenderness ratios in a sequential manner with particular height limitation for each (see Figs. 5 and 6). Thus, in effect, he demonstrated that the structural system should be optimized at a global level from which member sizes can be optimized at a local level. Khan arranged the structural systems in the form of charts on the basis of structural efficiency for simple rectilinear form of buildings. However, with the change of expression in architectural form, many innovative structural concepts were introduced later to meet the new requirements.

As we saw before, Khan identified the tube as optimum structural form for maximum stiffness of tall buildings to resist lateral loads, and thoroughly researched and developed the mechanics of structural behavior for framed tubes. He also developed influence charts for the aid of designers in engineering offices (Khan, 1974a). The main challenge facing him was the question of how to minimize the shear lag phenomenon and increase the cantilever component of the lateral sway of the building. He realized that circular, hexagonal, square or similar plan shapes would offer the best possible tubular effect and elongated shapes or irregular shapes the least. Although the horizontal configuration of a tall building need not be of a regular shape, it is, however, necessary that the shape be compact and closed to offer tubular behavior. He experimented with the configurations of tube layouts which eventually gave rise to different typologies within the tubular paradigm. A major innovation by Khan was the braced tube that resulted in a very stiff structure for supertall buildings. The well-known bundled tube concept, developed later for very tall buildings, where the building footprint must have large dimensions to keep the slenderness ratio under control, is an outgrowth of this search for the best system. The bundled tube is essentially a multi-duct tube shaft with direct wall-to-wall junctions. It is one of the three major large-scale stabilization systems in multi-tube structural form that largely surpass the capabilities of the single tube. Two other combinations are tube-in-tube with multi-casing tube shaft and a rigid tube frame consisting of individual tubes linked by bridge units (Engel, 1997).

When Khan had been working on the Brunswick Building, he became aware that the exterior columns exposed to severe temperature changes would shorten relative to the core, which is under controlled temperature condition during occupancy. Anticipating building movements that could result in racking of floor girders and consequently in major structural damage, Khan developed a sophisticated analytical approach to handle this column exposure problem in collaboration with Mark Fintel of Portland Cement Association (PCA), (Khan and Fintel, 1968a). Based on a rigorous thermal effect analysis for the Brunswick

Building, it was decided to release the rotational restraint at the rigid moment connections between the floor slabs of the upper twelve stories and the core by making the slab edges bear on neoprene pads on a ledge provided around the core wall (see Chapter 6). Similar thermal analyses were also performed for steel buildings (Khan and Nassetta, 1970).

An interesting innovation by Khan regarding the tubular concept that he used on major steel buildings like the John Hancock Center (braced tube) and the Sears Tower (bundled tube) is its identical application to concrete buildings. He employed the bundled tube and braced tube concepts to, respectively, the One Magnificent Mile and the Onterie Center—both concrete buildings located in Chicago (see Chapter 6). Another diagonally braced concrete building to which Khan made a significant contribution is the 50-story 780 Third Avenue Building in New York. Khan predicted that bundled-tube concrete buildings could be efficiently designed for up to 100 stories (Khan, 1974b).

Khan had been searching for a solution to the recurring problem of transfer of axial loads from the closely spaced exterior tube columns to widely spaced columns in lobbies and lower levels of tall office buildings. The need for the welcoming nature of entrances to buildings at the street level, and the desire for the occupants to have an open unobstructed view of the street from inside, encourages architects to space columns more widely than the typical maximum of 15 ft. (4.5m) on center. Furthermore, the requirement of providing loading docks at ground level demands the elimination of some columns. When the ground floor is used for retail space, the owners want people to have an open view from both inside and outside. Parking of cars at basement levels also demands elimination of some of the columns at ground level. Also, when underground high-rise construction is extended to property lines for additional parking space, some of the exterior columns from the high-rise building's superstructure need to be terminated below to facilitate easy traffic flow. All these factors that disrupt the tubular behavior of the building at its base warrant a structural solution that will ensure the expected efficiency of the structural system. (We note here that closely spaced columns at the ground floor have the advantage of protecting a building from terrorist bomb attacks. Perhaps, in 1995, many lives could have been saved if the Alfred P. Murrah Federal Building in Oklahoma City had had many closely spaced columns at the ground floor. Also, closely spaced columns in the tubular World Trade Center in New York probably saved many lives in 1993 when a terrorist bomb exploded in it.)

This problem bothered Khan until his death. A principal approach to overcome this problem is to introduce deep transfer girders and transfer trusses to ensure the transfer of columns at ground level. Fintel (1986) pointed out in this regard after he visited a concrete building accompanied by Khan:

> From conversations with Khan, I knew that he was on the lookout for a different solution to the ever-present problem of shift of loads from the closely spaced peripheral columns to the widely spaced columns required in lobbies of high-rise office buildings, which was accomplished by means of heavy transfer girders. I invited Khan to visit a newly completed

30-story apartment building in which every other column in the ground floor was eliminated without adding a transfer girder. The entire 30-story elevation of exposed columns was handled as a vierendeel truss (a truss without diagonals). We happened to visit the building after a rain, and the shear cracks in the spandrel beams of the lower stories were visually amplified by the rain. This picture was not lost on Khan as shown in the two approaches he subsequently used to buildings he designed.

Without the benefit of having a definite solution to the problem, Khan adopted some creative approaches to divert the loads gradually to the lower level columns by introducing heavier spandrel beams above the transfer girder. This eliminated an abrupt transfer of column loads from above to the transfer girder, although this still negatively affected the tubular behavior. He used arch action for the two buildings (Two Shell Plaza in Houston, Texas, and Marine Midland Bank in Rochester, New York) creating a natural structural expression that accentuated the aesthetics of the building's facade (see Chapter 6).

Although such arch action and "tree-like" transfer of loads created a visually dominant structural solution to the problem, the tubular action for lateral load was still impaired especially for buildings of greater height. He expressed this concern when I met him in his office for the last time prior to his departure for Korea and Saudi Arabia. In the course of our conversation, he reached for a small notebook in his coat pocket and showed a few rough sketches using a new system in which columns would be widely spaced and he would use hidden trusses in the space between the window sill above and the lintel below, which is usually clad throughout the building facade for the entire height. The discussions were very preliminary and brief. He wanted me to carry out research on this and promised that he would discuss this matter in more detail upon his return. It seemed to me that his main objective was to substantially increase the column spacing throughout the entire height of the building by magnifying the spandrel stiffness in relation to that of columns using a perimeter truss concept and other structural articulations.

A major innovation by Khan in the mid-1960s in the realm of tubular design is the composite system (Khan, 1974b; Iyengar, 1977; Taranath, 1997). In a nutshell, this system combines the advantages of the speed of erection of steel members and the rigidity and fire-resistant property of poured-in-place reinforced concrete peripheral wall comprising large spandrel beams and columns. The tubular behavior of the system relieves the steel members from the need to provide lateral resistance, thereby allowing for simple connection details. Moreover, the steel structure could be erected at its usual speed and the composite system could result in cost saving. Khan (1974b) explained the reason of why he conceived the composite tube system in the following way:

> In tube-in-tube structures the central shear wall core can drastically reduce the flexibility in planning and utilization of the area. For instance, when elevators drop off at different height levels, the free space cannot be retrieved in an efficient way because the shear walls cannot suddenly be eliminated. In tall steel structures the most important advantage, of course,

is that the structure can be built at a relatively fast speed, generally one floor every three days, whereas in concrete construction even one floor every seven days is an optimistic projection. In steel buildings the central cores are much more flexible than in the concrete building, and any free area due to dropping off of the elevators can be immediately utilized as a fully rentable area by adjusting the partition walls as necessary. Why not combine the advantages and eliminate the disadvantages in a Composite System. This is what led the author to the Composite System, consisting of the structural steel columns, beams and floor construction; whereas the exterior closely spaced columns and spandrels together with the curtain wall is formed of reinforced concrete.

A further innovation by Khan, and something that is not as well known, is his original concept of dissipating energy at the lower story of buildings in seismic zones. He worked with Fintel on this concept. He thought of a shock absorbing soft-story concept in which "stability walls," neoprene pads, and deformable cables would be used in the lowermost level in a predetermined fashion such that during an earthquake the lower level would dissipate energy and isolate the upper floors from any damage (Khan and Fintel, 1968b). Thus, instead of designing the entire building to resist high earthquake forces, the bottom story of the building is allowed to distort with the earthquake, thereby screening out most of the forces there. The upper part of the structure remains unaffected and behaves as an elastic system, whereas the lower story behaves as an elasto-plastic bilinear system. The lower story is pre-designed for calculated lateral distortion and can be readjusted and repaired after a severe seismic event. Around the same time, in 1971, a major earthquake in San Fernando, California, caused severe damages to the Olive View Hospital in which the lower floor was very "soft" compared to upper levels without any mechanism to dissipate the energy that Khan envisioned. In this building, a soft two-story system of rigid frames supported a four-story stiff shearwall and frame structure as well as a penthouse. During the earthquake, the upper stories moved so much as a unit that columns in the lower level could not accommodate such a huge displacement between their bases and tops, and failed. The term "soft story" thus received bad publicity on the west coast and the idea of using it, even with shock absorbing capability, was discarded. Fintel has told me, however, that the concept of shock-absorbing lower story using cables as proposed by Khan and Fintel was used by Chicago architect Bertrand Goldberg (the designer of Marina City in Chicago) for a hospital building in the north-west region of the United States.

While discussing with Fintel this topic of a shock-absorbing lower story in seismic zones, he mentioned that following an earthquake in Yugoslavia in the 1960s, he saw a few damaged buildings where the bottom story was excessively deformed. This triggered the idea of the shock-absorbing lower story in his mind, which he had later discussed with Khan and eventually they came up with this innovation. But Fintel, a good friend of Khan, was quick to add: "don't give me any credit for it . . . give it all to Faz."

The concept of base isolation is a popular approach for earthquake-resistant design. In this system, the energy is dissipated at the base of the building rather than in the bottom story. The base isolation technique for seismic design is in a way an extension of the idea of shock-absorbing lower story conceived by Khan and Fintel.

Khan, together with Michael Hogan, an associate of SOM, and Iyengar, studied the dynamic characteristics of modern floor construction that often produces lighter, more flexible and longer spans. Measurements of floor vibrations were taken on a number of common types of floors. The results were compiled and plotted using parameters of acceleration and damping as a measure of the dynamic response. A practical method of evaluating a floor design was developed using an empirical approach. According to Iyengar, this study was never published.

Nick Isyumov of the University of Western Ontario, who knew Khan for 15 years and worked with him on many projects including the Sears Tower, the One Magnificent Mile, the Haj Terminal and major hangars in Saudi Arabia, recognized Khan's extraordinary ability to realize that civil engineering structures are often dynamic rather than static systems. He put it this way, "Dr. Khan's philosophy was to search for structural systems which performed well in situations of dynamic loading and requied no premiums for resisting such additional effects as wind action. This required not only a firm and clear understanding of how different structural systems act but the genius to innovate and find new and better systems."

Since Khan was a visionary, he realized the potential of integrating computer technology with tall building design; he was able to convince his architectural partners to support this viewpoint. Doug Stoker, a structural engineer and computer specialist who worked at SOM from 1970 to 1989 and became a partner in charge of computing, referred to Khan during his conversation with me as the "spiritual leader" and "godfather" of technology at SOM. He recalled that when Khan bought his very first $450 HP calculator in the early 1970s, he was so proud of it that he would invite people to his office to demonstrate it. He was a great proponent of computers and he wanted a computer terminal at his office as soon as it became available. He liked to use computers whenever he could, but during his latter days, he had hardly any time left to work on his computer for a prolonged period.

In 1981, at SOM, I worked on a 60-story steel office building for Los Angeles called Pacific Plaza. This building had a pentagonal footprint and had a tube-in-tube structural system. It had a 5-story steel low-rise structure at the base of the tower and a 14-story separate concrete parking garage. It was never built in its original form, but was revised to a shorter building renamed Citicorp Plaza. Others primarily involved in the original project were John Zils, Mohammed Iqbal, and Sarv Nayyar, with Khan as the structural partner in charge of structural design. The analysis and design portion of the 60-story tower were assigned to me. During the course of this project, Khan always wanted to investigate different aspects of tubular behavior. For example, under his direction, we used heavier spandrel sizes at the corners to see if this would reduce the shear lag in this tubular structure. It did not help as much as we had hoped for. We also tried haunched girders for the spandrels. Again, no noticeable reduction of shear lag or increase of cantilever drift component resulted. It appeared that for framed tubes, reduced column spacing is the most important parameter to achieve efficiency.

I had a jolt in my career while working on this project. At this time, I was not aware of the problem of "quartering wind", that comes from a diagonal direction, faced by renowned structural engineer William J. LeMessurier, for the Citicorp Center in New York—which he designed. His firm inadvertently overlooked this wind force— a design flaw in the lateral bracing system was a result. LeMessurier discovered this conceptual error in 1978 after the building was constructed and occupied, but was able to fix the deficiency with necessary changes. Ours was a large project in a severe seismic zone. During the wind load analysis, we considered the wind forces along the two perpendicular x and y directions. Normally we do not apply lateral loads diagonally on rectangular buildings. For a regular building, if the structural framework is found to be adequate for wind load in the two principal orthogonal directions, it is taken to be adequate for wind load applied in any other direction. But this pentagonal building had a diagonal face at 45 degrees to the x and y directions. For this building, structural members were proportioned for lateral wind load applied in the x and y directions alone. However, wind load should have been applied on the diagonal face which had a much wider sail. This later proved to be more critical in terms of the building's sway, which resulted from a relatively lower stiffness of the structure in that direction. We did the same thing for the lateral seismic load, although this did not affect the design since wind rather than seismic load was found to control the overall design outcome. When this omission in the computer analysis was detected by Khan during his review, I was shaken and embarrassed. I tried to explain my case when this matter was discussed in his office, in the presence of Zils and Nayyar. Khan listened intently, noting that I was young and relatively inexperienced in tall building design; he never expressed the slightest frustration or anger towards me. Construction drawings were still not prepared, although preliminary drawings were completed. Khan suggested some innovative solutions to this problem to keep the total quantity of steel used in the preliminary structural system the same, while satisfying the building code. To my great relief the problem was easily resolved.

▲ ▼

In addition to his innovations in connection with professional practice, Khan undertook many academic investigations on tall buildings at IIT following the tradition of Mies and Goldsmith. In 1938, Mies van der Rohe became the director of the School of Architecture at IIT and established a new curriculum at all levels. Mies had long governed the thinking of faculty there since then. It is natural that Khan would be inspired by that. The school continues to derive much of its strength from research. Theories were tested and refined through its graduate thesis program, which were then applied to practical projects. Design, engineering, and aesthetics were brought together through research to create new and significant architecture. Khan had much to do with it.

Khan's work with Goldsmith started in 1962, when Khan joined the faculty there as an adjunct professor at the invitation of Goldsmith. Further assistance in the thesis program was provided by architect David Sharpe and structural engineer Mahjoub Elnimeiri. Khan and Goldsmith continued work on the idea of scale for long-span buildings. They investigated several nineteenth-century three-hinged arches, such as the Gallery of Machines in the 1889 Paris Exposition and the 1893 Manufacturers' Building in Chicago. Based on extensive studies of a large number of long-span systems, they concluded that long-span roofs had their own scale of structure. This was, of course, known intuitively. Although for short-span structures the efficiency of different systems was not much different, for longer spans a wide divergence in their efficiencies was observed. For very long spans, however, certain structural systems that were inherently much more efficient than others did exist. These long-span systems include trusses, rigid frames, domes, cable systems, and arches.

As part of his contributions to education, Khan had supervised a surprisingly large number of graduate students in architecture at IIT as an adjunct professor (Goldsmith, 1986; Blaser, 1987). In the projects in which Goldsmith and Khan were involved, a continuing investigation of new structural types and their expression was conducted. A significant number of new building types of that era warranted consideration of increasingly larger scale. Therefore, the theoretical research concentrated on long-span and high-rise buildings. This research resulted in several innovative research projects that became prototypes for many practical structures since realized. The study of long-span buildings culminated in the advent of the two- and three-story grid-systems and cable supported spans. Likewise, the study of tall buildings led to the development of such systems as diagonally braced tubes in steel and concrete, belt truss structures, and the superframes. The thesis projects discussed here show the broad range of possibilities for structural systems and their architectural expression. The source of many of the innovative structures designed by Khan and subsequently by others and built to date can be traced back to these germinal projects.

The first Master's Thesis was by David Sharpe in 1962, in which Goldsmith was the principal adviser and Khan the structural adviser. Sharpe produced a chart showing how the weight of a steel structure increases with the increase in its span. The study was conducted for 166 long-span varied structural systems in steel that included rigid frames, trusses, domes, arches and space frames. It was found that as the spans increase beyond 100 ft. (30m), the different types increasingly diverge, and it becomes evident which type is efficient for which span range (Blaser, 1987). With the assistance of Khan, Sharpe, who joined the faculty at IIT, subsequently received an AISC grant in 1968 to update his thesis work. Khan also advised and guided him on this funded project. In a 1963 thesis, Phyllis Lambert carried out an investigative study on 175 long-span reinforced concrete roof structural systems for her Master's Thesis paralleling Sharpe's study for steel systems under the supervision of Goldsmith and Khan. This study included flat spans, folded plates, barrels, hyperbolic paraboloids, domes, suspension systems and cantilevers.

Another very early study of significant nature—and the first thesis on tall buildings under the advisership of Goldsmith and

Fig. 9: Sasaki Project, Photograph of Model [Courtesy: Graham ResourceCenter, College of Architecture, Illinois Institute of Technology (IIT)]

Fig. 9

Fig. 10: Glyniadakis Project, Plan View

Fig. 11: Glyniadakis Project, Photograph of Model
[Courtesy: Graham Resource Center, College of Architecture, IIT]

Fig. 12: Glyniadakis Project, Photograph of Model Removing
Structure to Show the Relationships of the Various Functions
[Courtesy: Graham Resource Center, College of Architecture, IIT]

Khan—was a 1964 diagonally braced tower by a student, Mikio Sasaki. The tower was a 700-ft. (213-m) high office building that would be subjected to severe wind and seismic forces in Tokyo, Japan (Fig. 9). A steel structure was selected with a square plan 168 x 168 ft. (51 x 51m) with columns spaced 28 ft. (8.5m) apart around the periphery. It is based on a 4.67-ft. (1.4-m) module in plan with a central core which contains elevators, stairs, toilets, and the vertical building services systems. To resist lateral deflection, the building is braced by three giant 18-story high X-braces on each face. In the absence of sophisticated computer programs in those days, Khan and Sasaki tested structural models for different load conditions. This braced tube structure was a forerunner for the John Hancock Center designed by Khan.

In a 1964 thesis, Emmanuel Glyniadakis worked out a wide range of public sports facilities in a project that explored the concept of universal space (Figs. 10-12). An arena with a capacity of 13,000 spectators, a track and field area accommodating 2,000 people, a swimming pool with seats for 2,000 spectators, and a large flexible area for other sports were all combined in this project. The building is 810 ft. (245m) square in plan, with a two-way grid roof structure of 17-ft. (5-m) deep steel girders spaced 45 ft. (13.5m) apart, carried by nine steel cruciform columns forming four 405 x 405 ft. (123 x 123m) bays. Glass is used for both

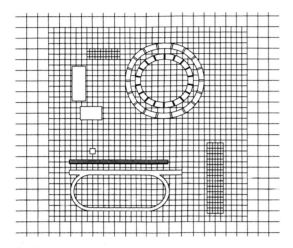

Fig. 10

Fig. 11

Fig. 12

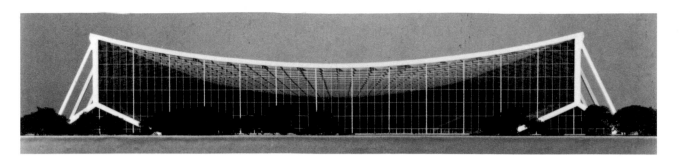

Fig. 13

perimeter walls and roof. Khan, Goldsmith, and Sharpe were the advisers for this thesis. The same year, Khan also supervised Melville Leopold von Broembsen, who carried out an investigation into the architectural expression of a long-span multi-story building in steel—its specific function being an exhibition hall of industrial machinery.

In a 1965 thesis under the advisership of Goldsmith, Khan, and Sharpe, Peter Doyle designed an enclosed stadium with a seating capacity of 65,000 people for football and other events (Figs. 13 and 14). A large number of configurations were studied. This stadium encompasses an area of 650 x 900 ft. (197 x 273m) with bundled catenary steel suspension cables spaced 50 ft on center. The cables are encased in precast concrete and are post-tensioned for providing stiffness. The catenary beams are supported by inverted Y-shaped bents 125 ft. (38m) tall. A diagonal tension member is provided to join the top of each bent with the ground to absorb the inward thrust of the catenary beams. Precast prestressed concrete beams are placed 27 ft. (8m) apart between the catenary beams, and the spaces between them are filled with glass.

In a 1966 thesis project, A. G. Krishna Menon attempted to derive an optimum structure by pushing the slenderness ratio of a 90-story apartment building toward its extreme limit. Measuring 94 by 185 ft. (28.5 by 56m) in plan, the building is 816 ft. (247.5m) tall and has a slenderness ratio (i.e., ratio of height to least width) of 8.7:1. The concrete flat slab floors are supported by interior columns spaced at 18 ft. (5.5m). Columns at the perimeter are spaced at 6 ft. (1.8m) and taper off toward the top. The concrete structure is a framed tube stiffened additionally by two full-width shear walls at one-third and two-thirds points of the long sides.

In a 1968 thesis under the advisership of Goldsmith, Khan, and Sharpe, Lawrence Kenny designed a suspended cable-stayed roof for consolidating the passenger train traffic for Chicago in a single glass-enclosed hall 600 ft. (182m) wide, 900 ft. (273m) long, and 65 ft. (19.5m) high (Figs. 15 and 16). The roof structure is carried by steel masts 150 ft. (45.5m) apart and projecting 25 ft. (7.5m) above the roof. Thirty-six cables radiate downward from the top of each mast to support the intersections of a two-way grid of steel beams spaced at 30 ft. (9m). Twenty additional cables radiate upward from the mast to the edge of the 150 ft. (45.5m) grid to stabilize it. This project was later used for a competition proposal for the United States Pavilion in Osaka. Prior to this, in 1967, another student, Dorman Anderson, investigated a similar long span roof for a university project with 100-ft. (30m) bays in precast concrete.

Fig. 14

66
67

Fig. 13: Doyle Project, Plan View
[Courtesy: Graham Resource Center, College of Architecture, IIT]

Fig. 14: Doyle Project, Photograph of Model
[Courtesy: Graham Resource Center, College of Architecture, IIT]

Fig. 15: Kenny Project, Roof Plan
[Courtesy: Graham Resource Center, College of Architecture, IIT]

Fig. 16: Kenny Project, Photograph of Model
[Courtesy: Graham Resource Center, College of Architecture, IIT]

Fig. 15

Fig. 16

Fig. 17: Hodgkison Project, Photograph of Model
[Courtesy: Graham Resource Center, College of Architecture, IIT]

Fig. 18: Hodgkison Project, Floor Framing Plan

Fig. 19: Hodgkison Project, Elevation and Section of 50-ft. (15-m)
Floor Beams (see Fig. 18)

Fig. 20: Hodgkison Project, Bracing Details

Fig. 21: Hodgkison Project, Bracing Details at Corner

Fig. 22: Pran Project, Photograph of Model
[Courtesy: Graham Resource Center, College of Architecture, IIT]

68

Fig. 17

69

Fig. 18

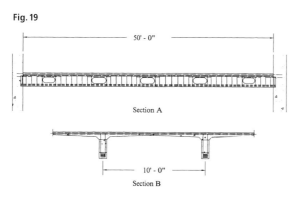

Framing plan | Alternative framing plan

Fig. 19

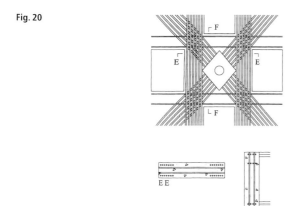

50' - 0"

Section A

10' - 0"

Section B

Fig. 20

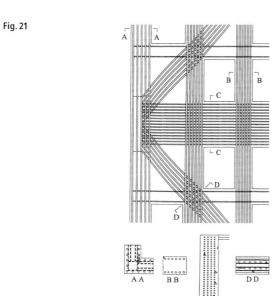

F

E | E

F

E E

F F

Fig. 21

A | A

B | B

C

C

D

D

A A   B B   C C   D D

Fig. 22

Also in 1968, Robin Hodgkison worked on an interesting project in which he tried to find an alternate solution in concrete for the World Trade Center in New York and to suggest an alternative to the proposed development of the Illinois Central Railroad site. This development project proposed a large number of medium-sized high-rise buildings. In the thesis, four buildings of higher density were proposed including three 116-story concrete office buildings (Fig. 17). The goal was to demonstrate that high-density development projects undertaken with many mid-rise buildings could be redesigned with fewer high-rise buildings of this type. Towers are square in plan. The perimeter of the building consisted of an array of columns spaced 10 ft. (3m) apart and spandrels that are 3 ft. (0.9m) deep, rigidly connected to the floor system (Figs. 18 and 19). The building has a slenderness ratio of 6.5:1. The exterior tube is diagonally braced similar to Sasaki's thesis. The diagonals are created by infilling between the columns blocking two window openings at each floor on each side of the building (Figs. 20 and 21 for bracing details). All lateral loads are resisted by the diagonals similar to those of the John Hancock Center. The proportions of the columns, walls, and blocked out windows were structurally feasible, architecturally acceptable, and buildable. Khan later used this concept using concrete as the structural material for the diagonally braced Onterie Center in Chicago.

Peter Pran's project of 1969 used a system of catenary cables to support the roof of a large exhibition hall (Fig. 22) with a clear span of 1000 ft. (303m). The 13 main cables were spaced 167 ft. (51m) apart along the 2000-ft. (606-m) long building. Each cable was slung between two cast steel saddles placed atop steel columns 240-ft. (73-m) high. The cables are extended diagonally downwards from the columns and anchored below grade. The roof is made of 8-ft. (2.4-m) deep steel trusses, hung from the main cables by suspender cables spaced at 20 ft. (6.1m). An investigation of the roof system showed that this system was more economical than other possible long-span systems in terms of material consumption.

In 1970, Khan and Goldsmith supervised Alfonso Rodriquez, who worked on a form-stiffened apartment building (Fig. 23). In this thesis, the plan of the building was deformed into a compound curve along the building's height. This deliberately provided curvature of the building stiffened it against lateral forces

Fig. 20

Fig. 24

Fig. 23: Rodriquez Project, Photograph of Model
[Courtesy: Graham Resource Center, College of Architecture, IIT]

Fig. 24: Hayashida Project, Photograph of Model
[Courtesy: Graham Resource Center, College of Architecture, IIT]

Fig. 25: Tanaka Project, Suspended Roof Elevations

Fig. 26: Tanaka Project, Photograph of Model
[Courtesy: Graham Resource Center, College of Architecture, IIT]

so much so that a 60-story structure became feasible that would be otherwise about 30 stories in height for a building with a conventional shape and the same efficiency.

Khan advised another student, Mahen Panchal, who completed his thesis in 1971. On this project, Khan joined Professor Daniel Brenner. It involved a 2-story concrete library building located in a tropical climate with a terrace garden on the roof. He helped the student develop important structural details, and provided architectural insight as well. Another thesis project by Heinz Sieber, also in 1971, raised some interesting possibilities of fenestration for multi-purpose buildings. The basic premise of this project was that the entire building would be designed by the structural engineer and the supervising architect, and once the building skeleton was decided upon, segments of the building for different functions or use could be given to separate investors and architect-engineers to design in an overall manner by collaboration.

In a 1972 thesis by Michael Breitman, Khan joined another professor, Alfred Swenson, and investigated into the idea of the superframe. The steel building was divided into 15-story units, carrying the loads to the outside of the building. The visually expressed diagonal on the outside connects the facade in its entirety so that the structure acts as an exoskeleton braced tube. This project led to complete and comprehensive analysis considering various structural parameters. It went deep into structural implications of different proportions for superframes, showing the effect of height on structural steel weight. This study proved an important point that with the basic trussed-tube superframe, the premium for height is relatively small for ultra-tall buildings.

In 1974, another of Khan's students, Masami Hayashida, worked on a multi-use high-rise building in steel (Fig. 24). Interestingly, this thesis investigated an 88-story building project using the bundled tube concept from the Sears Tower. This building had six modular tubes at the base up to the 15th floor, four in the middle up to the 46th floor, and ended with two tubes up to the top. The columns were spaced at 15 ft. (4.5m) similar to Sears and belt trusses were provided at the stepback locations and at the top. Khan wanted to see through this project if the bundled tube concept could be used for a multi-use

73

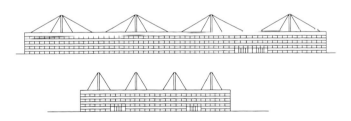

Fig. 25
Fig. 26

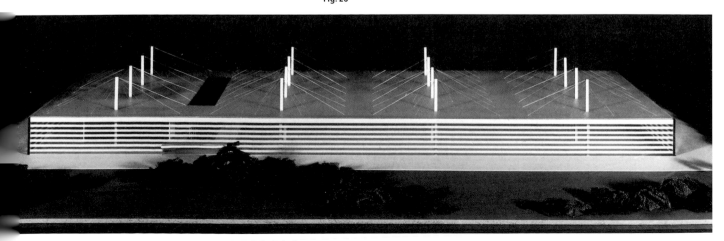

building in which lease spans change for hotels and apartments relative to the offices.

Khan also advised Mineo Tanaka on a suspended exhibition hall in Japan in 1978 (Figs. 25 and 26). In this project, a cable-stayed roof system was used. The spans were on the order of several hundred feet. It became apparent that for spans in the range of 300 to 400 ft. (91 to 121m), only a few systems could compete in material weight with a cable-stayed system. However, when the system was extended to the range of 600 ft. or more, no other system could compete with the cable-stayed roof system. As we noted before, Peter Pran's thesis study reached similar conclusions for a 1000-ft. (303m) span that used catenary cables.

A late student project was that by Wayne Petrie in 1981. He proposed a 43-story office building that would occupy a quarter block next to the Xerox Building in Chicago (Fig. 27). Two goals were established for the project. One goal was to build a tower that would solve the problem of proximity to the property line of the adjacent 43-story Xerox Building and to relate to it architecturally and yet to keep a separate identity. The other goal was to design a steel-framed tube structure which increased the usual 15-ft. (4.5m) column spacing on the exterior frame to as much as 50 ft. (15m), to eliminate the architectural disadvantage of close column spacing at lower levels in tube buildings. Khan anticipated tubular behavior by providing 6-ft. (2m) deep full-depth trussed spandrels connecting widely spaced columns. This was a scheme that he was never to realize in practice. As mentioned before, when I met him in his office a few days before his death, this issue was on his mind and he wanted to investigate this or a similar system in detail on his return from overseas. Goldsmith and Khan seemed to disagree on whether to express the vertical columns. Goldsmith strongly argued that it looked better not expressing the columns because they could be seen in the ground floor anyway. He agreed in retrospect that Khan was right and that the columns should have been exposed (Goldsmith, 1986).

Another late student project was a multi-use office and apartment building by T. Bok in 1982. In this work a diagonally braced and irregularly shaped building with large setbacks expressing the diagonals was studied. The following are a few other thesis projects that Khan supervised: "Train Exhibition Hall" by Meiji Watanabe (1962); "City Hall in Germany" by Christoph J. Sattler (1965); "High-Rise Concrete Masonry Building Structure" by Faramoz Shoai (1973); "Consortium Hangar for B-747-S" by Dick Ling (1974); and "Pre-fabricated Concrete—60-story Hotel-Office" by D. Kwong-Wah Lai (1975).

While reviewing certain structural properties of masonry, Khan was struck with the idea that it had not yet been used by engineers as a significant structural material to its full potential (Khan, 1974b). With a grant from the National Concrete Masonry Association (NCMA), he started working with two graduate students at IIT. The project consisted of three buildings: a 60-story apartment building, a 60-story hotel, and a 50-story office building. A testing program was undertaken at the PCA Lab sponsored by NCMA. The goal was to determine long-term stress redistribution between vertical steel reinforcement, grout, and hollow concrete blocks. The test results validated the design approach. These studies demonstrated that

Fig. 27: Petrie Project, Photograph of Model
[Courtesy: Graham Resource Center, College of Architecture, IIT]

74

Fig. 27

masonry could be used up to 60-story-tall, residential buildings. Concrete masonry, as a distinct material for construction, seemed to produce its own natural forms and shapes of buildings, both for residential and commercial occupancy. Khan also developed new approaches for precast concrete systems for tall buildings (Khan, 1976).

Khan was always at ease with his students. He took time to read their theses thoroughly and make grammatical and stylistic corrections. He took seriously his involvement with these thesis projects and considered them as the breeding ground of new ideas and concepts, which he attempted to realize in practice. He took keen interest in every project and every student and would go out of his way to help his students. On one occasion he invited his graduate students, Mahen Panchal and Heinz Sieber, to his home on Christmas Eve to discuss their projects. He could make very complex problems simple and communicate his ideas to his students clearly and in understandable language. He always carried a small slide rule and a 6-in. (152-mm) ruler with him. During his conversation with students he made necessary calculations quickly whenever a fast numerical answer to a question was desired. He continued to carry the slide rule for awhile even after hand calculators had become available. Following Goldsmith's death, David Sharpe and Mahjoub Elnimeiri, both faculty members in the School of Architecture, have continued the tradition set by Mies, Goldsmith and Khan at IIT in collaboration with SOM personnel such as William Baker and Ahmad Abdelrazaq.

In dealing with his students, Khan encouraged them to explore structural and architectural ideas and to avoid the temptation of trying spectacular structures where simple structures would suffice. According to Sharpe, most of the student projects were done by Khan's initiation on structures. Computer analysis of the structures was often performed at SOM's office. Khan never allowed the thesis to stop with concepts alone but would insist that it be comprehensive in its detail through its calculations and structural design, so the project was actually buildable. He would often say: "Some day, we will find a building where these ideas will be used." He required the best of his students and gave his best. Just before he left for his last trip, he was correcting a student's thesis, not only for content but also for style, grammar and spelling. This was his basic nature: whatever he did, he did thoroughly. Characteristically for him, nothing was too trivial for his full attention and care.

▲ ▼

Returning to Khan's innovations in his professional practice, his imagination did not stop with tubular design. He was continually searching for newer systems for buildings of great height. Those of the 1930s and 1940s had reached great heights, but they were heavy and were held down by masonry walls and stone cladding. Khan realized that modern buildings with light partition walls and cladding, and glass exterior had less resisting capability against overturning caused by lateral forces. If a building gets unusually high, it may demand a stronger material than the conventional materials like steel and concrete. Khan did not think seriously about light but strong synthetic structural materials but certainly he could have been aware of them and would presumably address this issue had he been alive today. At any rate, the problem of overturning due to lateral forces will only be aggravated if the building becomes taller and lighter.

In a tubular system, since the perimeter columns are closely spaced and the floor loads are primarily carried by interior columns, the tributary area of tube columns is rather limited. Khan realized this problem. In the early 1970s, he started investigating structural systems where more gravity loads could be introduced to these columns that resist overturning of the structure. This is possible if the total weight of the building can be collected on the perimeter columns. Although there are major implications of this from an architectural point-of-view, structurally speaking, large trusses transferring the floor loads to exterior walls in a certain fashion and by introducing deep spandrels for closely spaced perimeter columns or diagonal braces for widely spaced columns are feasible. Khan demonstrated that by progressively relocating the exterior columns to the corners of a rectangular braced tube, the structural efficiency can be greatly enhanced. An "ultimate structure" for a rectangular building then will have only four corner megacolumns interconnected by massive diagonals. With such a system the crowding of the tubular columns at the base of the building could be avoided. In his own words (Khan, 1972a):

> The ultimate possible improvement of the structural efficiency is to go from a multi-column concept to a square tower having only four large corner columns. Logically, this can be arrived at simply. The moment of inertia and the effective section modulus of the entire tubular characteristic of the building are successively increased from the trussed tube (John Hancock) type to megastructure type truss tube, and finally to the four-corner column type truss tube. This then is the ultimate high-rise steel building. It means that at every 20 floors or so there would be transfer trusses both on the exterior and interior of the building, thereby guaranteeing that all gravity loads in the building flow into the four corner columns. These corner columns are not going to be small in size, and facing the reality of the situation, one should make the four corner columns the service cores for the building.

Khan predicted 150 stories to be the optimum height of buildings and suggested that although greater heights for tall buildings could be structurally feasible, the three factors of building cost, zoning requirements and foundation capabilities would ultimately determine the height limit (*Modern Steel Construction*, 1972). His prediction of 150 stories as the optimum height was also reported in a feature article in the March 7, 1972 issue of *Montreal Star*. *Chicago Tribune* published many articles on Khan and his work in 1972 and 1973.

The principle of superframe was conceived by Goldsmith in his 1953 Master's thesis at IIT. He worked on a detailed example of a concrete 80-story office building (Blaser, 1987). Gravity loads were carried to the ground by a superframe in which eight columns forming three bays supported six horizontal platforms or macro floors spaced fifteen stories apart. From each platform, seven floors were hung below and seven supported above, leaving the floor midway between the platforms free of columns.

Fig. 28
Fig. 29

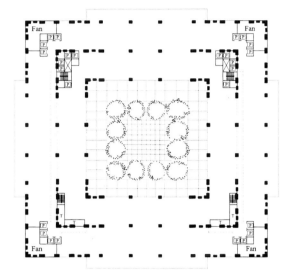

77

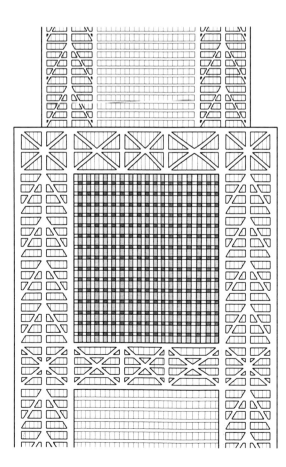

Alfred Swenson also studied superframes extensively that included the "pylon superframe" (Swenson, 1971; Chang and Swenson, 1974).

While working with the building corners, Khan, however, developed his concerns into the superframe concept differently—a superframe that consists of trussed elements used as columns that are interconnected by deep trusses similar to his idea of the ultimate structure. He sought a better cantilever behavior and more flexibility in the building's facade and a reduction of the denseness of columns at the base of the tube structure. As noted before, Khan developed the notion of trussed-tube superframe through a student project at IIT by Michael Breitman in 1972. He discussed the topic of superframe in a widely read paper in which he made predictions for tall building systems in future cities (Khan, 1972a). It is worth noting that at about the same time in 1973, structural engineers Paparoni and Holoma had designed the Parque Central Towers, a high-rise office complex, in Caracas, Venezuela, using the superframe concept with macro-structural floors (*macrolosas*). The two towers, each rising 56 stories, have since been built as planned. The superframe as a potential structural system was thus amenable to various possibilities.

The concept of superframe can be used in various ways for supertall rectangular or square buildings by providing four basic corner megacolumns as envisioned by Khan or more than the four corner megacolumns and for high-rise buildings not so tall. The ultimate goal of using corner megacolumns interconnected by trusses for supertall buildings was conceptually realized by Khan on a 168-story building proposed for the Chicago World Trade Center shortly before his death (Figs. 28 and 29). This building was, however, never built. The structural team led by him performed a number of structural system studies by rigorous computer analyses. He related these systems to the architectural requirements of adequate space for mixed use and forming the basic atrium on the inside of the structure. The project was very challenging from an architectural point of view in that new space planning concepts were introduced to complement this novel structural system. At one point a maximum height of a dizzying 2,700 ft. (823m) was under consideration for the building. The corner megacolumns of the 168-story building were composed of individual columns arranged in an L-shaped layout and connected by large K-braces over four stories at a time. Iyengar (1986) wrote on this project, "The natural evolution of a 150-story to 200-story structure was the tapered form. . . . So Khan devised a series of steps and series of superframes, in fact, which telescoped within each other . . . creating not only the atriums on the inside but also the basic structural form, which was then applied on the exterior of the curtain wall. . . . It shows some of the bracing elements of the superframe." What a wonderful concept indeed!

An interesting aspect of the Chicago World Trade Center project was that three large holes were provided to create an aerodynamically efficient structure resulting in a dramatically low acceleration from wind forces. This was confirmed by model tests at the Wind Tunnel Laboratory at the University of Western Ontario under the supervision of A. G. Davenport. The holes were provided in one direction and were found to reduce the vortex shedding and laminar flow of wind by creating turbulence around the building. As a means of reducing total wind forces, the three wind portals completely passed through the structure, significantly improving the cross-wind oscillations. The size of holes must be optimally large enough to get this effect and hence improvement in the aerodynamic performance of the building. The superframe, like the tube, offers improved stiffness and lateral-load resistance because the structure is placed on the outside of the building. Also, the concentration of structural material in the corners of the building improves its torsional resistance to lateral loads. While discussing this building with Iyengar, he told me, "This supertall building is still a tube in a way. It is, after all, an exterior system." Khan was not able to realize this concept of superframe on a practical structure during his lifetime.

The superframe not just gave a supertall building of enormous scale its necessary strength and stiffness from the structural point of view, but in visual terms, the interplay between the superstructure and substructure presented new opportunities for architectural expression. The superframe enables the architect to create internal spaces and atriums at different levels, allowing daylight into the interior of a skyscraper and making more livable the vast floor areas that result from great height (Tucker, 1985). On the advantages of the superframe, Iyengar (1986) remarked:

> This provided a great deal of architectural freedom with respect to the interior spaces. The atrium was becoming quite an asset in tall buildings, and a stacked multiple atrium could lend itself very well with this concept where the interior atrium could find access to the exterior of the building through these portals in the superframe. This then lends itself to the idea of megaframes where the idea was the total frame being conceived in superframe and secondary structure superimposed into these portals.

Khan had deep insight into the structural planning aspects of high-rise buildings and the stability of tall, thin buildings (Khan, 1972a). For very slender buildings, he conceived the idea of curving the entire shape of buildings in the form of a folded plate, a channel, or a fluted shape. He also predicted that concrete as a structural material would have limitless possibilities because of its moldability into various forms and shapes, and would lead to the concept of megastructure in which various kinds of multi-use buildings could be planned. Because of his profound understanding of the structural system in relation to the architectural, and mechanical/electric systems of a building, he can be truly called an ultimate structural planner.

Khan would tell his associates to be bold on certain issues and exercise caution on others. He advised them to design brackets, joints, and such weak links in the chain of structure very conservatively, but to design the structural members optimally when they had enough information and confidence. His love for research showed up when he would preach: Save money on structures and spend money on research and development. When designing One Shell Plaza, he saved money on the structure, showed it to the client, and requested that money for research and development.

Like many dedicated researchers, Khan was open to new ideas. Shankar Nair, a well known structural engineer, gave an example of his openness. Nair proposed a new way of analyzing the lateral stability of tall buildings at a Structural Stability Research Council Session in 1981, where Khan was present. Khan received the proposal well and promoted the concept later at SOM. Nair put it to me this way, "Typically, top-rung engineers at these events listen politely but do not expect to learn anything. But Fazlur immediately took the idea back to his staff to test on ongoing projects." He had a mind that was full of curiosity. He availed himself of every opportunity to learn new ideas. John Rankine, an Australian consulting civil and structural engineer, described it thus (Rankine, 1997):

> It is interesting that on one occasion when Dr. Fazlur Khan . . . visited Australia he came over to our office on a friendly visit. He was surprised at the amount of work we had and asked if he might wander round to every engineer and draftsman to see what they were doing. He graciously made many helpful and useful comments which were a great help to us. Also, he said he appreciated the opportunity of doing this whenever he could as he would often pick up ideas.

Khan was a prolific writer, and he made every attempt to write and publish papers on his projects. Although he died at the early age of 52, he authored and presented about 100 papers, of which 35 were published in professional journals. His written work is highly respected by the profession. I once asked him how he found time to write so many papers amidst his busy schedule. He replied, "During evenings and weekends." His advice: "Always try to publish your work so that it is documented." Research and innovation went hand-in-hand for him. As Iyengar (1986) observed,

> . . . whatever Fazlur Khan has introduced as a concept, had a much, much broader impact around the world as a system, and a much broader application. And in studying Khan's work, we find an enormous offering of concepts to sustain us for quite some time, and that's something you could use to build on.

Fazlur R. Khan reviewing a student thesis project in studio
at the Illinois Institute of Technology
[Courtesty: SOM/CTBUH]

Fazlur Khan in a reflective mood in his office at SOM, Chicago
[Courtesy: SOM]

Eugene E. Weyeneth, publisher of *Engineering News-Record*,
presenting *ENR*'s Man of the Year Award to
Fazlur R. Khan in 1972
[Courtesy: *Engineering News-Record,* copyright
The McGraw-Hill Companies, Inc. All rights reserved.]

Fazlur R. Khan receiving the honorary Doctor
of Engineering degree at Lehigh University (1980)
[Courtesy: CTBUH]

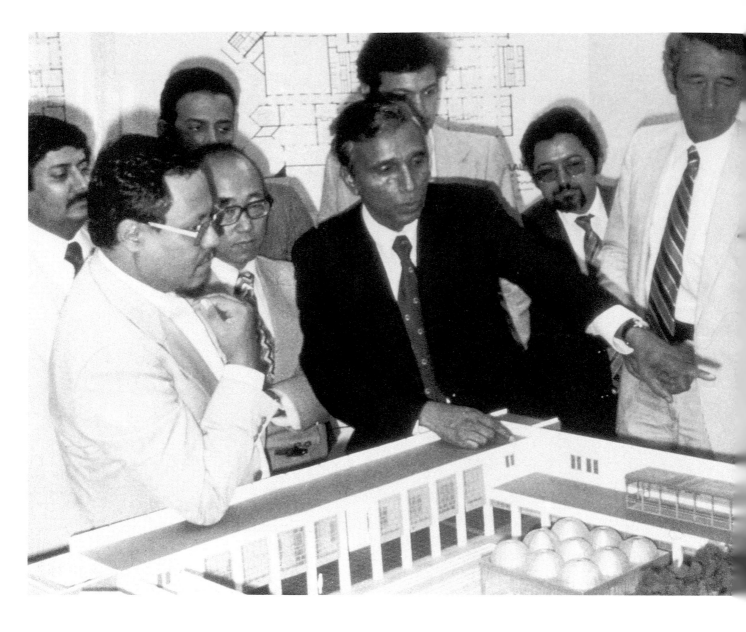

Fazlur R. Khan describes the Makkah University Plan
(Bruce Graham seen standing on Khan's left)
[Courtesy: SOM/CTBUH]

Fazlur R. Khan
[Courtesy: Reprinted from *Engineering News-Record*
(February 10, 1972), copyright The McGraw-Hill Companies, Inc.
All rights reserved.]

chapter 6   ADVENTURES IN DESIGN AND ACCOLADES

"There exists . . . a fine equation involving the interaction of two mysterious forces. One force is Faz Khan. The other is the complex body of dedicated anonymous workers in SOM within which framework Faz accomplished new heights in creative design through the use of enhanced engineering principles working collaboratively with his architectural peers."

—Nathaniel A. Owings (*Khan Tributes*, 1982)

Fazlur Rahman Khan's accomplishments are many, and at a professional level they include many exciting projects that he had worked on during his 25-year career at SOM (1955-57 and 1960-82) and the recognition he had received during his lifetime and after his death. He engaged in over forty projects involving structures in concrete and steel. Some of these projects of significant nature are briefly presented here and have been described variously in the literature (Iyengar, 1986; Fintel, 1986; CTBUH, 1995; IABSE, 1982).

Successful designing leads to conquering space through construction. It is an ever-changing challenge that is an exciting adventure in which problems are defined and resolved, skills are learned and applied, tribulations are surmounted, and risks of structural failure are assessed and overcome. Construction must be practical, within reach, and, above all, the professional reputation of the designer must remain intact. The rugged world of the construction industry demands hard work, discipline, good judgment, courage, and resourcefulness. The designer's survival depends upon possessing the above qualities, as well as relentless prodding of ingenuity and inspiration to succeed in every project. Each new project was a thrilling experience that Khan gladly undertook.

It would be wrong to give full credit to Khan for the successful design of the buildings that are discussed in this chapter. It was indeed the teamwork of the structural engineers and architects that led to the success of the projects described below and those not presented here. Bruce Graham, Fazlur Khan, and Hal Iyengar worked together as a team on most of these projects. While Graham acted as the principal architectural designer and Khan as the principal structural engineer, their objectives and design ideas generally overlapped across the boundaries of their respective architectural/engineering disciplines. Although Graham is an architect, he was much inclined to express the structure of the buildings that he designed. Likewise, although Khan was a structural engineer, he was very sensitive to the aesthetic and architectural needs of these buildings. There was naturally a cross-fertilization of ideas. In some cases the building form and the structural planning of buildings were proposed by Graham which Khan adopted and further developed to meet their structural requirements. In other cases Khan contributed to the architectural aspects of the projects by discussing them

84
84
84
84
84

Fig. 30: DeWitt-Chestnut Apartment Building, Chicago, Illinois.
Apartment building designed by Khan as the first known tube structure
[Courtesy: Skidmore, Owings and Merrill (SOM); photo by Hedrich/Blessing]

Fig. 30

with Graham and his other architectural peers. Khan and Graham acted as collaborative partners with mutual respect and understanding of each other's viewpoints and their design philosophies seemed to be generally along the same track. Undoubtedly, Khan was often inspired by, and benefited from, Graham's intuitive understanding of structural forms. Similarly, he benefited from the technical skill of Iyengar who worked with Khan on the structural analysis and design of the buildings. Iyengar's true professional allegiance to Khan's expertise and his in-depth understanding of structural behavior as well as his rigorous and pragmatic execution of the structural design process supplemented Khan's goal for successfully completing the projects.

▲ ▼

DEWITT-CHESTNUT APARTMENT BUILDING: The 43-story DeWitt-Chestnut Apartment Building of 1965 in Chicago is of historical importance (Fig. 30). This is where Khan used, for the first time, the tubular principle involving a peripheral tube without a core structure for resisting lateral loads. This reinforced concrete apartment tower employing the framed tube concept was built in the vicinity of two elegant buildings by Mies—860 and 880 Lake Shore Drive. A traditional tower would have allowed the designers to go about 28 stories high, thereby ruining the relationships of these two buildings. Khan's ingenuity made it possible to build a much taller 43-story structure for the same cost using the tube concept. In this building the perimeter columns are spaced at 5 ft. 6 in. (1.7m), supported on a deep transfer girder near the base and the spandrels are 24 in. (600mm) deep. Since the columns are closely spaced, the structure is more like a perforated tube. Building elevations using closely spaced columns connected by spandrels were not unknown at that time since, from an architectural point-of-view, such an arrangement eliminated the need for additional mullions for windows. Khan, however, realized that such beam-column relationship in the perimeter created the required resistance to lateral loads. He was perceptive enough to recognize the benefits of three-dimensional response of the structure to lateral loads rather than the commonly assumed two-dimensional response for reasons of simplifying the calculations and the fact that most of the columns could be removed from the inside of the building creating flexible open space inside the building. He recognized the problem of shear lag around the corner of tube buildings that demanded special consideration. He was able to convince his architectural counterparts to use the tubular concept for other projects.

An important outcome of a tube building is that the structural frame is exposed. The exterior concrete frame has a light appearance as a result of the relative thinness of its members. Therefore, this building conforms to the surrounding context of similar lightweight structures such as the Lake Shore Apartments adjacent to it. Some significant outcomes of this tubular configuration are that the floor slab, particularly the flat plate, which is highly efficient for apartment buildings, is relieved of participation in the lateral load resistance process, other than as a diaphragm in its own plane, and the tubular arrangement provides an honest visual expression of the structure.

Fig. 31: Brunswick Building, Chicago, Illinois
[Courtesy: SOM; photo by Hedrich/Blessing]

Fig. 31

BRUNSWICK BUILDING: The 38-story Brunswick Building (now called 69 West Washington Street Building) of 1965 in Chicago is essentially a tube-in-tube reinforced concrete office building, although its structure was not designed as such (Fig. 31). The shear wall-frame interaction principle was applied here for the first time by Khan considering the planar frames and core walls in the plane of these frames jointly resisting the wind forces. Historically, this building's design precedes that of the DeWitt-Chestnut Apartments. The tubular concept was still not known. The perimeter columns for the Brunswick Building were closely spaced primarily for an architectural reason, that is, for the ease of window treatment. All design calculations were manual and without any regard for the three-dimensional tubular response; as such, considerable intuition by Khan was required for this building's structural design. This building is not, therefore, a true tube-in-tube system, whereas for DeWitt-Chestnut, the three-dimensional resistance of the structure, was recognized. The exterior frames parallel to the direction of wind were analyzed for shear racking, whereas a cantilever analysis was performed to capture the three-dimensional behavior. Most structural calculations were carried out manually although some computer analysis was also performed. The original scheme for the Brunswick Building was for a structure in steel. However, Graham changed it to a concrete structure to provide architectural conformity with the nearby Chicago Civic Center (Daley Center). The facade was originally thought to be covered with travertine, but because of the high cost it was changed to paint.

The outer tube-like frame of Brunswick Building is composed of columns spaced at 9 ft. 4 in. (2.9m) on center connected by 24-in. (600mm) deep spandrels and the inner tube is the concrete core. A perimeter transfer girder 24 ft. (7.3m) deep and 7.5 ft. (2.3m) wide resting on large 7-ft. (2-m) square columns spaced 56 ft. (17m) apart was provided at the third floor. The core walls are 24 in. (600 mm) thick at ground level and diminish to 12 in. (300mm) at roof level. Below the transfer girder, the core is designed to carry all the lateral forces. One-way ribbed joists are used for the floors, and at the corners a two-way waffle slab system was employed. Lightweight concrete was used for floors. A 1:12 scale model of the deep transfer girder was load-tested at the University of Illinois at Urbana-Champaign. The deep girder is integrated with the columns above as they extend below and flare outward. There is a lack of integration, however, between the columns above and below the transfer girder. The deep girder and the large lower-level columns offer a powerful visual base, and is balanced by the tall mechanical story at the roof. The widely spaced columns at the base offer a large open space welcoming pedestrians and connect the building spatially with the streetscape. Also, this created a gesture to the open plaza of the Chicago Civic Center across the street—an architectural notion conceived by Graham and embraced by Khan.

Attention to the exposed structural detail of the exterior facade adds greatly to the visual and architectural characteristics of the building. The columns also act as mullions and the glass is inset deep into the frame exposing the columns about 70 percent of the area. It was evident to Khan that, under the extreme temperature variations caused by Chicago winters, the exterior columns would shorten relative to the inside of the building where the temperature is controlled and kept constant. A detailed temperature analysis was performed in collaboration with Mark Fintel by considering the heat transfer through the column and the restraining effects of the floor slab system. Based on this investigation, it was decided to sever the moment connections between the slabs of the upper floors (29th floor and up) and the core by making the slabs rest on neoprene pads on a ledge around the core perimeter as shown in Figs. 32 and 33 (IABSE, 1982). Observations on the building show that these hinging details are functioning well and no problems—either architectural or structural—have been encountered.

The Brunswick Building project proved Khan's mettle in another way. This was the first time he was the project engineer for a major building with shear wall-frame interaction behavior and with such a deep transfer girder. Khan carefully looked at everything where Murphy's Law could apply. He produced 500 charts to capture its behavior under all conditions. Despite his precautions, he got his first professional shock. One day, right after lunch, he received a phone call from the SOM Chief Engineer telling him that the building was being shored because it was "on the verge of collapse." Large "cracks" were seen in the floor slabs. Khan, who was normally very composed and confident, was flustered. He and others from SOM immediately went to the job site. He was greatly relieved to see that the "cracks" were actually slots deliberately cast in the slabs' corners to relieve stress during the building's vertical movements.

Brunswick Building represents a very early collaboration between Graham and Khan. It received a Citation of Merit bestowed by the Chicago Chapter of the American Institute of Architects (AIA) in 1966.

ONE SHELL PLAZA: Another major project in Khan's career was the 52-story One Shell Plaza of 1971 in Houston, Texas (Fig. 34). This is a tube-in-tube concrete building in which the exterior tube is formed by columns spaced 6 ft. (1.8m) apart connected by spandrel beams 4 ft. 3 in. (1.3m) deep with a rigid shear wall core. Each floor joist is supported on the exterior column (see Fig. 35). This simplified the spandrel beam design and detailing (Khan, 1970). A 9.5-ft. (2.9-m) deep transfer girder was used at the second floor to create larger openings at Plaza level. The project was originally envisioned as a 35-story building due to foundation limitations. But when it was found that if high-strength lightweight concrete was used in conjunction with a tube-in-tube design, a 52-story building would then be feasible for the originally projected unit cost of a 35-story building. This building reigned as the tallest concrete building of the world for a number of years, and is still the tallest lightweight concrete building. Similar to the Brunswick Building, the floor system consists of one-way joists with two-way waffle slabs in the corner regions. The column depth was progressively increased at two locations on each face of the building where the columns carried heavier floor loads at the exterior end of the waffle slab column strips. Graham was instrumental in proposing the idea of enlarging the heavily loaded columns to the outside, rather than to the inside. This structural feature, appearing on the outside of the building, created an undulation effect. It saved interior floor space and created a unique aesthetic impact. Despite the

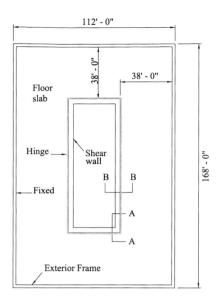

Fig. 32

Fig. 33

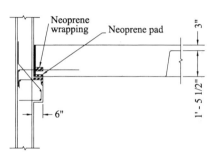

Section A - A:
Hinge at waffle section

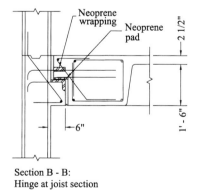

Section B - B:
Hinge at joist section

Fig. 32: Brunswick Building, Schematic Plans of Top Floors

Fig. 33: Brunswick Building, Hinge Details at Top Floors
(see Fig. 32)

Fig. 34: One Shell Plaza, Houston, Texas
[Courtesy: SOM; photo by Ezra Stoller/Esto]

Fig. 34

resulting complexity in the structural design of the facade frame, Khan embraced this idea to create an exciting visual image of the building. The spandrel beams were made of variable width to match the variable column depths. The core shear walls are 24 in. (600mm) thick at the base and reduce to 10 in. (250mm) at roof. The building was designed to resist hurricane wind pressure. A lightweight concrete mat foundation was used for supporting the structure.

The temperature effect is less significant in One Shell Plaza compared to the Brunswick Building. Houston is located in a warm climate and the thermal effects are less critical. The columns are insulated on the outside and clad in travertine. At any rate, a thermal analysis was carried out for all columns, and the glass line was located such that the maximum relative movement at the top of the building under the most severe winter conditions should not be greater than 0.75 in. (19mm). The resulting glass line follows the column profile rather than the conventional straight line and creates an interesting visual effect. This building was the very first tall building in which a refined creep analysis was performed. Two factors were thought to be critical. The first factor is that of differential shortening between the six highly stressed interior columns very close to the core walls, which are at a lower stress level, are rather lightly reinforced, and have a high surface-to-volume ratio as compared to the columns (Fig. 36). Since the core walls with low steel percentages creep more than the columns, Khan installed a diagonally reinforced short beam capable of transferring the heavy loads from the walls into the columns. Thus, the shear walls could transfer the loads on the columns over a period of time through the short beams and the columns, in effect, acted as part of the core wall system. The other factor is that some of the columns would receive higher loads from column strips in the two-way waffle slab system. Following Graham's idea, Khan increased the column sizes incrementally to the outside under the anticipated heavier loads, thereby equalizing the stress level in all columns and eliminating the potential differential creep problem.

At this point, some of the details surrounding the mat design will be discussed because of the special nature of the foundation. The site has primarily over-consolidated clay extending down to a large depth below the ground level. A floating type mat was found to be quite suitable. This means that the weight of the soil excavated must be approximately equal to the weight of the building—a concept known as foundation compensation. This required a 60 ft. (18m) deep excavation, which was also a practical maximum limit for excavation. The solid concrete mat was 8 ft. 3 in. (2.5m) thick and measured 160 x 220 ft. (49 x 67m) in plan. A thorough analysis was conducted based on long-term behavior and soil-structure interaction. Also, large diameter (No. 18) reinforcement details had to be developed to avoid lap splices of such large bars in tension. Khan viewed these problems from various levels of the overall behavior of the mat rather than from a simple mathematical solution. He was able to convince the owner of the building, Gerald Hines, to authorize a substantial sum of money to install pressure cells under the mat to check foundation pressure distribution over a period of at least three years. Electric strain gauges were also applied to the reinforcing bars.

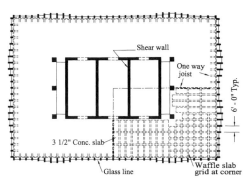

Fig. 35

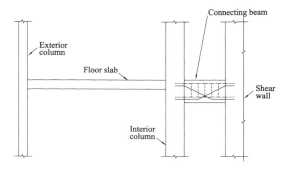

Fig. 36

Returning to the visual effect of the building, an unusual aesthetic quality emerges from the undulating façade. It occurs for the entire height of the building (see also Chapter 11). Expression of the structural action on the outside rather than on the inside created the undulating, rather than routine, planar facade. Although the two undulations are symmetric on each face of the building, the shadows created by sunlight are asymmetrical and accentuate the verticality of the building. The tall windows over the transfer girder merge well with the massive base. A solid base is used under the undulations where the vertical loads are the heaviest. The solid base is also undulated along with the columns in the taller stories above the transfer girder. Thus, the undulation of the facade continues from top to bottom of the building creating a visual expression of the elevations that breaks the monotony of closely spaced columns.

The structural design of One Shell Plaza is a major accomplishment of Khan in concrete building design. He showed innovative daring and depth of understanding of concrete as a material that went beyond many of his contemporaries. When it was built, he was repeatedly told that he could not build the tallest concrete building in the world on such poor soil conditions. Against these odds he demonstrated his courage and confidence by designing it successfully. His design concept made it possible to bring the unit cost of this 52-story building down to that of the traditional shear wall structure of only 35 stories (Khan, 1974b).

Two other examples of concrete buildings where Graham and Khan used the structural form to exhibit the nature of load transfer near the base of the building are Two Shell Plaza and the Marine Midland Bank building (Khan, 1972b).

TWO SHELL PLAZA: The 26-story Two Shell Plaza of 1972 in Houston, Texas, designed primarily as a parking garage in concrete, where office space was added later, shows the logical solution for the load transfer from the closely spaced columns to widely spaced columns at the ground floor (Fig. 37). Instead of using a heavy transfer girder, Khan handled the problem of load transfer by intuitively anticipating the natural flow path of the load. The transfer is accomplished over the course of several stories by gradually bringing the loads to the widely spaced columns simply by widening the columns as they descend and

Fig. 37

Fig. 35: One Shell Plaza, Floor Framing Plan

Fig. 36: One Shell Plaza, Connecting Beam Between Column and Shear Wall

Fig. 37: Two Shell Plaza, Houston, Texas [Courtesy: SOM; photo by Ezra Stoller/Esto]

Fig. 38: Marine Midland Bank, Rochester, New York [Courtesy: SOM; photo by Ezra Stoller/Esto]

Fig. 38

deepening the beams towards the base. The spandrel beams are also incrementally increased in depth along their spans toward the column lines over the widely spaced columns resulting in an expression of shallow arches in which the strong spandrels transfer vertical loads through shear. The building elevation thus received its strong visual expression from this type of transfer of vertical loads through the skillful manipulation of horizontal and vertical members to control the force flow (see also Chapter 11). The bottom of the building is the principal region of visual interest since, unlike the Brunswick Building, there is no similar visual expression at the top. Use of several widely spaced columns at the bottom facilitate the smooth transfer of loads from above, but still provides openness below to integrate the building with the street level.

MARINE MIDLAND BANK: The 21-story Marine Midland Bank, a concrete building of 1970 in Rochester, New York, similar to Two Shell Plaza, is another example of transferring vertical loads from closely spaced columns above to widely spaced columns below without the use of deep transfer girders (Fig. 38). By gradually enlarging the spandrel beams towards the main columns, Graham and Khan created the impression of single-story arches to achieve the load transfer. Unlike Two Shell Plaza, however, the load transfer here takes place both in and out of the plane of the facade, thereby creating an undulating form. The columns above, carrying loads to the main columns below, become heavier as they descend. As Graham put it to me, "we wanted to demonstrate how to make a building land." There are no main corner columns at the base creating a special imagery of the facade where it is interrupted at the corners, yet its verticality is maintained by the large widely spaced lower level columns branching out into multiple columns at the tall second story. The tall mechanical story at the top of the building caps the verticality of the building with thin, closely spaced columns and provides a visual balance with the tall lower story in the building elevation (see also Chapter 11).

Similarly, for the 31-story 1010 Common Street Building of 1971 in New Orleans, Louisiana, Khan introduced transition columns within the tall first story, changing from a wide section at the top to a narrow and deep section at the bottom of that story to get additional space between the exterior columns. It created an exciting aesthetic feature at the lower level of this concrete building.

▲ ▼

Khan's major steel projects are described below. Hancock and Sears buildings will be discussed in Chapters 7 and 8, respectively.

BUSINESS MEN'S ASSURANCE TOWER: The 19-story Business Men's Assurance Tower of 1964 in Kansas City, Missouri, is another early project in steel to which Khan contributed (Fig. 39). Graham and Khan were much influenced by Maillart's design approach for concrete structures. Maillart showed, through his bridges and flat slabs of the early twentieth century, how engineering works could be expressive and artistic. In some of the concrete buildings that the Graham-Khan team designed we already saw how they achieved it. We also saw that Khan worked on the problems of exposed concrete frame subjected to temperature changes in Chicago climate in collaboration with Fintel. He continued this pursuit at the Business Men's Assurance Tower project in steel instead of concrete (Graham, 1986). Here the building's rigid steel frame fully defined the facade. The purity of the structure of the building is fully expressed.

The problem of temperature movements in the fully exposed frames demanded an original engineering approach (Khan and Nassetta, 1970).

The delicate steel frame provides both a facade and a shading for the office spaces behind. Within the facade, there is also the expression of structural and architectural components of the building. The columns are taller at the base, and the entire area is open with the frame and a core of the building landing on the ground. The taller columns of the top mechanical story complement those in the first story resulting in a visual balance. An odd number of bays eliminates the necessity of a column in the center resulting in an open bay there and giving the facade a balanced appearance.

INLAND STEEL BUILDING: An important steel building that Khan had contributed to is the Inland Steel Building (Fig. 40). The 19-story office tower of the Inland Steel Building of 1958 in Chicago, Illinois, is an early example of Khan's competence in his younger days. It was one of the few tall buildings to be constructed in the Loop after the Great Depression. Its sleek skin of stainless steel and glass, together with immaculate detailing make it exemplary as an application of Miesian modernist architecture. Located at the corner of Monroe and Dearborn Streets, this office tower's major facade offers a visual backdrop to the east side of the First National Bank Plaza. Seven steel columns on each side of the office space support 60 ft. (18m) long steel plate girders spanning the entire width of the building. The columns are spaced 26 ft. (8m) on center and wrapped with stainless steel. The inner relationship between column and beam in a clear-span high-rise like this was difficult to define. Khan's contribution was to design the beam-column connections. Invited by Graham to conduct this design, he completely resolved the challenging engineering problem of connecting the vertical columns to the horizontal floor system. The challenge stemmed from the fact that the columns are located outside the main building and the building core is pulled out from its traditional location in the center of the building. The core is at the rear of the building and is clearly visible as it rises above the building. There are no main structural columns reaching the ground on the shorter sides of the building, although the columns that are on the building face are located outside the plane of the window. The well-expressed columns, the volumetric simplicity and functional clarity of the building, and the excellent detailing have made it a remarkable office tower.

FIRST WISCONSIN CENTER: A significant steel building by Khan is the 42-story First Wisconsin Center of 1973 in Milwaukee, Wisconsin (Fig. 41). The structural system was selected for this building to create a light open-frame type structure on the exterior

92

Fig. 39

Fig. 40

with columns spaced 20 ft. (6m) apart. This spacing exceeds the conventional 15 ft. (4.5m) spacing for tubular behavior and is thus rather inefficient as a tube structure. However, the interaction between the vertical core trusses and the frames creates, in steel structures, what is known as shearwall-frame interaction for concrete structures, although the potential for the core trusses to fully develop lateral resistance could be restricted due to the fact that the depth of the truss is often limited to the depth of the core. The core truss systems in this building are connected to three belt trusses at the 3rd, 15th, and the topmost story by outrigger trusses. This engages the exterior columns in cantilever action and minimizes the frame racking component of total lateral sway. When the shear core wants to bend, the belt trusses connected firmly to the core by outrigger trusses introduce direct axial stresses into the exterior columns, which, in turn, resist the deflection of the core. Thus the core fully develops the horizontal shears, and the belt trusses transfer the vertical shear from the core to the facade frame via the outrigger trusses (Schueller, 1990). The outrigger trusses then effectively act as stiff header beams inducing tension and compression in exterior frame columns with the assistance of belt trusses that distribute these tensile and compressive forces to a large number of frame columns. Further, there is improvement in vertical differential shortening and elongation characteristics at the belt truss levels. For this building the increase in stiffness against lateral sway was found to be about 30 percent due to the introduction of the belt trusses. The belt truss at the third floor also acts as a transfer truss to allow for a 40 ft. (12m) column spacing below that level. A schematic diagram of a belt truss system is shown in Fig. 42.

The employment of the open transfer truss in combination with the widely spaced columns below lightens the base, which is desirable for making a transition between the tower and the low-rise building at the base. This lower truss also balances the uppermost truss in the building elevation. The location of the intermediate truss at about one-third of the way up reinforces the verticality of the structure, rather than breaking it in half. On the whole, the structure is elegantly expressed in this building.

For this project, both rolled and built-up sections were used for main beams and columns. The spandrel beams are 36 in. (915 mm) deep and column depth varies from 14 in. (355mm) at top to 36 in. (915mm) at the base. Structural steel of different strengths was employed to optimize strength and stiffness and to minimize weight. The spandrel beams wrapping around the building horizontally complement its vertical expression.

In addition to the aforementioned projects, Khan engineered the Wolf Point Apparel Mart in 1976, a steel addition to the Merchandise Mart. This facility contains apparel showroom space, a hotel, convention facilities and an exhibition hall. The owner wanted a structure proportional in height to the existing 24-story Merchandise Mart that would satisfy all space requirements. The resulting building was a structure with two connecting towers, 13 and 23 stories high, which rise from a 4-story masonry podium. A steel structure was used because it reduced the size of the foundation, was lighter in weight, faster to erect and slightly less expensive than its alternative: concrete.

In 1981, I began working in a team under Khan on a project called Pacific Plaza in Los Angeles, which involved a 60-story

Fig. 41

Fig. 41: First Wisconsin Center, Milwaukee, Wisconsin [Courtesy: SOM; photo by Ezra Stoller/Esto]

Fig. 42: Schematic Diagram of a Belt Truss System

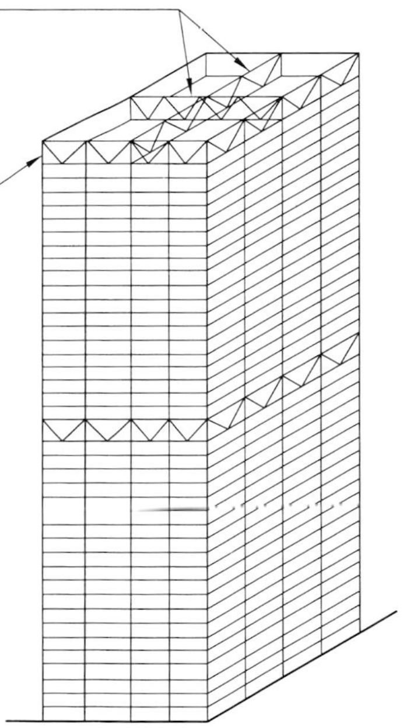
Outrigger trusses typical each way at each bay
Belt truss typical

Fig. 42

steel office tower. Khan was the partner in charge of structural design, while Graham was the architectural partner in charge of the project. Although this building was never built in its originally conceived form, it was unusual both due to its approximately pentagon-shaped plan with a tube-in-tube system and its location in UBC Seismic Zone 4. For both the perimeter and the core tubes, columns were spaced at 15 ft. (4.5m) on center. Khan would occasionally lead the project team meetings. These meetings were of immense benefit to the participants, including myself, who would learn what Khan's thoughts were.

During the course of this project, Khan appeared always to be at ease and he tackled difficult situations without losing his composure. He was casual in his approach but well prepared, as well as being quick in thinking and attending to what was at hand. When we posted the drawings on the walls, he just looked at them and instantly commented on the areas of concern. To him viewing the entire building was as simple as an average engineer examining a beam or a column. His deeply perceptive nature and very high level of intuitive understanding on the subject, far above the average, were apparent. Of course, this was a time when he had already reached the pinnacle of his success. With all the major innovations behind him it was unlikely that any structural problem was a great challenge for him anymore. But he was never complacent and he never stopped thinking. Once he put an idea to rest, he moved on to the next one. He was never intimidating and his modest and pleasant nature made us feel comfortable in his presence. When he discussed highly technical matters, his language was always clear and easy to understand.

For tube building construction, the most natural material to construct the perimeter frame is concrete because it can be readily molded into a perforated wall. Khan argued in the late 1960s that the exterior concrete frame could be combined with simple steel framing for the floor system and interior steel columns, resulting in a mixed or composite system. The 20-story Control Data Center of 1971 in Houston, Texas, was his first modern composite building, followed by the 36-story Gateway III Office Building of 1972 in Chicago. The Gateway Building (now called 222 South Riverside Plaza) was conceived as the very first composite system although its construction was completed after that of the Control Data Center. It thus has a unique historical significance since it became the forerunner for other future high-rises employing mixed steel-concrete systems. For the Control Data Center, the structure was built as a conventional steel frame except for the use of small steel erection columns for the exterior columns. The steel frame was erected about eight floors ahead of the concrete placement in the columns and beams of the exterior frame. Precast cladding was used as formwork for the exterior concrete. Another major building using this system constructed around the same time is the One Shell Square building in New Orleans.

ONE SHELL SQUARE: The 52-story One Shell Square office building of 1972 in New Orleans, Louisiana, is a remarkable application of the composite system by Khan (Fig. 43). This building is one of the first structures in which composite tubular concept was put into practice. This mixed steel-concrete construction, like other similar projects, eliminates labor-intensive field work, such as concrete floor framing and steel joint welding, required if only one material is used for the entire structure. As is common with this type of system, to keep the rate of construction equal to the usual rate for a steel building and also to separate the structural steel and reinforced concrete trades, the structure in steel was built ahead of the exterior concrete framing. A separation of eight to ten stories between steel and framed tube working levels was generally required. The framed tube is formed by 4-ft. (1.2m) wide columns spaced at 10 ft. (3m) on center along the building perimeter. Column depth is 3 ft. 9 in. (1.1m) at the base which reduces to 2 ft. 7 in. (0.79m) at the 18th floor and remains constant thereafter up to the roof. The continuity and rigidity of the spandrel beam-to-column joints are derived from the monolithic nature of the concrete. The exterior tube and interior steel gravity columns are connected by 40-ft. (12.2m) long simple span steel beams spaced 10 ft. (3m) apart. Composite steel deck with lightweight concrete was used for the floors. The structure was designed for hurricane loads. The tower is clad in travertine marble and reflective glass. The foundation comprised precast, prestressed concrete piles out of which more than 500 piles were driven to a depth of 210 ft. (64m). The piles were tied together with an 8-ft. (2.4m) thick reinforced concrete mat to stabilize the structure and to evenly spread the load.

▲ ▼

Khan not only excelled in the design of high-rise buildings. He was equally comfortable with low-rise structures. The most remarkable example is the Haj Terminal (see Chapter 9). He once mentioned this point to me by saying, "There is a misconception that SOM only does tall buildings." An excellent early example is the Spectrum Arena of 1967 in Philadelphia, Pennsylvania. Another example is the United Airlines Executive Office building of 1968 in Elk Grove Village, Illinois, an addition to the existing United Airlines Building.

BAXTER LABORATORIES DINING HALL: A significant low-rise project of Khan is the Baxter Laboratories Dining Hall (1975) in Deerfield, Illinois (Fig. 44). This is a 2-story building used as an

Fig. 43: One Shell Square, New Orleans, Louisiana
[Courtesy: SOM; photo by Hedrich/Blessing]

Fig. 44: Baxter Laboratories Dining Hall, Deerfield, Illinois
[Courtesy: McShane-Fleming Studios]

Fig. 43

Fig. 44

Fig. 45

97

employee cafeteria and lounge. It was designed as a cable sup-ported roof system in order to generate large column-free spaces. The use of tension characteristics of steel cable facilitated the employment of a light, thin, plate-like roof framing. Khan worked with Goldsmith on various cable schemes for the project at IIT. Two masts supporting the deck, laid out symmetrically, result in a balanced cantilever system, that reduces the cable stresses. The cable-supported structure not only created a large 144 x 288 ft. (43.6 x 87.3m) open area but also offered unique architectural features. The open perimeter permitted light win-dow wall to be easily installed. 48 tension cables 1.375 in. (35mm) in diameter suspended from each mast carry the solid roof deck at each node of the roof's 24-ft. (7.3m) square element. The roof is stiffened by 24 lower cables 0.75 in. (19mm) in diam-eter on the underside of the roof. These cables stabilize the roof against wind uplift forces. Further, 36 vertical cables run between the building perimeter on the underside of the roof at the 24 ft. (7.3m) nodes and the foundation to minimize any edge move-ments caused by the rotation of the roof about its horizontal axes. These perimeter cables are hidden in every fourth mullion of the window wall. The masts rise 35 ft. (10.7m) above the roof and bear on caissons that are 80 ft. (24.4m) deep. The lower seg-ment of each mast is a cast-in-place cylinder 6 ft. (1.8m) in diam-eter. At the second floor level, the mast extends upward as a steel shaft tapering off to 3 ft. 9 in. (1.1m) diameter at its top. This upper segment is filled with concrete. All roof girders and diago-nal elements are 18 in. (457mm) deep steel sections. The roof framing has a metal acoustical deck topped with gravel and tar. The frame is exposed on the inside. The deck was placed diago-nally in order to increase the diaphragm rigidity and to reduce its span. Vertical slip joints were provided to allow for movement between the roof and the curtain wall. These joint units that con-tain fluorocarbon pads, are installed at the top of each mullion to permit vertical and a slight lateral movement. To provide better control over tolerances, the roof was fabricated in place rather than at the ground level. During fabrication the roof was sup-ported by scaffolding at each node.

Khan was involved in several other projects in the United States and overseas. He worked on the National Life Building in Nashville, Tennessee and Latter and Meltzer Building in New Orleans, Louisiana. He received early recognition from Pablo Picasso in the 1960s for his work—the design of a 30-ft. (9.1-m) high steel structure representing Picasso's "BIRD" (a 12-in. [305-mm] high sculpture) at the Daley Plaza in Chicago (Fig. 45). Architect Bill Hartman of SOM was in charge of the project. Khan assigned the structural design task to Joseph Colaco and asked him to check the stability of the sculpture. Colaco suggested triangular stiffeners to reinforce it which Khan approved. Khan added some curves to it to make it aesthetically more elegant. Like several other architects of SOM, Hartman began to like Khan after knowing him better and would always support him in his bold experimentation with new structural systems. According to Colaco, Khan had plenty of political skill when dealing with architectural partners, and his objective was always to get the things done right. If he believed in something, he could find his way to accomplish his goal by keeping everyone happy. Picasso was happy with the design and wrote a personal

Fig. 45: Steel Sculpture replicating Picasso's "BIRD" at the Daley Plaza in Chicago [Courtesy: Ifat Ali Boles]

letter to Khan congratulating him on the transformation of his sculpture into a steel structure.

Khan worked on the Solar Telescope project at Kitt Park, Arizona with Myron Goldsmith and the US Air Force Academy in Colorado Springs. Another project was the King Abdul Aziz University, Makkah (more widely spelled as Mecca) Campus of 1978. He worked on the campus master plan. The academic complex was to have two separate campuses to accommodate a student population of 10,000 men and 5,000 women and to be expanded by another 50 percent if there was a need. Housing for 60 to 75 percent of the students and faculty was to be provided on campus. The master plan reflected traditional Islamic urban settlements. He worked with Bruce Graham and Richard Dober of Dober and Associates, Belmont, Massachusetts. Dober acted as the chief educational consultant. Khan was concerned about two critical issues—being sensitive to the local culture and taking into account the close proximity of the campus to Mecca, the center of the Islamic world. There were a number of massive low-rise buildings in concrete for the various academic units. When I joined SOM in 1980, architects and engineers were working on two buildings, *Dawa* and *Sharia*, for this project. This was toward the end of the project schedule. This university project was never implemented by the Saudis. Khan was also involved in the "Suez Master Plan Study," an SOM proposal of 1974 for the master plan of the cities of Suez and Port Towfik for the Ministry of Housing and Reconstruction of the Egyptian government.

Khan worked on a few other overseas projects that included a 40-story project, the BHP Corporate Headquarters building (1967) in Melbourne, Australia. In this building, Khan used the belt truss system at two levels, one at mid-height and the other at the top of the building. He also worked on the initial design phase of the Arab International Bank in Cairo, a 38-story building complex of bank and apartments. According to Graham, the architect of the building, the project started in 1973 and was completed in the 1990s. Another overseas project was the National Commercial Bank of 1984 in Jeddah, Saudi Arabia, a building on which Khan started working with architect Gordon Bunshaft of SOM's New York office. Iyengar had also been responsible for the project since 1975 when he became a partner of SOM. The project reached its climax in 1982 and was completed by Iyengar. In the 1970s Khan worked on the Pahlavian Treasures Building in Teheran for the late Shah of Iran. This building was, however, never built because of the Shah's loss of monarchy as a result of the Islamic Revolution in Iran in 1978. Further, Khan engineered the World Trade Center (1975) in Hong Kong. Another one of his projects is the Tobacco Processing Plant and Corporate Headquarters of W. D. & H. O. Wills (1974) in Bristol, England. Influenced by Isambard Brunel's nearby grand Clifton Suspension Bridge, trusses, that were structurally functional, were installed above the roof in this building to compliment the grand engineering tradition of the country.

▲ ▼

Two other concrete high-rise buildings engineered by Khan, towards the end of his career, were the One Magnificent Mile and the Onterie Center, both in Chicago. Construction of these

Fig. 46

Fig. 46: One Magnificent Mile, Chicago, Illinois. Bundled tube building in concrete [Courtesy: SOM; photo by Hedrich/Blessing]

was completed after Khan's death. One Magnificent Mile is an application of the bundled tube concept developed earlier for the Sears Tower, and the Onterie Center represents an application of the trussed tube concept developed for the John Hancock Center. The effectiveness of the bundled tube concept was also tested earlier on another of Khan's buildings, the 30-story Ohio National Bank Building of 1976 in Columbus, Ohio. Here tubes with wall-like characteristics are constructed in concrete and the interior framing is of structural steel.

ONE MAGNIFICENT MILE: One Magnificent Mile (1983) is a 57-story multi-use building comprising office, residential, parking, and commercial spaces (Fig. 46). This concrete structure bundles together three tubular towers 21-, 49-, and 57-stories high. The site is L-shaped facing Lake Michigan with a diagonal vista at the northern end of Michigan Avenue of Chicago. Graham and Khan collaborated extensively on this project to integrate the salient architectural and structural features of this building. A free-form structure was conceived that could be shaped around the angular site, and that would provide vertical modular relationship to match office and condominium spaces. Thus, the building floor plans and three hexagonal shaped modules were developed to take full advantage of the small L-shaped lot and the logic and structural possibilities of a clustered tube reinforced concrete system. The structural system was developed to provide for parking at lower levels and condominiums in the two taller tubes above the twenty-first story. The building contains commercial space on the first three floors, offices on floors 4 to 19, and luxury condominiums at the top. The tube geometry and arrangement of the three towers were determined from a comprehensive study of desirable views for the condominiums, and the possible shadow cast over the nearby park and beach. The 57-story tower in the middle of the cluster is capped with a sloped, glazed roof with a view to the beach and lake. The facade shapes permit different orientations to respond to views and to relate to the nearby buildings.

The 21-story tube has a 2-story mechanical floor at the top and this band is carried across the other two towers, creating a clear division between office and condominium floors. This band also creates a special visual effect by breaking the monotony of the perforated tubes of the two tall towers. The exterior fenestration relates to the function in the interior and therefore has a different treatment above and below this band.

The structural planning aspects of this building are instructive. An optimum interior column spacing of 30 x 30 ft. (9.1 x 9.1m) was selected for the west 21-story tube. In the north 57-story tube, where all the elevator cores are located, the location of the interior gravity columns was determined purely from the most desirable space allocation plan for the apartments. In the south 49-story tube, a staggered 20 x 30 ft. (6.1 x 9.1m) layout of columns was determined to be the most efficient because, while it met the apartment layout scheme for the upper levels, it also was very satisfactory for the office spaces and the parking levels below. As far as the peripheral tube frames are concerned, because of architectural requirements, column spacing varies for different functions. At the apartments, it ranges from 2 ft. 6 in. (0.76m) to 9 ft. (2.7m) whereas for the office floors it is 10 ft.

Fig. 47

100

(3m) and at the commercial and parking levels it is 20 ft. (6.1m). All interior tube columns are spaced 10 ft. (3m) apart. The structural efficiency of the bundled tube system allowed for the free-form massing and made the selection and design of the form a logical preference over other systems. Flat plate was used in apartments and flat slab with drop panel was used in office, commercial, and parking floors. The exterior spandrel beams at the apartment levels had to be upturned, which called for special attention to detailing. Along the interior column line between the north and south tubes, a few beam segments were, however, down-turned to allow for a hallway to pass through. It was because of Khan's flexibility in design approach that all these variabilities in this project could be successfully handled. This building certainly represents a promise for future multi-use buildings where the architect could use a wide variation of forms to match functions yet maintain the necessary structural integrity.

ONTERIE CENTER: Another major project engineered by Khan, completed in 1985, is the Onterie Center in Chicago (Fig. 47). This is a diagonally braced concrete multi-use building complex located on the Lake Michigan shoreline. It consists of two components—a 58-story main tower with a 12-story auxiliary building. The idea of concrete diagonals on the building perimeter was born in the late 1960s, when graduate students at IIT asked Khan: since it is possible to brace a building in steel, why not in concrete? Khan had tried this idea of diagonally braced concrete building as early as 1968 for Robin Hodgkison's thesis at IIT (see Chapter 5). Since then he had been waiting for an opportunity to apply the concept on a practical structure.

Onterie Center became an instant "landmark in its own right" in the City of Chicago (Zils and Clark, 1986). Use of diagonals for concrete buildings was delayed because no developer had so far accepted the idea, particularly because of the problem created by blocking the windows by diagonals. According to Graham, this concept of using diagonals for concrete buildings was proposed earlier for the One Shell Square office building in New Orleans. This was, however, not approved by Gerald Hines, the developer for that project. For the Onterie Center project, Khan had been away from Chicago during its initial phase. Graham proposed the idea of a concrete building with diagonals to Chandra Jha, developer of the project. Jha was concerned about the X-bracing in the apartment facade and the cost. He wanted to wait for Khan and hear his opinion also. On his return to Chicago, Khan readily embraced the proposal of using diagonals for the building and convinced Jha of the idea. Graham and Khan came up with the notion of blocking window openings with concrete infill in a lively and aesthetic pattern such that the extent of blocking would be minimum and only one window in each apartment would be blocked. Jha accepted their recommendation. Jha told me, "I am glad I accepted the idea of diagonals. It was less expensive and the building was completed ahead of schedule." He explained to me why he took the risk of trying out this new concept: "I had confidence in Faz because of my past acquaintance with him and his previous structural accomplishments." He emphasized, however, that Graham "sold the idea" to him and also had a major role in convincing him. He found that Khan and Graham reinforced each other's ideas.

Fig. 47: Onterie Center, Chicago, Illinois. Braced tube building in concrete [Courtesy: SOM; photo by Gregory Murphey]

Jha, Khan, and Graham discussed different schemes and finally agreed on the one that was actually implemented.

Khan did not live to oversee the completion of all structural design details for this building. He, however, completed the initial design phase of the building after which the project went on hold for some time. During that time, Khan passed away. Therefore, the construction of the building took place after his death. Iyengar carried out the final design and concluded the project. As a result, Khan was the primary structural designer for this building, which is generally regarded as his last major project.

The main public lobby and commercial space are located on the ground floor of the main tower and the connecting auxiliary building. The basement and four floors above the lobby are used for parking accommodating 380 cars. Floors 6 through 10 of the flared base and floors 2 through 11 of the auxiliary building are assigned to offices. Floor 11 includes a health club, swimming pool, and mechanical equipment space. Apartment floors begin at the 12th floor sky lobby and continue up to the 58th floor. The peripheral concrete structure is painted and infilled with gray-tinted double-glazing, which offers the facade a distinct character and expresses its concrete structure. Perimeter columns are laid out at spacings varying from 4 ft. 6 in. (1.4m) to 6 ft. 5 in. (2m) on center. The columns are 19 in. (483mm) wide in elevation and the spandrel beams are 19 in. (483mm) deep. The exterior wall comprising columns, spandrels, and infill panels is typically 21 in. (533mm) thick. The exterior of the building is fully exposed architectural concrete. The floor system is flat slab and interior column spacing is 22 ft. (6.7m) on center. The building has a slenderness ratio of 8:1. The structural system determines the aesthetics of the building.

The lateral load-resisting system was achieved by closely-spaced columns and spandrels in conjunction with infilling window openings with concrete in a diagonal pattern on elevation. These infill panels also act as shear panels at the different stories. These diagonals tie columns and spandrels together and help to evenly distribute the gravity loads to the columns. They also reduce the shear lag effect in the tube frame. An infill panel detail is shown in Fig. 48. The tower's center part on its long side is set back and not braced diagonally. This results in discontinuity of the diagonals across the broad face and creates two well defined braced shafts which form channels in plan creating partial tubular systems (Fig. 47). The webs of the channels form on the short faces of the building and are provided with X-bracing whereas the long faces have zigzag diagonal braces. A solid top floor without the setback brings the two shafts together both structurally and visually. The base of the tower splays out in front to create more office space with much sunlight below. The diagonal bracing is continued below to the street level thereby maintaining visual continuity. Since no core wall is used in this braced tube system, any differential creep between core walls and columns for such a tall building is automatically eliminated.

A design complexity is introduced by the fact that the horizontal component of the axial force in the diagonals creates a thrust at each bracing panel corner (Fig. 49). In a steel braced-tube structure like the Hancock Center, the outward thrust is contained by a tension spandrel, which runs continuously around the perimeter of the building. At Onterie Center this

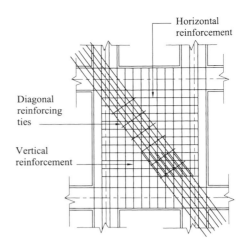

Fig. 48

Fig. 49

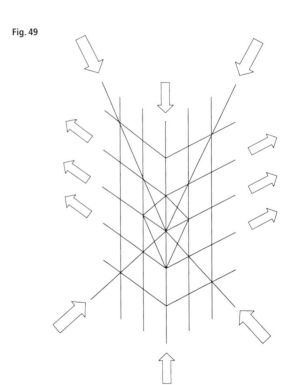

102

Fig. 48: Onterie Center, Typical Infill Panel Between Spandrels and Closely-Spaced Columns Showing Reinforcement Details

Fig. 49: Onterie Center, Force Flow at Panel Corner showing Horizontal Outward Thrust

Fig. 50: Onterie Center, Quadrant Computer Model

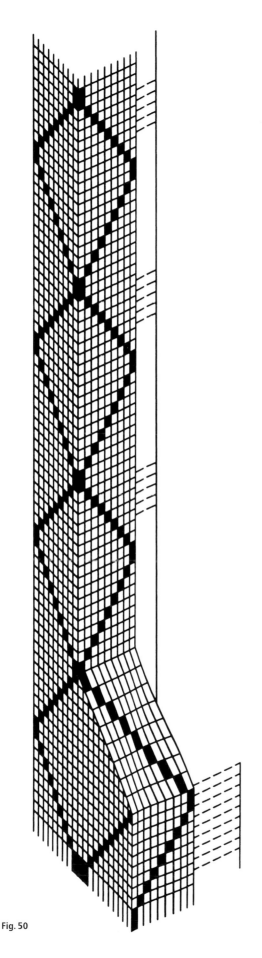

Fig. 50

thrust is restrained by increasing the slab edge and spandrel reinforcement in zones of these floors. A much larger thrust occurs at the sixth floor, that serves as the base of the inclined channel frame. Gravity forces from above flow downward along the inclined face of the structure. The horizontal component of the inclined force was contained by thickening the sixth floor slab and designing it as a horizontal diaphragm.

A sophisticated computer analysis showed that the building was sufficiently stiff against lateral wind load despite the fact that it is quite slender. The analysis was performed on an unlumped three-dimensional quadrant model representing one-quarter of the entire structure (Fig. 50). Standard loading combinations of dead and live load as well as lateral wind load, thermal loading, creep and shrinkage were considered for the analyses. Special attention was given to the load flow in the structure because of the unique and complex nature of the system and the effects of temperature (Zils and Clark, 1986). This project demanded a lot of collaboration among the developer, architect, engineer, and contractor. Since this was a new concept in concrete that was used earlier in steel for the John Hancock Center, a lot of questions about structural details and constructability came up, which were, of course, successfully resolved. The building was constructed on an average three-day per floor cycle, although quality control of the architectural finish in the exposed concrete in the building's facade was equally important as the speed of construction.

According to Jha, the shape of the building was created to respond to a new architectural vocabulary prevailing in the 1980s. Khan had a definite opinion on the building. He said to Jha, "This is very much a Chicago building, one in the tradition of the Chicago school. The inherent character of the structure is expressed, just as the columns and beams of the early 1900s' buildings in the Loop are expressed clearly, while the windows are infill" (*The Times*, 1984).

A parallel contribution of Khan is the 50-story diagonally braced concrete tube, the 780 Third Avenue Building of 1984 in New York City. Khan acted as a consultant to Robert Rosenwasser, structural engineer for this project. Raul de Armas of SOM, New York was the design architect. This building was completed before the Onterie Center, although the initial design concepts for Onterie preceded that of 780 Third Avenue. This narrow building has also a slenderness ratio of 8:1. Form and function are harmoniously blended in the elegant structural system of this building. It closely resembles the John Hancock Center in Chicago, its steel counterpart. The structure of the building becomes the architectural expression of the building. Like the Onterie Center, the diagonals that increase the stiffness of the building, are created by filling in window openings in a systematic manner with reinforced concrete covered by dusty red stone rendering them highly visible. The bracing is on all four sides, and the rectangular plan employs X-braces on the long sides and zigzag braces on the short sides. Unlike the 780 Third Avenue Building, however, the Onterie Center has thinner diagonals that result from the more closely spaced columns, forming smaller windows. As a result, the Onterie Center has a more sleek and delicate appearance.

Aesthetically, the Onterie Center is a superb creation of Khan-Graham collaboration. It also represents true collaboration among the developer, architect, and engineer. It is a piece of artwork. It is a highly geometric building. It has introduced a new and exciting architectural vocabulary for reinforced concrete high-rise buildings in which the structure provides a clear visual impact. Its architecture is based on its structure as is revealed on the facade. Its mind is as lovely as its body. The handsomest interior feature of Onterie, as noted by Paul Gapp in the October 12, 1986 issue of the *Chicago Tribune*, " ... is its marvelous glazed ceramic tile floor done in several shades of blue and gray in diamond and other diagonal shapes that echo the patterns on the building's facades." As part of a national architectural trend, Graham wanted that the floors should be lively. French-born artist Juan Gardy Artigas beautifully created the floor mosaics that run throughout the building's interior ground level areas and harmoniously blend with the oak paneling applied to walls and other areas. On the whole, the environment within this building is extremely pleasant. A walk through the main lobby and around the building is a delightful experience.

▲ ▼

Khan's many projects and contributions to his profession did not go unrecognized. The impressive list of awards bestowed upon him for outstanding accomplishments is a long one, and begins when he set foot on U.S. soil with the Fulbright and Ford Foundation Scholar award in 1952. He was recognized by his alma mater, University of Illinois at Urbana-Champaign, by conferring the College of Engineering Alumni Award for Distinguished Service in Engineering, UIUC, in 1972 and by the Distinguished Civil Engineering Alumnus Award a decade later in 1982.

Among the many prestigious professional awards, some important ones are the Wason Medal for most meritorious paper from the American Concrete Institute (ACI) in 1971, the Lloyd Kimbrough Medal from the American Institute for Steel Construction (AISC) in 1973, and the Oscar Faber Medal from the Institution of Structural Engineers, London, also in 1973. The Wason Medal was awarded to him by ACI for the paper that he co-authored with Mark Fintel on "Shock Absorbing Soft Story Concept for Multistory Earthquake Structures." The Lloyd Kimbrough Medal was conferred by AISC to only five previous recipients in its 35-year history before 1973. ACI also bestowed upon him the Alfred E. Lindau Award in 1973 for his "outstanding contributions in advancing the art of reinforced concrete construction in high buildings."

The American Society of Civil Engineers (ASCE) conferred on him the Middlebrooks Award in 1972 and the Ernest E. Howard Award in 1977. Also, the Cleveland Section of ASCE bestowed on him the G. Brooks Earnest Award in 1979. Further, ASCE honored him with the Chicago Civil Engineer of the Year Award in 1972. The Illinois Council of the American Institute of Architects (AIA) conferred on him the State Service Award in 1977. The Chicago Chamber of Commerce honored him in 1970 by awarding him "Chicagoan of the Year in Architecture and Engineering."

In 1965, the then 35-year-old Khan gained editorial recognition by the *Engineering News Record* (*ENR*) for his innovative design concept of the Hancock Center in Chicago. In 1972, Khan was selected by *ENR* as the "Construction's Man of the Year,"

(*ENR*, 1972). An article on him was published together with his picture displayed on the magazine's cover. In the editorial "Fazlur Khan: Man of the Year," *ENR* wrote: "In singling out Khan as Man of the Year . . . *ENR*'s editors were impressed, of course, by his innovation upon innovation in the field of structural engineering of high-rise buildings. But beyond the height records and the weight savings and cost savings of his designs, beyond the technical genius of this man, a sensitive student of the urban environment stands forth." The editorial concluded: "Fazlur Khan is a leader among the world's designers of great buildings. In this new era of the skyscraper, in this time of concern for human safety, comfort and convenience in high-rise homes and offices, he is a philosophical leader of thought. He is construction's Man of the Year." Before this, in 1966, 1968, and 1971, he was cited by *ENR* among the "Men Who Served the Best Interests of the Construction Industry."

Khan was elected to the National Academy of Engineering (NAE) in 1973. NAE was established in 1964 under a charter from the National Academy of Sciences, as a parallel organization of outstanding engineers. Election to the NAE is among the highest professional distinctions in engineering.

Khan was honored by three universities that conferred honorary doctorate degrees on him. He received an honorary Doctor of Science from the Northwestern University, Evanston, Illinois, in 1973; an honorary Doctor of Engineering from the Lehigh University, Bethlehem, Pennsylvania in 1980; and Die Eidgenossische Technische Hochschule (ETH), Zurich, Switzerland, conferred an honorary Doktors Der Technischen Wissenschaften (Doctor of Technical Sciences) in 1980.

He received the 28th Progressive Architecture award in 1981 for the Haj Terminal in Jeddah, Saudi Arabia. He also received several honors and recognitions posthumously (see Chapter 15).

It is clear that Khan got the highest and most prestigious awards that an engineer could ever expect to get. People have suggested that he would certainly win a Nobel Prize if there were one in engineering disciplines. But such rare honor made this humble man more humble and only inspired him further to perform even better and focus on his search for structural logic, truth, and justice. He got media publicity not only from *ENR* but also in *Newsweek*, *New York Times*, and the *Chicago Tribune*. His name appeared in other professional magazines and books in the USA and throughout the world. Anytime there was a discussion on tall buildings, his name just came up. He was in great demand as a speaker at various universities, conferences, and meetings worldwide. On one of his trips to Europe, he was scheduled to give a single presentation in London. Before Khan left Chicago, word had spread in Europe that he would be in London. Engineering and architectural groups from Paris, Stuttgart, Munich, Vienna, and Milan invited him requesting his talks, and he ended up giving eight presentations.

His international outlook, like his buildings, was monumental. His concern for human issues added a new dimension to the effectiveness of structural style and aesthetics of his engineered buildings. It was this preeminence that led the International Association for Bridge and Structural Engineering (IABSE) in 1982, just three days before his death, to vote him for its most prestigious "International Award of Merit."

chapter 7

THE TOWER OF STRENGTH

"An optimum structural system using a combination of the minimum number of diagonals along with exterior columns and spandrels made it structurally feasible to build a 100-story building for the equivalent unit cost of a normal 40-story framed structure."

—Fazlur R. Kahn (1967)

106
106

The 100-story John Hancock Center of 1970 in Chicago is the first major steel skyscraper designed by Bruce Graham and engineered by Fazlur Khan. Robert Diamant was the architect acting as the studio head. It is an investment-type multi-use building consisting of parking, commercial, offices, and apartments in a single building. The building provides approximately 1,000,000 sq. ft. (92,900m^2) of office space, 1,000,000 sq. ft. (92,900m^2) of residential space, and 800,000 sq. ft. (74,320m^2) of parking and commercial areas. It is 1127 ft. (342m) high and has a tapered form like a very tall truncated pyramid elongated vertically with a large base. Dozens of such shapes were studied resulting in the final shape that exists today. The ground floor has approximate dimensions of 160 x 260 ft. (49 x 79m) and the clear span of floor, from the central core consisting of columns carrying vertical loads only, is about 60 ft. (18.3m). The building top measures 100 x 160 ft. (30.5 x 49m) and the clear span diminishes to 30 ft. (9.1m). The building is thus a diagonally braced, tapered tube making it very stiff to resist lateral loads. Adoption of this efficient structural system resulted in a total structural steel quantity of 29.7 lbs per sq. ft. (145 kg/m^2), which represents a very efficient low-premium-for-height system as compared to 42.2 psf (206 kg/m^2) for the 102-story Empire State Building. The total amount of steel varies from tier to tier as shown in Fig. 51.

The project was initially conceived as two separate buildings using the traditional framed construction—one for the office and the other for the apartments—in order to meet the basic total area requirements. This would obviously create a higher congestion of the site with rather small setbacks from streets and very little plaza area at the ground floor. A thorough investigation was carried out in terms of architectural-structural integration and seeking a structurally efficient, cost-effective, aesthetically acceptable, and constructable solution that would cater to the user needs. A new structural system was developed that combined the two buildings into one. Initially a 95-story building was considered, which was changed to a 100-story structure at the insistence of the developer (Fig. 52).

Another motivating factor was to place the apartments on top of the offices. In apartment space planning, deep space from window wall to building core cannot be effectively utilized, since proximity to windows for natural light and viewing is very important to the occupants. Offices, on the other hand, could

Fig. 51

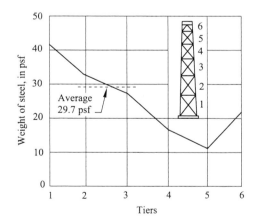

Tiers

Fig. 51: John Hancock Center, Variation of Steel Weight from Tier to Tier

Fig. 52: John Hancock Center, Chicago, Illinois. Khan's first braced tube building
[Courtesy: SOM; photo by Ezra Stoller/Esto]

107 107 107 107 107

accommodate a much deeper space away from the windows. Thus, apartments have to be above the offices in a "wedding cake-type arrangement" with a broad building at the bottom and a narrow one above. A tapered building form evolved out of this consideration as a logical consequence, where the largest feasible apartment floor could be located at the 46th level. Apartment floors containing 2-bedroom and 1-bedroom efficiencies in the building continue up to the 94th floor. Typical apartment floor framing is shown in Fig. 53. Offices are located from the 18th to the 41st floor. There is an observatory on the 94th floor. Also, an apartment sky lobby is located at the 44th-45th floors. The 95th and 96th floors contain a restaurant. Other floors are for parking, retail, and mechanical spaces. By tapering the building, a continuous structure on the exterior facade could be generated

Fig. 52

without disrupting its tubular behavior. An earlier scheme for the building was a tube structure without diagonals. A diagonally braced tube structure was finally selected. This is the first steel version of braced tube concept ever built.

The special nature of the structural system used for this building is underscored by the fact that only a few diagonals installed in the plane of the facade create a rigid box effect. The structural system causes all exterior columns connected to the large diagonal X-braces in the plane of the columns to act as an equivalent rigid bearing wall. Vertical loads are gradually redistributed to all of the columns through the diagonals and spandrels (Fig. 54). The diagonals, columns, and spandrel beams all meet at their centerlines, thereby eliminating any secondary moments caused by eccentricity. Heavy tie beams were placed at the levels where the diagonals intersect the corner columns so that the structure would not stretch outward at that level, and the diagonals participate in carrying the gravity loads and distributing the loads to the columns. The diagonals remained in compression under wind loads, which simplified the member connections. Because of this even distribution of loads, all exterior columns in each face were made equal in size. The structural system, in Khan's own words, can best be described as an "optimum column-diagonal truss-tube." The columns, diagonals, and ties were fabricated to an I-section consisting of three plates welded together. The maximum plate thickness is 6 in. (152mm) and the maximum overall dimension of column is 36 x 36 in. (914 x 914mm). The main ties along with the X-braces constitute a tier and there are a total of six such tiers including one at the top which has a chevron bracing.

A question arose during the design process: From where in the base should the diagonals start? Should they start from the top of the foundation or from the ground floor? Investigative studies of different options led to the decision to start the main X-bracing at the second floor. The lowermost floor was X-braced in the two corner bays at each end of each face of the building. A single transitional diagonal brace was added at each corner bay in the floor immediately above this lower-most floor (Khan et al., 1966).

As earlier noted, Khan had already tried this diagonally braced system on a thesis project of Mikio Sasaki at IIT. Although a simple model test generally validated the assumptions of the thesis, no detailed theoretical analysis was performed to confirm the various assumptions for the load flow. Since the structural system and the underlying concepts marked a complete departure from previous orthodoxy, it was decided that at least three independent computer analyses would be made, and unless all three analyses yielded similar results on stress levels in all members, member design would not be finalized. The results of the analyses actually indicated similar stresses in all members although some differences between a frame-type and a truss-type analysis were observed as would be expected. Because of Khan's departure from the conventional structural systems for such a large project, concerns were raised from within SOM in regard to whether another structural firm should be consulted on this project. (This will be examined later.) It may be noted here that when Myron Goldsmith studied diagonally braced systems in his Master's thesis, it was not known that such systems could act

Fig. 53: John Hancock Center, Typical Apartment Floor Framing
Fig. 54: John Hancock Center, Load Flow
Fig. 55: John Hancock Center, Computer Coordination Flow Chart
Fig. 56: John Hancock Center, Typical Tier

Fig. 53

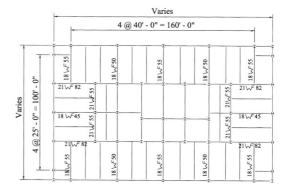

108

Fig. 54

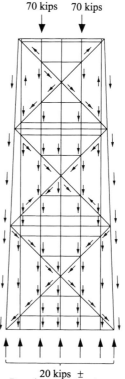

Concentrated load
70 kips   70 kips

20 kips ±
Reaction at each column

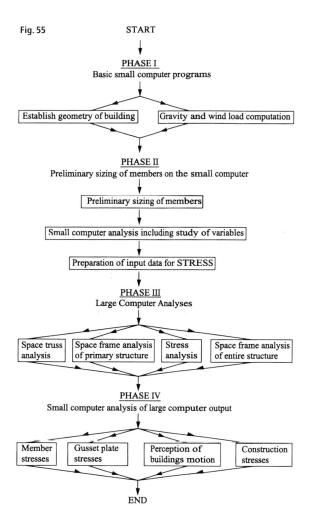

Fig. 55

```
                    START
                      │
                      ▼
                  PHASE I
         Basic small computer programs
          ┌───────────┴───────────┐
          ▼                         ▼
┌─────────────────────┐  ┌──────────────────────────┐
│ Establish geometry  │  │ Gravity and wind load    │
│ of building         │  │ computation              │
└─────────────────────┘  └──────────────────────────┘
          └───────────┬───────────┘
                      ▼
                  PHASE II
    Preliminary sizing of members on the small computer
                      │
                      ▼
       ┌───────────────────────────────┐
       │ Preliminary sizing of members │
       └───────────────────────────────┘
                      │
                      ▼
  ┌─────────────────────────────────────────────┐
  │ Small computer analysis including study of   │
  │ variables                                    │
  └─────────────────────────────────────────────┘
                      │
                      ▼
     ┌────────────────────────────────────┐
     │ Preparation of input data for STRESS│
     └────────────────────────────────────┘
                      │
                      ▼
                 PHASE III
           Large Computer Analyses
   ┌──────┬──────────┬──────────┬──────────┐
   ▼      ▼          ▼          ▼
┌──────┐┌─────────┐┌───────┐┌──────────────┐
│Space ││Space    ││Stress ││Space frame   │
│truss ││frame    ││analysis││analysis of  │
│analysis││analysis││       ││entire       │
│      ││of primary││      ││structure     │
│      ││structure││       ││              │
└──────┘└─────────┘└───────┘└──────────────┘
                      │
                      ▼
                 PHASE IV
   Small computer analysis of large computer output
   ┌──────┬──────────┬──────────────┬──────────┐
   ▼      ▼          ▼              ▼
┌──────┐┌─────────┐┌──────────────┐┌──────────┐
│Member││Gusset   ││Perception of ││Construction│
│stresses││plate   ││buildings     ││stresses   │
│      ││stresses ││motion        ││           │
└──────┘└─────────┘└──────────────┘└──────────┘
                      │
                      ▼
                    END
```

in a tubular mode. The braces were placed as simple wind bracing in planar frame systems. The braced tube concept truly evolved with the design of the John Hancock Center. But it is clear that Goldsmith did, in fact, consider a braced steel facade as early as 1953 in an attempt to develop a new architectural vocabulary for tall buildings.

In the early 1960s, computer capabilities were rather limited. Computers were slower and had low memory capability. SOM had only a small computer (IBM 1620) with a 20,000-digit memory capacity. As a result, the general scheme for analysis was segmented into analysis and design work in terms of large and small computer capability (Khan et al., 1966). A flow chart depicting the computer coordination procedure was developed (Fig. 55). This flow chart shows that the major part of the computer usage involved the small computer for doing the preliminary analysis and design of portions of the whole structure. The large computer was used for the analysis and design of the entire peripheral wall structure of the building. A few programs were developed for the small computer to define the basic geometry of the building and the loads on it.

The program dealing with the geometry set up the rigorous geometric discipline in the arrangement of the columns, spandrels, and the diagonals. The constraints imposed by the building's taper and the requirement that the exterior columns intersect with the diagonals at a floor level where a main spandrel tie could be placed, resulted in variable story heights in order to maintain acceptable story heights between the floors. The exterior framework, bounded by main ties and the corner columns with diagonals in between, together with other columns and spandrels at levels where the diagonals intersect the columns, was defined as a "primary system," whereas the "secondary system" was defined by the floor beams between the primary floors (Fig. 56). Architectural programming required story heights of 9 to 10 ft. (2.7 to 3m) for apartments and 12 to 13 ft. (3.7 to 4m) for office and parking. Different combinations of input variables, namely, number of tiers, column spacings on each side at the top of the last tier taper about one axis of the building, and typical story height for the tier, were investigated using several combinations of these variables. The program computed the required taper about the other axis, odd floor heights at the top and bottom of each tier, plan dimensions at each floor, and the floor areas. The final geometry of the structure was thus achieved.

Gravity loads and gravity load increment at each floor level were determined for the exterior columns using the column load program. Again, the building's taper necessitated the use of this program to avoid tedious load take-off calculations for columns with variable floor tributary loads. Likewise, the wind load program was used to compute and tabulate the wind shears and overturning moments at each floor resulting from the applied wind pressures on the exterior wall in accordance with the provisions of the Chicago Building Code, as well as the 1/7 power law of velocity variation. The Chicago Building Code wind load was increased in the final design by 25 percent on the basis of wind tunnel tests and meteorological records. Subsequent checks

09

Fig. 56

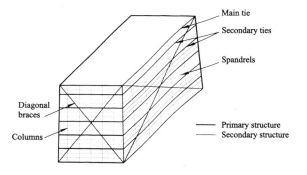

Main tie
Secondary ties
Spandrels
Diagonal braces
Columns

── Primary structure
── Secondary structure

proved that even with a 40 percent increase in the Chicago Code wind load, the design of structural members was not influenced by wind load effects.

Preliminary sizes of exterior columns, diagonals, and ties were determined by the structural team in the following way. Columns were sized for gravity and wind loads making simplifying assumptions. Diagonal braces in each tier were proportioned to limit the shear racking to 20 percent of the total lateral deflection, that is, the building's lateral stiffness was derived primarily from a cantilever mode, with 80 percent of the lateral deflection due to column shortening. The main ties were designed to limit the horizontal stretch of the building to a range of 0.250 to 0.375 in. (6.35 to 9.53mm), caused by the horizontal component of the forces in the diagonals. Typical floor spandrel beams were sized to satisfy the floor load requirements.

Because of the limitations of the small IBM 1620 computer, a planar module comprising half the face of the building three tiers high with appropriate boundary conditions was used as a computer analysis model and analyzed as a truss with pinned joints. This plane truss program helped to provide a better understanding of the structural behavior of the system. Some important conclusions were drawn. For example, it was found that there was a tendency for the vertical loads to be shared by the columns in proportion to their areas, that is, the behavior was more like a wall than a group of separate columns. All columns on a face of the building at any floor in the lower four tiers were made the same size. The corner column would normally require a smaller size for gravity loads alone, but to achieve maximum efficiency against wind loads, the same size for it as the other columns was used. A change in the size of the main ties did not influence the forces in the columns, but influenced their own internal forces due to a change in the deformation characteristics. Because the acceptable performance of the window wall and the structural floor slab require a restriction on the tie elongation, its size was governed by its deformation properties. The areas of other floor spandrels or secondary ties were found to have smaller effect on either the load distribution or the deformation of the main ties. These ties were, therefore, less effective in creating the tubular action of the peripheral walls.

Once the preliminary design was completed, refined analyses of the structure were carried out on large computers (IBM 7094). Four different types of analysis were performed: space truss analysis of the primary structure; space frame analysis of the primary structure; STRESS analysis of the primary structure; and space frame analysis of the entire structure, including the secondary floor spandrels and the core framing.

The space truss analysis was done on a module involving one-quarter of the building frame consisting of columns, diagonals, and primary level ties. The three load conditions considered were gravity, wind on broad face, and wind on narrow face. For the space frame analysis, the primary system module was used as above, except the joints were considered rigid with six degrees of freedom. The STRESS analysis program developed at MIT in 1964 was used to analyze a quarter of the three-dimensional structure for gravity and wind loads considering the structure as a frame. The last analysis type was the space frame analysis of the entire structure. This was also done on a quarter model but the secondary spandrels were considered to be hinged at both ends. A program was specifically written to solve the frame analysis problem. It was therefore possible to optimize the input data and reduce execution time by taking advantage of members having equal sizes. All results of the space frame analysis of the entire structure agreed closely with the results of the STRESS solution for the primary structure. [See Khan et al. (1966) for full details of the analysis.]

The use of computer as a computational tool was a primary factor in the analysis and design of such a major innovative structure. In the early sixties, modern digital computers were still in their infancy. Huge numbers of punched cards were prepared for running the computer programs. Computation running time was excessive. For example, the running time for the space truss analysis on the large IBM 7094 computer for each solution was 2 minutes, and that for the space frame analysis was about 10 minutes. The execution time for each STRESS solution was about 90 minutes—an astronomical amount of time by today's standards! For the space frame analysis of the entire structure, this time was about 21 minutes. Khan was a believer in the power of computers. He recognized and stressed that without the aid of computers, refined analysis and optimal design of supertall buildings would be unthinkable and so would be any parametric studies on them. But he always cautioned his co-workers that too much dependence on computer output results is counterproductive and inhibits logical thinking. One needs to check such results by simple manual calculations. Numerical and analytical reasoning should never be replaced by sheer number-crunching.

The output results from the large computer were used to check the adequacy of the members in the peripheral frame to meet the AISC 1963 specifications. A program was developed to check the stresses in these members. Whenever members were found overstressed, they were redesigned and rechecked. The program greatly aided in a fast and systematic check of all member sizes.

The stresses in the gusset plates at the locations where the diagonals meet each other at the middle of the tiers and at the corners where they intersect with corner columns and the main spandrel ties, were determined by a program. The plates were irregular in shape and a few simplifying assumptions were made for the analysis procedure. The method of analysis was elementary and involved the division of the gusset plates into a grid. The program pinpointed locations of high stress. The program is a simple version of the more sophisticated finite element programs that are so widely used today.

Because the building is so tall, Khan was concerned about its dynamic response to wind gusts. Tall and slender buildings can vibrate excessively in wind. The maximum displacement of a building during oscillations depends upon its geometry, materials of construction, and damping characteristics as well as the wind speed. Modern-day steel-and-glass buildings are relatively more susceptible to lateral displacements caused by wind than their previous counterparts. Such displacements or sways up to maximum critical limits would not be dangerous from a structural point of view, but are undesirable for the comfort of the occupants. Natural frequencies for the first few modes of vibration using the lumped-mass model of the Hancock Center were computed by an analysis on the large computer. A program for the small computer was written to obtain the dynamic response of the building under wind gusts. This program determined the displacement, velocity, acceleration, and the rate of change of acceleration in the prescribed time intervals. These results of the dynamic response were later verified by tests on human subjects.

There was also some concern about the effect of load application on structural members during construction. Four solutions were obtained to study this aspect considering one tier, two tiers, and three tiers with loads on single tier only and, in one case, three tiers with loads on all three tiers. The resulting construction stresses were found to be inconsequential.

With his experience in temperature effects for exposed columns in tall concrete buildings, Khan decided to focus on this aspect for this steel building also. He recognized that the prevailing trend of glass-steel construction for tall buildings offering an expression of technology in architecture could give rise to problems of temperature movements. For Hancock, he decided that the best way to resolve this problem was to avoid it. An anodized aluminum jacket with integral insulation and fireproofing was designed for the exterior structural system such that hot air would circulate inside the jacket and maintain a minimum temperature of 69 deg. F. (20.5 deg. C.) in winter. This would also ensure that a maximum temperature differential of about 5 deg. F. (3 deg. C.) between the exterior system and the interior columns would be maintained at all times. (The conversion of 5 deg. F. to 3 deg. C. represents the differential and not absolute value of conversion from US units to SI units.) Additional details to allow air circulation in the jacket by gravity were provided. The details consist of an air slot on the column jacket inside the building at the induction units and also an air slot through the column jacket in the ceiling space. By providing these openings at the top and bottom of the columns, cold air in the column space flows down into the induction units, whereas warm air replenishes the space from the ceiling area, thereby keeping the air temperature around the column very close to the inside temperature of the building (Khan and Nassetta, 1970). The jacket was tested successfully on full-scale mock-ups to ensure that the heating system was fail-proof. The mock-up tests of the detail just described showed that a 2-in (51-mm) thick insulation and gravity air circulation would maintain the aforementioned temperature differential of 5 deg. F. (3 deg. C.) under the worst winter exposure of -10 deg. F. (-23 deg. C.).

Because of preplanning and appropriate coordination, complete analysis and design of the building took only a year. Khan was very much concerned about the constructability of the building because of its departure from the traditional beam-column frame construction. Therefore, the details were developed in close collaboration with steel subcontractors. After the project was awarded to American Bridge for the fabrication of steel, the final details were refined and fully developed in cooperation with this company. To avoid field welding, the large gusset-plated joints at the intersection of the columns and braces were prefabricated in the shop by welding and the principal connections between the gusset plate assembly and members were made by bolting. Since the diagonals seldom went into tension under gravity and wind loads, they were treated as columns and the connection details were made simpler by making a bolted butt connection on the upper end and a bolted splice connection at the lower end. The simplified detailing for the structure resulted in a floor erection cycle time of about 3 floors per week. A view of the building during its construction is shown in Figs. 57a, 57b.

As usual, Khan worked very hard on this project, and it was against many obstacles. When the project began, Al Picardi was the Chief Structural Engineer to whom Khan reported. Khan was still a young, relatively inexperienced engineer for such a large project. The project structural team primarily consisted of Khan, Iyengar, Colaco, and M. H. Shah. Colaco carried out most of the analysis and design computations. The space frame and space truss analyses were conducted by Paul Weidlinger, Consulting Engineer, New York, and Professor John Goldberg of Purdue University. Assistance was also sought from Professor Steven Fenves of the University of Illinois at Urbana-Champaign and Professor Robert Logcher of MIT. Ammann and Whitney acted as a consultant to the owner.

Once the braced tube concept was proposed by Khan, Bruce Graham strongly supported it and saw some merits in it not only from a structural point of view, but also in terms of architectural programming and space planning. Hartman, an architectural partner, wanted a well known New York firm to work on this major project instead of SOM under Khan's direction. Khan, confident of his own abilities, totally opposed this idea. It was decided that SOM would do the design but Ammann and Whitney would review it. The engineering group for the Hancock project moved around this time to the Carson Pirie Scott Building. Meanwhile, Picardi left SOM for better prospects knowing that he was leaving the project in good hands. Following his departure, the engineering department was disbanded, and an integrated studio concept was introduced. This did not affect the nature and influence of Khan's work or contributions to the firm. He took over the firm's engineering component and became the undisputed structural leader of SOM.

Picardi and Khan once went to see Professor Biggs who taught at MIT and was also a principal of Hanson, Holly and Biggs of Cambridge, Massachusetts. Khan was not too enthusiastic about it. At Biggs' office, Khan and Picardi met him to discuss the matter. When Biggs stepped out of his office for a few minutes, Khan walked around the office and found that all books, reports, etc. displayed in that office were by professors from the University of Illinois at Urbana-Champaign. Biggs subsequently submitted a report showing very high wind loads. Khan did not like the report. He consulted A. G. Davenport of the University of Western Ontario and Ammann and Whitney and got a different perspective in the matter. But Biggs would not budge from what he presented in his report. Khan was able to handle the situation diplomatically discussing the matter in terms of building drift and ultimate stresses in the members and eventually convinced Biggs to modify his viewpoint. It was finally agreed that the wind loads determined by Biggs would be considered as ultimate loads.

To get a better understanding of the building's response to wind, wind tunnel tests on pressure models were undertaken in a steady state wind tunnel as contrasted to boundary layer wind

Figs. 57a, 57b: John Hancock Center under Construction
[Courtesy: McShane-Fleming Studios]

tunnel available at present. The purpose was to determine the magnitude of static wind loads at various levels.

A major concern about wind loads was whether the lateral movements at the upper part of the building where the apartments were located would create discomfort to the occupants. Although a steady high wind would result in the maximum lateral sway, objectionable vibratory movements could be caused by relatively sudden gusts. Louis Schmidt, of the US Naval School, Monterey, California, carried out a research study on this. He concluded that the Strouhal's Number for a building like the Hancock Center should be 0.17. It was also concluded that resonance under extreme wind conditions would not occur to this building. Study of wind gust showed that for a 50-year wind the maximum acceleration in the building was on the order of 0.3% g, where g is the acceleration due to gravity, and for a 2-year wind, this value is 0.25% g. To compare the anticipated performance of Hancock, ten other buildings, including the Empire State Building and Chase Manhattan Building in New York and 860 Lake Shore Drive and Marina City in Chicago, were studied. Khan, however, wanted to examine the problem of motion perception with some practical experiments. At that time, the idea of human perception of motion in a tall building was still not popular. But Khan was concerned about the human aspects of the design solution. To check motion perception, he carried out experiments on weekends at the Museum of Science and Industry on a large revolving table 20 ft. (6m) in diameter used for the Maytag Washing Machine Exhibit there. Nine people were subjects of this test. They represented a fair spread of variation in age and occupation and included Khan himself. Needless to say, this novel idea of the test was entirely Khan's and he organized it in collaboration with D. M. McMaster, Director of the Museum; John Wiss of Wiss, Janney, Elstner and Associates; and others.

A program of measuring actual movements of an existing building (860 Lake Shore Drive in Chicago) was undertaken to verify the theoretical assumptions involved in calculating the response of buildings to strong wind. This 26-story steel apartment building, designed by Mies Van der Rohe, is a somewhat flexible structure. An Impact-o-Graph was installed in the top floor in an apartment occupied by Phyllis Lambert, who offered her help in the instrumentation. The instrument would be switched on whenever motion was perceptible. Fortunately, there was a 70 mph (113 km/h) windstorm in the early hours of August 27, 1965 in the Lake Shore area. The acceleration was recorded by the instrument. Based on the comparative theoretical studies of ten other buildings, the experiment at the Museum of Science and Industries and the measurements at Lake Shore Drive building, Khan concluded that the maximum accelerations expected in the John Hancock Center were below the disturbing level even at the peak of wind storms.

After the Hancock Center was occupied, there were some minor complaints from occupants. In one case, a woman living in an apartment had complained that the chandelier in her living room would swing back and forth whenever there was gusty wind. Khan visited the apartment and added a brass tube to stiffen the vertical suspended stem of the chandelier and solved the problem. Also, the wine racks in the restaurant on the 95th floor would shake during gusty winds. Shaking of wine diminishes its quality. Khan and Colaco tried isolators to minimize the problem. Now the wine racks are kept in the basement and when a customer orders wine, it is fetched by express elevators.

He had the unusual sense of visualizing the movement of the building during high winds. On one windy Saturday he went to the apartment sky lobby of the building to watch, for himself, the waves of water in the swimming pool there. He anticipated such wave-like movements of water and put the gutters higher in the specifications. But he had to satisfy himself with his own visual observations.

Khan had encountered one major crisis during the construction of the building in March, 1966. One day, Earl Towery, the construction supervisor, called Colaco to say that a column had sunk by 1 in. (25.4mm). Colaco informed Khan who immediately instructed Towery to check the movement of the column at every level and also that of all other columns. It was found that only the one column in question sank by 1 in. (25.4mm). At that time, the building construction had reached the 10th to 12th floor height. Ironically, it so happened that in December 1965, the famed fortune teller and psychic Jeane Dixon predicted that the John Hancock Center would tumble down. Khan, however, demonstrated unusual calmness under the circumstances. The columns were all supported by machine-drilled caissons. Every caisson was cored and sonic tests were performed across the caissons. Al Lockett was the Project Manager who cooperated with him and Clyde Baker represented STS Consultants. According to Colaco, it was found that concrete in the caisson prehardened, arched, and split when the casing was lifted up. Clyde Baker, on the other hand, put it this way, "the problem is generally thought to be due to a fast-setting concrete. They (the workmen) cut the top half of the casing and attempted to pull it. The combination of casing and concrete acted as a plunger and sucked in soil and water below and the concrete finally broke free." According to Chester Siess who visited the site, a "truckload of weakened concrete" was removed from the damaged caisson to make room for pouring fresh concrete for replacing it. Siess had a preference for the Chicago method of pouring the caisson concrete over the drilled-caisson method. He recalled that he had asked Khan why drilled caissons were chosen for the Hancock project. Khan's response was that the contractor convinced him in this matter by telling him that time and money could be saved using the mechanized technique. It took six months to resolve this problem. It may be stated here that this problem arose due to the contractor's method of pulling the casing at his own risk. SOM never recommended it. At least one of the 57 caissons went 191 ft. (58m) into bedrock, the deepest sunk up to that point in time in Chicago.

A similar case-in-point is the collapse of a caisson at 500 North Michigan when the building was completed to about the 15th floor. In this project, a chunk of clay caved in to the concrete which was found when the concrete was cored. Khan did not, however, follow the conventional approach to investigate into the structure's foundation; he rather performed a detailed stiffness analysis before the building was shored and two new caissons were added to bridge over the defective caisson.

Colaco recalled that he had seen Khan falter only once. When Colaco found by a computer analysis that the gravity loads created almost equal stresses in the columns at the base, he asked Khan about it. Khan's intuition seemed to have failed and he said it was wrong, and that the columns, with larger tributary areas, should carry more loads. However, after checking the results thoroughly, Colaco went back to him. Khan came around quickly to realize that the diagonals and the exterior columns were creating a bearing-wall-type effect that distributed the loads uniformly towards the base.

Khan felt strongly about the John Hancock Center and had more liking for it than the Sears Tower. He once took his daughter Yasmin to the roof of the building. She later recalled: "When he took me onto the roof of John Hancock Building in Chicago, it was not to impress me with the extent of his innovation, but rather to share with me the exhilaration of the challenge."

Khan not only had a mystic understanding of the load sharing in structures, but also a microscopic vision of the connection details. For example, in a bolted beam-column connection using a cap plate on the beam, the bolts are normally spaced uniformly in a rectangular grid pattern. While working on such connections, however, he recognized intuitively that due to the shear lag effect the bolts that were far from the beam's cross-section were ineffective. Therefore, for bolted plate detail, he placed all the bolts around the beam's cross-section following the shape of the section. Likewise, when a continuity plate in a beam-column joint is welded between the beam flanges and columns, the weld between the end of the plate and the column web is ineffective. Forces are resisted by the welds connecting the two sides of the continuity plate and the inside surfaces of column flanges. His intuitive understanding in both cases was validated by tests. In addition, he had a bolted splice connection for the large diagonals tested at the University of Illinois under the supervision of Professor William Munse. The tensile test was conducted to evaluate the effectiveness of the ASTM-490 bolts used in the bearing-type splice connection. The test specimen was fabricated by the American Bridge Company. The test was carried out on January 11, 1966. Again, Khan realized that he was dealing with large diagonals in a large building and he wanted to assure himself that he would not take any chances on a project of this magnitude.

The John Hancock Center, nicknamed "Big John," was not without controversy in terms of its public image. The building's expression was pristine and more structural than architectural. Both its structural system and aesthetics represented a radical departure from those prevailing at that time. Its tapered shape and the X-braces make it reminiscent of the Eiffel Tower in Paris except that the perimeter is clad in glass and metal, and the structure accommodates people who could work, live, and shop there. Like the Eiffel Tower, this building, when completed, was a tower of strength. Graham (1989) wrote on this building:

> John Hancock insisted on producing a tall building with residences above, office and commercial uses below. The search for a new kind of structure which would accommodate multiple uses and also express the scale and grandeur of a one-hundred-story tower, led Dr. Khan and me to the diagonal tube. It was as essential to us to expose the structure of this mammoth as it is to perceive the structure of the Eiffel Tower, for in Chicago, honesty of structure has become a tradition.

117

Hancock declared the dominance of technology, and was ruthlessly criticized as industrial, super-rational and representative of machine age architecture. For example, here are some remarks by critics: "It [John Hancock Center] proudly, almost arrogantly, displayed its structural reinforcements—huge X-braces cutting across the facade. It was a building of swagger, of enormous strength, although its shape made it a less than compatible neighbor on North Michigan Avenue. The tower seemed like a looming giant, a great cowboy stalking the town. Skidmore's attempt to make the form gentler by sheathing the bottom in travertine did little to help; in truth, it only added an uncomfortable, awkward tone to the structure" (Goldberger, 1989); "Chicago is building an ugly steel-braced colossus . . . which promises to disrupt not only the appearance but the urban ecology of the downtown area" (von Eckardt, 1966); "Hancock's tapering one hundred stories serve primarily as support for these big-dollar TV masts" (Newman, 1970). Another critic was more blunt: "as a symbol of Chicago the tower is superbly expressive. But shouldn't the tallest landmarks in a metropolis be part of a larger plan? In a typically, tragically American way, John Hancock Center is not" (Dixon, 1970).

Reacting to the early comments on the building, Billington (1983) wrote, "For the critics the Hancock is mere technology, the result of purely utilitarian urge, whereas works of the designer from the Bauhaus are likened to things that arose in the past in societies that were not democratic. What critics sensed about the Eiffel Tower: it is not architecture in any traditional sense. But the Hancock goes beyond the Eiffel Tower in that it directly symbolizes a new city life—a life that escapes the image of control." Of course, today the Eiffel Tower symbolizes Paris. Sears and Hancock symbolize Chicago. Hancock is a town in itself and represents sky-high living. It is an exemplification of the megastructure concept in which people can live, work and play. People who live at the Hancock like it because almost every service they need is there. The building gives spatial understanding to people and represents what Graham called "people's architecture.

The building visually expresses the efficiency of the structure that was built economically and that offered a new meaning by its highly visible and unique structural expression. Although the building may not appear to be cute or pretty, its majestic presence, look of strength and stability accentuated by the larger-than-life diagonals, and lightness due to the exposure of its structural system through transparent glass gives it an unusual aesthetic quality that defies the temporary fashion of the time and makes it define undisguised and rational architecture. Its architecture stands apart from the routine, and the tower itself stands apart from the crowd of buildings nearby like a lion, the king of the jungle, standing apart from his other subject animals. A look upward by an observer standing next to the building from the plaza at its base strikes one with awe and wonder! People who live and work there love it and the commercial area is full of lively activities. According to John Zils, "It is almost like a status symbol, now, to have a 'diagonal' in your apartment. It symbolizes that you live in the Hancock." Others who occasionally visit inside or pass by the building are elated by the cheerful environment. The diagonals are not always readily accepted by some occupants, however, as they do not look logical from within and obstruct the views to outside at some locations. This sacrifice had to be made for gaining the structuralist architectural expression of the building and for structural efficiency. The view of Chicago from the top of Hancock is panoramic; according to some it is even better than that from the Sears Tower. One can get a more complete and spectacular view of the shoreline of Lake Michigan and the scenic Lake Shore Drive.

The visual expression of the tower is simple and without intricacy. Visible steel elements elegantly show the force flow and reveal the structural logic of the building form. The overall form demonstrates a strict discipline of structural design. Thus it is a building that has a structural rather than a conventional aesthetic facade, and no emphasis is placed on a bright, jovial, or romantic color scheme. Although the scale of the building seems amplified in relationship with surrounding buildings in terms of height and width, the diagonals and the main ties on the facade cut down the scale of the building by separating it into tiers which are within conceivable limits, and the visible floor structure reduces the scale of the building even further by bringing it down to an acceptable human level. The building's overall proportions are interestingly balanced. The gentle slope and the lightness and thinness of members add to the visual effect, structural clarity, and aesthetic quality of the building. The visual effect does not represent an extravagant, fanciful sculpture or exuberant romance. Pompous beauty is totally absent in the building's aesthetic appeal and there is no attempt to tone down the structural expression with non-tectonic ornamentation and decor on the facade, except for the sheathing at the bottom in travertine. According to Graham, the original base was to be clad in granite, but John Hancock Insurance Company had changed it to save money. Elaborate cladding elsewhere was avoided to express the metallic structure and its joints. The exterior cladding comprises black anodized aluminum with tinted bronze glass.

Graham once remarked that the building was intended to project the "gutsy, masculine, industrial tradition of Chicago where structure is the essence" (Dean, 1980). When I interviewed Graham, he spent a great deal of time talking about Hancock. He focused on the diagonals and felt that they gave a sense of scale to Hancock, because as he put it, "as you go higher in the building, the diagonals become smaller." Thus the diagonals give a different character to the building. He lamented that the diagonals and the exterior columns could not be expressed even more by placing them outside the plane of the window glazing. Dean (1980) described the scale and the diagonals of the tower thus:

> …the Hancock doesn't look grossly out of scale, except when viewed from the southwest corner (North Michigan and Chestnut Street), where two sides of the 260 x 160 foot rectangle are in full view next to the much smaller neighbors. Even here, however, the taper of the form helps reduce the feeling of bulk, as does the fact the building is set back from North Michigan…. The 'Xs' formed by intersecting diagonals, which diminish in size as they soar, tend to exaggerate perspective, making the building to zoom upward all the faster and higher, or descend with a great rush, depending on how you perceive it.

Although this trussed steel tube reminds us of the Eiffel Tower, it also repeats the singular image of the Washington Monument, the 555 ft. (168m) tall earliest known solid "tube" in the USA made of marble and granite completed in 1884. Both Hancock and this monument are obelisks of giant proportions representing strength and stiffness.

About Khan's ability to convince architects of his ideas, Graham said, "Faz's forte was the ability to talk to the architects and be understood of his structural ideas." According to Graham, structural engineers should take lesson from this and the architects should get inspired to work with structural engineers to develop appropriate forms for buildings. This needs a spirit of collaboration and team work. Hancock is a remarkable example of Khan's collaboration with the architectural design team. He was a firm believer in team work and promoted the idea that the design process of a tall building must be multi-disciplinary in nature. While discussing Khan's contributions to the Hancock Center and Sears Tower projects, Billington (1983) wrote:

> I have spoken of these buildings as if Khan were *the* designer just as Eiffel was for his tower. However, Khan's designs were collaborations between him and one of his architectural partners, usually Bruce Graham. Khan always emphasized his role as collaborator rather than principal designer. He repeatedly urged that 'the design process of any major building . . . must be multi-disciplinary in nature', . . . His argument for collaboration, in short, was a reaction against the idea of the architect alone producing the visual design and the engineer merely making the work safe and inexpensive.

At one stage of development of the building form, the architectural team in response to the owner's concerns wanted to remove the diagonals above the 90th floor (Khan, 1982b). Khan opposed this idea and won the argument. Graham agreed with Khan that "the integrity of the structural-architectural expression of the building was indeed enhanced and recaptured by continuing the diagonal scheme all the way to the top of the building." Such a spirit of collaboration between the engineer and the architect had resulted in a logical architectural statement from the bottom to the top of the tower. A beautiful passage from one of Khan's last publications speaks of his idea of collaboration thus (Khan, 1982b):

> The process of design for major architectural projects often does not take advantage of team effort of all disciplines working together to create the most relevant engineering/architectural solution. *A priori* architectural facades unrelated to natural and efficient structural systems are not only a wastage of natural resources but will also have difficulty in standing the test of time. The author, in this particular case, has attempted to highlight the structural/architectural team interaction which has resulted in this significant architectural statement based on reason and the laws of nature in such a way that the resulting aesthetics may have a transcendental value and quality far beyond arbitrary forms and expressions that reflect the fashion of the time.

Hancock made Khan instantly famous and gave him media publicity. As early as in 1965, Khan gained editorial recognition from the *ENR* magazine for the Hancock Center, the tallest building of the world since the Empire State Building and remained so for a short time until the World Trade Center and then the Sears Tower were built (*ENR*, 1972). The conceptual design of Hancock was started that year and Khan was 35 years old then. He established himself as a world leader in tall building design once the building was completed in 1970. From a structural engineer's role he gradually moved on to become an engineer-architect. He became a form-giver of buildings. He revived the tradition of Jenney and Root, of Maillart and Nervi. More challenges for him were yet to come. With his experience and confidence, he was now prepared to accept them. His next major project—the Sears Tower—was just waiting for him. In the meantime, Khan, who had been an associate partner since 1966, was promoted to the rank of a partner in 1970—the first structural engineering partner after Merrill, who was also a structural engineer, in the traditionally conservative SOM. He and Graham were later instrumental in getting other engineers promoted to the rank of partner and thus paved the way for engineers to have a say in the firm's major policy issues.

The John Hancock Center was awarded the 25-year Architectural Excellence Award by the American Institute of Architects (AIA) in February, 1999. The award is bestowed to a building whose architecture has stood the test of time and after 25 years retains its original excellence. This is a great recognition for Graham and Khan indeed.

According to Billington, the Hancock Center was Khan's favorite building (Billington, 1983). Interestingly enough, Graham also seemed to love Hancock more than Sears, because he spent most of his time with me talking about that building. Also, I found how elated he became by referring to the Hancock Center and its tapered form and its great diagonals! I guess that was the first major project for both of them that they did so successfully and that boosted their careers and established their reputation. Hancock represents a successful solution to the conflicts of land and occupancy. It has a symmetric, wholesome elevation on both its broad and narrow faces. It is near the lake. It still remains a unique Chicago landmark with its powerful diagonalized expression despite the presence of the Sears Tower built a few years later in the southwest of the Loop.

chapter 8

A TUBE OF TUBES

"Next came the Sears Tower, a bundled tube structure, in which we were able to shape the structure to respond to varying tenant conditions, from a very major occupant, Sears Roebuck, to very small tenants."

—Bruce Graham (1986)

One of the most famous projects generally attributed to Khan's name is the 110-story Sears Tower building of 1974 in Chicago (Fig. 58). The John Hancock Center was a great leap forward in the application of the tube concept to tall building design. As for the John Hancock Center, Graham was the design architect and Khan was the structural engineer of this major Chicago landmark. For the Sears Tower the Khan-Graham team pushed the idea of tubular design even further to what came to be known as cellular tube, or more commonly, as bundled tube. At 1454 ft. (442m), it broke the short record of the World Trade Center in New York as the world's tallest building and then enjoyed the title of the world's tallest building until 1996. It has become the most dominant structure—even a symbol of Chicago—and has been a significant addition to the Chicago skyline. It also became the largest private office complex in the world. The total development contains 3.9 million gross sq. ft. (362,000m^2) of office space.

The project occupies a full Chicago city block in an area bounded by four major streets on the southwest side of the Loop. Sears Roebuck and Co. selected the site considering its growth potential, closeness to the Chicago Loop, and proximity to city transportation. With the way Chicago's downtown area is laid out, rapid development was happening around the north side of the Loop where the John Hancock Center is located. From there it was projected that commercial activity would spread southward of the Loop. Since Hancock was already there, Sears Roebuck did not want to locate another major office building on the north side. Instead, they were looking for a location that had not yet fully grown but looked as though development would take place in the near future. It was anticipated that a supertall tower, more toward the south of the Loop, would become a south anchor for the city, and the existing Hancock Center would be the north anchor—an idea fully endorsed by the City of Chicago. Between the two towers, business and commercial activity would flourish. Gordon Metcalf, Chairman of Sears, Roebuck and Co., Chicago mayor Richard Daley, and Bill Dunlap, SOM partner in charge of project management—all agreed to the final location. Mayor Daley, in particular, helped Sears in making this decision, and took great personal interest in this landmark project for his city.

The Sears Tower occupies about 40 percent of its site area and the rest is designed to be an open plaza paved with granite to service the 16,500 users of the building and the pedestrians of

Fig. 58: Sears Tower, Chicago, Illinois.
Bundled tube building, tallest ever engineered by Khan
[Courtesy: SOM; photo by Ezra Stoller/Esto]

Fig. 58

the city. The space below the plaza level extends to a maximum depth of about 50 ft. (15.2m) below ground and contains three full basements.

The building is a large tube consisting of smaller tubes that are terminated at different heights creating a non-prismatic structural form and an eccentrically organized configuration from a spatial point of view (Fig. 59). To promote clear structural expressionism and to create a unique visual effect, symmetry of the building form, viewed in elevation, was not sought. The form chosen, a significant departure from the usual symmetric shape of tall structures, also met the space planning requirements. A total of 47 schemes of the project ranging from 60 to 120 stories were studied. The shape of the building was a direct consequence of space requirements and responded to the basic necessity that it would allow for a large area of office space for the Sears Corporation, which occupied about 60 percent of the tower. The remaining 40 percent would be rental office space. Thus the Sears Corporation required large floor areas, whereas, in contrast, the office rental space required a more flexible and efficient layout that needed a much smaller plan area.

It is interesting to trace the process of design development. Once again the active and friendly collaboration between Bruce Graham and Fazlur Khan during the initial conceptual stage resulted in the idea of a cellular building. According to Iyengar, Khan had been thinking for some time of utilizing cross walls or cross frames in a building, by which the three-dimensional response of the structural skeleton could be improved both in terms of strength and stiffness. Graham and Khan started brainstorming, and noting that a large perimeter tube surrounding a large floor area needed to be somehow stiffened with cross walls or interior framed webs to reduce shear lag, accidentally hit upon the cell concept. Graham had a deep structural vision and even though he practiced as an architect, he believed that structural concepts played a key role in the generation of building forms. He generally attempted to make it easy for the structural engineers to develop the appropriate structural system rather than create hindrance by imposing difficult architectural constraints.

When I met Graham at the Chicago Club Lounge, he recounted the story of how the bundled tube idea was conceived during a conversation between him and Khan. He pointed to a table a few feet away from where we sat. "That's where Faz and I sat as we were talking about various options related to the project," he said. Holding together a bunch of cigarettes in his hand to show me, he recalled, "I put together a few cigarettes like this and showed him. I said to him `will this work if we have several tubes together, not just one'? Faz responded to this by saying that it was a hell of an idea worth pursuing." The concept of bundled tube defining an assemblage of multiple tubes of various heights arranged directly next to each other was thus born. Khan and his structural team worked on this concept. Their main challenge was to figure out how the individual tubes could be integrally connected to each other so that they would collectively behave as a single unit. This was successfully resolved by providing a single line of frame where the individual tubular lines abutted each other. In the original scheme a megatube consisting of fifteen individual tubes tied together was envisioned. This was later revised to nine tubes at the base as can be seen in the building's present form (Fig. 59). Each of these nine modular tubes is square in plan. Following Graham's example, Khan later demonstrated the bundled tube concept to others with nine cigarettes representing the nine modular tubes of the Sears Tower (*Time*, 1973). This modularity of tube design had far reaching consequences in terms of introducing a new architectural vocabulary in building form. The individual tubes need not be necessarily square or rectangular and buildings could be made of varied forms simply by manipulating these modular tubes in plan and in elevation. Sears represents the first application of the bundled tube concept. Khan estimated that $10 million was saved by using this concept (*ENR*, 1971).

The basic shape of the Sears Tower building consists of nine modular areas 75 ft. (22.9m) square, for an overall floor area of 225 ft. (68.6m) square up to the 50th floor. These larger floor areas cater to the needs of the Sears Corporation. Termination of the large modular tubes at floors 50, 66, and 90 created a step-back system and a variety of floor configurations ranging from 41,000 to 12,000 sq. ft. (3,800 to 1,100m²) in floor area. Thus starting with nine cells at the base, the building diminished to seven cells at level 50, five at level 66, and finally just two at level 90 that continued to the roof. In this way, more perimeter space next to the window walls was created and the non-prime space away from the windows was virtually eliminated above the 50th floor. Such modular planning of space maximized rental revenue. SOM determined that the braced tube concept of the Hancock Center was not an appropriate solution for this project because of this set of particular space requirements. Although a Hancock-like building form was structurally conceivable, such an idea was immediately discarded simply because Sears Corporation wanted to build a unique building and not a duplicate of the John Hancock Center in downtown Chicago. Nor did Graham and Khan want to prominently display another Hancock in Chicago. They sought contrast and so for Sears they searched for a distinctly different form, which would be no less rational than that of Hancock. Thus, the bundled tube concept was an outcome of the architectural-structural integration developed through the collaboration of an eminent architect and an outstanding structural engineer.

Investigations on typical exterior frame tube systems have indicated partial loss of cantilever efficiency due to the shear lag phenomenon. Cantilever efficiency is defined by the ratio of the cantilever component to the sum of cantilever and frame-racking components of lateral deflection. In the bundled tube system of the Sears Tower, the shear lag effect is reduced and the interior or core columns that are integrated within the overall lateral load-resisting system become useful in carrying both gravity and wind loads. A three-dimensional plot of the column axial stress distribution at the base caused by the wind load revealed that the integrated behavior of the bundling of individual tubes had essentially been to provide two interior web frames in each direction (Fig. 60). These two additional frames transfer the wind shears at four points on each flange face. "The result has been to lift the sagging axial load distribution line of the exterior framed-tube into peak points at the intermediate frame locations . . ." (Iyengar and Khan, 1973). The shear lag effect of the entire structure is consequently reduced thereby resulting in an

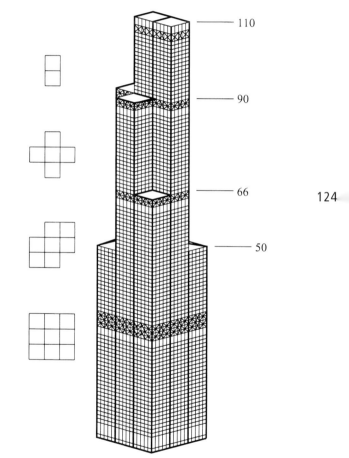

Fig. 59

124

improved behavior of the overall structure. The high efficiency of the modular tube system resulted in a low structural steel consumption of 33 lbs. per sq. ft. (161 kg/m2) for the building. This figure compares well with the structural steel quantity of 29.7 lbs. per sq. ft. (145 kg/m2) required for the 100-story John Hancock Center. Interestingly, it represents a substantial saving (approximately 22 per cent) in steel consumption compared to that of 42.2 psf (206 kg/m2) for the 102-story Empire State Building. The average lateral sway due to design wind load is about 0.3 in. (7.6mm) per story (IABSE, 1982), implying a total approximate sway of 2 ft. 9 in. (0.84m) at the top of the building relative to its base.

The perimeter of each modular tube is composed of columns at 15 ft. (4.6m) on center and deep beams connecting these columns at each floor. All beam-column connections are fully welded. Two adjacent modular tubes share one column line. At floors where the floor area is reduced, step-back is achieved by discontinuing the columns belonging to the particular tube while the remaining columns shared by adjacent tubes continue upward.

Belt trusses composed of diagonal members between columns were provided by the structural team at three mechanical levels and of two of them were planned to occur immediately below the step-backs at the 66th and 90th floors, that is, at the 64th to 66th floors and 88th-90th floors; and the third one at the 29th to 31st floor mechanical level (Fig. 59). Additional belt trusses were provided at the 31st to 33rd, 104th to 106th, and 106th to 109th floors. (Working drawings prepared by SOM included key plans to indicate location of belt trusses and a schedule of connection design forces for members in belt trusses. These details are too intricate to be discussed here. Interested readers may obtain full information on the belt trusses and connections from SOM.) Outrigger trusses were provided at all floors containing belt trusses except at the 31st to 33rd level where no outriggers on interior lines were feasible because of the presence of chillers. All diagonal members of the belt trusses were connected to gusset plates installed at beam-column joints with A-490 bolts. The belt trusses served as vertical shear diaphragms and were instrumental in reducing the general dishing effect brought about by differential column shortening at the step-backs, while at the same time providing an efficient means of absorbing the large member shears in the immediate vicinity of locations where the modular tubes are terminated (Iyengar and Khan, 1973). In addition, the overall lateral stiffness of the framed tube was increased by about 15 percent. This was so because the shear-racking displacement over these floors where mechanical equipment was placed was virtually eliminated. The overall tubular efficiency also increased as a result due to vertical shear diaphragm effect at those levels. Iyengar put the concept of adding belt trusses this way: "When a tube drops off, there's an abrupt increase in gravity forces on the remaining tubes. The trusses smooth out the shear stresses and help the building act more like a real cantilever, our aim in tubular design" (ENR, 1971).

In a tubular building, the efficiency of the structural system depends upon column spacing and beam-column proportions. Clearly, close column spacing with the deepest spandrel members

Fig. 60

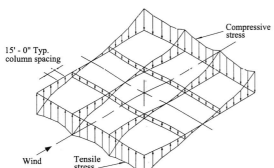

Compressive stress

15' - 0" Typ. column spacing

Wind

Tensile stress

Fig. 59: Diagram of Sears Tower
Fig. 60: Sears Tower, Stress Distribution in Columns due to Wind Load

would offer the maximum efficiency. However, space continuity between the modular tubes, a reasonable glass proportion on the window walls, and the cost-effectiveness of steel fabrication influenced the project team's decision to use a 15-ft. (4.6-m) column spacing typically for the building. Column depths were 39 in. (991mm) and beam depths were 42 in. (1,067mm) for the entire structure. All beams and columns were built-up members with three plates welded together to form I-sections. Typical column flanges vary from 24 x 4 in. (610 x 102mm) at the bottom to 12 x 3/4 in. (305 x 19mm) at the top and those of the beams from 16 x 2-3/4 in. (406 x 70mm) to 10 x 1 in. (254 x 25mm). All floor trusses carrying gravity loads were made 40 in. (1,016mm) deep (Fig. 61). Sizes of columns, beams, and trusses were kept uniform for the ease of fabrication and simplicity of detailing. The repetitious characteristics of the modular tubes also permitted the efficient use of shop fabrication.

Shop fabricated units that consisted of a two-story column with half-length beams welded to either side of the column forming a "tree" unit were used (Fig. 62). These modular units were transported to the site and field bolted for shear only with splice plates at the middle of the beam span (Fig. 63). The shop fabrication eliminated 95 percent of field welding and contributed to the economy of construction. For ideal conditions, the theoretical point of inflection in a beam belonging to a frame due to lateral load is at its mid-span. However, from a practical point of view, some nominal bending moment develops there due to the irregularity of loading and the positive moment caused by gravity loads. It was decided to lower the bolted connection by lowering the splice plates on both sides of the beam web so as to deliberately create an eccentricity of the centroid of the bolts with respect to the centroid of the beam section (Figs. 62 and 63). Thus the composite floor assembly comprising cellular metal deck and lightweight concrete topping could develop a compressive force and the bolt group could develop a tensile force thereby creating an increased moment arm of the couple due to the lowering of the splice plates and the bolt group. Column splices consist of field-bolted web connections with minimum partial penetration bevel welds for flanges (Fig. 64).

Structural steel was erected by standard S2-type stiff-legged derricks capable of lifting modular units weighing up to 45 tons (40,770 kg). Four such derricks were used up to the 90th floor. From the 90th floor to roof a guy derrick was added at the 90th floor for steel erection. The derricks were lifted to the next position after four stories or two tiers of steel erection. The lifting was accomplished in about 20 to 30 minutes by use of slow-speed, electric winches operating from cathead beams supported on the highest level of steel just erected. The erection speed was about eight stories a month for a total scheduled erection time of fifteen months for the building. On May 3, 1973—just three years after the project was begun—the last beam at the top was put into place. The entire project was completed on time in 1974.

It is important to review the preliminary analysis and design process for such a large project. According to John Zils, the project engineer for Sears, analysis of such a large structure for its full size was not possible then on the computer available at SOM. Lumping technique developed at SOM in which a reduced analytical model of the structure could be generated by lumping

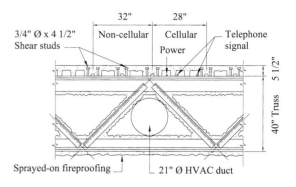

Fig. 61

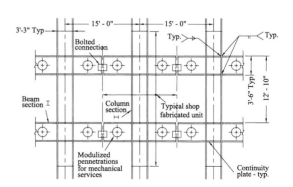

Fig. 62

127

Fig. 61: Sears Tower, Metal Deck - Truss Assembly
Used for Floors

Fig. 62: Sears Tower, Prefabricated Beam-Column Modules
Fig. 63: Sears Tower, Beam Splice Detail
Fig. 64: Sears Tower, Column Splice Detail

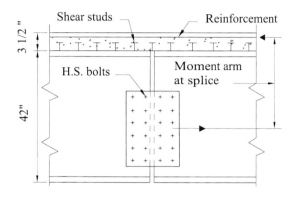

Fig. 63

Fig. 64

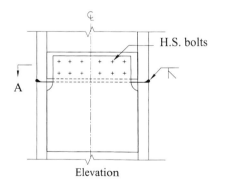

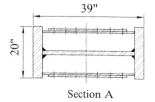

the properties of beams and columns of a few stories into those of an equivalent single story, was used for the analysis. The preliminary design was performed in two phases. The first phase dealt with the framed-tube behavior and optimization of key parameters. The overall geometry, together with column spacing and member proportions, was determined. Two-dimensional frame analyses were carried out on the web and flange frames. The study was then extended to three-dimensional tubes of different plan dimensions to correlate the size effect. The shear racking and cantilever components of the lateral deflections for wind loads were calculated separately from the gravity and wind load calculations for preliminary member designs. The second phase of the preliminary analysis and design process was conducted on a more sophisticated basis using three-dimensional frame analyses to verify the overall behavior of the bundled tube. The unsymmetrical geometry required a division of the building structure into two vertical segments. The lower part was based on two diagonal symmetry lines and was applicable from the 3rd basement floor below the main floor to floor 66 and a portion of structure from floors 67 to 90. The upper part had one axis of symmetry and was applied from floors 67 to the roof (Iyengar and Khan, 1973). The frame analyses involved 2,094 members in the lower part and a smaller number in the upper part.

For the final verification of the analysis, a contract was initially awarded to McDonald-Douglas, who had the STRUDL program. They were, however, unsuccessful even after 24 hours of computer run. CDC Corporation was then retained to carry out the analysis on the full structural model. Lo Hua of CDC Corporation performed this analysis at the IIT computing center. The full building structure was modeled by lumping technique, that is, and as already mentioned, a vertical combination of several stories to formulate the equivalent computer analysis model. The total structure of 10,000 joints and 21,000 members was reduced to an equivalent structure of 4,000 joints and 10,000 members. The structure was analyzed for gravity and four wind load cases. Two wind load cases corresponded to Chicago Building Code wind load distributions and the other two to wind pressure distributions obtained by statistical wind study and wind tunnel tests. Results of the refined analyses by CDC matched satisfactorily with those of the preliminary analyses performed by SOM. According to Iyengar, the full building solution was not completed in time and that the first tier of steel up to 28 stories was released based on results of analyses on partial structural models.

Zils pointed out the limitations of computers and the complexity of post-processing operations during that era. All input data for the project were generated manually. Because of the repetitive and modular nature of the structure, it was decided to calculate loads and other input data manually. These calculations took several months. Iyengar recalled to me that John Goldberg of Purdue University was also contracted as a consultant for the analysis. He, however, finished the work when the construction of the Sears Tower had already started. Results of the full structural model analyses were used to verify the member and connection designs. Small computer programs were used for the final design of columns, beams, column and beam splices, moment connections, and panel zones of beam-column joints.

Zils recalled an interesting story in this regard. After the construction of the building started, Sears Corporation decided to add antennas on the roof. As a result, the building was reanalyzed. U.S. Steel was already fabricating the steel and there was a deadline to be met for this reanalysis. Zils and his co-worker, Doug Stoker, went to IIT one day to run the computer program on its large UNIVAC machine. In those days computers were slow and a whole load of punched cards had to be read by the computers. At midnight they got the results of the computer analysis. They were dumbfounded to see that the lateral sway of the building was some 350 ft. (107m)! They went through all computer printouts to find the mistake. At 3:00 a.m. when they were still unable to do it, Zils gave up, decided to tell Khan and Iyengar what had happened, and left for home. At 4:30 a.m. he reached home and as soon as he stepped in his house the phone started ringing. It was Stoker who was still at IIT and did not yet give up. He discovered the mistake. For some inexplicable reason the value of the modulus of elasticity of steel got drastically altered in the input data. He ran it again with the right value and got results that made sense. They met Khan and Iyengar at 8:00 a.m. to show them the results.

Stoker related to me the same story. According to him, he just made a trivial mistake in the input data for the modulus of elasticity of steel by punching fewer zeroes for its value. He also described his general experience with Khan when he met Khan with the results of his computer analysis for different projects. He put it this way, "Faz could tell right away what was happening to the structural frame simply by looking at results. He would look at deflections first in the back pages of the output results to see if they made sense. He was very fast and he grasped quickly the structural behavior from deflections. He could also grasp the meaning of other numbers and saw in his head what that meant to the structure. He then checked some numbers manually. Faz had the unusual sense of picturing how it all fit together." Stoker further noted, "He could connect very well with technical people. He seemed to know everything. He could lead people to concepts very quickly. He wasn't just good with numbers, he always applied intellect to everything he did."

The structural design of such a supertall building for wind forces required both analytical and experimental verification of static and dynamic behavior. The analytical part corresponded to structural analysis, optimization studies, and design of framed-tube members. The experimental part involved extensive wind tunnel investigations that consisted of three phases: statistical analysis of meteorological wind data for the Chicago area to determine frequency of occurrence, speeds, and critical directions of wind for the site and verification on a 1 in 2,000 scale terrain model; wind tunnel studies on 1 in 400 scale rigid pressure model to determine curtain wall pressures; and dynamic behavior studies on 7-mass aero-elastic model representing the mass and stiffness properties of the prototype.

The dynamic properties consisting of modes of vibration, frequencies, and damping factors were used to assess the dynamic behavior of the building under wind load and also for the construction of the aero-elastic wind model. The fundamental period was found to be 7.8 seconds. The torsional mode obtained by a separate analysis resulted in a fundamental torsional period of 3.3 seconds. Frequencies of the translatory modes in the two principal directions were identical. The wind tunnel tests were done at the University of Western Ontario, London, Ontario in Canada by A. G. Davenport and his associate N. Isyumov. The model for the surroundings was made by SOM at its model shop. Zils flew it with him to London, Ontario. The building model was done at the University of Western Ontario.

The objective of the wind tunnel study was to investigate and provide reasonable predictions of certain wind effects significant in the design of the structure, especially the loads and movements of the building as a whole and the pressures on the cladding and window glazing. Measurements of the various design parameters on aero-elastically scaled models in a boundary layer wind tunnel were obtained. These measurements were combined with "a statistical description of the wind climate developed for the site" thereby obtaining the statistical predictions of the quantities needed for design. Results of the model tests revealed that the dynamic response was characterized by the fundamental sway mode of vibration. Due to some coupling effect between the two principal directions the response exhibited the characteristic bi-directional displacement excursion even when loads were applied from one direction.

A set of two-level wind pressure criteria was developed from the wind studies. One corresponded to the "design level" with the usual factor of safety for the design of members in accordance with the AISC Code; and the other to a "limit-state level" which represented the extreme wind case. The design level was 1.25 times the Chicago Code wind with a return period of 4,000 to 6,000 years, whereas the limit-state level was 1.8 times with a return period of 10,000 to 100,000 years. The limit-state design was done to limit the maximum stress to within the yield stress of steel. Evaluation of the perception of dynamic motion caused by wind gusts was carried out analytically. The basic approach for this was to compare perception behavior with that of the John Hancock Center for which performance was already known to be acceptable.

A damping level of 1 percent was assumed for structural evaluations. This was based on field measurements on the John Hancock Center that resulted in damping factors of the order of 0.6 percent at very low amplitudes. Since the bundled tube concept of the Sears Tower is based on interaction of a considerable number of moment connections and members, a larger value for damping was deemed more appropriate. It is indeed interesting to observe that field measurements on the partially completed structure of Sears Tower, up to the 76th floor, indicated damping factors in the range of 1.1 to 1.2 percent. The idea of installing visco-elastic dampers was also considered, but later discarded to maintain inherent structural stiffness to ward off any undesirable vibrations of the building.

We noted before that Khan was always concerned about column exposures to extreme temperature variations. For the Sears Tower, the average temperature of the exterior column for an outside temperature up to -20 deg. F. (-29 deg. C.) was restricted to be within 7 deg. F. (4 deg. C.) of the inside temperature of 75 deg. F. (24 deg. C.) to reduce the effect of exterior column shortening. The columns were detailed to include 4 in. (102mm) of Thermofiber insulation behind the cladding and gravity circulation of inside air through the column covers. Tests were performed by the curtain wall contractor to determine the effectiveness of insulation by simulating the worst possible thermal conditions.

Caissons to rock were typically used to support all columns of the tower. The caisson diameters vary from 7 to 10 ft. (2.1 to 3m) and their lengths are 65 ft. (19m) on the average. Permanent steel casings were used for all caissons. The caisson tops are tied together by a 5-ft. (1.5-m) thick concrete mat. The 50-ft. (15.2-m) deep excavation was retained by a 30-in. (9-m) thick diaphragm wall system constructed by the slurry trench method. This wall bears on hardpan clay at a depth of 55 ft. (16.8m) below ground and was retained by a set of horizontal struts diagonally at the excavation corners and inclined rackers in between. 20- to 36-in. (508- to 914-mm) dia. pipes were used for these struts and rackers. Unlike the John Hancock Center, the foundation construction for Sears went smoothly. A 15-ft. (4.6-m) dia. sewer pre-existed right across the job site, which was dismantled. The sewer line was rerouted around the site.

In addition to Iyengar, who led the group, and John Zils, the project's other structural team members were Navin Amin, L. Carpenter, D. Stoker, E. Shlemon, and A. Zasadney. The full team, at peak time of the project, consisted of about eight people while the average number of people throughout the project was about five or six. Out of these, two to three people were engaged in the analysis process. Iyengar was involved in the design process from the beginning and was also responsible for getting the job done and, as usual, worked very hard on this project. Because of a strict time schedule, he and his group completed the structural steel drawings in about three months, a process that would take eight months under normal circumstances. The project team worked overtime and used computers extensively. Khan gave the ultimate leadership as the structural engineering partner and reviewed all the major decisions.

As a partner, Khan had to give his time to other ongoing projects and could not spend full time on this project as he did on the John Hancock Center. The Sears project team was located at 33 North Dearborn Street. However, he maintained a very active role even though his office was in the Inland Steel Building where Graham was also located. Khan and Graham collaborated with the structural team either together or individually as needed. Bill Drake, a senior architectural designer working closely with Graham, became a close friend of Khan. Bill Dunlap played an important role in the project as its project manager.

Khan was consistently able to achieve a close relationship with both structural engineering and architecture through his teaching, his research and his professional work. In the Sears Tower, the structure responds to the architectural needs of the building and the architecture expresses the structure. With mutual support and collaboration, Graham, Khan and the structural team formulated the shape of the building that would express the structure. This is what he thought should happen in a design office. He argued, "Many architects are brought up to think that they are the only creators and the engineers are technicians. This must stop. The engineer has to be an architect

to the extent that the architect has to be an engineer so that in combination they produce the creative building" (*ENR*, 1972).

The step-backs in the building and the eccentric form, although necessitated for space planning and modular arrangement of the tubes, effectively provide the building with an elegant and interesting form that contrasted with many of the monolithic buildings of the contemporary era. It also presented the city with a landmark, the elevation of which changes as one moves around the building giving the viewer a rare opportunity to appreciate the building's exciting features. The Sears Tower, exceeding the maximum world height record of the World Trade Center in New York, drew considerable media attention nationally and internationally. It was reported in magazines like *ENR*, *Time*, and *Newsweek*. Articles and news features were also published by *Chicago Tribune* in 1972 and 1973.

Khan not only reinforced the natural affinity between architecture and structural engineering, but also brought the professionals from the two disciplines together. *Newsweek* magazine published a story about him with his picture against the background of the Sears Tower calling him the "Man at the Top," applauding him as the "designer of the world's tallest building" (*Newsweek*, 1973). He wrote a letter to *Newsweek* in which he emphasized the role of collaboration in designing tall buildings, and particularly referred to the important role that his architect partner, Bruce Graham, had played. He subsequently told his brother Zillur Khan, "A complex building and its translation into reality requires significant team work and collaborative efforts," (BAGC, 1998). He simply could not accept the fact that he was getting full credit for the Sears Tower.

On Sears, Graham (1989) wrote:

> Tall buildings are man-made. Towers have historically been the pride of their temporary owners, but of their cities as well. So the Sears Tower, one more mountain, was created for this city on the plains. Sears is very direct in its structural solution, a new concept of cluster tubes.... The Sears Tower itself is much like the idea behind San Gimignano, but unlike most tall buildings in New York, it is a tower of the people, not the palace of a bank.

Sears majestically stands out in its surroundings and has truly become an icon for the City of Chicago. A drive along Interstate 94 makes this point clear. It creates a great impact on the observer about its vertical edges and stepped levels. The tower makes a lively expression from a distance, whereas from nearby it is exalted in scale but not as expressive. As Billington (1983) points out, "Its visual interest is greater from a distance than from close up, where the great expanse of glass and metal wall has little differentiation." The Hancock building, on the other hand, is more expressive from nearby as the massive diagonals become clearly visible and less expressive from afar as they become practically invisible. From a distance, Hancock's mass looks monolithic and dramatically tapered.

The Sears Tower was originally planned to be rectangular in plan rather than square to accommodate a hotel, which was later abandoned. A rectangular plan was very much liked by Graham, because the increase in wall area per unit volume allowed more

Fig. 65

sunlight and it offered a more interesting view of the building. Even though, from a structural point of view, a square plan is preferable for economy and balanced load distribution, Khan appreciated the architectural advantages of a rectangular plan and was supportive of it, putting aside the structural and economic gains. Also, the open plaza and the main lobby of the building have become very lively and interesting places.

Goldberger (1989) criticized SOM's architectural intention in toning down the form at the ground level for both Hancock and Sears. On Sears, he remarked, "Sears was no better at ground level—once again, there was an uneasy travertine sheathing, as if to hide the fact that these architects did not know how to make the skyscraper join the ground. It is far better in the sky." About the tower itself, he continued: "The building's structure is unusual—it is in effect a set of square tubes, virtually separate towers, bridled together. The tubes stop at different heights, giving the building a varied, stepped-down profile. It is a splendid allusion to the elaborate tops of old, but it emerges directly and logically out of structural expression. So at Sears, architects found a way in which the modernist idiom could be used for the creation of a romantic and rather non-modernist result, the ornate top." Apart from such architectural concerns, the termination of tubes at different heights not only creates a structural expression of the building, but also the bundling of the tubes becomes highly visible. When asked whether there was any reason other than space planning for choosing the eccentric form for the tower, Graham replied, "We could have come up with a symmetric design for the entire building height if we wanted. But we deliberately chose to use the eccentric form so the tubes could be expressed clearly and uniquely. Otherwise, it would look like any other tall building. Nobody would know that we were using the bundled tube concept for the building where the individual tubes were held together." Iyengar, on the other hand, viewed the shape from a purely structural engineering perspective and stated to me: "The two-module upper part contributed to better dynamic performance under wind load. The cruciform shape below the top form was very active dynamically due to torsional response. The unsymmetrical top clearly reduced the torsional response as per the wind tunnel results."

When further asked why he used the dark color for the facades of both the John Hancock Center and the Sears Tower, Graham's reply was, "In winter, dark color absorbs heat from sun and therefore offers energy efficiency." He added, "There is also an architectural reason. Dark buildings have a tradition in Chicago. Monadnock is dark. There are many other dark buildings in Chicago. Mies also did it. Look at his dark buildings next to Lake Michigan. Every city is different." I was quick to ask, "If that is so why then don't other architects do it? I see many bright and light-colored buildings around too." Graham responded by saying, "That does not mean I am wrong."

Sears Corporation wanted a building that would show off their commercial dominance and status within the city. Even they, perhaps, did not expect such a grand public response to the building that they received. The Sears Tower now serves more than 1.4 million tourists each year who want to experience the view from the skydeck defining the highest spot of the city's urban habitat. To accommodate such a large group of people that was not clearly anticipated in their original program indeed became a difficult challenge. The building's entrances were originally designed primarily with security in mind and no emphasis was given to the matter of way-finding by newcomers who had never been there before. Also, since the wind is obstructed by the large mass of the building near its base, air turbulence and wind gusts around the building cause discomfort to the pedestrians outside the building and to those who try to enter the building on windy days.

Beginning in 1985 the Sears Tower underwent a major $25 million renovation of its ground floor (*Progressive Architecture*, 1986). The entrance on Wacker Drive was provided with a barrel-vaulted entry that signaled a welcoming public entrance and also reduced the tremendous wind pressures at the entry. This entrance, however, does not seem to be integrated well with the building's original aesthetic and structural features. The south entrance was provided with benches and landscaping to allow more interactions with the street life. The original tower was built with security in mind and its plazas were restricted to employee use only. The remodeled Sears is more public-oriented and is more attuned to the sidewalk. Basement floors were reorganized to accommodate enough space for those waiting for elevators to the skydeck. More significantly, the traffic of employees and tourists was separated and more well defined to avoid confusion.

The Sears Tower had its share of ups and downs. Although it is a main tourist attraction in Chicago, the original notion of creating a commercial anchor on the south end of the Loop did only partly succeed. The areas surrounding the building have not achieved much density since it was built, and commercial activity did not increase at a rate that was expected. The status of the economy and the pattern of growth within the city did not allow for it. Sears Corporation moved its location out of the tower to take advantage of less expensive suburban office space. The building was left with about 60 percent occupancy. In 1990 Sears sold the building to a number of insurance companies and a Boston firm by the name of Aldrich, Eastman and Walch (AEW). In 1996, AEW sold their interests in the building to TrizecHahn Office Properties; this new owner was confident in the investment showing courage by taking over the building's ownership. Fortunately for TrizecHahn, the city got involved in a building revival program and it experienced great economic success soon thereafter, which had pushed the occupancy rate to a comfortable 90 percent.

Concern for people and the social and visual effects of tall buildings was one of the cherished goals of Khan. He once said, "The social and visual impact of buildings is really my motivation for searching for new structural systems" (*ENR*, 1972). A building of this size also has other environmental implications. Its construction required Federal Aviation Administration (FAA) approval. Also, according to Zils, a question arose: what would this tower do to block Hancock's TV transmission? Channel 7 moved to Sears whereas others stayed at Hancock. The problem of blocking TV transmission from Hancock was of major concern and was never actually resolved until the structure was built. It was subsequently discovered that the problem did not really exist because it did not affect Hancock's TV transmission in any way.

Some minor problems in such a large glass box-type building are worth mentioning. On very windy days, the floor system has been reported to creak and make noises similar to a creaky boat. Occasionally, the doors creak and the windows shake vigorously making a rattling noise. Some occupants from the upper floors have reported that when the building sways the water in the toilet has been found to swish and wave back and forth. These are things that are to be expected for such a tall structure. Despite these few complaints about the building, occupants say they get used to these and they do not mind working there. The overall impression of the public is that it is a great place to work and employees enjoy the prestige of working in such a well known city symbol. Sears Tower will continue to be a proud landmark of the City of Chicago.

Its title as the tallest building in the world was stripped by the Petronas Towers in Kuala Lumpur in 1996, following a decision by the Council on Tall Buildings and Urban Habitat. The Council's decision was based on some technicality concerning the spire, and the matter became controversial in many minds. At the April 18, 1996 interview with WPWR TV "Night Show" in Chicago, Lynn Beedle defended the Council's decision by stating that the Council adopted 25 years ago Khan's definition of the height of tall buildings as the distance from the ground level at the main entrance to the top of the highest structural element of the building. By this definition, the top of the spire of the Petronas Towers, which is integrated structurally with the building's main structure, should be considered as the highest point of the building. In the same interview, Hal Iyengar disagreed and remarked that he occasionally discussed the issue of height of tall buildings with Khan. He felt that the highest usable floor which is functional and "over which people can walk" should determine the top of the building. Iyengar suggested that this old criterion should be reviewed. He further added that Khan "paid a great deal of respect for truth and logic, and if he would be alive today, he would fight for maintaining the title of the tallest building for Sears Tower." The highest occupiable floors in the Petronas Towers are 150 ft. (45.7m) below that of the Sears Tower. Despite such initial controversy, the professional communities and the public at large have eventually accepted the Council's decision.

Although the Sears Tower has lost its title as the "tallest building" on earth, it still holds a few other records. It has the world's highest elevator ride (*New York Times*, 1996). According to Noelle Gaffney, spokeswoman for Chicago Mayor Richard M. Daley, "While there is a dispute over what qualifies as the tallest building in the world, there is no disputing the fact that Chicago would still have the highest observation deck in the world." The Sears Tower remains a world class structure, the biggest supertall office building with the highest occupied floor and highest roof in the world, and a major U.S. icon.

At any rate, Khan's name is permanently associated with both the John Hancock Center and the Sears Tower. These two towers will constantly remind the present and future generations of the fruits of his structural innovations right in his adopted city, Chicago, where he lived and worked. Sears and Hancock are two powerful skyscrapers that moved the business centers of downtown Chicago to the areas surrounding them. Sears especially draws public attention since it is near the expressway welcoming visitors to the city from a distance. Despite the fact that Sears and Hancock represent International Style prevalent at that time, they are not merely glass boxes. They have their own inherent geometric expression. Moreover, as Khan said, "Sears established that the bundled tube is a vocabulary, not a system, as at Hancock. We have extended it, made it more flexible. We can now let the tube happen on the basis of program and site; it has become a moldable shape" (Dean, 1980).

Although the Hancock Center was Khan's favorite, Sears remains the centerpiece of his professional career. His collaboration and friendship with Graham became further cemented by the Sears project. Architects and engineers should emulate them with the same spirit of collaboration to create successful, well-integrated buildings. Khan and Graham rose fully to the promise of making Chicago a great city once again since the days of Jenney, Root and Sullivan with the stupendous design of the Sears Tower. They once again demonstrated that finding an appropriate form for each structure was the worthiest goal of the engineer and the architect, as it always has been since antiquity.

chapter 9

THE GATEWAY TO MECCA

"...in my opinion, it (the Haj Terminal) should evoke the spirit of Haj and that's all it should do. It creates a spirit, it gives you a feeling of tranquility and a sense of continuity, of transition into the real place, which is Mecca."

—Fazlur R. Kahn (*Progressive Architecture*, 1982)

"We took a rather high technology roof to produce a low technology terminal. That sort of paradox is the key to the thing."

—Raul de Armas (*Progressive Architecture*, 1982)

One other major project in Fazlur Rahman Khan's career is the Haj Terminal of the King Abdul Aziz International Airport at Jeddah, Saudi Arabia (Fig. 66). This was a different type of project than for what he is generally known—the high-rise. This project, in a way, brought him to a new and different world—a mixed world of architecture/engineering, Arab desert culture and Islamic spirituality. He worked hard on this project and enjoyed it thoroughly. He had previous experience with cable-supported structures when he supervised his graduate students at IIT and from the design of Baxter Laboratories in Deerfield, Illinois. Form-finding was a natural and inherent instinct in him. Therefore, the Haj Terminal was not a major structural challenge for him from that point of view, particularly with the availability of sophisticated digital computers to perform the complex structural analysis. His real challenge was—and he was a master of this art—how to put it all together for this largest roof structure of the world in a harsh desert environment with sensitivity to the local Arab-Islamic culture and spirituality.

Internationally known architect Hassan Fathy of Egypt has been the most prominent and persistent leader of a modern movement in Islamic architecture, that in some cases, preserved traditional forms and construction techniques, and, in other cases, adopted new technology in the construction of modern buildings based on traditional forms. Fathy promoted a culturally and environmentally sensitive architecture and believed in the use of appropriate, sustainable technology for building construction. Reviving the time-honored traditions of arches, domes, courtyards, mud brick construction, and an approach to modern urbanism emphasizing the Islamic principles of oneness and unity, Fathy has influenced many Muslim architects. Khan accepted Fathy's philosophy and applied it to the design of buildings that are well-suited to the Middle East but are also greatly dependent on Western technology. Khan felt that Western technology created a temptation to accept it without transformation, which made structures irrelevant. This transformation meant adopting Western technology to the sociological and climatic conditions of the people who would use or live

136

136

136

Fig. 66

137

137
137
137 137
137
137

Fig. 66: Haj Terminal, King Abdul Aziz International Airport, Jeddah, Saudi Arabia. Largest roof structure of the world [Courtesy: SOM; photo by Jay Langolois/Owens-Corning Fiberglas]

in the buildings created from it. Thus he viewed the Haj Terminal roof as a system of separate, suspended tents—a modern version of traditional desert dwelling.

One of the richest aspects of Islamic religious thought and practice is that of haj (also spelled as hajj) or pilgrimage. The Islamic community has developed a strong sense of its literal and symbolic centrality through this international assemblage annually in Mecca. Thus haj epitomizes Muslims' sense of identity as a unique community of faith. Perhaps more than other basic Islamic traditions, haj symbolizes the community and equality of individuals before God, and embodies the strong feeling many Muslims have for a humanity healed of its ethnic tensions and divisiveness. In the year 630, after the triumphant return of Prophet Mohammad to the Holy City of Mecca from Medina leading his Muslim followers, one of his first acts was to cleanse the Ka'ba ("cube"), that Muslims believe was built by the prophets Abraham and his son Ishmael, of its 360 idols. When the Prophet returned to Mecca in 632 to make his "Farewell Haj," he sanctified the Ka'ba, the House of God, and the sites in the vicinity of Mecca. The Ka'ba is a cube-shaped stone structure empty inside except for a few hanging lamps. It is 43 ft. (13m) high with its four sides ranging in width from about 36 to 43 ft. (11 to 13m). The Qur'an commanded the believers who can afford to make haj or "Greater Pilgrimage" at least once in a lifetime and made it integral as a major ritual with the Islamic faith.

The haj represents, for the Muslims, a metaphor for return to the center. Being a Muslim and a philosophically inclined spiritual person himself, Khan realized the importance of the Haj Terminal in Jeddah even though it is located 70 kilometers west of Mecca. To him this was the gateway to the Holy City, where the pilgrims came by air from all corners of the world to participate in the annual haj event. These pilgrims can enjoy the terminal's acres of comfortable shade provided by the great tent-like structure without being aware of how these were made possible by a man's unique understanding of built forms, the same man who developed the important structural and visual features of the Sears Tower and the John Hancock Center in Chicago.

Haj is one of the five "pillars" of Islam. For the devout, it is an occasion when people suspend their worldliness and totally focus on God. The number of pilgrims has always fluctuated with the prevailing international circumstances; the jet age has resulted in a great increase of aspiring pilgrims. In the 1930s about 30,000 people made the pilgrimage every year when the estimated worldwide Muslim population was 350 million. With the present Muslim population of over 1.2 billion (about one-fifth of the human race) the number of pilgrims has risen to more than 2 million. About one-half of them pass through the international airport at Jeddah. This increase is a symptom of not only population explosion and improved transport opportunities, but of a general increase in religious consciousness among the Muslims worldwide (Ruthven, 1984; *Aramco World Magazine*, 1974).

In response to this increasing demand for serving passengers from all around the globe during the haj period, and to reinforce the legitimacy of the Saudi ruling family as guardians of Islam's holy places, the Saudi government invested about $5 billion in developing the new King Abdul Aziz International Airport near

Jeddah. It occupies an area of about 35 square miles (100 square kilometers)—larger than the international airports of New York, Chicago, and Paris.

The airport's most spectacular feature is the Haj Terminal, comprising vast tented halls making up the world's largest fabric structure, enclosing its largest covered space. The tent clusters forming the roof and hung from cables and steel pylons high above floor level very much resemble the great tented city of Arafat where the pilgrims gather at the climax of the haj ceremonies. As a remarkable example of contemporary design as can be found anywhere in the world, it is an apt symbol of the Saudi rulers' ambition to boost traditional values with the latest technology. Viewing the scene from an airplane landing at the airport, one can see the bright tents of the Haj Terminal glow in the sunshine over the desert land. When exiting from the airport's regular passenger terminal during the off-haj season, a visitor to Jeddah can hardly miss the sight of this structure as a cluster of large, white, umbrella-like tents, surrounded by the towering pylons.

Jeddah is the only large commercial city close to Mecca. All air traffic bound for Mecca arrives there and pilgrims proceed by land to the Holy City. Regular airport facilities can handle this traffic except at the time of the haj event when, during a six-week period, 700,000 Muslim pilgrims arrive and depart (Khan et al., 1980). A separate terminal facility of about 500,000m^2 was necessary to process the haj pilgrims. It was projected that by the year 1985 the terminal would handle about 1 million people en route to Mecca during the six-week period, accommodating 50,000 of them at one time for periods that could last up to 18 hours during arrival and 80,000 Pilgrims for periods up to 36 hours during departure.

The entire terminal complex, an "airport within airport," comprises a linear, air-conditioned terminal building adjacent to the aircraft parking aprons and a large, sheltered support complex adjacent to the terminal building. It has 50 hectares of apron to hold 20 wide-body aircrafts at 20 terminal gates and another 26 in holding positions, 150,000m^2 of air-conditioned terminal building, and about 45 hectares covered by fabric canopy to serve one million pilgrims twice over a two-month arrival and departure period. This scheme offered a short walking distance for the pilgrims from the airplanes to the air-conditioned terminal. This terminal building accommodates all formal processing and baggage handling operations. Pilgrims next move on into a naturally ventilated support area where they will organize for land travel to Mecca by bus. The Haj Terminal and support complex not only fulfill the requirement of its functional program, but also provide a moving and uplifting spiritual experience to inspire the pilgrims as they set foot on the land of Saudi Arabia—Islam's heartland.

Because of the extreme environment in the Jeddah area, the support complex was protected from the sun. It was obvious that only a long span, lightweight structure with translucent material could adequately respond to the overall environmental needs of this space. Just any material was not going to be suitable for the project! The material had to be correctly chosen so that the structural components could be prefabricated and erected quickly to beat the deadline of 1982. The Saudi Government was asking for a speedy completion of the project.

Fig. 67

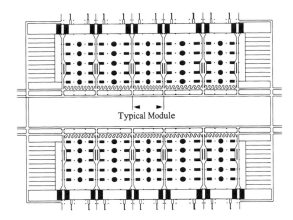

Typical Module

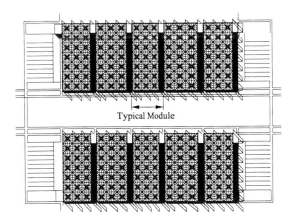

Typical Module

Fig. 68

Fig. 67: Haj Terminal, Ground Floor Plan
Fig. 68: Haj Terminal, Roof Plan

The Haj Terminal plan itself went through an evolutionary process. An earlier design of 1965 was modified and was used only for support facilities for the final design. The holding area, which was at a remote location originally, was made integral to the new plan. A partial plan of the ground floor is shown in Fig. 67. The roof structure of the pilgrim's temporary stay area evolved from concrete mushroom forms through a previous fabric form to the final modular fabric form developed by SOM (Fig. 68).

Khan was the structural partner in charge of the project assisted by Zils as the senior structural engineer and Mohammad Salem as the project engineer. Khan started looking at alternative structural systems and materials. Until that time, the most common form of long span lightweight system had been the two-way cable net structure with a non-structural infill covering or skin. Such a system was used on the German pavilion in Montreal for Expo '67 and the Olympic Stadium in Munich, Germany, for the 1972 Olympics. Many cables and numerous connections between cables were used to develop a grid network. Upon reviewing those projects, it was decided that this system would not be cost-effective for the Haj Terminal. Also, new and improved membrane materials allowed the development of an appropriate structure as a two-way interactive system of cables and fabric membranes. Such a system can be erected quickly and different shapes could be generated from it for structural efficiency and aesthetic expression. However, SOM had not been involved in similar membrane-type structures before. Therefore, this was something totally new for the firm itself since traditionally it has been known for designing tall buildings with a few exceptions.

Unlike most SOM projects in which the architects and engineers from the same SOM office usually collaborate with each other, the arrangement for this project was different. The architectural design partner in charge was Gordon Bunshaft of SOM, New York office, who had designed many important New York buildings. He could be considered as the counterpart in New York of Bruce Graham of SOM, Chicago office. Gordon Wildermuth was the partner in charge of project management. Roy Allen, a senior architectural partner, also worked on this project for a few months and was a key supporter of the project. Bunshaft wanted Fazlur Khan from the Chicago office to work on this project because of Khan's reputation and, in Graham's words, "probably because Faz was a Muslim." He felt confident of Khan's ability to handle such a large project involving a special structure.

Initially there was no idea of what shape should be used for the roof structure. Khan realized that to be used as a structural element, the membrane material had to satisfy a number of performance criteria. In the past, fabric membranes had a rather short life span; as a result, they were employed in temporary structures. The Haj Terminal, on the other hand, was expected to be a durable structure and its fabric membrane should last for a minimum of 30 to 40 years with the least maintenance. Because of the continuous exposure to ultraviolet degradation and a highly hostile and corrosive marine environment, the material's lifetime requirement was very crucial. Also, the fabric membrane had to satisfy numerous other criteria. It had to be self-cleaning to insure good visual appearance. It had to be relatively lightweight, yet capable of carrying large tensile forces without unacceptable long-term creep. It should be a good thermal insulator to protect the pilgrims and be translucent so that the area it covers is naturally illuminated during the day. The membrane should also be non-combustible and should not shed any toxic gases or fumes when under fire. Finally, it should be easy to fabricate and install and, of course, should be repairable on site, when repair becomes necessary.

From a structural point of view, form and tensioning of fabric roofs have significant influence on structural strength and stability, reduction of flutter and vibration, capacity to carry applied loads, ease of fabrication and erection, and the cost-effectiveness of the structure. Deviation from the correct form for form-based structures jeopardizes the functioning of the system warranting additional mechanisms that compensate the deviation. The structural form in such systems should ideally coincide accurately with the flow of stresses. These systems, therefore, reflect the *natural* path of forces in the surface material. The natural stress trajectory of the tensile systems is the funicular tension surface determined by the forces acting on the system as well as the rise or sag and the distance of the supports where critical horizontal stresses develop. Any change of loading or support conditions alters the form of the funicular surface and results in a new structural form. Lightness of the flexible suspension cables is a structural demerit of such systems. The cables can, however, be stabilized by prestressing. These are some of the critical issues to be considered in deriving an appropriate form of such structures. For their long-span qualities, these systems have a particular significance for mass congregation with its demand for large open spaces.

After intensive investigations under Khan's guidance, it was determined that the fabric that met all these requirements was a teflon-coated fiberglass. The fiberglass provides structural strength and the teflon coating offers improved resistance to degradation and protects the fabric from hostile environmental assaults. Once the basic material for the roof was selected, an extensive investigation into the shapes and forms that were aesthetically satisfying and structurally acceptable were conducted. Shapes like hyperbolic paraboloid (hypar) and others with high and low points were considered. Experiments on simple models revealed that wide variations of shape could be achieved by changing the elevations of the peaks and the spans. Eventually the tent shape evolved, although it did not start that way.

The cultural heritage of Saudi Arabia was kept in perspective. The tent tradition is a familiar form in the Middle East. Throughout the history of Saudi Arabia, tent structures have provided comfortable shelters by shading while allowing the breeze to pass through. Even under the intense heat of the sun, being in the open under an umbrella is preferable to being in an enclosed hot building. This simple lesson helped in making a decision for an open roof structure. The SOM designers visited Saudi Arabia in the mid-1970s in connection with this project. They were inspired by the temporary tents constructed in the valley of Meena. That inspiration was never lost. They wanted to create an environment similar to that at the Plain of Arafat while designing the terminal to receive incoming pilgrims. In the end, a system of permanent "tents" was used for the roof of the Haj Terminal.

According to Reginald Jackson, Vice President of Morley Builders in Santa Monica, California, who worked in the structural group at SOM, Chicago on this project, "shape of the roof structure was an issue. The fabric should have equal strength in all directions and stressed evenly. We needed time to figure this out. Once this was established the question arose: how many cables should be employed?" Jackson was also engaged in the design of the large reinforced concrete masts and their foundations. Regarding Khan, he made the following observation: "Dr. Khan pulled full weight of partnership. He generated business and had many Middle-Eastern contacts. A number of other projects in Saudi Arabia were supervised by him. The Saudi Air Force Facility, airport hangars, etc. are some examples. Computers and technology were way advanced at SOM in the 1970s." He went on to say, "he gave young people an opportunity to do things. He gave them responsibility."

It was apparent to Khan that the fabric's real strength and stability under upward and downward wind pressures lay in the creation of a two-directional curvature. Also large flat areas in membranes are to be avoided since enormous prestressing forces would be required to maintain the areas under normal loads. He realized that there was no reason to create this form of fabric structure with the classical grid pattern of the cables because the type of fiberglass to be used was very strong. Based on the properties of this fabric he was convinced that he should be able to use the fabric in a tent form that would give the necessary structural strength and stiffness. He further determined that a double curvature would guarantee tension in the fabric under any load condition with only adjustment needed in the level of tension in one direction or the other depending on whether the wind pressure was upward or downward. To ensure that the fabric would remain taut and stable, an appropriate initial tension could then be determined (Khan et al., 1980). Khan also realized that there was an infinite possibility of creating forms "simply by pushing and pulling at different locations to achieve a two-directional curvature." The fabric could theoretically have an infinite number of forms. As long as a negative-positive surface curvature was created, it could be built. Zils recounted to me in this connection: "Faz and I traveled to New York from Chicago frequently. We built models in Chicago and flew them to New York. We took about two trips a week. We tried different shapes. Finally, the tent shape evolved. It was a good structural shape and it made meaning to the local culture. It took months to come up with this." The models were quite useful for studying the various geometries during preliminary design stages. Transition zones between upward and downward curvatures had been particularly problematic and could be specially studied with the help of the models.

After a number of studies on forms and proportions, the final configuration selected for the roof system was a two-way grid of pylons from which the high point of the tent, where a tension ring was located, were suspended and the low corner points were anchored (Figs. 69 and 70). The double curvature tensile membrane surface was generated by holding the membrane at the pylon locations and raising the tension ring thereby elongating and pretensioning the membrane. This shape provided for rainwater drainage at the pylons and also induced a natural flow of air out from within the tent space through the opening at a high point at the center tension ring. Zils, who once

Fig. 69

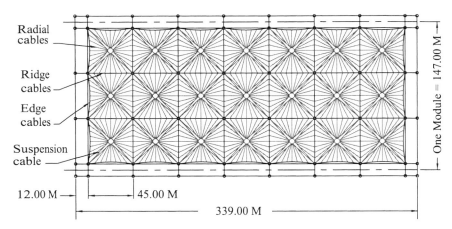

Fig. 70

142

ascended to the top of a tent, related his experience this way: "I was standing at the top near the tension ring. A lot of air was flowing out of the big hole just like wind blowing in a wind tunnel." Thus a high technology roof using a sophisticated material and sophisticated engineering techniques was created for a tent-like primitive form.

During the planning process, initially a mezzanine level for resting was briefly considered and then discarded. It was thought that people would like to stay on the ground level. Therefore, a one-level terminal was designed, with the only exception of the two levels used in the arriving area of passengers. The passenger then passes over a bridge and descends to the level below to pick up baggage. From that point onward, all activities are in the ground level. For the tent roof, a 45 x 45m unit representing a tent was established (Fig. 69). Each module is comprised of 3 units by 7 units for a total of 21 units per module (Fig. 70). A longitudinal section of a single module is shown in Fig. 71. The overall plan is grouped by 10 modules, of which 5 form a row on each side of a central roadway. Therefore, the entire roof has a total of 210 tent units with 4.6 million sq. ft. (422,350m^2) of approximate covered area with provision for an additional 5 modules on each side. 45m high steel pylons are located at the corners of each unit. The roof fabric forms the tent shape springing upward from a 20-m height at the pylons to 35m at the center of the tension ring (Fig. 69). Initially, the tents were analyzed in a simplistic manner. A least surface structure that would be optimum in nature was generated. This, however, looked aesthetically unattractive. The shape was then modified based on aesthetic considerations by introducing gentle curvature to the tent controlled by the radial cables.

Fig. 69: Haj Terminal, One-Module Fabric Roof Plan
Fig. 70: Haj Terminal, Fabric Roof System
Fig. 71: Haj Terminal, Longitudinal Section of One Module

43

A total of 32 cables per unit extend radially from the center tension ring to the edge or ridge cables on the four sides of each unit connecting the pylons at the intersection of adjoining roof units (Khan et al., 1980). The suspension cables extending down from the top of the pylons to hold the center tension ring in place are arranged in four pairs. Double cables for suspension were used instead of single cables to provide a second line of defense in the unusual event of cable failure. Additional protection against collapse was ensured by providing for each unit four stabilizing cables that extend from the lower center ring down to the pylons at the elevation where the edge and ridge cables are connected to the pylons (Fig. 69). These cables retain the center ring in place should a unit's membrane lose its tensile characteristics. The edge cables were used to stiffen the free edges and to allow a more uniform tension field to be developed in the membrane itself. The ridge cables perform similar functions. The pylons provide the primary high points by acting as large compression masts and were designed as beam-column elements. The entire structural system is stabilized and supported by a special arrangement of the pylons around the perimeter of the modules. A 4-pylon frame is installed at the four corners of two major contiguous roof areas, giving a total of four such frames. Along the perimeter of these areas, that is, all the ten modules, a 2-pylon frame is installed including the common row of pylons between adjacent modules. The stiff edge and separation between modules makes them independent of each other and permits modules to be added or removed. Moreover, this system guarantees that a failure in one module will be isolated and would not affect the adjoining module. The roof thus provides structural safety, stability, and redundancy at three levels of the system: individual cables, individual units, and the modules.

Khan was confronted with a number of challenges related to the complexity of structural form and behavioral intricacy of fabric structures. As alluded to earlier, these structures rely on their skin to carry loads. All internal forces developed are tensile forces as a result of membrane action. They are built with adequate pretension so that under various combinations of applied loads the structure does not become slack at any location. The tensioning of the fabric must be even. They derive their strength and stiffness from their shape and the amount of built-in tension. This pretension and the provision of a double curvature surface offer the strength and stiffness to the fabric structural system. Surfaces with a greater curvature are stiffer than those with less curvature for the same amount of tension. Determining the exact form of a stretched skin is complex, as is actually making doubly curved surfaces from real materials. Since such surfaces are normally not developable, the use of naturally flat material sheets to make the surface is problematic. These surfaces are usually made of smaller non-uniformly shaped strips that are

Fig. 71

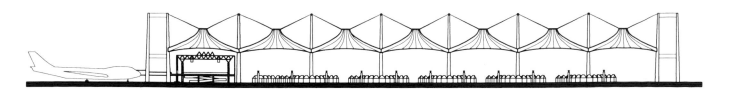

specially cut. Finding the shapes of these strips is a challenging task by itself. These structures, moreover, deform under loads and change their geometry because of the large displacements that they experience. A structural analysis must account for this together with the amount of curvature and prestress they have and is thus inherently complex. Computer programs must also account for the material non-linearity since the fabric material's stress-strain diagrams are nonlinear in character. Another complexity arises due to the fact that the biaxial deformation properties of the materials need to be accounted for in the computer analysis (i.e., differences in stress-strain characteristics in the warp and weft directions in fabrics must be considered).

In addition to the above complexities of structural analysis, the interconnectedness of the tents in the Haj Terminal made the analysis by computer most challenging and tedious compared to the case when each tent would be supported on a center-pole and designed as an isolated unit. The connectivity of the units rendered each terminal section as a large roof and the structure highly indeterminate with "ripple effects from unit to unit and module to module" (*Architectural Record*, 1980).

The NONSAP is a nonlinear large displacement computer program that can handle both static and dynamic analyses. This program was originally developed at the University of California at Berkeley, and was modified for the analysis of the haj fabric roof. Mohammad Salem was responsible for the computer analyses. The modifications made were primarily intended to overcome the difficulties encountered in the membrane analysis: shape finding, numerical instabilities, and the large amount of data stored, retrieved, and displayed graphically during the analysis-design iteration process. An elastic, flexural, finite-element analysis procedure was also included in the program (Khan et al., 1980). A computer model used for the roof analysis involved the surface within a single unit represented by a set of intersecting curved finite elements in the radial direction and in the hoop or circumferential direction (Fig. 72). The unit's shape was mathematically established in the following sequence. The shape of the radial cables was first established. An initial estimate of the shape of the interior unit was made by assuming an axisymmetric shape generated from the radial cable. A computer analysis was carried out to establish the equilibrium shape of the roof unit. A few iterations were necessary to obtain this shape of both the roof and edge and corner units.

Effect of wind loads on a fabric roof of this size is major; so the wind load criteria were important. Both downward and upward wind pressures were considered for the analysis. As expected, the structural design was primarily controlled by wind loads. A static pressure model test at the University of Western Ontario by A. G. Davenport established the wind load criteria of pressures on a localized 7.5m^2 area, on one roof unit and on one 21-unit roof module. A finite element analysis with mesh representing a complete module was performed to check the wind load effects. Suspension cables were designed so that if one cable in a pair fails, the remaining cable will temporarily support the center tension ring until repairs can be made. Stabilizing cables were designed to pick up the tension lost by the fabric roof in the event that the fabric should accidentally lose its tension capability. Cable sizes ranged from 5/8 in. (16mm) diameter for a radial

Fig. 72

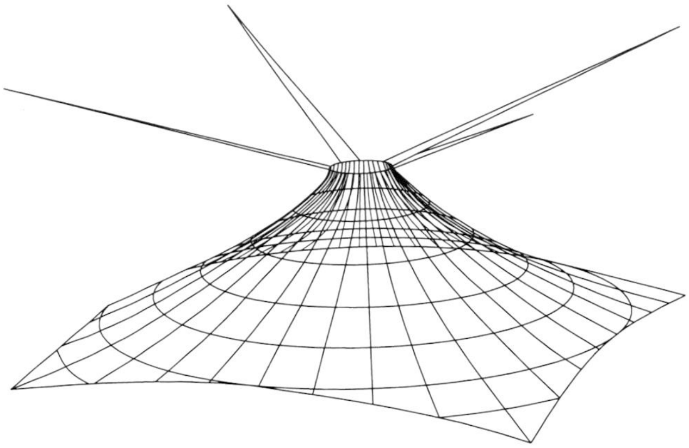

144

Fig. 72: Haj Terminal, Computer Model Used for Roof Analysis Showing the Intersecting Curved Finite Elements

cable to 2-1/2 in. (64mm) diameter for a ridge cable (Khan et al., 1980). Galloping vibrations caused by wind were also considered. Dynamic analyses were performed on a single roof unit and on a single roof module. The possibility of any resonance-type behavior was ruled out under the design conditions on the basis of the analysis of the tents. An aero-elastic model consisting of 3 x 3 units and simulating the dynamic properties of the full-scale structure was built and subjected to a wind tunnel test under a simulated wind speed of 95 mph (153 km/h). The structure was found to be stable without experiencing excessive vibrations.

As stressed before, Khan was a firm believer in experimental verification. Anytime he was faced with a unique and challenging structural problem, he was not satisfied with analysis alone, even if it was a sophisticated computer analysis. After all, computer analysis can be performed merely on an idealized structural model assuming idealized material properties and load-deformation characteristics. Therefore, as part of the final verification for this structure, a full-scale prototype of two of the tent roof units was constructed. Apart from the validation of the results of the analysis, another reason for doing this was to verify its constructability. The prototype was built by Owens-Corning Fiberglass, subcontractor for the project. It consisted of a corner and edge unit. The tent pylons were designed with tie-back cables so that pylon deflections could be controlled to approximate the behavior of the actual pylons. All roof membrane patterning, fabrication, and shipping techniques were duplicated in a manner expected for the project. Based on a series of tests carried out at Owens-Corning's technical center in Granville, Ohio, it was found that the roof structure performed as predicted with no loss of unit stability or strength. A series of fabric rip tests showed the system's redundancy regarding loss of membrane stress and also the fabric's anticipated repair procedures.

Upon erection and final tensioning of the two roof units to the full stress level, ground and aerial surveys were carried out to verify the final shape of the membrane. The overall behavior was thus evaluated with respect to the theoretical model and minor adjustments were made for the actual construction of the Haj Terminal roof.

Three bids were received for the construction of the fabric roof system: Owens-Corning, a consortium from Germany and Switzerland, and a Japanese contractor. The Japanese bidder later dropped out. According to Zils, the German-Swiss Group never fully understood the shape and its justification for the structure. They did not like the idea of raising a built-up tent in the air, the way SOM and Owens-Corning planned. Instead, they wanted to build the tents at the final elevation using scaffolds. They even questioned the engineering design and wanted to redesign. After discussion, they accepted the design but not the mode of construction. Bids were submitted in seven copies by the two firms. Each submittal was voluminous and was put in trunks. The German-Swiss bid was opened first and their bid amount was double the estimated cost of the project. This was a great frustration to Khan and others. Then when Owens-Corning's proposal was opened, it was found to be within the budget. Everyone was relieved. The work was awarded to them.

John Zils recounted the following interesting story regarding how the final decision was made about the project.

Brigadier General S. Y. Amin, director of the project and in charge of construction, represented the client, the Kingdom of Saudi Arabia. During an important meeting, the Haj Terminal project was presented to the client by SOM. After a one and one-half day presentation, Khan, Amin, and Zils were discussing the matter. Amin could not decide what to do, that is, if he could confidently go ahead with the proposal. He asked for Khan's opinion. Khan simply said, "If I were you I'd take it." Amin immediately made up his mind. As Zils put it, "At the end, it was the meeting of two minds . . . human interaction of just two people that made all the years of work fruitful."

Zils recounted another interesting story about this project. At one point, a number of technical problems cropped up that needed immediate resolution. Owens-Corning got frustrated and wanted to have a problem-solving meeting that would include themselves, Hochtief (general contractor), Geiger-Berger Associates (engineering consultant), Birdair Structures, a division of Chemfab (fabric roof fabricator), and SOM. Khan agreed to such a meeting to be held in Toledo, Ohio. Khan, Zils, and Salem were received at the airport and they boarded a van for a prearranged trip to the meeting place. The van soon left the city area and headed for Lake Erie. Khan was totally surprised and shocked by viewing the wilderness around him along the way. Zils quipped, "He looked like he was going to the moon. I never saw him with such an expression of surprise on his face." They were then ferried to an isolated island in Lake Erie where there could be no interruptions of any kind during the meeting. The meeting was to be held for as long as needed until the issues were settled. All parties met for three to four days and the problems were resolved. The scheme worked.

Geiger-Berger was retained by Owens-Corning Fiberglass to reconfirm the structural engineering done by Khan and his team and to do the engineering for connections, clamps, and other hardware. To simulate the complex behavior of the highly indeterminate roof structure, the largest computer storage system in the U.S. was used for a comprehensive and sophisticated engineering analysis, which was part of Geiger-Berger's contract as structural engineering consultants. According to architecture professor James Simon, who had been teaching and researching on fabric structures at the University of Illinois at Urbana-Champaign for many years, David Geiger of Geiger-Berger was a modern-day guru of fabric structures. Geiger's name is associated with the design of a low-profile, air-supported roof covering 100,000 sft. ($9,181m^2$) at the U.S. pavilion at Expo '70 in Osaka, Japan. He held more than a dozen patents, all of them related to long-span membrane roofs. He also developed the cable dome—patented in 1988. Khan's design was, as expected, found most adequate by Geiger-Berger.

The Saudis were very concerned about the time span to build the airport and make it operational. The airport construction proceeded on schedule and was completed in 1982, four months ahead of schedule, and was operational the same year. The structure was erected in a 29-month period. A view of its roof structure under construction is shown in Fig. 73. Although the beauty of the Haj Terminal can be partly captured in photographs, its immensity cannot be comprehended without actually seeing it. I myself visited Jeddah and viewed it in 1999. It is indeed vast, beautiful, and magnificent!

At the early stage of the project, a small mosque was to be included in the Haj Terminal, but it was eliminated later. It may seem that the terminal is not a sacred space that could evoke spirituality in the pilgrims. Richard Rush, a senior editor of *Progressive Architecture* raised this question in an interview (*Progressive Architecture*, 1982). Raul de Armas of SOM responded to this by saying that the Saudis asked "we would like this to be the gateway to the Holy Land, the gateway to Mecca." He continued, "It is the gateway you penetrate before you get to Mecca . . . in looking back at that request . . ., personally speaking, I feel the gateway was created. I would assume that someone arriving at the facility after a long trip—with that bright light coming through, those white tents of that scale and that form— if they don't feel something tingling inside, I'll be amazed. That's the best way I can describe it." Khan then gave this response during the same interview: ". . . I would say the Haj Terminal does not have to be religious; in my opinion it should evoke the spirit of the Haj and that's all it should do. It creates the spirit, it gives you a feeling of tranquility and a sense of continuity, of transition into the real place, which is Mecca."

When we look at the Haj Terminal closely, we find that its structure is truly the architecture. This is what Khan once again accomplished in this project consistent with his life-long search for structural logic and the expression of the structure's inherent strength. SOM did not attempt to add any ornamental, religious, or other features to the natural-looking tent structures. Khan thought the fabric forms were powerful enough, although he recognized that the low building form could have been made somewhat more evocative of Saudi architecture or the kind of reference that the tent structure was intended to have. "Architects wanted to keep the shape and form *absolutely simple*" he said (*Architectural Record*, 1980). The architect wanted to make a very strong design element out of the support structure. The lofty pylons on the long sides of each module can call forth some of the magnificence and monumentality of the tall minarets the pilgrims may view at the Grand Mosque of Mecca and the Prophet's Mosque at Medina.

Unlike other projects, Khan was dealing with a different architectural partner and in a different environment and setting. Gordon Bunshaft was known to be a strong and domineering partner and, unlike Bruce Graham, was not a proponent of structural architecture. Khan did not get the same accommodation of his structural concepts from Bunshaft that he always got from Graham. But that is precisely the point. He gave leadership to the entire project team and was able to get Bunshaft excited about his ideas and to accept them. He was able to make the structure become the aesthetic expression of the tent roof by communicating well with Bunshaft and being understood.

Because of the openness of the structure, natural ventilation augmented with mechanical fan towers was used in this complex. SOM's environmental engineering partner, Perry Gujral, analyzed the temperature levels of the air in the structure from top to bottom with smoke tunnel tests. He found that the top was constantly being ventilated. Khan was very concerned about the comfort of the thousands of pilgrims following a tiresome journey by air. He

Fig. 73

collaborated with Gujral on this issue. He reported (*Progressive Architecture*, 1982): "body heat from people and some internal reflection of the heat gets stuck in the ground level. So, at this level, actually, temperatures are a little higher. The coolest temperature is in this upper level. So what we did was, in fact, create a technique using fans to move the cool air from above down to the human level and push it out again, taking advantage of the coolest layer rather than refrigerating any air."

The perception of pilgrims about the Haj Terminal is positive. To them it is a beautiful place with all the needed facilities available. The terminal itself is usually comfortable, particularly due to its proximity to the sea. There could be a few thousand people gathered at one time but things move fast. People arriving during the daytime who can catch buses for Mecca do not usually have to wait there too long. Those who arrive in late afternoon or at night remain there under the roof. The haj is meant to symbolize a great sacrifice, and no one minds spending the night on the hard floor which had been built under the roof. People cannot really sleep here; they spend their time in prayer and meditation, and in anticipation. When the pilgrims return from performing the haj, the experience is reversed and they reflect on the haj that they have just performed. Some pilgrims have reported that being under the roof is like being in a forest: cool, breezy and pleasant in the hot desert. This is due to the provision of continuous natural ventilation under the open tents (*Architectural Record*, 1980). Other pilgrims, on the other hand, have reported hot and humid conditions under the fabric roof, particularly in the afternoon. After all, it is an open structure and despite the presence of a roof and the natural ventilation, the harsh desert climate cannot be totally overcome. In spite of the hot weather and the physical hardships they go through during this period, people are spiritually reawakened and reborn and they feel like going there again and again to experience the connection between the human and the Divine. An inside view of the Haj Terminal during the Haj season is shown in Fig. 74.

The Haj Terminal project has a truly international character. It serves an international airport handling passengers from around the globe during the haj period. The fabric structure came from foreign countries. The fabric came from the United States, the pylons from Japan, and the cables from France. Likewise, the architects, engineers, contractors, sub-contractors, suppliers, and manufacturers came from different countries, primarily from the United States though.

After working with Khan on this project for a long time, the Saudis developed a high regard for him. Khan's involvement in this project created his interest in the Arab-Islamic culture and particularly in Islamic architecture. He was appointed to the Advisory Committee of the Aga Khan Program for Islamic Architecture at the Harvard University and Massachusetts Institute of Technology (MIT). He was also invited to contribute to one of the seminars associated with the Aga Khan Award for Architecture. Had he been alive today, we would most certainly see his major contributions to this area of architecture, in addition to other successful innovations in tall building design.

In addition to the Sears Tower and the John Hancock Center, the two skyscrapers that dramatically changed the Chicago

Fig. 74

skyline forever, and brought this windy city to the level of New York City, the immensity of the tent roof of the Haj Terminal will keep his memory alive in the building and construction industry. The Haj Terminal is indeed a technical marvel!

In a way, Khan unwittingly fulfilled the dream of Frei Otto, the German structural engineer who is credited for developing the principles and methods of modern membrane construction. Otto convincingly demonstrated the possibilities of new tent construction methods with structures of complex forms. Some of his tents were intended for mass production, whereas others were designed for a specific purpose and location. The injection of fresh life into the art and science of tent construction by Otto was not a direct development from traditional tent-making, which was historically known as part of the nomadic culture of the Middle Eastern people, but was inspired by his ideas and awareness derived from the systematic study of structural engineering, suspended roof and bridge structures, and other natural objects and phenomena. Although Otto worked on the development of mass production of temporary tent structures, he always regarded this as a step towards the development of more permanent tent structures (Rowland, 1965). Otto did the first tent structure for the 1967 World Fair in Montreal, which was dismantled and taken to the Lightweight Structures Institute that he headed in Stuttgart. He later used tensile membranes as "permanent" architecture with the construction of the tent-like roofs for the Munich Olympics in 1972. Khan's enormous Haj Terminal realized Otto's aspirations for a permanent tent structure to a scale beyond what Otto perhaps originally envisioned. Khan's innovative contribution thus pushed the state-of-the-art of tent construction to a new frontier. After a visit to the Haj Terminal, Otto wrote a letter to Khan on June 3, 1981, congratulating him on the success of the project and calling it a "masterpiece." He praised its precise craftsmanship. He also commended "the exactness, the form, and the engineering" of the structure that combined "classic proportions with the tradition of Islamic architecture."

Khan himself went on the haj in 1976. He won the 28th Progressive Architecture Award for this project in 1981. In 1983, after his death in 1982, the Haj Terminal was awarded the Aga Khan Award for Architecture. The award was reported in the September, 1983 issue of *Architectural Record*. Here are the jury's words:

> The brilliant and imaginative design of the roofing system met the awesome challenge of covering this vast space with incomparable elegance and beauty. The Hajj Terminal structure pushed the known building technology beyond its established limits, while demonstrating that such a massive structure can still be light and airy, a 21st-century echo of the traditional tent structures that have worked so well in desert climates. The scale of the structure and the uniqueness of the hajj phenomenon that prompted its erection place it beyond the pale of direct replicability, but it will undoubtedly serve as a source of inspiration throughout the Muslim world for generations to come.

chapter 10

THE SUPREME INTEGRATOR

"The office records of Villard de Honnecourt, in the year 1235, make it clear that the 'master builder' of medieval times was still both architect and engineer, and from Leon Batista Alberti's definitive architectural treatise of 1451-52, we learn that the Renaissance brought no division of labor. The many-sided Renaissance man, in fact, considered all art his province, and all engineering a part of art—as witness the remarkable Leonardo, whose particular genius only magnified the accepted attitudes of his time."

—Ada Louise Huxtable (*Pier Luigi Nervi,* 1960)

150 150 150 150 150

Huxtable (1960) points out in the biography of Nervi that even though the questions of whether architecture is art or structure, aesthetics or engineering—or, a mix of all these—are timeless, the confusion about them is actually of recent origin. The eighteenth century laid the groundwork for what we may now call the professional engineer. The nineteenth century brought highly accelerated development of the scientific concepts of structure. Huxtable wrote, "In America . . . no dream was too big, no ideal too ambitious for practical realization. The field of experimental, progressive construction, of untried techniques and unfamiliar forms, belonged exclusively to the engineer—the builder of bridges, factories, railroad sheds and exposition halls. The schism was complete. The architect, disturbed by, or oblivious to, the unorthodox methods and effects of his 'scientific' colleagues, withdrew in self-righteous superiority to the peculiar refuge of the time: the ivory tower of the arts." Thus the nineteenth century set art and science against each other and "Architecture, once the master of all the building, mechanical and structural arts, was reduced to a correct veneer. Engineering was excluded from the respectable realm of art" (Huxtable, 1960).

It is the nature of the building projects that makes the architects interact with the public more than the engineers. After all, architecture deals with space and a building's spatial quality characterizes architecture. All too often owners or developers approach architects first for new projects. Thus architects become more readily accessible to public than engineers, who usually join the project team later. Architects are largely viewed by society and themselves as artists. Contrary to this, engineers view themselves as individuals with the faculty of quantitative reasoning. The engineer's primary concerns are to economize the design and to implement the notion of load-sharing in the structure in a rational way. This is where the paths of the architect and the engineer seemingly depart from each other. Of course, there are exceptions to this.

The technological revolution of the mid-1800s, however, brought about significant changes in the zeitgeist of the era. The French architect, scholar, and theorist, Viollet-le-Duc, developed a theory of building in which he emphasized the importance of construction and structure stating "architecture and construction must be taught, or practiced simultaneously . . . construction is the means, architecture is the result" (Viollet-le-Duc, 1895). Many of the great monuments of the nineteenth century were, in fact, built by engineers who were pushing the limits of structural expression in new materials such as cast iron, steel, and concrete. Thomas Telford designed iron bridges in England, Gustave Eiffel built his tower in Paris, and John Roebling designed and built suspension bridges, such as the Brooklyn Bridge, in the United States. These engineers are noteworthy because they had the rare ability to combine technical expertise with great aesthetic sensibility.

Joseph Paxton, who was a gardener, not an engineer or architect, designed the Crystal Palace of 1851 as the dramatic centerpiece of the Great Exhibition in London. In this huge structure, large open spaces were framed with "light, standardized, and prefabricated iron pieces." Glass was lavishly used as a building material and form determinant, triggering an explosion of glass-roofed structures. Structure and form were the same, and "conventional 'architecture' was relegated to exterior trimming" (Billington, 1983).

Beginning with the late nineteenth to early twentieth centuries, engineers and architects were exploring the aesthetic and structural possibilities of concrete. Among these was the great Swiss bridge engineer Robert Maillart whose designs represent the epitome of structural form raised to artistic perfection. Other noteworthy architects and engineers include Antonio Gaudi, Eduardo Torroja, and Felix Candela from the Spanish School. For Gaudi, who preceded others and began working in the late nineteenth century, form and structure were integral to building. Torroja was an engineering educator and designer who, like Gaudi, applied the integration of form and structure to the design of concrete vaults. Inspired by the work of these men, Candela, an architect with strong mathematical skills, created new forms in concrete. The Italian engineer Pier Luigi Nervi would bring aesthetic innovations to the design of concrete buildings.

Khan was a complete designer in the sense that, even though he was a structural engineer by training and skill, he was very much comprehensive in his outlook. Many people around the world erroneously think of him as an architect; but he took pride in being a structural engineer and, indeed, did not like being depicted as an architect. But he loved architecture. He told me this when I just began work at SOM in 1980. He advised me to develop knowledge and interest in architecture. He said, "In the building industry, you can't remain just a structural engineer. You need to interact with architects and contractors. Develop interest in architectural details and learn the architect's language. Also, read magazines on construction to understand how buildings are built . . . what problems are involved. You may design buildings, but if they can't be built economically and sensibly, what good is the design?" Later I understood he was, in fact, advising me to be well-rounded, and to know how to collaborate best with other professionals.

Khan was a supreme integrator. Because of this he has been often labeled as a "master builder" (*ENR*, 1982; Fintel, 1982, 1986; Taranath, 1988), and justifiably so. Iyengar explained it to me in a private communication this way:

> He was a master builder, not in a literal sense, but in the sense that he incorporated qualities of all disciplines to bring wholesomeness to his concepts. Khan was a visionary engineer who devised various structural forms and systems that were structural first, but had great architectural qualities. He understood well that to create newer forms, one has to go beyond engineering. This thought process led him to understand architecture, the nature of aesthetics, and planning and societal issues. In order for him to excel in devising structural concepts, he had to have knowledge of all relevant disciplines. He was careful, however, to allow other professionals to utilize their expertise to play the roles in the collaborative team effort. While he absorbed the essence of various disciplines and while this knowledge helped him to evolve relevant systems, his primary success was in innovation of structural forms and systems and his design contributions in other areas.

A master builder has to have a broad awareness and in-depth understanding of issues. Buildings are enclosed spaces in an urban setting. Bruce Graham defined architecture to me as essentially urbanism dealing with exterior and interior spaces. For example, "the relationship between Hancock and Sears is primary," Graham told. He continued, "Sears, Amoco and Hancock buildings are truly space markers. Faz understood that." This is where Khan differed from most structural engineers. He was concerned about the city, the streets, the people, the environment, and the mutual relationship of tall buildings with each other in a dense downtown area. He was concerned about both the vertical and horizontal scales of cities (Khan, 1974b). He realized that the architect should meet with ordinary citizens as well as with city officials. Because he was architecturally inclined, he made such contacts an important aspect of his career, even though most structural engineers usually avoid them.

Viollet-le-Duc's rational approach to design was based on materials, technology, and aesthetics. Since his time, the design of tall buildings has so grown in complexity that the responsibility of the architect and the engineer in designing buildings is greatly amplified. William Le Baron Jenney designed a number of high-rise buildings in Chicago in the late nineteenth century, including the first Leiter Building of 1879 that "marked the beginning of skeletal urban form whose facade consisted only of glass and structure." Jenney was deeply influenced by the works of Viollet-le-Duc. Then, in the 1960s and 1970s, the large number of buildings were created in the United States following the structuralist and modernist notions of Mies van der Rohe and promoted by SOM under the Graham-Khan leadership. After this came the era of Post-Modernism and sculptural architecture. One condition, however, remained constant throughout these periods. As a project became larger and more complex, so did the number of professionals who must collaborate to make the project a success. This is especially true in the planning, design, and construction of tall buildings.

In the Middle Ages, a master builder would plan, design and execute the construction of buildings—large or small. The master builder was a single person who combined the aesthetics of form with the technology of structure and environmental control. The act of building a monument, shelter, or an enclosed space was more like "craftsmanship" and the master builder, the craftsman, would coordinate the project by leading the masons, carpenters, and other skilled workers. His forte was to envision the total building entity. We do not have master builders today in the original sense. The role of the earliest master builder has now been divided into that of professionals from different disciplines. It has shifted from the endeavor of an individual to that of a team of professionals. When asked how he would define the term master builder, Iyengar put it to me this way, " . . . the term master builder evolved from middle ages where the artist, the architect, engineer, and contractor was the same person. I do not believe this term has a great deal of relevance in a contemporary industrialized construction process. The demands of technical and scientific knowledge required of engineers and the highly industrialized shop and field construction methods have separated themselves into separate disciplines as contrasted to space planning, aesthetics, and other artistic endeavors of the architect. In effect, the overall design and construction has become a collaborative effort."

The building industry has now become professionally fragmented moving toward specialization, but the notion of master builder latently persists. From time to time, such master builders have appeared on the building scene, but the late-nineteenth-century sophistication in technology divided the master builder into four distinct entities, namely, the architect, the structural engineer, the building services engineer, and the contractor. The transition was evolutionary rather than revolutionary. Khan recognized that this separation of roles was often counterproductive in that it resulted in architecture that was inefficient and uneconomical, as well as dishonest in its visual effect. He took up the challenge of reunifying structural engineering and architectural solutions, treating the structure as an integral part of architecture that would synthesize function and visual expression to create new possibilities in forms and proportions of buildings. Khan had his own views on the nature and role of a present-day master builder. According to him, architects only became artists in the nineteenth century, "going around sketching Roman columns, and so on; they became aesthetically oriented." At SOM, he said, "we have tried to bring engineering and architecture back together. We like to think we are bringing back the idea of the master builder, but this time as a team effort" (*Civil Engineering*, 1980).

With Graham's association and influence, Khan recognized well that the process of choosing a structural system for a tall building may depend on some criteria other than structural (Khan, 1972c). Since the structure is an integral part of the total scheme, the design process has to be multi-disciplinary. For example, the insertion of a new tall building into a neighborhood will influence transportation systems and the movement of all its people. He was sensitive to the fact that such a project must consider the needs of pedestrian, auto, and other traffic, as well as the overall need for space at the ground level. While an open plaza may be a viable solution under certain climatic and planning conditions, it may not be a logical solution where weather conditions are extreme—either in winter or in summer. The structural system must respond to these conditions appropriately. Similarly, climatic conditions should dictate the size of windows and consequently the selection of the structural material and the structural system. It goes without saying that the shape and structure of a building also will be governed by zoning requirements, allowable floor area ratios, and the size and shape of the site.

Khan was concerned with the new scales of cities, of tall buildings and their influence on the skyline. He knew how significantly tall buildings shaped the urban space. He believed that "the building of tall structures simply for their own sake does not make economic sense, nor does it enhance the total environment of our cities. It seems meaningless to develop structural systems for high-rise buildings if the results do not have a positive effect toward creating better cities and better environment" (Khan, 1972a). He further wrote:

> In the final analysis, the development of tall buildings closely
> follows the development of the urban centers of America. It
> is undoubtedly the concentration of population in these cen-
> ters, combined with the high cost of land, that results in build-
> ings with high-density population. Tall buildings, however,
> are recent phenomena in the history of civilization and have
> been possible only because the vertical transportation
> problem was resolved by Elisha Graves Otis in the middle 19th
> Century, and because new high strength materials, both in
> steel and concrete, have been developed to carry heavy loads.

Although an architect's primary concern may be the scale of the building including its interior spaces and functions, he or she cannot ignore a heavy responsibility for the building's physical presence in the urban space, as well as its impact on the urban environment. Great architecture is a blend of art and science in which creative, abstract, and sublime imagery crystallizes into the reality of visual forms. While the scientific side of architecture is objective, verifiable, and quantifiable, its artistic side is subjective, emotional, qualitative, and sometimes even irrational. This is the major dilemma of architecture challenging the designer on how to mix these two polarities (or perhaps two worlds), into one (Ali, 1990). Because the architect has delegated the technical and practical aspects of a project to the specialized professionals his/her role as a master builder has been lost. Sadly, many engineers only deal with the technical issues, assuming that the architects should develop the conceptual design, architectural style and aesthetics; that they should define and allocate spaces, and derive the geometric composition of the building. With such an assumption, the structural engineer's influence as an integral part of a project team is also undermined.

Khan recognized that the tall building is a form-function-material continuum in which several design criteria must be satisfied and integrated. Some of these criteria are: geometry and scale, urban context, social effects, structural system, architectural function, building services and environmental systems, constructability, and safety. Out of these criteria, geometric composition is likely the most difficult one because aesthetics, structuralism, functionalism, and symbolism are very closely intertwined. Although Khan did not have the technical expertise in areas such as planning, interiors, and mechanical and electrical engineering, he nevertheless was eager to involve himself in all design criteria and demonstrated his aptitude for these and other related issues (Khan, 1974c). He appreciated the architect's will, but he strongly believed in cross-fertilization of ideas between architects and engineers. He never felt subordinated; he always made his ideas on design criteria known to other professionals in the design team.

A keen sense of aesthetics was natural to Khan. Once in SOM's office, I saw him examining a model of a building and its surrounding terrain. Although placed on a low table, he looked intently from every possible angle to see whether the building had the right geometric proportion and the right relationship to its setting. He read books on aesthetics, such as Santayana's *On the Nature of Beauty* (*Khan Tributes*, 1982). It's no wonder that the forms he created were natural to the material as well as to the physical forces developed in the structure—and thus they also became elegant shapes aesthetically meaningful. While Khan was concerned about form, scale, aesthetics and social effects, his basic thinking focused, of course, on structural systems, and in this, he rigidly followed scientific methods. His ultimate goal was to discover knowledge and then to deal in objects, not in abstractions. But this did not keep him from crossing boundaries of thought from one area to another—from subjective to objective, from abstraction to reality.

To Khan, architectural treatment of buildings did not mean adding superficial features to structures or modifying logical structural shapes and forms with texture, grooves, offsets, and other such cosmetics on the facade. Rather, he used engineering dictates to generate form thus providing a prime basis for design. In other words, his dictum was: let stresses in materials shape the structure. He firmly believed that beautiful structures which complemented their sites can be designed at little or no additional cost by following sound structural and architectural principles. For Khan, mathematics, engineering, and art had to be blended in a harmonious manner.

He once questioned the shape of the Marcel Breuer cantilever chairs in the office of SOM, chairs that were recognized as "modern classics" (*The Economist*, 1998). Khan questioned the rationale behind making these chairs cantilevered, when the loads on them could be more readily carried by four legs. His architectural colleagues suggested that the cantilever added springiness to the chairs. Khan remained unconvinced and argued that Breuer had designed these chairs with such shape not for springiness but for novelty. As always, Khan's mind abhorred novelty unless it could be coupled with rational engineering principles.

When I talked with Graham, I found him to have exactly the same views. Like Khan, he disliked unnecessary architectural features to his buildings. He encouraged structural expression—so close to Khan's heart—and spoke passionately about it. Out of the strength of such convictions came buildings like the John Hancock Center, the Sears Tower, and the Onterie Center, whose structures are so honestly expressed! When structure and architecture are so wedded, their geometry becomes so vivid! As Zils put it to me, "A child can easily draw sketches of these buildings, because their form is so clear. Ask the child to draw some other buildings where the structure is not so clearly expressed and see what happens."

Myron Goldsmith and Bruce Graham had a major influence on Khan's career and the development of his affinity for architecture and building aesthetics. Goldsmith was a firm believer in structural architecture and demonstrated this in most of his projects. A dedicated engineer-architect, and someone who never stopped thinking or working until his last days, Goldsmith lent a new impetus to the Miesian mode of architectural expression. He balanced contemporary design standards against the great building traditions of Chicago. His association with Nervi added another dimension to his career by offering him further insight into the development of the modern movement and the International Style. He collaborated with innovators like T. Y. Lin and finally with Khan. Khan deeply appreciated Goldsmith's conviction that complex problems could be broken into simple parts for resolution by a clear, logical approach. Goldsmith believed in teamwork and rejected high-tech formalism in architecture on the pretense of expressing the structure. While speaking at a special seminar session organized by the Committee on Aesthetics and Design of the American Society of Civil Engineers (ASCE) in Houston, Texas, and dedicated to the memory of Khan, he noted, ". . . I come to the popular, mostly British movement called high-tech, exemplified in the Hong Kong and Shanghai Bank in Hong Kong. . . . In this case there was a preconceived idea that was not structurally efficient, and that structure was used regardless. This building is but one example of several in which a very expensive structure is used for expressionism. Khan often discussed these ideas, opposing them as strongly as he could. He always tried to connect the architecture, aesthetics, and structural efficiency" (Goldsmith, 1986).

William Le Messurier, a distinguished structural engineer and an admirer of Khan, made important observations about him and high-tech architecture at the same ASCE session when he said (Goldsmith, 1986):

> . . . I was deeply influenced by Khan myself. In addition to working with architects, he looked at the way buildings actually get built and he understood the construction process,

and everything that was done had an enormous practicality, unlike the case of that Hong Kong monster. That is the third dimension in this triangle. There is a builder with the construction techniques, there are architects, and there are structural engineers, and Khan put them all together.

Unquestionably, Khan immensely benefited from his association with Goldsmith and the thesis projects that he and Goldsmith supervised at IIT. Both were great Chicagoans and had a personal chemistry and both understood the nature of the growth and expansion of Chicago's skyline. They were visionaries and great innovators. I had a brief opportunity of dealing with Goldsmith in SOM's office when I discussed some technical problems with him and also later when he contributed to a chapter of the book *Architecture of Tall Buildings* (CTBUH, 1995) together with David Sharpe and Mahjoub Elnimeiri. I found out that he loved buildings and was constantly exploring new ideas and concepts.

As noted before, Graham also influenced Khan's career. Graham, a prominent American architect, was the architectural designer of many SOM buildings. He met Khan in connection with the Inland Steel Building in Chicago, in which Khan "resolved, very competently, the inner relationship between column and beam in a clear-span high-rise structure," (Graham, 1986). Graham told me, "Faz designed a special type of connections between the beams and the exposed columns. A Canadian firm had tried a similar design but the structure failed because the connections were not properly designed." Graham and Khan developed a close relationship as partners in business and as intimate friends. As of July, 1998 and March, 1999, in conversations with Graham in Chicago, I had the opportunity of having a glimpse into the inner thoughts of this outstanding architect and the man that he is. I realized why and how they could work together so closely. Graham's thoughts mirrored those of Khan.

At SOM's office, Graham had the reputation of being egotistical and domineering, like many famous architects. When I met him on July 7, however, I met a different person: a self-effacing, polite, humorous, warm, and humanistic individual. When we parted late in the evening, we had only gotten warmed up in our conversation. He suggested I could see him when he came to Chicago again. He spoke of many things, some anecdotal, his own philosophy of design, Khan's career, his projects with Khan, and what is wrong with present-day architecture and architectural education.

Although Khan may have exhibited a sense of aesthetics from his childhood, all indications are that refinements came gradually. During the early years of his career he focused primarily on structural analysis and design; he deferred aesthetic issues to the architects. But later, through his association with Goldsmith, Graham, and others he developed a great aesthetic sensitivity, expanding his horizon broadly to include issues of exterior and interior spaces. While he learned from architects, they learned from him about the importance of an inherently correct structural form for buildings. One SOM architectural design partner, Walter Netsch—with whom Khan worked on a few projects—was not, however, impressed by Khan's structural logic and wanted to create his own forms. But Khan was able to work in cooperation with most of the prominent architects at SOM. He was, in his more mature years, able to participate in the discussions and judgements on aesthetics and space with his architectural counterparts as an equal. He often brought to them a fresh perspective. On the whole, his broad vision enabled him to humanize technology and to present structure as an art form.

It is fitting to tell how Graham, an accomplished architect in his own right, worked so successfully with Khan. Graham believes strongly in expressing structures and lamented that many architects fail to appreciate structure. Architecture to him is closer to dance rather than to painting or sculpture. The building should look dynamic. If its structural form is not expressed, a building becomes stolid. I asked when he developed this notion, and, without hesitation, he replied "From my childhood." Even though he always intended to be an architect, he was drawn to structure. He studied civil engineering at the University of Dayton for some time before he went for studies at the University of Pennsylvania at Philadelphia to obtain his architecture degree in 1948. This comprehensive knowledge helped him to integrate aesthetics with structure. He joined SOM in 1949.

Graham has visions for Chicago. He knows well its great architectural traditions and the influence of Mies van der Rohe in shaping the architectural trends of the 1960s and 1970s. He is a proponent of Modernism and the International Style. He thinks the great body of fresh water of Lake Michigan is a source of great power to Chicago. Also, Chicago's location between the Allegheny and the Rockies is unique, representing the power of the United States. Architecture of Chicago should, therefore, reflect that power. Sears and Hancock do just that. He added that Khan shared with him this macro-vision of Chicago. That is precisely why they had a meeting of minds.

Graham was critical of present-day architectural education. He thought students should spend more time in architectural/engineering offices. The universities should facilitate this for students. Architecture is a professional discipline and students need to get a taste of professionalism during their academic learning period as part of their educational experience. He also felt strongly that students should be taught to be multidisciplinary—that building design needs the team effort of architects, planners, engineers, and contractors.

Other traits of Graham's character are his modesty and his humanistic ideals. Not once have I heard him boast of his own abilities as an architect. He simply noted his own contributions to architecture, giving due credit to Khan for the projects that Khan worked on as a structural engineer. It became clear how they would work in close collaboration for two decades since Khan was of a similar temperament. Graham was known for his corporate or commercial image, but to a surprising degree, he had a deep concern for common people and how architecture must relate to them. In his work for churches and for underprivileged groups, he had an altruistic thought in the back of his mind. He cared for the common man's opinion. At one point he said, "I asked a cab driver one day which building he liked most. He replied, 'The Hancock Building'. He is my best critic."

Like Khan, Graham also believes in both the preservation of cultural heritage and the diversity of civilizations. Buildings should be designed in congruence with local culture and its traditions. Over the centuries, humans developed their habitats to fit their own settings respecting their own values, climate, and environment. Current attempts to develop a single world civilization are contrary to all human experience.

Graham also noted a few personality traits of Khan, who had a great sense of humor. Creativity is often concomitant with a sense of humor. Although Khan was a modest person by nature, he was aggressive professionally. He was polite but not shy, aggressive but not offensive, in dealing with architects and contractors. His aggressiveness, coupled with his gentle demeanor and convincing soft tone, was one key factor that led to his great success. When I asked Graham whether Khan could be called a present-day master builder, as I wished to portray him, his direct answer was, "yes."

Returning to Khan, he was not only a visionary, but he also had a keen business sense. He had a comprehensive understanding of building construction. Being a pragmatic person, he always kept it in mind during design. He hammered it into his IIT students that buildings must be built in an efficient, practical and cost-effective manner, regardless of their design. He made it a point to discuss constructability issues with the contractors and listen carefully to their concerns and suggestions. John Tishman, executive Vice President of Tishman Realty & Construction Co. Inc., New York, construction manager on the Hancock Building, said, "Khan stands on no ceremony whatsoever. He is constantly willing to reevaluate his own decisions and works very closely with the contracting experts. We have tremendous respect for Faz, particularly his unusual designs and innovations" (*ENR*, 1972).

Another related issue is the fabrication of large steel members for tall buildings. He worked closely with the steel sub-contractor, American Bridge, for the John Hancock Center. He discussed with them the details of connections—the welding, bolting, and fabrication—the shipping and erection of members. Such collaboration resulted in details that were both workable and cost-effective. The steel fabrication and detailing for Hancock was especially challenging because of the tapered form of the structure. In the case of the Sears Tower, it is hard to imagine how such a magnificently tall structure could so readily be erected. But the concept that Khan developed, together with his associates, working with U.S. Steel, the steel fabricator, simplified the process. Since the building was composed of identical modular tubes, similar column spacing, and uniform member depths, it lent itself to a straightforward prefabrication process. It took only a month to complete eight floors of steel construction!

Khan concerned himself with the mechanical and electrical engineering aspects of tall buildings. The need to consider the total picture of the design process remained at the forefront of his mind, but mechanical and electrical services and products became increasingly important design criteria. He saw from his repeated experience with buildings how the mechanical ducts, elevator shafts, mechanical floor openings, plumbing systems, fire protection systems, mechanical equipment, cooling towers, and other environmental systems made ever more demands on the structural system and therefore, on the architectural planning, especially of tall buildings. Electrical systems involving vertical and horizontal conduits, bus ducts, and other components influence the building's planning. In his association with mechanical and electrical engineers, he quickly mastered the basic concepts underlying these systems. Such comprehension augmented the integration of complex overlapping systems and resolved many conflicts.

Raymond J. Clark, a mechanical engineering partner of SOM who was associated with Khan since 1975, stated that Khan was not only a brilliant structural engineer, but he also had a keen understanding of the mechanical. Clark worked with Khan on the Haj Terminal and Makkah University. To simulate the conditions of university dormitories in a hot desert environment, a dormitory room model was built at Gaithersburg, near Washington, DC. The room was provided with air-conditioning, coolers and other systems including wind shafts and towers. Khan was so insightful that he contributed to the design of the mechanical systems. Wind tunnel modeling was done in association with Dr. Hasan Naguib. Although Makkah University was never built, findings from these tests were used in other SOM projects. For the design of mechanical systems for the Headquarters Building for Lucky Goldstar in Seoul, South Korea, Khan helped design their building services systems, particularly their energy saving schemes.

Khan's contributions were validated by his participation in meetings involving the various disciplines. According to Clark, Khan provided mentorship to many people, including Clark himself. In this connection, he recounted a story about Khan. Once Clark was welcoming some new people who would start working at SOM's Chicago office at 33 West Monroe Street. Khan was also present. When Clark shook hands with everyone, he extended his hand to Khan. Khan shook his hand but was somewhat surprised and asked him why—they saw each other almost everyday at the office. Clark replied, "It is an honor to shake hands with you. How many times do I get such an opportunity?"

Khan cared about comfort levels in the building. David Wickersheimer, an architecture professor at the University of Illinois at Urbana-Champaign, who knew Khan from his own work at SOM as a summer intern in the 1960s, related to me the following story. Wickersheimer told of meeting Khan in the early 1970s at an engineering conference at the Pacific Palisades Center near Monterey, California. Khan spoke there on creativity while Wickersheimer gave a talk on the history of buildings. They rented a car and Wickersheimer drove Khan around. During their tour, Khan talked about buildings and explored the integration of systems. He stimulated Wickersheimer by his questions. Wickersheimer knew from his own time at SOM how Khan would pose technical questions politely, then steer respondents in the right direction. He and Khan were staying at the same hotel, and Wickersheimer found Khan at one time measuring humidity and airflow in his hotel room. When asked why, Khan replied, "what good is a building if it is not comfortable to its users?" Khan often carried meters and gauges with him when he traveled.

Beyond the comfort of occupants, Khan continued to demonstrate his interest in the energy efficiency of tall buildings. The energy crisis of the early 1970s was considered a clarion call to designers to minimize energy consumption. The extent of window glazing, the shape and orientation of buildings, the materials used, the location and layout of atriums should all bring about energy savings.

Regarding energy conservation, Khan (1974c) wrote:

> ... there are other changes taking place in our society and they in turn will affect our cities. The energy crisis is one, raising new demands for efficiency in heating, cooling, lighting, and operation of buildings. Compared to individual small offices and homes scattered all around the suburban areas, centralized commercial and living spaces are more efficient from the energy consumption point of view. Per unit floor area has less total surface exposure to heat loss and energy is saved by requiring total travel time and fuel if more people live and work within shorter distances.

Khan believed in the elegance of forms, not just how the structure would carry the applied loads. His aesthetic sensitivity combined with his expertise in structural engineering and concern for other aspects of buildings rendered a degree of uniqueness to his professional career. Although he did not have explicit control on architectural design, his architectural qualities and his mastery of the art of communication found expression through his structural design. His incessant longing for connecting the emotive beauty of the structure to the rational logic at its core provided him with the ammunition that he needed for his professional success.

chapter 11

A VOTARY OF STRUCTURAL ART

"The Eiffel Tower and the Brooklyn Bridge became great symbols of their age because the general public recognized in their new forms a technological world of surprise and appeal . . . that tower and that bridge are only two of the numberless works of recent engineering that constitute a new art form, structural art, which is parallel to and fully independent of architecture."

—David Billington (*The Tower and the Bridge: The New Art of Structural Engineering,* 1983)

162   162   162

One of Khan's major contributions to the design profession is his recognition and implementation of the *art* of structural engineering through his aesthetic experience. David Billington of Princeton University wrote the book *The Tower and the Bridge: The New Art of Structural Engineering,* in which he discussed the idea of structural art, then demonstrating that works of engineering constitute a new art form (Billington, 1983). In the opening paragraph of its preface he wrote the words quoted above to set the tone of his book.

Billington identified three fundamental ideals of structural art: a discipline of efficiency (to utilize minimum materials); second, a discipline of economy (to make for construction simplicity as well as ease of maintenance); and third, a search for structural elegance (an expression of beauty and aversion to ugliness). In addition, he identified three pairs of criteria to be met for achieving structural art: thinness and safety, integration and cost, and contrast and affinity.

The art of the structural engineer entails an aesthetically pleasing and meaningful arrangement of structural elements that demonstrates dexterity in the application of a system of rules and principles that facilitates skilled human accomplishment. Structural artists believe that structures can create art; that is, an in-depth understanding and appropriate application of structural principles should lead to the creation of beautiful forms. They use mathematical analyses for their structures, but are not

163 **163** **163** **163**

163

limited by them. Generation of structural form does not necessarily require that it be totally subservient to the scientific laws of mechanics. Great structural artists—Maillart, Nervi, Gaudi, Candela, Isler, and Khan—believed in their freedom to choose what system is rational structurally and most fitting aesthetically. They worked to harmonize nature's laws and material properties with the inherent aesthetics of a design. Santiago Calatrava, a contemporary architect-engineer and a structural artist, exemplifies such integration, but he is more inclined toward aesthetics than the ideal of correct structural form. He begins his design with aesthetic considerations, then makes it work structurally. There are, of course, structural engineers who are architects in their hearts just as there are architects who are structural engineers in their hearts. A majority of structural artists probably fall between these two poles.

Chapter 6 touched on the point of how Khan developed the forms from structural considerations and created an elegant aesthetic quality from these forms. Also, Chapter 3 told how the development of the modern skyscraper started with the contributions of the first Chicago School. The three great designers of this era were William Le Baron Jenney, John Wellborn Root, and Louis Sullivan. Sullivan, as a great architect, is still greatly applauded by architectural historians—and he deserves such applause. Although his buildings do not exhibit the same level of structural expression as Jenney's and Root's, his best-known work, Chicago's Carson Pirie Scott Building, strongly expresses its steel frame system. In the upper stories of this department store building, the predominate horizontality is based largely on the underlying grid of the structural steel frame. Sullivan further expressed the vertical structure in the Wainwright Building in Saint Louis and the Guaranty Building in Buffalo. Jenney and Root, both trained as engineers, became architect-engineers and designed buildings that exemplify early efforts of structural art in high-rise design.

Jenney began practicing as an architect in Chicago in 1868. He is recognized for his pioneering design of the first Leiter Building of 1879, the Home Insurance Company Building of 1885, and the second Leiter Building of 1891. The 180-ft. (54.7m) tall Home Insurance Building in Chicago is generally considered the first skyscraper of the world; it marked the beginning of the "American century" as measured by the world's tallest buildings. His engineering background strongly influenced the design of these elegant structural forms. Jenney's buildings were the progenitors of Khan's buildings of the 1960s and 1970s.

Root carried Jenney's concepts further. Although he was first and foremost an engineer, he was concerned with visual effects and was a practicing architect in partnership with Daniel Burnham since 1873. Like Jenney, he was influenced by the tenets of the French architect Viollet-le-Duc. Like Khan, he was a structural innovator. He developed concrete foundations with a grillage of steel rails to transfer heavy loads from multi-story buildings to a weak subsoil. He also used, for the first time, the metal skeleton as a complete window wall system for the superstructure. Root's most well known building is Chicago's 16-story Monadnock Building of 1892. According to Billington (1983), the facade of Monadnock Building "is an undecorated wall pierced by windows from base to roof." He further wrote, "... Root has designed a facade whose verticality is fully continuous and expresses what needs to be, a wall with openings . . . Root's form is original and rational in the sense of showing visually what it does protectively. At the scale of Monadnock, the wall is a weather protection and a source of light; it need not be a structure. . . . If the First Chicago School is parallel to the high Gothic, then Root is its climax and Sullivan its florid aftermath" (Billington, 1983).

Although the First Chicago School began to recognize that structure did not matter as an art form for the scale of a 16-story building, its proponents refrained from ornamentation and decorative treatment of facades. Structural art for high-rise buildings was still in its embryonic form as was the development of high-rises themselves in the late nineteenth century. The art of structure in the realm of tall building design did not truly blossom until the advent of the Second Chicago School seven decades later inspired by the structuralism of Mies and his protégé Goldsmith, supported by Graham and several other SOM architects and structural engineers led by Khan. Mies and Khan picked up where Root left off. Khan accomplished structural art with more meaning and clarity for buildings of immense heights where the structural form and its expression mattered most. Thus Mies and Khan were in intellectual company with Jenney and Root as well as the structural artists like Maillart, Candela, Nervi, and Isler.

Maillart left a deep impression on Khan's sense of aesthetics and his passion for the fusion of structural form and the principles of aesthetics (Khan, 1972b). Robert Maillart, a Swiss engineer, had a brilliant understanding of structural form in concrete and its multi-faceted potential. He was truly a revolutionary in structural art and was the first to treat reinforced concrete as a "discrete building material in its own right." Mostly known for his contribution to bridge architecture, he produced sleek, romantic, and graceful visual effects. He created three-hinged arch forms in spectacular settings which are both a pleasure to behold from a distance and to traverse. His search for thinness and elegance came out of a keen sense of structural efficiency and aesthetics, and it continued throughout his career. As an imaginative designer, he never lost sight of the fact that a principal ideal of design was to continually pursue economy in materials and cost.

Maillart also imagined new forms for three types of building construction—the flat-slab floor supported on columns, beam-supported roof, and thin-shell vault. His "Mushroom Floor" of the Giesshübel Warehouse of 1910 in Zurich shows the curvaceous column capitals that smoothly transfer the floor loads to columns giving a look of both grace and efficiency. His love for slenderness and elegance is also apparent from the Cement Hall for the National Exhibition of 1939 in Zurich—where he used a thin, pure structural form—and the Magazzini Generali Warehouse Shed of 1924 in Chiasso, Switzerland—where the truss-like roof structure meets the Y-shaped columns demonstrating efficiency, originality, and due proportions. Its entire structure visually gives a calm feeling of structural equilibrium, stability, and balance.

Like Maillart, Khan demonstrated structural and aesthetic integration of concrete in several buildings (see Chapter 6). He worked with Graham to enhance the visual interest by smooth shapes of structural members and connections. In this, Graham, the architectural designer of these buildings and himself an admirer of Maillart, played a crucial role in challenging Khan's aesthetic sensibilities and structural acumen in making these projects successful. In the Brunswick Building, Graham and Khan introduced a lively structural detail at the base of the exterior columns, where they carry the greatest load. They flared these columns outward from the plane of the facade to meet the heavy transfer girders that support them.

They went farther with the Marine Midland Bank, One Shell Plaza and Two Shell Plaza (see Chapter 6). For the Marine Midland Bank, where vertical load is transferred from many columns above to fewer, widely-spaced columns below, the force flow takes place both in and out of the plane of the facade, resulting in an undulating effect. Thus the building elevation visually displays a "tree-like" transfer of vertical loads near the base. On One Shell Plaza, the facade undulates similar to Marine Midland Bank. Here, however, the undulation continues throughout the entire height of the structure. The waving shape bears some resemblance to that on the facade of Root's Monadnock Building, even though the reasons behind them were different. Although overall ruggedness to the facade was introduced in this building, it is still visually pleasant because of the rational smoothness of its individual undulations. This is structural art at its ultimate. Structure and art are here embedded in each other, with one complementing the other.

For the Two Shell Plaza, the loads are gradually carried down to the widely spaced columns by widening the upper columns and deepening the beams toward the base. This created an arch-like effect, so that the load path becomes visually apparent. This technique, manipulating the use of horizontal and vertical elements to accommodate the force flow, bears some resemblance to Maillart's Warehouse Shed at Chiasso, where loads are carried by the horizontal and vertical members in a similar manner.

Another great architect-engineer who preceded Khan linking architecture and engineering, art and science, aesthetics and structural form, is the Italian Pier Luigi Nervi. He was a passionate votary of aesthetics and his passion was to create beautiful buildings. To Nervi, like Khan, the structure could be art if it stemmed from the "correct form, careful construction practice, and a conscious aesthetic intention." Like Khan, he was also a prolific writer and wrote several books and numerous articles. Structures, he said, "can be solved correctly only through a superior and purely intuitive re-elaboration of the mathematical results" (Nervi, 1956). He was skeptical of complex mathematical analyses—which, he thought, drove junior engineers away from intuition.

Nervi's approach to reinforced concrete design was similar to Maillart's; each was a builder of structures competing with one another in aesthetics and cost, and creators of new and exciting forms. Like Maillart, he sought to optimize the cost and efficiency of buildings, using minimum quantity of materials. He designed numerous structures including many vaults. One of Khan's culminating concepts was to be tubular design for tall buildings; for Nervi it was ribbed design for large spans over open spaces. The Exhibition Building of 1950 in Turin is another structure of exquisite beauty viewed from the interior. Its ribs and curvaceous columns and buttresses and the arrangement of structural elements to meet architectural requirements demonstrate Nervi's unparalleled creativity as a structural artist. For the Gatti Wool Factory of 1951 in Rome, Nervi designed a flat slab with column capitals, but unlike Maillart, he introduced two-way ribs. Ribbed dome systems were also used for the Little Sports Palace of 1957 and the Large Sports Palace of 1960, both in Rome. The intricate ribs created an exemplary visual interest and expressing actual stress trajectories. His domes are masterpieces in structural art.

No practicing professional in the twentieth century understood building structures better than Nervi before World War II and no one understood them better than Khan following that war. Each aimed for structures that were unadorned, ordered, and pleasant. As in Khan's case, in many of Nervi's buildings there was a collaborating architect, but the structural form and its open stylistic expression came from Nervi. Both Khan and Nervi were at their best when their structural intent coincided with the architectural requirements. But both were flexible when certain structural requirements needed to become subservient to complex architectural functions. Both had the rare quality of being deeply technical men with a keen sense of aesthetics, and they firmly believed that structural art could respond with several resolutions to any technical challenge.

Nervi and Khan were complete designers and master builders. Not only did they reunite architecture and engineering, but they looked at art in a more broad and purposeful sense than most. In their self-perception, they had one major difference. While Nervi thought of himself more as an architect and deplored the "art-engineering split that persists in architectural education and practice today" (Huxtable, 1960), Khan considered himself primarily a structural engineer. Khan intensely disagreed with architects thinking of engineers as mere technicians and helpers to architects; he vehemently argued that this practice must stop. In terms of their engineering judgment, they were similar in their outlook. Each was pragmatic and intuitive, and had a feel for the flow of force—through a structure. They used mathematical analysis only as a tool, a means to an end. They used their concepts and creative judgement with profound understanding of the structure; they drew on a comprehensive technical awareness to produce beautiful and truthful buildings.

In 1959, Nervi designed a high-rise, the Pirelli Building in Milan. Nervi and A. Danusso were the structural designers for the project. The building plan is a slim rectangle with chamfered edges giving a unique form and strong architectural expression. Rising 415 ft. (126.5m), it has the powerful appearance of a building soaring skyward, especially in its context. Although there is no unique structural expression on the outside, there is visual stability since the two solid end facades appear to firmly hold the structure in between. Although the architect developed the form, Nervi must have influenced it because its proportions gave elegance and thinness to the building both of which characterized Nervi's vision of architecture. Moreover, there is no particular physical ornamentation on the facade; it is clear and simple. Such characteristics resemble those of Khan's buildings, even though Khan had a much greater part in the development of forms. One significant difference between Khan and Nervi is that Khan was more occupied with the expression of the facade, whereas

Nervi was generally more concerned with the building's interior. Such emphases may result from the type of buildings they were given to design in their respective careers.

One other notable structural artist and master builder is Felix Candela from Madrid, Spain, best known for his shell structures in which he introduced a profusion of forms. He was inspired by natural forms in which he saw a definite potential for man-made structures. He demonstrated how aesthetics and utilitarian function could be combined for achieving innumerable possibilities of form.

Candela was an engineer-architect and a builder. He designed the Cosmic Ray Pavilion at the National University of Mexico with a very thin roof using a compound curvature to provide rigidity to a vaulted shell. This drew immediate attention and he was inundated with lecture invitations. Although skilled in mathematical analysis, he was more inclined towards intuitive understanding of structures. He emulated Gaudi and Torroja in his quest for novel forms; but in his own way he achieved new forms in concrete.

Candela's Xochimilco Restaurant Roof of 1958 near Mexico City had a thickness of only 1 5/8 in. (41.3mm). This extreme thinness is beautifully and clearly expressed in the roof structure made of eight hypar vaults. The lotus form of the structure spreads out dynamically, it is graceful and light. It represents a delicate concrete shell of unsurpassed design. Candela eliminated edge members in favor of free edges which "rise and fall" without any special reinforcement. Its geometry—symmetry in plan and double curvature—in conjunction with the presence of gullies in the shell, was skillfully utilized to refine the form. Regarding the special characteristics of concrete shells Faber (1963) wrote, "... there is a definite affinity between concrete shells and natural shells. . . . Reinforced concrete is not only very akin to the stuff of natural shells, but it can also withstand substantial tensile stresses. The properties of continuity and tensile strength of reinforced concrete offer us a unique opportunity to emulate the economy of material in natural methods of enclosing space."

Candela, like Khan, was a firm believer of structural efficiency coupled with aesthetic sensitivity. Like Khan, he believed in the moldability of concrete. Each was skilled in mathematical analysis, but would distance himself from it initially to exercise intuitive understanding of structures.

Candela designed numerous shell structures. Apart from church roofs, he designed a band shell at Seguro Social Housing Project in Santa Fe, a signpost with "flapping" wings in the wind at Lake Tequesquitengo, the Circular Bazaar at Los Abanicos, and an Ornamental Structure of sculptural quality at La Plaza de los Abanicos. Most of his structures are in Mexico.

Two Swiss designers were Heinz Isler, who designed many concrete shells and Christian Menn, who designed long-span bridges with aesthetic sensitivity. These men, contemporaries of Khan, were structural artists who experimented with concrete to generate new and interesting forms.

Santiago Calatrava has brought together a profound technical understanding and a keen aesthetic sensitivity which has resulted in his poetic structures. Practicing in Zurich since 1981, he has two other offices in Europe—one in Paris and the other in Valencia, Spain. Born in Spain in 1951, he studied art and architecture in Valencia, and did graduate work in urban studies and civil engineering. He obtained a doctoral degree in Technical Science from the Swiss Federal Institute of Technology. Among Calatrava's notable structures are the Stadelhofen Railway Station in Zurich; the Airport Railway Station of 1994 in Lyon, France; the Kuwait Pavilion, Expo '92, in Seville, Spain; the BCE Place Gallery and Square of 1992 in Toronto, Canada; and the Alamillo Bridge of 1992 in Seville.

Calatrava was deeply influenced by Maillart's ability to design structurally without compromising on aesthetics. Maillart had demonstrated, as his design progressed on bridges, that their aesthetics could be refined by reworking the structure until it was most efficient.

Calatrava's design is often based on organic forms; and he found great potential in concrete by imitating them. He was influenced by Antonio Gaudi to whom form and function should co-exist and not follow each other. One of Calatrava's contributions is his unusual ability to merge structuralism and symbolism; that is, achieving architectural space through ordering and geometrical manipulation of structure and communicating a meaning to space through combining structure, imagery, and form. He uses forms derived from nature. For instance, to convey a feeling of lightness and flight, Calatrava designs forms recalling nature's airborne creatures. He derives his structures in imitation of the structure within the wings of live birds and insects. His structures are thin and efficient but he would not compromise his original intentions of symbolism. In this, he follows an artist's approach by sketching an original scheme, turning it into three-dimensional conceptual models, then reworking and refining them. A few schemes retaining the initial intent constant are developed. Next comes the structural studies, the constructability of the project is investigated, and a final design emerges. His goal is to produce a building in which its structural system and its aesthetics mutually accommodate each other.

The Railway Station at Lyon is a good illustration of Calatrava's work. The roof structure is sheathed with a membrane designed as a shell, similar to the wings of an insect. The main hallways employ repetitive elements; they portray a sense of continuity. The angled piers supporting the roof are designed to match the flow of forces and to provide maximum stability. The corners and edges of the supporting frames are curved and smooth and create a visual effect.

Another Calatrava project, the Alamillo Bridge, uses a cable-stayed system in which a series of straight cables intermittently support a rigid horizontal member. The cables radiate from a common mast, avoiding complicated curved cables that are difficult to construct in bridge design. The bridge can be viewed as "static motion," giving the effect that something moving has been captured on film. The bridge depicts a heartful sense of balance and a delicate equilibrium. It is a beauty to behold. Calatrava's architecture is beautiful spatially with structure trimmed to barely achieve the desired strength and integrity.

Among these pioneers of structural art, Khan is the principal structural artist in tall building design. Since tall buildings are so large and of enormous complexity, Khan is unique in having to deal courageously with the ferocious wind forces that become more and more critical as the structure reaches so profoundly into the sky. It must be emphasized that he gradually turned into a structural artist through his interaction with and admiration for other professionals and by combining technical genius with aesthetic sensitivity and humanistic ideals. He did not want to create structural art simply for structure's sake (that is, on the rational basis of his structures), but because of his adoration of art as a motivation force for creative design.

Like Nervi, Calatrava uses ribs in his structures. Calatrava, like Khan and Nervi, wants to express his structure and is very much concerned about the creation of aesthetically pleasing forms. Calatrava starts design with a fixed aesthetic objective in mind and determines the best structural system that will integrate with that. Khan, on the other hand, started with a structural system that is correct in its form and then would seek the appropriate aesthetics to match that form. Whereas Khan was conscious about the simplicity of force flow in his structures, Calatrava seems to be preoccupied with animal skeletons and other organic forms in which it is often difficult to visualize the complex force flow patterns. Calatrava was educated both as an architect and an engineer. He is primarily an architect which Khan was not and he never claimed to be. Whereas Calatrava has full control of design, Khan had the difficult task of convincing his architectural peers of his ideas.

Khan had no formal academic training in architecture unlike the other structural artists mentioned here. He developed his aesthetic interests and judgement through his sheer innate understanding of the wholeness of building projects. He was, at the same time, a visionary and a pragmatist. He never intended to limit his creative efforts in only one direction. This is why he was able to evolve into a master builder even without a rigorous architectural education.

Peter Rice, an eminent contemporary structural engineer with Ove Arup, who then started his own practice in Paris in the 1980s and continued to work with Ove Arup as a consultant, was similar in spirit to Khan. Like Khan, Rice had been influential in helping many renowned architects all over the world in realizing their design goals. He is an epitome of collaboration between a creative structural engineer and architects. Rice is known for his in-depth philosophy on the nature of materials and for utilizing their attributes to the fullest of their potential. Some of his prominent projects are the Centre Pompidou in Paris, the Sydney Opera House, Lloyd's of London Redevelopment in London, Football Stadium in Bari, Italy, Pavilion of the Future at Expo '92, Seville and the Menil Museum in Houston. His structural vision, like Khan's, was largely instrumental in shaping the architecture in Europe today. In striking similarity with Khan, Rice was fond of poetry, philosophy and mathematics and had a wide range of hobbies.

The notable architect Eero Saarinen might be contrasted with Khan with regard to education. Saarinen was an architect by training but had structural vision. This is demonstrated by the Dulles Airport at Chantilly, Virginia, and his famous arch in downtown St. Louis, Missouri. In the Dulles Airport terminal, the inverted arch of the concrete roof deck restrains the cables in the roof. The sculpted outward-leaning concrete columns counterbalance the inward pull of the roof, and this static balance is visually evident. In a similar vein, Bruce Graham also belongs to this category of architects with structural vision. As we noted before, he was formally educated as an architect but he demonstrated his great intuitive understanding of structural systems while designing many of his buildings.

Although Khan engineered the Sears Tower and the Hancock Center in steel because of their enormous heights, his preference for concrete—like that of most structural artists—in which the art of structure can be better articulated, is not a secret and is amply demonstrated in many of his other projects. While predicting the future of high-rise buildings, he wrote (Khan, 1972a):

> Concrete is a moldable material and its character leads to many unusual forms, while retaining high efficiency in construction. It is through these newer forms that concrete probably will find its use in future ultra-highrise buildings for offices and housing in those urban areas of the world where steel is relatively expensive. Form may follow function, but certainly it can also give strength through shaping the entire building into structurally efficient and stable overall shapes."

He continued:

> The character of concrete as a plastic material naturally leads to different forms and shapes for ultra-highrise buildings than those of steel. One of these promising future forms could be a single cylinder or square tube of concrete wall from which residential and office complexes project. These projections could be on either side of the hollow tube.

He finally remarked:

> One thing becomes clear: the moldability of concrete has almost limitless possibilities in form and shape, and can lead to the concept of a megastructure in which various kinds of multi-use buildings can be planned to create the 24 hr exciting environment.

Needless to say, many supertall buildings have been built in concrete since then. Khan saw the greatest potential for concrete for tall and slender apartment buildings where the width has to be limited to about 90 ft. (27.4m). The disadvantages of slenderness for such buildings taller than about 700 ft. (213.4m) could be circumvented by curving the "entire shape of the building in the form of a folded plate, a channel or a fluted shape." He suggested that it would be necessary to "create an equivalent thin plate out of each exterior face of the building." This can be achieved with "closely spaced columns on each face of the building, connected by relatively deep spandrel beams running along the facade" (Khan, 1972a).

Beyond and underneath all the intricate issues dealing with the engineering and architecture of tall buildings, Khan had a deep appreciation of the social and psychological aspects of design. He never wanted to take architectural design away from the architect. He simply indulged to it and thus could contribute to the grand scheme of things. Billington (1983) succinctly clarified this point well when he wrote:

Sometimes the architect is thought to be like the symphony conductor, directing all the instruments and shaping the results to his own vision. Khan, by that analogy, is like a great pianist, playing a concerto with his architectural partner conducting the orchestra. The concerto obviously makes no sense without the orchestra; but it only becomes transcendental when the soloist is a great artist.

Khan will always be remembered for his tubular form for tall buildings, Maillart for his bridges and flat slabs, Nervi for his ribbed vaults and domes, and Candela for his smooth ribless hyperbolic paraboloid vaults and shells. Nervi counted on ribs for stiffness; Maillart counted on arch action; Candela on compound curvatures; and Khan on three-dimensional tubular action. Like the other great innovators and form-givers discussed here, Khan was indeed a watchful observer of nature, a creator of forms, a believer in the building's natural strength; and above all, a devoted structural artist among structural artists.

chapter **12** # THE TALL BUILDING COUNCIL AND OTHER AFFILIATIONS

"Fazlur Khan was a true giant in the tall-buildings field, and he was a perfect representative of the Council on Tall Buildings and Urban Habitat. The Council's central attribute is that it is interdisciplinary and international. Dr. Khan transcended all the usual engineer/architect disciplinary distinctions, and he was international in his outlook."

—R. Shankar Nair (*BAGC*, 1998)

172 172

172 172

The above statement is part of a message sent on the occasion of dedication of a street corner in Chicago to Khan on June 16, 1998. Nair became the Chairman of the Council on Tall Buildings and Urban Habitat (CTBUH) in 1997. He referred to Khan as "a perfect representative" of the Council. Fazlur Rahman Khan was interdisciplinary and international in outlook, and that is exactly what the Council stands for. Khan was associated with a number of professional organizations and was very active in several of them. Because of his keen interest and involvement in tall buildings, he had a special role in the Council.

CTBUH is an international organization dedicated to research and dissemination of information related to tall buildings and their impact on the urban environment. The members of the Council are professional specialists in the areas of planning, designing, building, and operating tall buildings. The Council does not promote tall buildings, but where such buildings are

172 172

173 173
173 173

173 173
173 173

173 173
173 173

feasible as a solution to urban needs it encourages the use of the latest information and makes it available to its membership and other interested parties. The Council's Headquarters are located at Lehigh University in Bethlehem, Pennsylvania.

The Council fulfills its mission of technology transfer through publications, congresses and conferences worldwide, and its databases and membership resources are intended to provide answers to questions. It is sponsored by a number of professional societies, that include the International Association of Bridge and Structural Engineering (IABSE), American Society of Civil Engineers (ASCE), American Institute of Architects (AIA), American Planning Association (APA), International Union of Architects (IUA), American Society of Interior Designers (ASID), Japan Structural Consultants Association (JSCA), Urban Land Institute (ULI), and International Federation of Interior Designers (IFID). It functions through topical committees organized into eight groups.

A major strength of CTBUH is its series of monographs published periodically. The monographs are prepared by the topical committees and are aimed at documenting the state-of-the-art of various aspects of tall buildings and the urban habitat. The first five monograph volumes were published by ASCE during 1978-81. This was followed by the McGraw-Hill Series after the Steering Group of the Council decided to publish monographs prepared by individual topical committees rather than groups. As Chairman of the Council's Committee 30 - Architecture, I was actively involved in the preparation of a monograph on tall building architecture during 1990-95, and found it to be a remarkable experience. I found it gratifying to be able to contact and work with committee members and contributors to the monograph from around the world. Such contacts coupled with the tasks of compilation and editing of the book made me more informed of the architectural trends and the local socio-cultural traditions of the various regions of the world. Unquestionably, these aspects and the Council's World Congresses, where I interacted with prominent architects and engineers of the world, offered me an opportunity to broaden my horizon and stay informed about up-to-date knowledge and ideas worldwide. Further, my frequent contacts with Lynn S. Beedle, the founding father of the Council, who is highly revered internationally, enriched my understanding of issues and widened my vision at both professional and personal levels.

Another major strength of the Council is the holding of World Congresses at intervals of about five years in major cities of the world. The World Congresses and international conferences draw people from different countries and offer an opportunity for exchanging ideas.

The Council also maintains a high-rise building database. This website contains statistics of more than 8,000 buildings around the world. The Council has now grown into a major international organization with affiliations all over the world.

Behind all this is Lynn S. Beedle, a university distinguished professor at Lehigh University and the Director Emeritus of the Council. He served as Director until he retired in December, 1999. He directed the university's Fritz Engineering Laboratory for 24 years until 1984. Beedle is internationally known for his structural steel research, but perhaps more so for his great networking abilities and human relationship skills and has been continually devoted to the Council's mission since its inception in 1969. In fact, CTBUH is the brainchild of Beedle. Fazlur Khan had also been actively involved in it from its early days. Beedle and Khan worked together in the Council, where Khan was instrumental in defining some of the Council's tasks and criteria on tall buildings.

Regarding the birth of the Council, Beedle (1992) recalls:

> It all started with the IABSE.... The afternoon of Friday, September 13, 1968, at the 8th Congress of the IABSE in New York. Professor H. Beer of Austria was summarizing the theme 'Tall Steel Buildings', and I was struck by the significant tall building research he was describing. This research was not being coordinated or evaluated in a form useful to the designer. It spoke of the need for an international effort to bring information together.

In February, 1969, at a meeting of the US Group of IABSE in New Orleans, Elmer Timby sought suggestions for a topic that would lay the basis of bringing together professionals from overseas and result in fruitful exchanges of ideas. The notion of preparing and updating of a monograph that would offer a "focus for continuing exchange" was immediately implanted. It was agreed that a "Joint Committee on Tall Buildings" would be formed formalizing a joint activity between IABSE and ASCE. Approval by both these organizations came in 1970. National Science Foundation (NSF) funding was approved and the Headquarters was established at Lehigh University. The formation for such a Joint Committee was justified by the increasing urban population throughout the world requiring more high-rise buildings, the question of livability and quality of life, and avoidance of unnecessary wastage of precious natural resources by cost-effective construction. By this time mounting socio-economic pressures started demand for more efficient land use to create a more desirable urban habitat. Khan was very much involved in the founding of the Joint Committee and was a member of its first Steering Group.

Khan had much to do with formulating the philosophy of the Council. Of particular importance was his leadership in the Joint Committee's discussion of the first criteria defining a building, a tall building and the height of a tall building.

At an important Steering Group meeting during the early stage of the committee activity, the question "What is a tall building?" was addressed. Fazlur Khan and Les Robertson debated this question vigorously to seek an official definition of tall buildings. It was decided to define a tall building like this: "A tall building is not defined by its height or number of stories. Rather, the important criterion is whether or not the design is influenced by some aspects of 'tallness'. It is a building whose height creates different conditions than those that exist in common buildings of a certain region or period." Such a formal definition was essential before the work of a monograph on tall buildings could be started. As a practical matter, the Council concentrates on buildings 10 or more stories in height, although users of the Council's database will find a shorter building—primarily when it is the only one in the region.

The above definition of tall buildings was further refined and presented in the 1981 monograph titled *Planning and Environmental Criteria of Tall Buildings* in which it is stated in the *Foreword* that a tall building "is a building in which 'tallness' strongly influences planning, design, and use. It is a building whose height creates different conditions in the design, construction, and operation from those that exist in 'common' buildings of a certain region and period."

In 1976, the "Joint Committee" under the leadership of Khan changed its name to the Council on Tall Buildings and Urban Habitat. The reason for this change was the participation of additional organizations (such as AIA and APA) that reflected its broader scope. Along with a few others, Khan was the prime mover in shifting the Joint Committee to its new name. The word "international" was not included in this name, although the Council is an international organization. I have been involved with the Council since 1990, and I found that somewhat awkward since I have to always explain to people who hear about it the first time that it is an international organization. I have found people referring to it occasionally as the International Council on Tall Buildings and Urban Habitat. I brought this up once to Beedle, who consulted with the then chairman of the Council, Gilberto do Valle, and responded to me by saying that this matter was once deliberated by Khan and others and they felt the title was appropriate without the word "international."

The Council had originally been concerned with research on engineering aspects, since Beedle, Khan, Robertson, and its several other founders and early proponents were structural engineers. It soon became clear that architecture, planning, and other disciplines could not be excluded when discussing tall buildings in an urban context. Thus other architectural, planning, and interior design organizations were invited to join the Council in 1973, and by 1976 a number of such organizations became sponsoring societies of the Council. In 1979, CTBUH was admitted to UNESCO as a non-governmental organization.

With the dedication and untiring leadership efforts of Beedle, two major conferences were held, one in Bled, Yugoslavia in May 1971, and the other in Chicago in November 1971. These meetings were held as preparatory to the first major international conference (now called World Congress) at Lehigh University in August, 1972. The conference in Bled, a holiday resort on a lake in the hills of Slovenia (then part of Yugoslavia) brought together specialists from all over the world to decide what the first monograph would entail. Each of the topical committees (26 at the time) reviewed abstracts of the state-of-the-art reports that would be presented at the meeting. The three days of the conference allowed the IABSE members and the delegates from the United States and other countries to know each other in the scenic environment of Bled. The meeting in Chicago in November was a follow-up one to this.

The First International conference at Lehigh University held from August 21-26, 1972, brought together more than 700 participants coming from 30 countries. The conference was run in six parallel sessions, and 27 pre-print volumes totalling more than 5,000 pages were available to participants. Later these were edited and published in a 5-volume set of Proceedings (a best-seller, according to ASCE). Towards the end of this conference, Beedle informed the participants that the 27 specialist committees that had organized the technical sessions would prepare a monograph. The monograph containing a total of 4,478 pages dealing with topics covering the design of tall buildings in a comprehensive manner also comprised five volumes successively over the period 1978-1982. It took over nine years of intensive compilation and editing to produce the complete set of this historical monograph by the Council. The "Lehigh Conference" was thus the trend-setter for the Council for future Congresses and the original monograph paved the way for the Council to become a unique and firmly established international organization dealing exclusively with the issues related to tall buildings. From 1972 to 1998, five World Congresses and over 70 conferences were held in different cities of the world that were either organized or co-sponsored by the Council. Khan participated in the Second World Congress held from November 21-25, 1977 in Paris, France, in which he played a prominent role. He also attended many of the conferences, such as the ones from January 14-17, 1974 in Cairo, Egypt, and from October 7-9, 1975 in Athens, Greece. He actively participated in a two-week Council seminar from July 7-20, 1980 in China held in the cities of Beijing, Guangzhau, Hongzhau, and Shanghai. Before his death in March, 1982, he was planning to participate as a guest speaker in the Council's Asian Regional Conference on Tall Buildings and Urban Development from August 17-20, 1982 in Kuala Lumpur, Malaysia.

The Council expanded its scope of publications by aiming for a monograph by each topical committee organized within its eight groups. Eight have already been published and more are on their way. In addition to the monographs, the Council has published proceedings of its conferences and Congresses together with additional publications. It has an impressive record to date of publishing more than 100 proceedings, monographs, and reports. This has been accomplished entirely through the voluntary efforts of some of the world's eminent tall building and urban habitat professionals. It also produced two educational videos. It regularly publishes a newsletter, *The Times*, outlining the activities of the Council and the latest developments in the realm of tall buildings and urban habitat. An electronic journal titled *CTBUH Review* was launched, in May, 2000, by the Council to stimulate scholarly discourse and record research results and case studies.

The Council enjoys a high level of respect from the professional community. Beedle and the leadership staff of the Council are held in high esteem by building professionals and academics around the world. I myself have been privileged to work with the council in the capacity of Committee Chairman and later as a Group Leader. I have always been impressed by Beedle's untiring efforts and leadership. He has a very fertile mind and an excellent memory. His ability to remember people's names, times, and places is exceptional. He can absorb and transmit information with unparalleled speed and efficiency. Beedle's, the Council staff's, and other Council leaders' efforts have made the Council the source for information on tall buildings, recognized by the media, the public, and even the *Guinness Book of World Records*.

Several new issues that were initially included in a limited manner were added to the agenda of the Council. The structural design technology has advanced so dramatically, thanks to the innovations and breakthroughs by Khan and others, that architectural and environmental issues have now become more critical. The Council now serves not only the professionals in various disciplines, but also the academic community nationally and internationally.

Moreover, the technological revolution of the nineteenth century resulted in a materialistic philosophy of life and hence in excessive utilitarianism and insensitivity toward the value and essence of beauty and rights and aspirations of the common people. In the twentieth century the two World Wars caused tremendous devastation of the built environment and resulted in economic backsliding in many parts of the world. Following World War II, however, there was enormous scientific, technological, and economic progress and a new age of awareness and understanding arose about the quality of life as the public became more conscious about the environment and socio-psychological aspects of urban life. A move towards humanizing the built environment started. The focus is now on better working and living environments thereby improving the social and health effects, and on sustainable development.

Khan predicted as early as 1971 that 100-story buildings would soon become commonplace and by 1980 the usual height of skyscrapers would increase from the 30- to 50-story range to a range of 40- to 70-stories. This is evident because of the exploding population worldwide. Thus sky-high living and working are becoming inevitable although some social and environmental groups are questioning the proliferation of tall buildings in major cities. There is an urgency in addressing the socio-economic and philosophical issues that surround the city and its infrastructure. The Council has expanded its focus on this—the urban habitat side of its mission. The creation in 1999 of a new group in the Council, namely "Urban Systems," and the adoption by the Council of a theme "Cities and the Third Millennium" for its Sixth World Congress in Melbourne, Australia in March 2001, clearly point to this trend. However, its emphasis on the technical aspects of tall buildings is still intact. The Council has essentially evolved into an international organization with a multi-disciplinary strategy to tall building design in the urban context. And this is what Khan would always emphasize in his speeches and writings.

Another important issue in which Khan was directly involved is the definition of height of tall buildings. In the early stage of the Council during the early 1970s, following Khan's suggestion, the criterion for the height was established as the distance from the street level at main entrance to the top of the structure. This definition of height was used as the criterion in 1996, for declaring the Petronas Towers in Kuala Lumpur as the tallest building of the world by the Council.

In addition to being a member of the Council's Executive Committee and its Steering Group, Khan also served on some other important committees of the Council. He attended a number of committee meetings in New York, Washington, DC, and other places until his death. He was the Chairman of the Implementation Committee and a member of the Finance Committee, which was Standing Committee S7. Further, he was twice elected to be the Group Coordinator for Group SC - Systems and

Concepts. In that capacity he led the editorial work of the 1980 Monograph Volume SC - Systems and Concepts. In addition, he was a member of the Editorial Committee of the Council.

Khan became the Chairman of CTBUH in 1979 and continued in that capacity until his death in 1982. During this period, he gave his positive and purposive leadership of the Council. Because of his association with the Council since its inception, he had a thorough understanding of the Council's role and mission, and was able to steer its activities in the right direction. In collaboration with Beedle, he left a lasting impact on the Council's present and future objectives. Following the death of Khan the Council collected all the available speeches on Khan delivered at the memorial session and compiled the "Khan Tributes." Beedle was instrumental in founding the "Institute for the Study of the High-Rise Habitat" at Lehigh University in 1982, which published *Technique and Aesthetics in the Design of Tall Buildings* in 1986, covering the Proceedings of the Fazlur R. Khan session on "Structural Expression in Buildings." Khan acted as an advisor to the Institute. The High-Rise Institute no longer exists.

The Council has grown rapidly over the last three decades. 27 topical committees in 3 groups have become 68 committees in 8 groups. Its height criteria are referred to world wide. Khan's legacy continues at the Council.

▲ ▼

In addition to the Tall Building Council, Khan was affiliated with several other professional associations. He was a Fellow of both ASCE and the American Concrete Institution (ACI). He was a member of the American Institute for Steel Construction (AISC) and had served on the AISC Beta Factor Task Committee on LRFD. He was the Chairman of the AISC Committee on Tall Building Study until his death, and had been very active on this committee. He was also the Chairman of a Special Task Committee under the AISC Specifications Committee—a position to which he was appointed in January, 1979. The Committee was charged with the task of reviewing possible areas of improvement of the AISC specifications and commentary in light of the monograph on steel structures of CTBUH.

He believed in serving on committees and contributing to the profession through committee activities and emphasized this point to others. Through committee work one could stay on top of things and interact with others interested in the same area. He felt strongly that information, once learned and gathered, should be put together in a form that could be used by others. This is what he believed committees need to strive for.

Khan was a member of IABSE, American Welding Society (AWS), and Prestressed Concrete Institute (PCI). He was elected to the National Academy of Engineering (NAE) in 1973. The NAE was founded in 1964 and it operates under the National Academy of Sciences that was incorporated by a Congressional act and signed by President Abraham Lincoln in 1863. The NAE is, however, a private, independent, non-profit organization of peer-elected membership. Membership in the NAE is the highest professional honor an engineer can receive. These members must have been instrumental in bringing about most of the major engineering accomplishments and innovations prior to their admission to this prestigious academy.

He became a member of The Chicago Architectural Club and was elected President of the club just before his death. He served on the Advisory Committee for Aga Khan Program on Islamic Architecture at Harvard University and MIT. Derek C. Bok, President of Harvard University and Jerome B. Wiesner, President of MIT invited him in August, 1979 to serve on the prestigious Advisory Committee for the Aga Khan Program when it was first established. The broad purpose of the Aga Khan Program is to ensure the continuity of research and teaching in Islamic art and architecture and to develop ways of furthering the architectural tradition of the Muslim world and of making contemporary Islamic architecture more responsive to values and aesthetics of Islamic culture. Khan was granted the advisory position because of his role in the design of the Haj Terminal and the master planning of the Makkah University and because of his deep sensitivity to Islamic culture, art, and architecture.

Khan left his legacy in another way on the Chicago skyline. His vision of Chicago as the birthplace of tall buildings and his leadership role of the second Chicago school convinced him to spearhead, together with a few others, a separate committee on high-rise dealing with the tradition, challenges, and prospects of tall building construction in Chicago. He helped in founding the Chicago Committee on High-Rise Buildings and was its prime mover. The committee is still active today and is an affiliated group of CTBUH. He was also a member of the Mayor's Advisory Committee on Building Code Amendments for the City of Chicago.

—chapter **13** **A LOVER OF HUMANITY**

A LOVER OF HUMANITY

"The technical man must not be lost in his own technology. He must be able to appreciate life; and life is art, drama, music, and most importantly, people."

—Fazlur R. Kahn (*ENR*, 1972)

180
180
180
180
180
180
180
180
180
180

These are the words of Khan that are inscribed on the memorial plaque that was installed in the main lobby of Khan's "final work," Onterie Center, in Chicago after its completion in 1986. This plaque was dedicated to his memory by Michael T. Woelffer, Director of the Illinois Department of Commerce and Community Affairs, on December 14, 1983 on the occasion of the groundbreaking ceremony. The plaque was designed and made by the French-born artist Juan Gardy Artigas. The full inscription originally intended on the plaque, which was later slightly modified and reconfigured, read:

"The technical man must not be lost in his own technology.
He must be able to appreciate life,
and life is art,
drama, music, and most importantly, people."

Dr. Fazlur Rahman Khan

IN MEMORIUM
Dr. Fazlur Rahman Khan
(4/3/29 - 3/27/82),

world-renowned structural engineer, whose lasting
contributions to architecture illuminated all our
paths. We dedicate this plaque, with gratitude to
Dr. Khan for his leadership in engineering practice
which culminated in this structure, Onterie Center
— his final work
Gratefully,
James R. Thompson
Governor, State of Illinois
Michael T. Woelffer
Director, Illinois Department of Commerce
and Community Affairs
Chandra K. Jha
for PSM International Corporation
Bruce J. Graham
for Skidmore, Owings and Merrill

Khan was a staunchly technical man. He was also a structural artist who had a deep appreciation of architecture and aesthetics. But unlike many others of his stature and technical competence, he was also a humanist and a philosopher. He was deeply concerned with the interests and values of mankind and could easily reach out to people. He touched many lives.

In a statement made on the occasion of the dedication ceremony of "Fazlur R. Khan Way" at the corner of West Jackson Boulevard and South Franklin Street by the City of Chicago, on June 16, 1998, part of the message of Chandra Jha was (BAGC, 1998):

> When people wanted to know about his monumental buildings, he did not talk about concrete, steel or technical design but talked about his co-design partner, clients and how that particular solution came about. He always talked about the human aspects of design or solution. When it was not even heard of or popular, he conducted experiments on weekends at the Museum of Science and Industry to understand people's perception of motion in a tall building. He struggled to make the building a more humane and livable space. That was his way—Fazlur R. Khan Way.

Although Khan is known for the structural design of skyscrapers, and he felt that tall buildings were "tremendously exciting," he never lost sight of the human aspects associated with tall building design. He was never enslaved by structural engineering. Economy was important, of course, but an overriding motivation for seeking new structural systems was the "social and visual impact of buildings." He recognized that typical high-rise buildings could have some adverse effects on public spaces because of their shadows and their channeling of wind; he believed that an increase in the volume of buildings in a city must logically be compensated by an expansion of the public domain. His response was to go tall with his structures, leaving maximum public space for a surrounding plaza. He and his design partner, Bruce Graham, gave close attention to what happened at "ground level where people and a city's facilities come together." They wanted to ensure that public or semi-public interiors at street level were provided in the buildings to create an exciting environment and a lively interaction between the plaza and the street life.

During his presentations on high-rise buildings, he inevitably brought up issues of 'people' that were so close to his heart. He presented buildings as part of the urban fabric: "skylines in the daytime, the glow of lighted buildings at night." *ENR* (1972) wrote in this regard,

> Invariably, when Khan lectures on high-rise buildings, he first goes through a brief slide-supplemented history of tall buildings, and then explains the details of some of his innovations. Suddenly, shots of crowded, smog-covered Chicago and New York City appear on the screen. Khan then cuts to shots of buildings with tree-filled, people-filled plazas. While this is going on Khan expounds on how designers have got to face up to urban problems and let their consciences push them in that direction.

181 181
181 181
181 181

Apart from Khan's outstanding achievements in structural engineering, what really makes people remember and respect him today is his concern for people and his motivation for designing building structures for the benefit of the society. People from all walks of life who have come in contact with him have sensed his altruistic motives; they have been impressed by the depth and breadth of his humanity. "Whatever you do it must be useful to people for whom you are doing it," he told me once, "whether you are writing a theoretical paper or designing buildings for clients." His own work was all people-centered. In 1981 I wrote a paper on the mechanics of masonry for the Canadian Congress of Applied Mechanics held at the University of Moncton in Canada. I showed Khan a draft of the paper and sought his comments. After reviewing it, he commented, "This is good. But try to concentrate on practical aspects of brick masonry. For example, if you can come up with a better shape or size of brick that gives more strength of masonry, makes it easy to build a wall, and is economical, it will be more useful to people." His emphasis was clearly on "people," the end users.

Khan appreciated life. He was content with himself and enjoyed working and living. Every day was a good day to him. He saw only the good side of people's nature. Despite his demanding schedule, he found time to show his warmth and concern to his family, friends, and colleagues. "The miracle of this man, Fazlur Khan, was his wholeness and his intense interest in people," said Beedle (1986), "It reflected itself in his work and projects." Beedle noted that the location of Khan's office in Chicago and the position of his desk told much. At both Inland Steel and the 33 West Monroe buildings, where SOM's offices were located at different times, he arranged to have an office near the windows, and he positioned his desk so that frequently he could see one of the busiest spots of downtown Chicago, the plaza of the First National Bank Building. He did this because he was concerned not only with the building but also with its role as part of the urban scene. I know that he enjoyed the view. Once when I visited him in his office, I found him sketching the First National Bank Building and its surroundings. He probably wanted to capture the scene he loved during a moment of reflection.

Khan was a person with great human relationship skills. He understood people's problems—even trivial ones—and had a unique way of addressing them. He could resolve small problems between his associates and co-workers using his wit. Joseph Colaco related to me such a story. In the early 1960s, SOM employees had to clock in. Colaco disliked this strict regulation. Occasionally late to work, he became frustrated and decided to find employment elsewhere. When he told Khan of his intentions, Khan persuaded him to drop this idea and tactfully handled the matter. Shortly afterward, to Colaco's relief, the clocking-in was discontinued. It is not known whether Khan had any influence on this decision by SOM.

David Wickersheimer told of a secretary at SOM who complained of headaches that she got only when she worked at her desk. Elsewhere, she felt fine. SOM administrators who investigated the matter thought her headaches were because of floor vibrations or "sea-sickness" due to the building's movement. Floor vibrations were tested without any definitive conclusion.

Other investigations also failed. Khan decided to investigate it himself and to sit in the secretary's chair to do his own work. Soon he found himself sick. Through the window he saw a billboard directly outside that featured a large arm moving back and forth. He turned the desk around and the problem was solved.

Khan could relate to people of every level because of his politeness, his simplicity of character, and his unassuming nature. He had no pretensions. Jane Quinn (formerly Wiehn), his secretary during his last few years, knew him well. Following Khan's death in 1982, she said Khan was the "sweetest boss" she'd ever had and doubted if she would ever get his equal. In 1998, when I met and conversed with her about Khan, she reiterated that and said, "He was calm, sweet, kind, and funny." She continued, "I had great respect for him, he was always a perfectly sweet and gentle man, and so unassuming even with all of his degrees, awards and fame. Everyone adored him and recognized him as the man and the genius that he was." Jane added, "I used to make all his travel arrangements and organize his articles. Never did I see him angry or raise his voice."

Even though Khan was aggressive professionally with architects and contractors, he was still soft-spoken and pleasant. With others, he was self-effacing and listened attentively. He made the other person the center of his universe. He inquired of building custodians about how to clean a floor nicely and asked women for recipes. He could communicate with anyone regardless of age, color, social class, or sex. Once on an airplane ride, he sat next to an old woman. He felt at ease to strike up a conversation and asked her what type of detergent she used for washing her clothes. He could shift easily from the abstract to the practical and from the surreal to the down-to-earth. He could adjust to new environments readily.

Nadine Post, Staff Senior Writer of *ENR* recalled how Khan left a deep impression on her even though she met him only once. During a meeting, she sat next to Khan, who wanted to know about her, showing his utmost care for someone whom he had not met before. When one person in the group attacked him with some negative remarks about tall buildings, she noticed how Khan gracefully responded to him. During the course of the meeting, another *ENR* staff member took longer time than usual in the restroom. Post noted how Khan got terribly concerned and started enquiry about his wellness.

He connected with people very quickly. People with marriage problems and financial troubles sought his help and he would gladly help them, guide them and give them good advice. He knew how to make others feel comfortable. He knew how to converse with his architectural partners in office, and how to speak with farmers, students, or new immigrants to America.

Sabah Al-Rayes of Al-Rayes Group in Kuwait recounted to me how Khan treated him as if he was Khan's intimate friend. When they first met in the early 1970s in connection with a mid-rise hotel project in Kuwait that Khan had worked on, he felt as if Khan knew him for many years. "I found him a very loving and enjoyable person," said Al-Rayes. In the summer of 1980, when Al-Rayes was in Chicago, Khan personally gave his ten-year old son and eight-year old daughter a tour of the Sears Tower. Khan held the two on his two sides with his outstretched arms and explained to them during the tour how the building was designed and built. He communicated his ideas in such a simple language that they had no difficulty in understanding him. The two children were so deeply impressed by Khan's explanation that both eventually became architects. Al-Rayes emotionally recalled how he felt when he heard the news of Khan's sudden death while at work in his office. "I was devastated. I felt I had a death in the family", he said with a trembling voice.

Doug Stoker, who worked and interacted with Khan on many projects (including the Sears Tower and the Haj Terminal), considered him a "father figure." Khan encouraged and helped Stoker to pursue a doctoral degree at Carnegie-Mellon University. Stoker described Khan as "incredibly gentle and bright" and someone who had a "serene confidence in himself."

He also had a great sense of humor. Jane observed, "he would tell a lot of jokes and was a good storyteller." He captivated audiences with interesting stories. The first day I met him in his office, he spoke with me for a full hour and offered me tea. He not only talked about SOM, engineering, architecture and tall buildings, but also about Bangladesh, people, and expatriates in America. He even made some jokes. He was enjoying the conversation so much that his secretary came twice to remind him of an impending meeting. At the end of our conversation, he walked with me to the door to say goodbye. I could feel his sincere warmth, and when I came out of the office I marveled that a partner of SOM could take one hour of his busy schedule to spend with a junior engineer.

Just being around Khan was a pleasant experience because his warmth radiated and touched all he met. He looked at people as friends and believed in their goodness. That includes the heads of departments to janitors, male and female, people of all ages, ethnic backgrounds and nationalities. He believed that however people made their living, they stood on their own merits. He never discriminated against others and did not feel himself discriminated against by others.

When dealing with a special issue, he was always well prepared regardless of whether it was technical or social. People approached him for a variety of favors. He never dismissed them as inappropriate. He went out of his way to extend help to the needy, he gracefully put up with those who exploited his amiable nature. Some who were desperate and in distress could approach him and secure help morally as well. He never mentioned his acts of kindness and philanthropies to anyone.

Regarding Khan's state of preparedness, Colaco recounted the following story to me. He asked Khan to raise the toast at his marriage ceremony and to say a few words on the occasion. At first, Khan declined politely, saying he did not have experience in such things. When Colaco insisted because of his deep respect for him, Khan agreed. Being a Muslim, Khan was uneasy about what he should say at a Christian wedding. He consulted Christian ministers. But it was also a cross-cultural marriage (Colaco being from India and his wife from America); Khan prepared a thoughtful speech and delivered it at the wedding. According to Colaco, it had "a very philosophical and cultural theme." On the day of Khan's funeral, Liselotte told Colaco that he had given Khan a hard time on one occasion. Colaco was surprised and wanted to know when and what that was. She replied, "when you asked him to make the toast at your wedding." Liselotte must have seen Khan spending a lot of time preparing the speech. Whatever Khan did, he took it seriously.

Khan enjoyed travel. While most of his travel was for business or presentation of papers at conferences, he took advantage of such trips to learn about other cultures. He photographed buildings and their settings in many countries to record the spectrum of the human civilization in its totality. When visiting a new place, he reached out to learn all he could of its history, traditions, customs, and culture. He felt at home in every part of the world. To him all humankind was one. He had an unbounding appreciation of each individual.

Khan returned home from trips with a stock of pleasant thoughts. He would have conversed with local people, taking pictures with his camera that he always carried. He would inevitably carry a notebook with him to record his activities and observations. His notes contained as much vivid detail on indigenous customs and life as about buildings and monuments as noted by Lynn Beedle: "His description of an acrobatic performance. The highlights of an opera. His entry at a briefing about a housing project on a hot afternoon in China begins: 'At Briefing: six of my colleagues are sleeping' (and he records their names)" (*Khan Tributes*, 1982).

Returning from trips, he would show pictures and slides of people and culture, and not just of buildings and places. He viewed things with more sensitivity than most people. At a seminar by Khan that I attended at SOM's office following his China trip in 1980, he gave a slide presentation on the Chinese buildings, monuments, and sculptures; but his slides had the unusual quality of human scale—their dress, food habits and modes of transportation. He had photographed everyday people in the sidewalks, markets, parks and plazas, and he tied them together with commentary on their culture. With regard to the common belief that the Chinese government was an atrocious abuser of human rights, he pointed out that their police did not apparently carry firearms.

Khan loved classical music, especially music by Beethoven, and native Bengali music. The Bengali language, spoken by more than 200 million people in Bangladesh and in the province of West Bengal in India, has a rich heritage. During the Independence Movement of Bangladesh that began in 1971, *Time* magazine called Bengali, a "singsong language." The language had been immensely enriched by Rabindranath Tagore, a Nobel Prize Winner for literature and by Kazi Nazrul Islam. Poets and writers, they composed numerous songs with a wondrous musical quality. Khan was particularly fond of Tagore's writings, poems, and songs. He cherished the concept of unity for all of humanity, in the spirit espoused by Tagore. Even his handwriting in Bengali had Tagore's style. During travel, he constantly carried the collection of Tagore's songs called *Gitobitan*. As is common with many Bengalis, he would occasionally sing Tagore's songs with his family at the dining table before breakfast, lunch, and dinner. He deeply loved Tagore's songs, because these songs were replete with rhyme and rhythm, tones and melody, lyric and tune. They are distinguishable from other songs. Moreover, their themes of love, mysticism, spirituality, and nature—full to the uttermost with philosophical overtones resonated with his inner impulses and in his awareness of the world that

185

surrounded him. Occasionally, he organized or participated in *gaaner ashor* (musical assembly) of Tagore's songs with his friends during weekend evenings. Many remember him for his fine voice. One song he often sang to himself opened with:

Tomar holo shuru, amar holo shara
Tomaye amaye meelay emni bahey dhara

[This is your beginning and my end
The flow (of life) continues mixing both of us]

Khan took his professional work not just as a vehicle of self-fulfillment and success in his career, but as a service for the welfare of humanity. Khan thought of himself as a citizen of the world. A true internationalist, he kept up with current events. He was cultured and sensitive to ethnic differences. He knew that the size and character of living spaces in Hong Kong were significantly different from those in Saudi Arabia which were different from those in the Netherlands. Although, as is expected, he had a special affinity for his native country, Bangladesh, and his adopted country, America, he never felt restricted to geographic, racial, or religious boundaries. Even though his philosophy of life was man-centered, he also had a deep faith in the Divine. He went on the haj in Mecca in 1976. He could easily balance his outward concerns for the world and the society with his inward spirituality. Because of his concerns for people and their customs, if his work involved an unfamiliar culture, he would travel there before beginning to work at his office to study the old structures—both with regard to architecture and to structural systems—and to see firsthand the way people lived and worked. Beedle (1986) wrote, "It was my pleasure to be with him in the China Tall Building Seminar. In this two-week period he consistently demonstrated his interest first in the people and then in the structures that were created to accommodate them. He always came back at the end of a day of tours having absorbed the essence of the cultural factors involved in the particular day's activity."

Khan liked Chicago. He did not want an expensive house in an affluent suburb because he wanted to be close to his office and be part of the city. He lived at 3150 North Lake Shore Drive to get a full view of the downtown Loop and its skyline, and of Lake Michigan. He lived in an apartment to avoid the time-consuming chores of maintaining a house and yard. The city of Chicago matched his personality well.

He also loved America where he found outlet of his talents and where he could do freely what he dreamed of accomplishing in his profession. He was not restricted because he was foreign-born. "Look at Hancock Tower—a 100-million dollar project. I came up with an idea, and the people said okay. In another country, where they take a more conservative attitude, it might have been discouraged" (*Civil Engineering*, 1980). He went further: "Some countries have a more restrictive economic base, being mainly either socialistic or feudalistic/fascistic. Either way you must play a lot of politics. In the U.S., unless the job is a political appointment, a person is generally recognized on his merits—if you're good, you can make it."

Despite his enormous success in the United States, he never forgot his roots in the Indian subcontinent and his native country,

Bangladesh. He was proud of his Bengali and Muslim heritage as much as he was proud of being Asian and a national of his adopted country, America. He grew up in a deeply divided land. His people fought for independence from British colonialism, yet among themselves they were religiously and communally riven by differences. His "truly global humanity first took shape in his resistance—in the Bengal of the 1930s and '40s—to the constant pressure to narrow one's loyalties" said Ralph Nicholas of the University of Chicago. "Repudiating parochialism, he recognized the common humanity of all those who shared the motherland of Bengal. And although Bengal was divided in 1947 between India and Pakistan, he did not relinquish the sense that the whole Indic subcontinent was his homeland, that all its people were joint heirs with him of a rich and distinctive patrimony" (*Khan Tributes*, 1982).

While living in the city of Chicago, Fazlur Khan, the Muslim from Bengal, became a bosom friend of Chandra Jha, a Hindu from Bihar. These two became unfailing partners during Jha's leadership of the India League of America (ILA). They were like brothers devoted to meeting the needs and aspirations of the developing community of immigrants from the Indian subcontinent. Jha founded the ILA and got Khan involved in it as a director. Together they realized the commonality of the immigrants' children in America regardless of their origin in the Indian subcontinent. In later years they continued to serve on the Board of Directors of the ILA Foundation, the new name of ILA.

Jha met Khan in Chicago one day, by chance, and after striking up a brief conversation, liked him. He observed that Khan "did not talk about himself, what his education level was and what he did, but rather focused on philosophical issues and life in America as expatriates." Neither of them brought into their conversation the political problems of India and Pakistan. Their friendship was cemented as they came to know each other better.

Khan's vision for the Indian subcontinent was put to a severe test in March, 1971, when the military junta of Pakistan launched a brutal attack on his homeland and perpetrated atrocities against the civilian population there. Bengalis in North America were shattered by the news from their homeland and sought a sense of direction. During this catastrophe, Khan emerged as a calm, level-headed, confident leader around whom people could rally. People came to him, as to a "trusted elder brother," seeking counseling and leadership from him in understanding and overcoming the tragedy. Despite his heavy commitment to work in the midst of one of his busiest periods of professional life, he gave time, energy, and compassion selflessly, to this cause. He organized the Bengalis and their friends in America into the Bangladesh Defense League, a political organization, and the purely humanitarian Bangladesh Emergency Welfare Appeal. He presided over both of them. He raised funds for relief for the millions of refugees who fled to India from East Pakistan. He lobbied in Washington to convince the U.S. Congress and the Nixon Administration, who favored Pakistan, a U.S. ally, to discontinue shipment of arms to the Pakistani junta. He crowded into his living room—East Bengalis, West Bengalis, Muslims, and Hindus from other regions of the Indian subcontinent, and many Americans—for meetings. When he traveled on professional business, he invariably took the time to talk to

Bengalis and their supporters throughout North America and abroad about steps that would help secure the end of the armed repression of his country. He assisted innumerable of his countrymen, including many struggling students, who were stranded overseas during this period of uncertainty in their homeland. He gave unstintingly of himself and his personal resources to help develop in Bangladesh a society to assist in creating a respectable livelihood for everyone, including its abandoned women, poor farmers and fishermen. As Ralph Nicholas noted, "Probably no one who knew the masterful understatement of this leadership in the world of engineering and design would have doubted his capacity to handle the enormous responsibility thrust upon him by the Bangladesh crisis" (*Khan Tributes*, 1982). Justice Abu Sayeed Choudhury, the first President of independent Bangladesh wrote in his book *Probashe Mukti-Juddher Dinguli (Days of Liberation War in Foreign Lands)*, "Although Dr. Khan reached the zenith of his profession, yet he never forgot his roots. He led the Bangladeshis in America during the Liberation War and arranged meetings with Senators and Congressmen to apprise them of our War of Independence."

Khan was deeply touched by the plight of his fellow Bengalis in the hands of the Pakistani Army. When he saw a movie made of the military atrocities perpetrated on innocent civilians, he wept. He told Richard Kieler, Assistant Editor of the *ENR* magazine, "I feel very tragic about Bangladesh. The killing and the suffering there has affected me deeply" (*ENR*, 1972). His vision of brotherhood for the people of the East Indian race was dealt a severe blow, and it took time to heal his hurt. But realizing with his great wisdom that this crime against the Bengali people was committed by the Pakistani Army, he never expressed hatred or bitterness against the Pakistanis. With his forgiving nature, he tried to put it behind him once the war was over to concentrate on the betterment of life for the ordinary and disadvantaged people in the new nation of Bangladesh. After the repatriation of the millions of refugees, he focused on assisting the reconstruction of the country. He immediately moved to replace the interim organizations which he had created during the crisis with the establishment of the Bangladesh Foundation. Its objective was to help the needy and disadvantaged start small businesses and find other means of making a living. The new organization became a permanent legacy of his contribution to Bangladesh independence. He became its founding President and continued to lead it until his death. Following his death, his younger brother, Zillur Rahman Khan, Professor of Political Science at the University of Wisconsin, took his place. The Foundation continues his dream. After independence, Khan suggested that the new Bangladesh government change the name of their currency from "rupee" to the Bengali word "taka"; this was done.

In 1980, Khan became the founding president of the Bangladesh Association of Chicago, that brought together the small group of Bangladeshi families and students in Chicago on a social and cultural level. The first day I met Khan that year he told me of the association and invited me to its upcoming social event. Khan participated in the association activities with a passion and used to attend all the social events enjoying their Bengali songs, dances, and recitation of poems. He would enjoy himself very much during the performances. He would talk to all people freely without maintaining any distance from anyone. Every person he met quickly became his friend. Because of his unpretentious nature and approachability, unscrupulous people began to exploit the situation. On one occasion one man in particular persisted in asking for some business favors. Seeing how Khan was disturbed by the man's intrusions, I tried to moderate. Because of his gentleness and humility, however, Khan refused to reveal his annoyance.

At one event, I watched Khan talking to a six-year-old boy. From a distance, they looked like two friends having an intimate conversation. As I was nearby, Khan spoke to me and the boy ran to join his friends. Khan laughed, looked at me and commented, "Look, this guy has an infinite amount of energy."

He could relate well to women, who enjoyed conversing with him. He joked, then sought issues of interest to them. On one occasion, when one of his favorite Bengali dishes, *akhni polao* (rice pilaf with beef cooked in a special way), was served, he asked them how it was made. Actually, he cooked himself, entertaining friends with food he had personally prepared. Chester Siess recalled how Khan would prepare Sunday brunches to entertain his professional friends at his apartment. Jane Quinn related to me that at social and office parties, women "clustered around him." He charmed men and women alike with interesting and humorous stories. He had a pleasant and friendly way of talking with an individual or a group and he would never run out of words. His personal charm and charisma together with his excellent communication skill helped him in becoming a natural leader in a group.

Khan returned home to visit Bangladesh whenever he could. He gave seminars and connected with local engineering and architectural communities. He participated in preparing a Master Plan for Dhaka City; regrettably it was not implemented. He encouraged local builders, engineers, and architects to build high-rise structures to accommodate the problems of increasing population and congestion. He advised Mukit Hossain, a reputed Bangladeshi engineer to design the Secretariat building of the government as 21-story rather than 18-story. Based on initial studies, he suggested that buildings from 40 to 60 stories tall could safely be built in Dhaka. In 1979 the government of Bangladesh asked him to help design a 20-story World Trade Center Building in Dhaka, and to do a feasibility study on a large auditorium project. In 1980 he was consulted by Bashirul Haq and Associates, an architectural firm in Bangladesh, on a 20-story Bangladesh Chemical Industries Corporation office building for Dhaka. Haq, a reputed architect in Dhaka, who knew Khan well, recounted to me how Khan went out of his way to help him secure admission to a graduate program in architecture at a U.S. university. He expressed his deep gratitude to Khan for inspiring him and giving him support in many ways. About Khan's personality, he said, "He had an unassuming demeanor . . . a trait of character common to great people. He would not discuss technical issues at parties. He shunned mediocrity. I remember him for his humaneness."

Khan also advised Bangladesh Steel and Engineering Corporation for a 20-story office building on Airport Road, Dhaka. On November 12, 1977, at a meeting in Dhaka with sixteen local engineers, he offered a number of recommendations following a site visit. From the minutes of the meeting that M. Mujbur Rahman, Chief Engineer (retired) of the organization shared with me, it can be seen that Khan's recommendations ranged from site conditions and architectural functions to mechanical/ electrical and several structural requirements. He also suggested means of construction and the need for designing the building for seismic loading. He particularly stressed the need for overall planning of the Kawran Bazar Commercial Area where the building was located. In a letter to Rahman of August 28, 1978 after the foundation stone for the building was laid on July 26, he stated:

> . . . I have always been willing to help in the construction of a good quality high-rise building in Bangladesh and I do hope that our discussions in Dacca have enabled the architects and engineers to develop appropriate details of construction.

Khan helped the organization through his advisory role but refused to accept any kind of honorarium for his services.

The City of Dhaka now has many high-rise office and apartment buildings. Although tall buildings may cause occasional environmental problems, there are few alternatives because of crowding and exorbitant land prices. Enforcement of zoning and building code regulations is seriously needed to avoid the "canyon effect" and the creation of a "concrete jungle" in the city causing shortage of light and air. Such problems were a challenge to Khan. His love for Bangladesh was behind his dream of living there for six months of every year to serve his homeland following his retirement. According to Zeaul Huq, he even selected an apartment in Dhaka and had been making arrangements to purchase it. He wanted to work on low-cost housing, cyclone-resistant structures and cheaper construction for Bangladesh. Sadly, this wish was never fulfilled.

He was a born educator. Early in his career he taught in Dhaka and then during his SOM career, at IIT, Chicago. Not only did he influence students by his approach to architecture and structure, but he also showed personal concern for their education and well-being. Although he had a structural engineering background, he had no difficulty in teaching students of architecture. He had a broad, mature philosophy about architectural concept and conviction as well as the detailed and technical knowledge necessary to achieve the integrated product. He recognized that architecture concerned itself with the problems of humanity, and rarely did it provide a definitive solution to these problems. He also knew that education was essentially concerned with the individual and it must develop his or her intuitive and intellectual powers. Therefore, he attempted to instill orderly habits of inquiry into his students that would enable them to digest and employ information wisely exercising mature judgement during their future professional career. He accepted no money for his teaching job at IIT.

Peter Pran, a former student of IIT, and now a principal of the architectural firm NBBJ in the United States told me how he was greatly influenced by Khan. Pran, an eminent architect and educator, felt that his professional success was due to the inspiration that he had received from Khan. He recalled how Khan would often come to IIT on Saturdays to spend time with his students. He was also associated with Khan at SOM where he worked on the Jeddah International Airport project and on the schematic design phase of the Sears Tower. He recalled how Khan would always treat him as a good friend. He sighed and said, "The memory of Fazlur Khan is permanently deep-seated in my heart."

Similar sentiments were expressed by Wayne Petrie, another former student. Petrie is a Director of HPA, an architectural firm in Australia. He recalled how he was motivated by Khan, who impressed upon him the strong relationship between structure and architecture. Following Khan's advice he has always made it a point to integrate them in his design practice and has immensely benefited from this in his professional career.

He advised co-workers at his office on career decisions and noted their positive attributes. During slow times at SOM, he organized technical seminars to keep the engineers busy. Many who worked with him considered him as their mentor. He was a motivator, a peacemaker and a good judge of character.

He also took his art of enlightening others outside his office. He lectured worldwide. Because of his understanding of Arab and Islamic cultures (demonstrated during his Haj Terminal and Makkah University projects), Saudi universities invited him to lecture and to be part of conferences. The Saudi government also requested that he reform their engineering curriculum. Bangladesh University of Engineering and Technology (BUET) regularly sought his advice in evaluating faculty qualifications for promotion and tenure.

Khan had virtually no enemies. He had friends with different opinions and points-of-view, professionally and socially. He viewed people as individuals without categorizing them. According to Jha, when Khan differed with another he would make their point of contention sound so insignificant that it did not hurt. When someone agreed with his opinion, he "made it sound as it was in reality their opinion." For him, "it was never one or the other." When someone acted against his wishes, he was quick to forgive. Tolerance, forgiveness, and patience were primary attributes of his character. He could give and receive affection with joy and without effort and would believe in reciprocal happiness with others. Because he did not live in a prison of too powerful an ego, he could readily enjoy the world to the fullest and had the capacity for genuine affection of others. Zeaul Huq put it this way: "He had no pride. He was amiable. Success did not change him at all. He always thought about Bangladesh and how to reconstruct it." Abul Faraz Khan, a retired civil engineer and a consultant to an architectural firm in Dhaka at this writing, spoke to me of Khan's "childlike innocence" and "liveliness."

Mosharaff Hossain, one of Khan's best friends, described Khan this way: "He was full of life . . . never boring. He would enliven an environment. He was forthright but he never offended others. He had intuitive knowledge and a powerful mind. He used his high quality of mind rather than study of a subject as a basis to accomplish his mission. He was spiritual, a humanist with belief in God. He loved people and he deeply loved Bangladesh."

Fazlur Rahman Khan was a philanthropist. He was generous in giving. He supported many Bangladeshis when they defected from the Pakistani government during the Liberation Movement.

He was the first contributor of the newly formed organization *Gono Shaistha* (public health) dedicated to the health and well-being of the people of Bangladesh after the independence of the country. He donated a large sum of money to get the organization started. Dr. Muhammed Yunus, the founder of Grameen Bank in Bangladesh applying his own concept of microcredit, became its first Director. *Gono Shaistha* still exists today as a non-governmental organization (NGO).

Khan loved his family. Even though his work was demanding, he tried not to neglect his family. His secretary Jane told me that he often spoke of "my dear Lisl" and "my dear Yasmin." He was excited about Yasmin's decision to become a structural engineer. For the dedication ceremony of the "Fazlur R. Khan Way" in Chicago, his younger brother, Zillur Khan, wrote (BAGC, 1998):

> He was not only my big brother, but a confidante and dearest friend as well. Seven years and six months' difference between our ages had never created any gap in communication because of his sensitivity, straightforwardness, and consideration. He was truly a philosopher and guide to me in helping to find my being and becoming. Striking a balance between logic and compassion, my brother helped me to understand the need for systematic approach to solving problems, both personal and professional. He used to tell me to 'think logically and find the relationships which exist in every system, because it will help you understand nature itself, making living more meaningful and exciting'. I tried to follow his advice and never for a moment did I regret it.

Indeed, Khan found sets of relationships in prestressed concrete design during his doctoral study, in a tall building's structural system, and between architecture, aesthetics, and structural design. Finally, he found relationships in the problems and challenges of life—in his everyday interactions with people of different personalities, egos, and beliefs. It is not enough to say that he had only cultural interests and an interest in people. He was a humanist who had an attitude in which human ideals and the perfection of personality are made central. He was a lover of humanity.

93

Poster at the Bangladesh National Museum prepared by Bangladesh Emergency
Welfare Appeal, an organization founded and led by Fazlur Khan during the Bangladesh
Liberation War in 1971-72. Khan's office at SOM was located at that time at 30 W. Monroe
Street, 5th Floor, Chicago, IL 60603.
[Courtesy: Asif Iqbal with the permission of Bangladesh National Museum]

chapter 14

JOURNEY TO
THE ETERNAL WORLD

"The shining star of our community—Indic Community—has fallen. Today at twelve noon we buried Dr. Fazlur Rahman Khan and (he) is gone forever. It is like the lightning that strikes you at the middle of the day when the sun is shining and you do not know how and why it happened."

—Chandra K. Jha (*Kahn Tributes*, 1982)

194

194

194

194

194

194

194

Chandra Jha spoke the above words in his opening statement in an address aired on Indian Radio in Chicago on April 2, 1982—the day Khan was buried (*Khan Tributes*, 1982).

By the year 1970, Khan was at the peak of his career. He was self-assured and energetic. By 1980, he already completed his work on the Haj Terminal and was leading the Makkah University project. He was traveling frequently either on SOM business or to participate in or give presentations at conferences. He was active physically and mentally and seemed never to slow down.

Khan went to Mecca to perform haj in 1976—only a few years before his death. Although he had been in Saudi Arabia on business before, this was a new experience for him. The act of circumambulating around the Ka'ba, the cube revered by Muslims as the House of God and representing the center of the Islamic world, as well as sharing of his faith with thousands of believers from around the world, left a deep impression on him. Being philosophical, the pilgrimage was all the more a mystical one—a spiritual journey to the world of the Divine. Haj is obligatory on every believing Muslim who can afford it at least once in a lifetime, and each pilgrim has a different perspective of it. As part of the haj rituals Khan performed the rites, visiting the sacred sites in Mecca and Medina—the city where Prophet Mohammad lived and is buried. He described his haj experience with a slide presentation at a gathering of the Bangladeshi community in Chicago in the fall of 1981 on the occasion of the *Eid-ul-Adha* reunion which was preceded by the haj of that year. (In Muslim tradition, the *Eid-ul-Adha* commemorates the occasion of Abraham's intended sacrifice of his son to God. The annual haj is performed by devoted Muslims in Mecca at the same time.) Those who knew him most intimately saw a gradual but profound change in him in the late 1970s. He became still more inwardly directed—although he was already an introspective man—and he became more spiritual. He came to know that the truly integrated person was one for whom a spiritual dimension in life was important. Although he was not orthodox, and had a respect for all religions, he was loyal to his faith. He was a student of Islam, studying Islamic history and philosophy. When Joseph Colaco asked him about his religious belief, he replied "I have always been a Muslim." And when Chandra Jha and he discussed religious issues, Khan would quote from the Qur'an to make his point. He had a clear distinction between right and wrong.

It was his nature to carry every activity to its ultimate. Prabhas Nag, Khan's friend in Chicago and a contemporary from his student days at Bengal Engineering College, recounted that Khan loved to play ping pong in which he inevitably beat his opponent. They would often play at the International House, University of Chicago. He concentrated on the game, determined to win. He frequently went to an Indian restaurant in Chicago with Nag to order *Lassi* (pronounced laach-si), an Indian drink of sweetened yogurt, which he savored. Hem Gupta, another friend of his, also recalled Khan's visits with him to Indian restaurants. Gupta noted, however, that Khan was very careful about what he would eat.

In the early 1980s, Nag detected a mellowing in Khan's brisk and jovial nature. Occasionally, he appeared to be fatigued. At one point, he recalled to Nag his family's history of cardiac problems. A few days before his death, he noted the loss of his youthful energies during a conversation with me.

He also reported his feeling of loneliness at home to another friend as Lisl had been engaged in her doctoral research and Yasmin had already left home for her engineering studies. His physician had advised him to cut down his trips and take more rest.

In 1981, a rumor at SOM was that Khan would leave the firm soon and either start his own firm or go into full-time teaching. This rumor concerned the partners because they valued him and recognized him as the genius that he was. Khan cleared the air by telling his secretary Jane that he was not leaving; it was merely a rumor. SOM partners and his co-workers were relieved.

By this time, Khan found himself engaged in too many activities. He was a sought-after speaker, at home and abroad. At SOM, he was deeply involved in a number of projects, including two major ones in Saudi Arabia—the King Abdul Aziz International Airport at Jeddah, Saudi Arabia, followed by the King Abdul Aziz University at Mecca. He worked on the master plan for Universiti Kebangsaan Sabah Kampus at Kota Kinabalu in Malaysia. He traveled increasingly within the USA and overseas in connection with these projects. In 1981 he was involved in the Pacific Plaza project in Los Angeles and the Chicago World Trade Center. Some other projects that he immersed himself in during this period include the Lucky Building in Seoul, South Korea; One Magnificent Mile in Chicago; Columbia Presbyterian Hospital; US National Bank at Portland, Oregon; Onterie Center in Chicago; Trans Pacific Building in San Francisco; 780 Third Avenue in New York; and Gulf University.

Because of his close association with the Arab and Muslim worlds, he continued to be asked to speak, especially in the Middle East. In 1981 alone he presented five papers in Saudi Arabia. He had to turn down other invitations because of lack of time. In some of the papers he was able to deliver, he recorded his thoughts on Islamic architecture, drawing from visits to a number of Islamic sites, and advice from Islamic scholars such as Hassan Fathy and Titus Burkhardt.

Khan was an invited participant in a seminar on "Housing Design in Islamic Cultures" at MIT in 1981. Hasan Khan, Editor-in-Chief of *Mimar*, a Singapore journal in architecture and development, asked him to submit an article. An article on the Haj Terminal was published posthumously together with an obituary on Khan in this journal. He had begun to collect material on the Islamic faith, including a map depicting the spread of Islam in the world.

During 1980-81 he had been in constant contact with Bangladesh University of Engineering and Technology regarding such things as faculty promotion and tenure. Khan felt all along that he was obligated to his native homeland and wanted to repay his debt however he could.

As Chairman of the Council on Tall Buildings and Urban Habitat, Khan had been actively engaged in the activities of the organization. In July 1980, he attended the China conference on tall buildings. He was to give a presentation at the International Union of Architects Congress at Warsaw, Poland on June 19 of that year, but had to cancel his trip due to ill health. He continued to chair meetings of the Executive Committee of the Tall Building Council during 1980-81. In 1980 he worked on a bibliography and prepared a database on tall buildings. He was scheduled to be a guest speaker at the Asian Regional Conference on Tall Buildings and Urban Habitat in Kuala Lumpur, Malaysia, held from August 17 to 20, 1982. He was invited by the National University of Singapore to speak there at about the same time. Neither was to be.

In a meeting held on September 7, 1981, at Imperial College, London, Khan had noted the need to consider the "habitat" aspect of the Council in the planning and formation of new communities. He felt that habitat should be considered with respect to regional and societal aspects of the local situation. A proposed Cairo Conference on "New Communities and Urbanization Problems in Egypt" was planned in this context. Khan became a co-organizer. The conference date was tentatively set for January 23-29, 1983.

Khan visited Lehigh University and the headquarters of the Council on Tall Buildings and Urban Habitat during February 10-12. At a university auditorium he gave a lecture "How a Tall Building Evolves: The Influence of Changing Social and Economic Conditions" on February 11. This was reported in the Bethlehem newspaper *Morning Call* on February 16.

As if these commitments were not enough, he had been active with AISC. At a meeting on the theme "AISC-Partner in

Education" held during February 16-17, 1982, Khan was invited to lecture on his view as a structural designer. A meeting of the AISC "Committee on Tall Building Study," which Khan chaired, was to be held on April 16, 1982, at the AISC Headquarters in Chicago.

Khan had continued to teach at IIT and to supervise thesis projects. In 1981 he was deeply engaged in a student project by Wayne Petrie, and another by T. Bok, whose thesis was completed in 1982. Characteristically, before his final trip, he had been thoroughly correcting a student's thesis. At the same time, Khan had worked on a paper on the John Hancock Center in Chicago, which was to be his final statement on his idea of collaboration between architects and engineers (Khan, 1983). Shortly before he left for Korea in March, 1982, he completed still another paper. As incoming president of the architectural club of Chicago, Khan prepared this paper accepting his election. Although he would never deliver the address, the paper "Rise and Fall of Structural Logic in Architecture" was posthumously published in the club journal (Khan, 1982).

In late March, Khan prepared to go on his fateful trip to Korea and Saudi Arabia. He included a side trip to Bangladesh to visit his elderly mother, Zeaul Huq; other relatives planned a large welcoming party in Dhaka. A few days before this trip, as busy as he was, he gave time to me and candidly told me a few things—mostly in the form of advice and encouragement, and especially of his plans of still more research on tall buildings. He asked me to think about what he had told me about the new research project so that, upon his return, we could discuss the work in more detail.

After he left for Korea, a military coup d'état took place in Bangladesh. When Liselotte heard this news, she was able to inform Khan after his arrival in Hong Kong. Because of the political turmoil in Dhaka following the coup, Khan cancelled that wing of his trip, and went directly to Saudi Arabia. He arrived in Jeddah on the evening of March 26.

On the afternoon of Saturday, March 27, after attending a meeting in Jeddah about the implementation of the Master Plan for the King Abdul Aziz University, he was walking together with Khalil Khan, his colleague at SOM, and Munir Ahmed, Technical Director of the University. Then came the fateful moment. It was about 3:30 p.m. Khan turned to Khalil and said, "I don't feel so good." They saw that he was pale and feeble looking. As Khalil reached out to steady him, Khan collapsed. Khalil Khan and Munir Ahmed found themselves in an unexpected situation of a sudden emergency. Khan briefly recovered and gave them words for Liselotte in case he didn't survive. They were near the University Teaching Hospital where excellent medical facilities were available. A doctor was passing by across the street who immediately got him into the hospital. A full team of doctors attended upon him, but the heart attack was just too massive. While Khalil and Ahmed waited in tenseness, they were informed of his death. They were stunned in disbelief.

I heard the tragic news on Saturday at SOM's office when several of us were working overtime on the Pacific Plaza project. Several members of the project team were present. Sarv Nayyar approached me to ask "Did you hear anything about Faz?" His face was sad and gaze lowered. My first reaction was that Khan was involved in an accident or that he had fallen ill during his trip. I replied, "No, all I know is that he is out of the country." Nayyar murmured a few words but could not find it in himself to tell me. I insisted on hearing it. He said, "I heard bad news . . . Faz suffered a heart attack in Saudi Arabia . . . and they are saying he passed away. I hope it isn't true." In shock, he and I agreed that it had to be a false rumor. Rumors sometimes come and go out of nowhere. Other members of the team overheard our conversation and surrounded us. Everyone was stunned and speechless. We all lost our mood to work and wondered what to do next. Gloom prevailed. One person in the team tried to motivate us by saying, "Let's continue doing what we are doing. If he were alive that's what he would expect us to do anyway." But our spirits were destroyed. We began to leave. Before I left, however, I called friends of Khan whom I knew, heard the same news and, finally, began to accept the grim fact that it was not a rumor.

The news of Khan's sudden death spread like wildfire. His secretary Jane heard the news on Sunday. She came to work Monday morning; on viewing Khan's empty office, she burst into tears. Several people tried to console her. Bruce Graham hugged and comforted her. When another secretary came to Jane a few weeks later to tell her that the files and papers had to be removed from Khan's file drawers, Jane felt, "it was so cold." She went to Tom Eyerman and expressed her feelings. Eyerman immediately put a stop to the move. Jane told me, "That secretary did not realize that Dr. Khan was so famous. She didn't deal with Dr. Khan before. He was such a modest man. He was so humble that he once told me that he didn't like to preface his name with the title 'Dr.' He allowed it only for business and professional reasons."

Khan was 52 at the time of his death and would have been 53 on April 3, only a week later. He was survived by his wife Liselotte, daughter Yasmin, a stepson Martin, his mother, his brother Zillur Khan, his sister Masuda (Leena) Khan, and a host of relatives, friends, and well-wishers. Condolences poured in from around the world.

The Saudi government offered to honor Khan with burial at a sacred site in the holy land of Islam. Liselotte, however, chose to bury him in Graceland Cemetery in Chicago so that she and her family could pay their tributes to Khan by visiting the gravesite often. It may be that she wanted him to be buried in the cemetery where several other famous architects and engineers— as well as well-known personalities of Chicago—were buried.

His remains were flown from Saudi Arabia to Chicago. Bill Drake, of SOM, was in Kuwait at the time and he flew immediately to Saudi Arabia from Chicago to make the arrangements. Khan's final resting-place is in Graceland Cemetery at 4001 North Clark Street, Chicago. Main entrance to the cemetery is from the northeast corner of Irving Park Road and North Clark Street. Next to Khan is buried the ashes of his wife, Liselotte Khan, who, following Khan's death, moved to Albuquerque, New Mexico. She would never recover from her husband's premature demise and died there in February, 1995.

The Graceland Cemetery has historical significance. Established in 1860 and designed by Chicago landscape architect O. C. Simonds, the entire cemetery has a beautiful park-like environment. Massive broad-leaf trees such as oaks, elms and maples are scattered throughout the nearly 120 acres of land. The architecturally significant monuments and markers cover the cemetery creating a wonderful integration of natural and man-made objects. The cemetery is beautifully landscaped by an abundance of plantings with well-planned vistas and natural topographical and water features. It is indeed a peaceful, serene, permanent resting-place.

One can walk through the cemetery and see the graves of John Kinzie, one of the earliest settlers in Chicago; Potter Palmer, a business leader; railroad and automobile manufacturer George Pullman; and Cyrus McCormick, who revolutionized American agriculture with the invention of the mechanized reaper and other farm machinery. Other Chicago notables buried here are civic planners and builders Daniel Burnham and Charles Wacker; the retailing giant Marshall Field; meat packer Phillip Armour; and several Chicago mayors and Illinois governors. Renowned architects like John Root, William Holabird, Louis Sullivan, David Adler, Van Doren Shaw and Ludwig Mies van der Rohe are also buried here. The new addition to the constellation of these renowned people was Fazlur R. Khan—structural engineer, philosopher and humanist on April 2, 1982.

At the burial, following Islamic practice, each of those present threw a handful of soil onto Khan's casket before it was covered with earth. Jane recalled her own experience thus: "After Dr. Khan's coffin was lowered into the ground, we lined up to throw dirt on the casket. . . . At first I felt awkward but was determined to take full part in what was going on since the loss was mine too. But when I dropped the dirt down, I felt that I was connected to him even in death and that it was kind-of an all too real closure on that chapter of my life." Thus Khan reached the eternal world. Following the Islamic tradition of mourning for forty days, a memorial service was held on May 6 at the Auditorium Theater in Chicago. A four-screen slide presentation, entitled "The Works of Fazlur Rahman Khan," was shown. Speeches given by Khan's distinguished colleagues and friends captured various aspects of his illustrative life. The entire program of recitals, music, testimonials, and slide show moved the guests and participants. The auditorium was filled with people who came from all over the world to show their last respects to the beloved man.

Khan's death received wide coverage in the news media and professional publications. All three major civil engineering organizations—ASCE, AISC, and ACI—reported his death, printing special tributes. ACI published a eulogy on Khan by Fintel (1982), who wrote:

> Fazlur Khan will be sorely missed by his countless friends and admirers who are deeply saddened by his untimely death, but feel enriched because he touched their lives. His was a relatively short, but worthwhile, productive, and full life. His many contributions to the cities of his world and the millions who inhabit those cities will remain an everlasting monument to his memory.

AISC, with whom Khan had been actively involved, began their tribute with (*Modern Steel Construction*, 1982): "the structural engineering community has lost a great talent—and a warmhearted friend." And the AISC Tall Building Study Committee adopted a "Memorial Resolution to Fazlur R. Khan" on April 16. Some excerpts read:

—He (Khan) felt very strongly that information, once learned, should be 'implemented'—collected together in a form that would be useful to others. . . .

—In our profession, he did much for those of his same heritage—Bengali and Moslem. As they have often said, 'Because of his ability and success, people recognize that others of his origin can succeed too.' By being himself, he broke down barriers.

The Structural Stability Research Council adopted a "Memorial Resolution" on March 30, in which his frequent participation in its various activities and special panel discussions were noted with deep appreciation. AIA and many other organizations and professional societies around the world reported and paid homage to Khan.

News of Khan's death was reported in several newspapers. *The New York Times* reported it on March 30 with an article by Paul Goldberger. Both Chicago newspapers, *Chicago Tribune* and *Sun-Times*, reported his death immediately on March 29. The *Tribune* followed it up with a feature article by Paul Gapp on April 4. The article featured a picture of Khan and called him a "gentle giant" and a "megastructure man." It ended with the statement: "He was a man of warmth. He was deeply committed to the practice of science *cum* art. He was a giant." *Engineering News-Record* reported Khan's death in its April 1 issue and editorialized (*ENR*, 1982):

The sudden death of Fazlur R. Khan has robbed the world of an inestimable wealth of ideas, inspiration, and grand designs that were still to come from his wonderfully fertile mind. The mild-mannered man whose greatest ideas stand as monuments as great as Chicago's Sears Tower leaves marks of his genius all around the world . . .

Fazlur Khan was a philosopher among engineers, a master-builder among architects, a teacher among students, a thought leader in a world of followers. He was sensitive to the needs of people as he was respectful of the forces of nature. He was at once a resource and catalyst among those with whom he worked in Skidmore, Owings and Merrill. His influence spread from his Chicago office to their projects around the world. He leaves the firm a legacy of structural strength in his co-workers.

ENR concluded the editorial:

The design professions, the construction industry and the people for whom he performed his works of genius must be satisfied with his magnificent accomplishments to date. The consoling facts are that his structures will stand for years, and his ideas will never die.

His death was also reported in the May issue of *Building Design & Construction*.

The news of his death was prominently reported in the media in Bangladesh, India, Pakistan, and several other countries. The *Hindustan Times*, a widely circulated Indian newspaper, published a feature article on him in its May 9 issue. The newspaper called him "a towering personality" and recounted his association with Calcutta and how he had carried fond memories of his student days there during the late 1940s.

Were Khan alive today, he could certainly come up with innovation after innovation, and could have enriched humanity at large. Recognition of his works continued following his death. An academic chair was established in his honor at Lehigh University and he has been honored by others posthumously. He is still being fondly remembered by the profession and his friends and well wishers worldwide.

Khan was in this world but 52 years. He led a life of unique quality and greatness that can be captured in the couplet written by the Pakistani poet and philosopher Mohammad Iqbal:

> Live your life in such a way that,
> should death be eternal,
> God should be ashamed of that.

chapter 15

THE KAHN CHAIR
AND MORE RECOGNITION

"Beedle . . . is technically retired, but you'd never know it. He is now raising $1.25 million for the Khan Chair at Lehigh—a tribute to the memory and a perpetuation of the philosophies of one of the century's most eminent structural engineers."

—ENR (1989)

Shortly after the untimely death of Fazlur Rahman Khan, Lynn Beedle conceived the idea of establishing a Chair in his honor. One logical setting could have been the IIT in Chicago, where Khan had taught for two decades. However, when that did not happen, Beedle, who had worked with Khan at the Council on Tall Buildings and Urban Habitat, took the initiative to spearhead the program for establishing the Chair at Lehigh University. Beedle found immediate support from Lehigh's administrators of the importance of such a Chair as a fitting consummation of the efforts of the man who had chaired the Tall Building Council headquartered at Lehigh at the time of his death. Thus the program with a goal of $1.25 million for a fully-funded Chair was established in 1982.

The entire amount for the endowment was to be acquired through direct appeals. Beedle knew that it could only be accomplished by personal contacts and that it was indeed an enormous task. He assumed the role of the Coordinator of the Khan Chair and began his long-term efforts. For him fundraising for the Chair was a noble mission—a labor of his love for Khan. He told *ENR*, "I'm struck with the breadth of the man's abilities and the regard that people had for him" (Post, 1989). This was probably the first time an American had initiated and followed through such a major task of establishing a Chair for an Asian entirely out of donated money.

Known for his interpersonal skills and as a "polite pusher," Beedle began his fundraising drive by going almost door to door to people all around the world using his international connections, through primarily concentrating on those who had known Khan. He used his warmth and charisma to influence people and even to mobilize a small group of volunteers to work with him, with Chandra Jha as its leader. I was recruited to be such a volunteer in the summer of 1988—to work with Aminul Karim, an academic administrator and Chicago resident—to raise funds from Bangladeshis living in America. The eventual goal of this particular endeavor was to honor Khan by establishing a Khan Scholarship (subsequently renamed Fazlur Rahman Khan Prize) to be awarded to a meritorious Bangladeshi student studying at Lehigh, as part of the Khan Chair program.

In 1990, a Fazlur Rahman Khan Chair Advisory Committee was formally established with Chandra Jha as its Chairman. Committee members are: Muhammad Ridzuan Salleh from

Malaysia, Sabah Al Rayes from Kuwait, Jamilur Reza Choudhury from Bangladesh, Zuhair Fayez from Saudi Arabia, and Aminul Karim and Mir M. Ali from the U.S. As Chairman of this committee, Jha consistently assisted Beedle in funding the Chair.

The main purpose of the Chair was to honor a world-famous engineer. Additional core objectives were identified: to foster state-of-the-art teaching and research, stimulate closer ties with universities around the world, develop closer ties with professionals, stimulate the application of new knowledge to practice, accelerate the development of computerized databases.

The principal goal of the Chair was to perpetuate Khan's philosophy: To use the finest technology, to remember that designs are for people, and to share new knowledge with others. The results would mean a better life for urban dwellers through improving the built environment.

The Khan Chair program was ambitious in its scope and vision. It was established that the Fazlur Rahman Khan Professor—the faculty occupying the Chair—would be a member of the Lehigh faculty. The program consisted of ten main components. First, the Khan Professor would participate in the instructional program with special emphasis on the built environment. Second, the research focus would feature joint projects with other universities. Third, this person would undertake visits to various countries for worldwide lecturing and dissemination of information. Fourth, through international contacts, the holder of the Chair would encourage graduate students to participate in the regular programs as well as in those related to the built environment. Fifth, a visiting scholar program would be instituted in which scholars from other universities could collaborate with research teams at Lehigh through the auspices of the Chair. The remaining five components were identified as: the development of codes and standards; seminars and short courses both abroad and at Lehigh; exchanges between professionals at conferences, particularly through such opportunities provided by the Tall Building Council; the transfer of knowledge to spur learning to meet the needs of the local community; and development of a knowledge base throughout the world in the form of a comprehensive interactive information network.

In sum, it was envisioned that the Chair would promote educational activity, stimulate research, and provide a focus for the application of that research to suit the conditions of the particular environment and culture. All these issues were indeed very close to Khan's heart. A so-called Bangladesh program was also developed under the umbrella of the Khan Chair program. Under this program, a center named the "F. R. Khan Center for Study of the Built Environment" would be established at Bangladesh University of Engineering and Technology (BUET) as a counterpart to the Lehigh Chair. Jamilur Reza Choudhury, a professor of civil engineering at BUET, prepared a detailed proposal outlining the possible joint research activities by BUET and Lehigh University.

The "Bangladesh Program" was aimed at raising adequate funds so that every year the Khan Professor could spend up to a month in Bangladesh and a faculty member from BUET could be supported by the Chair to be a visiting scholar at Lehigh. A coordinating committee in Dhaka to follow through on the various initiatives was set up under the leadership of Zeaul Huq, a leading industrialist in Bangladesh. This committee, designated as the "Committee for the Fazlur Rahman Khan Foundation," had a broad scope that ranged from fundraising to advising the F. R. Khan Center at BUET.

Throughout the fundraising drive for the Khan Chair, Beedle left no stone unturned to make contacts with people from all walks of life. By 1989, he had secured over half of the $1.25 million amount in pledges and contributions representing the gifts of three governments, thirty firms, and over one hundred individuals (Beedle, 1990). Some major contributors from the industry have been ARAMCO; AISC; Bechtel; Hochtief; Ove Arup Partnership; Pan Arab Consulting Engineers; SOM; and Tishman Speyer Properties. Out of these, the most substantive gift was the generous subscription of $50,000 per year of his Royal Highness Prince Sultan bin Abdul Aziz, Minister of Defense, Saudi Arabia. The Government of Malaysia contributed $40,000. A special endowment fund was created to receive these gifts. Through the generosity of Prime Minister Mohamad Mahathir, an additional contribution of the Malaysian government was made to the Khan Chair. This opened the way to the establishment of a "Khan Collection" of books at the University of Malaysia and University of Technology, Malaysia.

Beedle retraced Khan's contacts in some twenty countries during his fundraising efforts. He even went to Khan's native country, Bangladesh. The Secretary of Industries of the Bangladesh government, A.K.M. Mosharraf Hossain, arranged a meeting of Beedle with President Hussain Muhammad Ershad, in 1989. Beedle explained to President Ershad how the Khan Chair would directly benefit Bangladesh and, in addition, bring recognition to it through tributes being paid to one of its most illustrious sons. In the meeting, President Ershad made a pledge for $100,000. Mosharraf Hossain wrote to Beedle on January 18, 1990 telling Beedle the President's view in the matter. Hossain informed him again through a letter of February 15 that the matter was under active consideration of the government and that he would advise Beedle soon about it.

Moudud Ahmed, Vice President of the People's Republic of Bangladesh, took the initiative in the matter which reached a stage when it could be presented to the President's cabinet for approval. However, the sudden political instability in Bangladesh at that time and Ershad's departure from the office of the President jeopardized the $100,000 Bangladesh contribution. The successive governments of Prime Minister Khaleda Zia and Sheikh Hasina have been either indifferent or have not been approached to remind them of the verbal pledge of President Ershad to Beedle. The matter remains, at this writing, in stalemate and needs persuasive efforts.

By 1994, 2 governments (the Saudi and Malaysian), 34 firms and 152 individuals were included in the Roll of Honor of Contributions to the Khan Chair, bringing the amount raised to 60% of the target of $1,250,000. The more than 20 countries represented in the list of donors demonstrated the wide influence and appeal of Khan. The Roll of Honor of contributors continued to grow.

Rather than waiting until the full endowment was in hand to enable Lehigh University to establish the full-fledged Chair and to recruit a distinguished professor, a number of initiatives have been undertaken since 1983, using some of the endowment income and with help from Lehigh.

Beedle, as the Coordinator for the Chair, gave lectures at King Abdulaziz University, King Saud University, and King Fahd University of Petroleum and Minerals in October, 1983. In November, 1984, he gave a lecture at King Faisal University. These lectures included the following topics: "The Philosophy of Tall Buildings," "Architecture of Tall Buildings," "Tall Buildings in Steel," and "The Tall Building as an Instrument of Urban Design." In addition, in 1984, a short course on "Tall Buildings in the Urban Context" was presented at King Fahd University of Petroleum and Minerals, in coordination with Zamil A.R. Mokrin of the University, and proceedings recording the presentations were issued.

As part of the educational mission of the program, lectures on "The Life and Work of Fazlur Rahman Khan" were given at universities in Bangladesh, Brunei, Hong Kong, Jordan, Korea, Kuwait, Malaysia, People's Republic of China, Saudi Arabia, and Taiwan. At each of the university visits made by Beedle, he emphasized the idea of exchange visits and joint research. The most intensive discussions took place in Bangladesh, Saudi Arabia, and Kuwait. A week-long lecture series was conducted in March of 1988 at BUET for university and leading industry personnel. Highlights of these lectures were reported in a one-day seminar in Brunei, a program chaired by Dr. Ismail, Minister of Development of Brunei.

Books and other publications on the built environment, resulting from the work of Lehigh's High-Rise Institute and the Tall Building Council, were collected. As of 1998, fourteen institutions have created the "Khan Collection." Four of these universities are in Saudi Arabia and two in Malaysia; the others are in Lebanon, Germany, Cyprus and the U.S. The collections were made available to a donor whose contributions to the Chair came to $25,000 or more.

As an educator at IIT, Khan had been especially understanding of the needs of students. Appropriately, then, support was provided to graduate students from Malaysia and Sri Lanka. Their work had added to several databases on the built environment. Moreover, Khan assistantships have been regularly awarded to undergraduate students at Lehigh University to provide for a work experience on projects—in a real world situation and related to the objectives of the Chair. They get a feeling for graduate study and many of them go on to attend leading universities for Master's and Doctor's degrees.

Khan recognized the importance of travel and the educational benefit it can provide to students. The Chair, therefore, provided "Khan Traveling Fellowships." The Chair has been providing such fellowships to individuals from countries such as India, Venezuela, the USA, and Poland.

The Khan Chair supported seminars at Lehigh University by two visiting lecturers: Jamilur Reza Choudhury from Bangladesh, on "Technology in Bangladesh;" and Zuhair Fayez from Saudi Arabia, on "Modern Islamic Architecture."

Professor Bill P. Lim of Queensland University of Technology, Brisbane, Australia, was appointed the first Fazlur Rahman Khan Visiting Professor at Lehigh University for the Spring of 1990. Lim delivered a series of special lectures on "Energy, Environment, and Aesthetic Considerations: Tall Buildings in

Singapore and Australia." The lecture series covered nine different topics which added a new dimension—that of improving the livability in tall buildings. These topics were assembled in book form (Lim, 1994).

A Khan Visiting Fellowship was also offered to a Malaysian specialist to support documentation on the legal aspects of high-rise development.

With a flurry of activities undertaken under the auspices of the Chair since its very inception, new knowledge has been generated and attempts are underway to make this knowledge available to academic institutions and to the profession worldwide.

By early 1998, the funds for the Fazlur Rahman Khan Prize secured from Bangladeshis living in America made its award possible. Aside from the generosity of individual donors, two major contributions by the Bangladesh Association of Chicago and the American Association of Bangladeshi Engineers and Architects (AABEA) expedited the matter.

The Khan Chair is a major step toward maintaining Khan's legacy in the disciplines of structural engineering and architecture. Together with his other professional accomplishments, it is an achievement for Beedle—an achievement that he is proud of, and for which he gave unselfishly and limitlessly of his time and energy. In 1999, in New York, he was awarded the Fazlur Rahman Khan Award by AABEA—an award well deserved—in recognition of his untiring efforts as the Chair Coordinator.

The holder of the Chair is expected to have a national reputation and a background in both academia and industry—as well as an appreciation for the built environment. In addition to teaching, research and supervision of graduate students, the Khan Professor would be responsible for traveling worldwide to give lectures, initiate and encourage joint research and exchange programs, and to promote Fazlur Khan's philosophy. At this writing, the search for the person to fill the Chair is expected to begin soon.

▲ ▼

Khan was posthumously recognized and honored not only by Lehigh University, but also by SOM and other organizations. SOM established in 1982 the Fazlur Khan International Fellowship for excellence in engineering supported through the SOM Foundation endowment fund. The primary goal of this program was to further the work and philosophy of Khan on an international basis through the identification and nurturing of engineering professionals capable of making professional and cultural contributions. Following Khan's death, in conversations of how to honor Khan's memory, which started at the funeral service, Bruce Graham brought into the Foundation's inner circle Stanley Tigerman, who, in turn, introduced other architects in the discussion, notably Thomas Beeby and Henry Cobb. These discussions resulted in the creation of the Khan award. The first award in this category went to Werner Sobek of Germany, and was announced in 1983. Two more awards were given subsequently to Himanshu Parikh of India in 1985, and to Santiago Calatrava, then living in Switzerland, in 1988.

To recognize Khan's contributions to wind engineering, the Wind Tunnel Laboratory at the University of Western Ontario established a Fazlur Khan Award given to outstanding graduate students who make significant contributions towards the study of the behavior of structures under wind action. Six students have received this award since its inception in 1982.

ASCE honored Khan by assigning a special "Khan Memorial Session" at its Annual Fall Meeting in Houston, Texas on October 19, 1983. The session was sponsored by the Committee on Aesthetics in Design, of the Structural Division of ASCE, and it brought together some of Khan's closest colleagues. This session was devoted to structural expression in buildings. As reported in the January, 1984 issue of *Civil Engineering*, speakers paid tribute to Khan, emphasizing his passion for structural expression. A book, *Technique and Aesthetics in the Design of Tall Buildings*, based on this ASCE session was published in 1986 by the Institute for the Study of High-Rise Habitat. The book contains a series of tributes to the work and character of Khan with recollections on some of his most important works relating to tall buildings.

A favorable review of the book by Paul Gapp of the *Chicago Tribune* stimulated significant response. The first printing was quickly exhausted, leading to a second printing. Publication of the book by the Institute for the Study of the High-Rise Habitat was made possible by a grant from the Fazlur Rahman Khan Chair. The book was edited by David Billington of Princeton University and by Myron Goldsmith.

Khan's work was also recognized through the 1983 Aga Khan Award for Architecture held in Istanbul on September 4 of that year, when the structure of the Haj Terminal was chosen in the category of technological innovation. The award ceremony took place in the second court of the Topkapi Sarayi, formerly the great palace of the Ottoman Sultan. The Aga Khan and President K. Evren of Turkey presided over the ceremony. The Haj Terminal was selected as one of 11 prize-winning projects. These projects were not selected for aesthetic quality alone or as perfected artifacts, but were viewed by the juries as stages of transition, experimentation and continued search. They were viewed as models for future projects. A substantial portion of the award money was allocated to the Fazlur Khan estate and to the SOM Fazlur Khan International Traveling Fellowship.

The Chicago residents of Bangladeshi origin honored their fellow countryman by collecting funds from among themselves to establish the Fazlur Rahman Khan Scholarship at BUET in Bangladesh in 1986. Efforts of fundraising and coordination with BUET were carried out by a committee led by Aminul Karim. The Scholarship is awarded annually to two meritorious students, one in civil engineering and another in architecture at BUET. In June, 1993, The Institution of Engineers in Bangladesh organized an International Conference on Tall Buildings in Dhaka with a special "Fazlur Rahman Khan Session" in which the life and works of Khan were presented through speeches and photographic display. In the late 1980s, the Fazlur Rahman Khan Foundation was established in Dhaka with Zeaul Huq, Bashirul Haq, Jamilur Reza Choudhury and others as members. The Foundation is dedicated to the propagation of Khan's idea of the development of Bangladesh and has been raising funds since then.

Because Khan was an integrator of engineering and architecture, he was greatly respected by both structural engineering and architectural communities. He had a profound understanding of structural, aesthetic and functional points of view. Acknowledging this, the Chicago Architectural Club had elected him as their president, and he was to have assumed those responsibilities shortly after his death. The Club's second annual journal was dedicated to him. The Chicago Committee on High-Rise Buildings announced in 1991 the annual award named "Fazlur Rahman Khan Award for Innovation in the Design and Construction of High-Rise Buildings" recognizing an individual or company or project team that has developed "an innovative improvement for the technology of high-rise buildings." Gerald Johnson, AIA of Fujikawa Johnson and Associates chaired the committee at that time.

The ultimate honor bestowed by the architectural community was the AIA's 1983 Institute Honor to Khan, a structural engineer. The announcement was made in the April, 1983 issue of the AIA Journal. The AIA recognized his innovations in high-rise design and "the distinguished achievements that enhanced or influenced the environment and the architectural profession." Khan's award was presented posthumously during the May, 1983 AIA Annual Convention in New Orleans, Louisiana. His nomination cited the following: "Rarely has an engineer played as key a role in shaping of architects' ideas and the shaping of buildings themselves as Fazlur Khan in the design of high-rise buildings." The AIA Jury on Institute Honors, chaired by Thomas S. Marvel, of Hato Rey, Puerto Rico, wrote in its comments, "Fazlur Khan's work and research had made him one of the most influential structural engineers of the century." The jury continued, "Besides his innovations in high-rise buildings, cable and tension structures, and teaching, he demonstrated a human awareness and commitment to structural and architectural design collaboration that has particular importance for architects today."

In a letter to the AIA Journal (May, 1983), Richard P. Geyser, an architect, summed up the feeling of architects by writing, "Faz's great qualities were humility, humane attitude, and concerned involvement. He was a great friend, an awesome competitor— competent beyond measure—and one who is sorely missed."

Fazlur R. Khan attending a conference in Athens, Greece in October, 1975
[Courtesy: CTBUH]

Fazlur R. Khan, Lynn S. Beedle and others in Paris where they attended the Executive
Committee Meeting of the Council on Tall Buildings and Urban Habitat on May 6, 1979
[Courtesy: CTBUH]

Fazlur R. Khan with Lynn S. Beedle and Richard Baum of Jaros Baum and Bolles,
New York, in Shanghai during the China Seminar in July, 1980
[Courtesy: CTBUH]

chapter 16

THE SPIRIT LIVES ON

"In tribute to Khan, architects and engineers continue to work together to reach new levels of thought and vision for our future, developing the technology to make our dreams come true."

—Anne S. DeHaven (1995)

"They stretch toward the sky, piercing clouds as they soar to spectacular heights, majestically mocking gravity and humbling everything on the ground below. The Empire State Building, the Sears Tower, the Petronas Twin Towers. These heavenly high-rises, surging well past 1,000 feet (300 meters), have been a striking testament to human-kind's technological strength throughout the 20th century."

—Alden M. Hayashi (1999)

Engineering is essentially the art and science of designing, constructing and operating systems and products for the benefit of mankind. Engineers usually work behind the scene and are almost taken for granted by the society. This lament is widespread in engineering circles and justifiably so (Ali, 1983).

In the preface of his book *To Engineer is Human*, Henry Petroski (1982) attempted to assign a reason for their lack of recognition: "Even the most elementary of principles upon which great bridges, jumbo jets, or super computers are built are alien concepts to many. This is so because engineering as a human endeavor is not integrated into our culture and intellectual tradition."

Though some engineers in the eighteenth and nineteenth centuries were widely recognized in Europe, that trend has become an exception rather than the norm. Engineers of today are as inventive and daring as their counterparts of the past. Historically, engineering, being more akin to science than it is to art, bypasses the cult of personality. Engineers believe in natural laws and pragmatic rationalism; they do not compromise their common sense and integrity to achieve art's immortality. Scientific principles are more important to them than the cultivation of personalities—they would choose the tune rather than the flute. This has made many of them introverted and least communicative with those who do not understand the engineering vocabulary. They prefer to stay behind a veil of seclusion and this isolates them from society. This lack of expansive personality and failure to identify with their work is their major weakness.

Fazlur Rahman Khan rose above this state of affairs. Not only was he highly competent technically, but he could also break the barriers of communication with other professionals and with society at large. He took an interest in human beings, designing buildings and structures less for the marvel of engineering but more for the comfort of humanity. He possessed and exercised a wide range of talents, not the least of which was skill in public relations. Unlike many of today's engineers, he never permitted himself to be totally involved in the demands of his formal education. Although he had to abide by unyielding scientific and technical principles, he did not cherish skepticism in his mind about the importance of such inexact fields as sociology, philosophy, psychology, politics and communications. This outlook encompassed a sense of exploration into other disciplines—not just structural engineering. This is where young structural engineers can learn from Khan's experience and his outlook on the building profession. Following Khan's advice that technical people must not be lost in their own technology, new generation engineers must come out of the shell of technology. They should consciously try to improve their communication skills in both structural and non-structural realms. They should interact with the public more often and develop a sense of aesthetic quality of structures that will meet the public demand of creating beautiful objects around them. If structural engineers want to get recognition in the society, they should seriously study Khan's works and his style to take lessons from them.

Even during his lifetime, Khan's influence on the engineering profession became apparent. Although he reached the pinnacle of his professional career around 1970 when he was recognized internationally as the leader in tall building design, he never consciously sought status. He was too occupied in creating engineering marvels that benefited society, and his accomplishments brought acclaim. And he believed so strongly in what he was doing, naturally he was driven to publish extensively and to lecture tirelessly.

By the early 1970s, structural engineers began to adopt Khan's tubular concept. Most of the tallest buildings that were built at that time used it. These included the Standard Oil Building (now called the Amoco Building) in Chicago and the World Trade Center in New York. A modified tubular principle was used for the Bank of China Building in Hong Kong and the Petronas Towers in Kuala Lumpur, Malaysia. Following Khan's death, the design of other skyscrapers in the Far East and other parts of the world have obviously been influenced by his thinking.

Dealing with the forces in a building and making them go where they ought to go gratifies the engineers. Obtaining the right sizes of beams and columns and making the building stand still fulfills their expectation. The engineers, by virtue of their training, are largely indifferent to the aesthetic appeal of the building, thereby isolating themselves from the public, who fail to understand and appreciate the engineering concept which is not visually obvious. All too often, the architect is recognized while the engineer remains anonymous, although it was not always so. Because Khan was able to break this barrier, he is applauded worldwide.

The establishment of the Fazlur Rahman Khan Chair at Lehigh University (see Chapter 15) is a great tribute to Khan and will perpetuate his philosophy. Khan's legacy is not just that he has left an indelible mark on civilization by creating the monumental towers, but also his ideas. People who design monuments are certain to be forgotten, but those who leave the imprint of ideas are remembered through posterity. Khan's ideas of tubular principle, structural art, designing for people's comfort, synthesis of engineering and architecture, and his concerns for humanity will always keep his legacy alive. Inclusion of human criteria in his designs projects them beyond the cold logic of structural mechanics. He applied such convictions to his towers; they testify as well to his feel for contrast and diversity, to his integration of economy with elegance.

Is this why Khan's projects were so successful? In dissecting a problem he was imaginative yet determined to look for alternate solutions. Such an approach excited architects and led them to accept his solutions. He was never shy to promote his ideas. His mathematical comprehension was incisive in the quantification of solutions, both in the creation of mathematical models of structural and material behavior and in the use of the computer to develop helpful charts. But he was a hands-on engineer depending upon intuition and test results rather than upon musty calculations. He attempted to know the crux of a problem before finding its solution. He could bring clarity to a complex subject. He did not become complacent after publishing and applying his revolutionary concepts of shear wall-frame interaction and tubular design. He was incredibly hardworking and driven to succeed. Often he came to SOM's office to work at 9:00 p.m., after teaching in the evening at IIT, to stay there until midnight or beyond. In addition, in delegating work to others, he instinctively challenged them to do their best. He enjoyed every moment of his working day and made the day rewarding and fruitful. His gentle manners and kindness allowed him to gain respect and admiration from his professional colleagues of diverse disciplinary backgrounds.

He treated his fellow engineers warmly, more as friends. Zils, who closely worked with him on several projects, put it this way: "Faz led people by example. He never urged me to work hard on a project, but seeing him so excited about the work, I wanted to do the same. His enthusiasm was contagious. He had a natural perception of things. He made everyone a better engineer who would just evolve that way under his leadership. I never saw him angry or heard him raise his voice. People would readily follow him. Behind all this, he had a strong technical background. This is a rare combination. He had something special in him." Mahjoub Elnimeiri, a professor of architecture at IIT, who worked with Khan at SOM as a structural engineer, echoed a similar sentiment: "I would be trusted. Faz treated me like a friend and asked for my opinion."

Khan intensified his research as well as lectures and publications. He used simple technical ideas to select structural systems and avoided supertechnical solutions. He could envision the parts and the whole simultaneously. He focused attention on elements sharing a building's loads, and worked toward a structure that would allow the most logical flow of loads. Interestingly, his encouragement of collaboration and team work was a human parallel, calling upon several people to be a part of the overall solution.

Myron Goldsmith, who was affectionate and collaborative with him, left a lasting influence on him. Goldsmith had a sound knowledge of structure and of its integral role in architecture. Khan absorbed that knowledge, expanded upon it, and put it into practice. Goldsmith worked with Mies and Nervi, but Khan had the benefit of building on their collective works. It was Goldsmith who invited Khan to teach at IIT. His contact with IIT professors and graduate students further stimulated him.

Bruce Graham had a strong influence on him in the design office. Graham is an ardent proponent of structural architecture. He admired structure as Khan adored architecture, so the two of them developed a unique chemistry. Khan was glad to find a superior architect of Graham's caliber who would work in harmony with him, who understood and appreciated structural concepts so well. Since they mutually strengthened each other, most of Khan's major projects were actually Graham-Khan projects. Khan's professional relationship with Graham was elegantly expressed by Graham himself in the following words (Graham, 1986):

> Once upon a time, engineers and architects were synonymous. They were tastemakers and pacesetters, socialites and poets. Once upon a time, I had such a partner . . . Dr. Fazlur Khan. We lunched, laughed and played together, but most of all we worked in tandem till at the end we could think for each other. This relationship grew not only because of sympathetic aesthetic preoccupations or the mutual respect with which we regarded each other, but also out of an indistinct vision of the city, of the city beautiful, the purpose of cities and of the pride of human existence.

Another key player was Hal Iyengar, one of the finest structural engineers that Khan was to have as an associate, who has a great reputation in his own right. Iyengar worked with Khan on numerous projects. Because of Khan's preoccupation with other projects in his role as a SOM partner, the Sears Tower project was primarily carried out by Iyengar in terms of structural design and detailing along with John Zils, with Khan's input and consistent guidance. The John Hancock Center was a project that demanded Khan's full attention because it was his first major building requiring a completely new structural system. Moreover, it became the tallest building of Chicago. There also Iyengar actively assisted him. After Khan developed the basic structural concept for Hancock, Joseph Colaco, another competent engineer, undertook the detailed calculations and computer analyses. Iyengar continued to work closely with Khan on subsequent projects and substantially contributed to them.

John Zils, a loyal associate of Khan, is an unsung hero in all these. He began his career at SOM working with Khan and continued Khan's design philosophy even after his death. He is one of those who have played a huge but relatively unpublicized role in the twentieth century structural engineering. Khan trusted him and gave him major responsibility of many significant projects. Zils' unfailing thoroughness and attention to details certainly contributed to the success of Khan's projects.

Mark Fintel is another top-notch structural engineer outside of SOM who collaborated with Khan on thermal movements of exposed concrete columns due to seasonal changes in temperature. Khan and Fintel also cooperated on providing new solutions incorporating material characteristics, particularly creep and shrinkage, made necessary due to the drastic increase in height of concrete buildings in the 1960s and 1970s to the 50- to 60-story range (the previously customary maximum was 20 stories). Khan had the benefit of cooperation with Fintel in concrete material behavior that he applied to various buildings. Khan profited in his work with such brilliant collaborators; he drew from all of them.

To sum up, Khan skillfully pushed structural form and architectural function to their limits. In spite of his being a structural engineer by training, he was able to break into architecture. He related well to those professionals with whom he had the most frequent dealings. He was attentive to the owner's viewpoint and demonstrated finer sensibilities than most to the architect. Importantly, he interacted well with the contractor by being conversant with the practical demands of construction.

Chicago as a city has a long history in architecture and structural engineering; it remains one of the top-ranking cities of the world from that perspective. Much of that status is the legacy of Khan, who remolded the cityscape, setting trends for the future. The Sears Tower and the John Hancock Center joined other landmarks of Chicago, but they go beyond to represent the crux of structurally significant architecture. Both reflect his loyalty to a notion that tall buildings release land at ground level, opening up space for plazas, fountains, arcades and for recreational purposes, thereby creating a humane environment around them. This concept seems so obvious, yet it has been disregarded by too many designers in large cities. Chicago has indeed a lively environment that a visitor should not miss. A walk in its downtown core will reveal a wealth of outdoor sculptures and plazas enhanced by the works of renowned artists like Picasso, Miró and Calder. But for its skyline, Chicago owes much to Fazlur Khan.

Following Khan's death, the Structural Engineers Association of Illinois (SEAOI) began an effort to erect a sculpture to honor him and to perpetuate his memory. Carlos Marinas, a reputed Spanish sculptor, was commissioned to create a bas-relief in stainless steel and bronze. Marinas' most well-known sculptures in Spain are works for the country's national government monuments and for private industry. He had won various awards and international competitions. His work is preserved in private collections and museums in Italy, Portugal, Germany and Switzerland. He also designed and built monuments and plazas in Arab countries.

The resulting 4 x 11 ft. (1.2 x 3.3m) rectangular piece features a bust of Khan as its focus surrounded by the Chicago skyline and the structural frames that include many buildings he designed. Khan's image is set in a rift between the two sides of the bas-relief, which are "offset as if sheared along an earthquake fault" (Petroski, 1999). An early rendering of the sculpture did not have any inscription, but the inscription added later reads:

> The Structural Engineers Association of Illinois
> recognizes Fazlur Rahman Khan as one of the great
> structural engineers of our time

To the right of Khan's head, on top of the skyline, are inscribed the words "structural engineer, humanist, educator and speaker." Each of these is staggered from each other so as to catch people's attention. The image of Khan does not exactly match what people remember. When some questioned this, Marinas explained that he viewed several photographs of Khan in different poses and moods, and attempted to reflect them all in a single image to evoke the many qualities of the man. As is often the case, the artist saw beyond the vision of others.

Here is the chronology of events surrounding the sculpture. In May of 1988 the sculpture was completed and shipped to Chicago from Spain. On May 20, 1988 at 5:00 p.m., SEAOI held a reception in the lobby of 222 North LaSalle in Chicago to announce its arrival and to honor Khan. Structural engineers, invited dignitaries, community leaders and admirers of Khan were present. Illinois Congressmen John E. Porter and Henry J. Hyde read statements into the U.S. Congressional Record on May 10 and May 17, respectively—announcing the reception and noting the achievements of Khan. Acting Mayor of Chicago, Eugene Sawyer, proclaimed Friday, May 20 as "Dr. Fazlur Rahman Khan Day in Chicago." Illinois State Senator Bob Kustra offered Senate Resolution No. 991 honoring Khan. At the reception, Jon Boyd, SEOAI President, recounted the legacy of Khan's work and called the occasion a celebration rather than a memorial. *ASCE News*, in its August, 1988 issue, reported this event and paid homage to him by referring to him as "one of the giants of the structural engineering profession." This was the first public exhibition of the Khan sculpture.

Shortly before its unveiling, a resolution recognizing the event and the role of Khan in shaping Chicago's skyline, was adopted by the City Council of Chicago on April 27, 1988. The resolution acclaimed Khan for his breakthroughs in efficient structural design of tall buildings. The Council paid special tribute to Khan for his "numerous contributions to man's built environment" and his "leadership and humanistic concerns for a better world." 222 North LaSalle was, however, only a temporary home for the sculpture. In fact, it was not going to be easy to find a permanent site.

The owners of the John Hancock Center and the Sears Tower did not entertain the idea of locating Khan's image in either of their lobbies despite the fact it was his design that made their buildings possible (Petroski, 1999). Likewise, the Chicago Academy of Sciences, the Museum of Science and Industries, the Chicago Art Institute, the Chicago Cultural Center, and the Chicago Historical Society all turned down the request of SEAOI. Even IIT, where Khan had been an adjunct architecture professor for many years, did not wish to have it. According to Petroski (1999), "Though their refusal may have been due in part to what they perceived to be the too prominent place given to the sponsoring organization in the inscription, thus blurring the line between plaque and sculpture, local structural engineers took the rebuff as a further example of the anonymity of engineers, their poor treatment by the media and their status relative to architects in the windy city."

After a display for only a few weeks at the LaSalle location, the work of art was put on display in the lobby of City Hall, again for a short period. After this, it was put in storage with the hope that a suitable permanent site would be found. After about a year, the proprietors of the Brunswick Building agreed to provide a permanent venue for the image in its plaza. The dedication ceremony was carried out with appropriate fanfare. Mayor Richard Daley formally dedicated the sculpture on May 8, 1989. In his address at the ceremony, the mayor said, "Chicago, a premiere city famed for its architectural excellence, owes much of this reputation to Fazlur Khan's genius and to his profession of structural engineering." Paul Gapp, *Chicago Tribune* architectural critic, said at the dedication, "This is a city where the names of Sullivan and Wright and Mies come easily to the tongue. Now, perhaps, the name of Fazlur Khan will be more clearly remembered as another giant of architecture and engineering." Bill Lavicka of SEAOI, whose tireless efforts made possible this homage to Khan said, "This is our gift to all Chicagoans. We hope that this sculpture will generate public awareness of this great man and his profession, structural engineering."

Unfortunately, Miró's 25-ft. (7.6m) tall Miss Chicago dominated the plaza so much that it overshadowed the much smaller bas-relief installed on the rear wall. After a few years, to add insult to injury, welding on the sculpture, exposed to the outdoor environment, began to rust and degrade. This was reported by the *Chicago Sun-Times* in its January 7, 1992 issue with the headline "Loop sculpture rusting on its laurels." Fortunately, however, the bas-relief finally found a suitable indoor site in the summer of 1993, after the new management at Sears Tower agreed to install it near the entrance to the skydeck ticket purchase area of the building close to the elevators, through which more than 1.4 million tourists pass annually on their way to the observatory on the 103rd floor. On their way back, many visitors stop to view the sculpture and to photograph themselves with the artwork in the background. Others view Khan's bust and read the inscriptions. Still others are often seen rubbing his nose for good luck. Because of the unflagging efforts of SEAOI, Khan was finally recognized in a worthy manner in the tallest and one of his best-known tube structures.

Although the structural engineers of Illinois voiced their utmost regard for him, both during his lifetime and after his death, engineers in his native land have been slow with similar recognitions. Khan emerged as a mysterious genius from his origins in Bangladesh to achieve international acclaim. Despite individual Bangladeshi engineers who have deep respect and admiration for Khan, the profession there has failed to adequately recognize his greatness in the past in a befitting way. Even the government of Bangladesh has been slow to recognize one of the most illustrious sons of the country, Khan, who not only put Bangladesh on the world map but also indefatigably demonstrated his utmost loyalty to his native homeland by contributing to its Liberation Movement.

The sentiment was well expressed by Hubert Francis Sarkar, a Bangladeshi resident of Dhaka, in a letter to the editor of a widely circulated local newspaper, *The Daily Star*, published on April 20, 1992. He wrote:

> We the Bangalees of Bangladesh know very little about a fellow Bangalee who achieved world-class distinctions. . . . During a magazine programme of BTV, Professor J. R. Choudhury revealed a sense of regret that many of the people even in F. R. Khan's motherland fail to appreciate such a formidable personality who once stirred the civil engineering firmament. . . . How does it happen that an architect-engineer of this soil is the designer of the tallest building of the world? We can be exultant enough that some vital innovative concepts of designs for tall buildings have been formulated by this gentleman. . . . [Recently, we came] to know of Mr. F. R. Khan's outstanding contributions to the War of Liberation in 1971. He raised funds for the refugee Bangalees and he did find it a graceful act for him to lobby the cause of his own people, the Bangalees. . . . I would salute this Bangalee architect-engineer who made real, big achievements. We have learnt somehow that this gentleman chaired many prestigious establishments and a statue dedicated to his memory is now situated in Chicago. Sad to note that he is not much recognized in Bangladesh. . . . It will be enlightening for present and future generations of architects and engineers to learn about the achievements in detail. . . . Trust, it is never too late to pay homage to a real super-achiever.

Finally, on March 25, 1999, on the occasion of Bangladesh Day, the Government of Bangladesh showed belated respect to him when the postal department issued commemorative stamps showing a picture of his face emerging from a brick facade in the background and an image of the Sears Tower on his left. The stamp was officially released in April, 1999. Also, at the same time, the government of Bangladesh has recognized him with the Independence Day Award for his contributions to "architecture" (we note again that in his native homeland, he is generally recognized more as an architect than a structural engineer). This national award carries with it a gold medal, some cash funds and a certificate of recognition. Khan was one of eleven recipients of this highest civilian honor who were recognized for their outstanding contributions to Bangladesh.

In addition to the above mentioned recognition, a students' hall of residence of the Bangladesh Institute of Technology at Gazipur, a suburb of Dhaka, has been named after Khan. The establishment of Fazlur Rahman Khan Center for Built Environment is yet to be realized, but according to Jamilur Reza Choudhury, it is in progress and some funds have already been raised. The Institution of Engineers of Bangladesh features an annual Fazlur Rahman Khan Memorial Lecture. Moreover, the Bangladesh National Museum in Dhaka displays a large portrait of Khan to honor him as a noteworthy "architect" of Bangladesh amongst portraits of other Bangladeshi notables.

Bangladeshi expatriates in Chicago had recognized Khan by raising funds for the Khan scholarship at BUET (see Chapter 15). Also, expatriates in the USA donated funds for the Khan

Prize at Lehigh University in his honor. Fundraising efforts for this prize had been carried out by Aminul Karim and myself in cooperation with Lynn S. Beedle and Chandra Jha for many years. AABEA organized a fundraising dinner in New York on November 15, 1997 for the prize. This event, organized by AABEA president Sufian Khondker and his associates, helped raise the remaining much-needed funds to launch the award of this prize. Beedle was the invited keynote speaker on the occasion. A souvenir booklet showing the buildings designed by Khan was published on the occasion. Messages from Khan's brother, Zillur Khan, and his daughter, Yasmin—none of whom could attend the event—were included in this publication. In her message, Yasmin stated:

> As this community remembers Dr. Fazlur Rahman Khan,
> it is an old familiar friend. By reminiscing about him, we
> keep him alive and surely, his presence is still felt within us.
> Everyone here may not have known him personally, yet, it
> seems to me, this does not lessen the special caring that
> one feels for him. . . . He loved life and people, and Banglades
> his can truly feel proud that such a man as Fazlur Rahman
> Khan was very deeply a Bengali.

Khan's public recognition was enhanced when the street sign on the northwest corner of the intersection of West Jackson Boulevard and South Franklin Street in Chicago named that corner as "Fazlur R. Khan Way." Few engineers get a street corner in a major U.S. city designated after them, but the City of Chicago did just that. The event was reported in the July 16, 1998 issue of the *ASCE News* and CTBUH's newsletter *The Times*. It prompted an article on Khan by Henry Petroski (1999).

Behind the remarkable dedication ceremony on June 16, 1998 were the concerted efforts of its coordinator Sadraddin Noorani, a Bangladeshi businessman in Chicago, and its organizers The City of Chicago and the Bangladesh Association of Greater Chicagoland (BAGC). They were assisted by SOM and TrizecHahn Office Properties.

A resolution was adopted earlier by the City Council of Chicago on April 1, 1998. In the resolution signed by Mayor Richard Daley, the 27th independence anniversary of Bangladesh on March 25, 1998 was recognized and tributes were paid to those who fought for its independence. The Bangladeshi citizens in Chicago were also recognized for their "enormous contribution to the civilized professions such as engineering and architecture." It further recognized that "one such Chicago resident was the great Fazlur Khan," credited for the design of the Sears Tower and the Hancock Building.

The same day, in a meeting, the City Council passed an ordinance in which the Commissioner of Transportation was authorized to "take necessary action for the standardization of the northwest corner of the intersection of West Jackson Boulevard and South Franklin Street as 'Fazlur R. Khan Way'." The event was reported in local newspapers. On June 15, it was featured in the *Chicago Sun-Times* under the heading "Chicago's Towering Intellect." Architecture critic Lee Bey discussed the upcoming event with a brief biographical sketch of Khan and by paying tributes to his memory.

21

The dedication ceremony started at 1:00 p.m. with a series of speeches at the outside plaza of the Sears Tower, where architects, engineers, Bangladeshis, news reporters, community leaders, and Khan's friends and well wishers gathered. After formally dedicating the street corner in Khan's name, another ceremony was held on the 100th floor of the Sears Tower where a few more speeches were delivered by Khan's friends and associates. A message from Chester Siess, who could not be present, was read. In it, Siess said in part,

> As a student at the University of Illinois, Faz was every professor's dream—he came to learn, not to be taught . . .

> Fazlur's accomplishments as an engineer are known to all, and it is impossible to recount them without using the word 'innovation'. But what is not always realized or mentioned is that Faz was not just an innovator—but a successful one. Not all innovations are successful, many are failures, and lead to failures of structures—I have investigated some of these. Successful innovation advances the state of the art. Faz had the rare ability to know just where the line was that defined the state of the art, and he never stepped over that line. He knew the limits of his knowledge and that of the profession, and before he 'innovated', he did what was needed to improve his knowledge—by tests or studies—before moving ahead into new territory. He never stepped over the line, he pushed it back. This is the key to successful innovation. We are indebted to Faz for demonstrating this as much as we are for his innovations themselves.

> I learned of his many humanitarian and philanthropic activities from others, not from Faz. This was typical of him. He was not only a great engineer, he was a great man.

A souvenir book (BAGC, 1998), commemorating the ceremony, was published and distributed to the attendees. Letters and dedications from officials and Khan's family, colleagues, friends and devotees were included in the book.

Greeting everyone who gathered in Chicago to honor Khan's life and achievements, President Clinton sent a message which said in part, "Architecture can define as well as reflect the spirit of a people, giving tangible form to the beauty of human expression and the power of human imagination. Drawing on the richness of his Bengali background and the vigor and energy of American culture, Fazlur Khan pushed the boundaries of modern architecture and dramatically changed the physical landscape of the great city of Chicago."

Illinois Governor Jim Edgar said in his letter, "The Sears Tower is a world renowned, architectural masterpiece that we are proud to have in Chicago's skyline. The innovative technologies that Mr. Khan utilized in designing the Sears Tower have been an inspiration to engineers around the world and have truly revolutionized the skyscraper construction."

Chicago Mayor Richard Daley wrote, "From the coastal region of Bangladesh, Mr. Khan's memories of the structural properties of bamboo enabled him to see a wholly new way to build. His pioneering design concept for the Sears Tower enabled the world's tallest building to be raised in Chicago and gave the art and science of construction an innovative technique for erecting towers to touch the sky. I am delighted to commend his unique gifts and outstanding vision."

Khan's principal project, the Sears Tower, now has the Khan sculpture within it and is located at the Fazlur R. Khan Way—a fitting recognition indeed! Meanwhile, his ideas on structural design continue to flourish and be used by others around the world.

An article on engineers, that appeared, ironically, in *The Economist* (1998) of London, pointed out that the civil engineering profession is in need of heroes. It described the achievements of European engineers, notably George Stephenson, Isambard Brunel, Thomas Telford, Robert Maillart, and Othmar Ammann. Some other names mentioned included Nervi, Torroja, Candela, Ove Arup, and Fazlur Khan. Santiago Calatrava is mentioned as the only living hero at present. Among the several references to Khan in the article is the following:

> Apart from bridges, heavy civil engineering projects and the concrete marvels of such as Nervi, the obvious engineering feats of this century are its skyscrapers. The leading exponent of these was Fazlur Khan (1929-82), an engineering partner in a top American firm of architects, Skidmore, Owings and Merrill.

But Khan is only one of the few American civil engineers named in the entire series of names. Other notable Americans mentioned are Othmar Ammann and David Steinman—both bridge designers. Like Khan, Ammann migrated to the United States where he was highly successful in his career. David Steinman, on the other hand, was born and raised in New York. Khan is the only building designer from America who seems to have caught the attention of the Europeans.

In the August 30, 1999 issue of the *ENR* magazine, Khan was recognized as one of the "Top People of the Past 125 Years." He was included in the same list that contained such names as Thomas Edison, the inventor, and Gustave Eiffel, the designer and builder of the Eiffel Tower, and other luminaries not mentioned here. In its citation on Khan, *ENR* said, ". . . he came to the U.S. on a Fulbright scholarship and combined technical genius with a sensitivity for people and where they work."

▲ ▼

Speaking about the structural design of tall buildings, it had remained stagnant until the end of the second skyscraper age, sometimes also referred to as the Art Deco period (see Chapter 3). Steel rigid frames with wind bracing were the primary structural systems for most of the buildings of that era. To summarize, it is due to Khan's innovations and vision that the ideas of shear wall-frame interaction, tubular design, composite tubular systems, and superframes with large corner columns were conceived and implemented on practical structures. In these, he laid the basis of the design of megastructures. Because of his work, multiple structural approaches to tall building design are now possible creating exciting architectural forms. Although he liked both steel and concrete, he enlarged the potential for concrete in particular as a material for tall buildings and used it for many of his projects. He enhanced the importance of concrete further by pioneering composite systems that have been primarily used for tall buildings in recent times. New variations of mixed construction have been developed for many of the latest buildings. They all, however, owe their origin to Khan's vision.

Through his brilliance and inventive designs, Khan has shown the way to build really tall. He has dispelled the myth of 'rigid frame only' for tall buildings. The technology is now there. Computers have now facilitated complex structural analysis. The height limit is dictated no longer by structure, but by life safety, environmental concerns, vertical transportation system and economic viability. Since Khan has truly revolutionized tall building design in the twentieth century, he may be aptly hailed as the 'father of modern-day tall buildings'. Anyone exploring the annals of structural engineering following the turn of the millennium will be unable to come away without happening upon the name of this technical genius who has changed forever the way we look at the tall buildings that we live and work in. The scope of his monumental work cannot be measured.

Khan realized that, despite the occasional opposition of skeptics, the urge to build as high as possible would remain a challenge and a common trait of human culture. The population growth in the great cities of the world will demand the construction of many more high-rise buildings. How true his vision has proven to be! Since his death, many high-rises and supertall structures have been built in Asia, Europe, Latin America and other parts of the world. The drive for height continues.

He had a majestic vision of the cities. While he predicted that urban centers of the whole world would inevitably undergo changes in their vertical scale, he recognized the importance of the horizontal scale and the need for a better awareness of the ground level environment (Khan, 1974b; 1974c). On the issue of the changing scale of cities, he wrote (Khan, 1974b):

> The changing vertical scale has indeed opened the possibility of a brighter future for the dense urban environment. What is now needed is a fresh look at the horizontal scale at the ground level. It is hoped that the engineering profession will join their hands with the planners and architects to create a more livable human environment with the upward changing scale of cities.

While he lived, Khan was a trend-setter of structural innovations at SOM. Since then, such work has continued under the leadership of Iyengar. After being elected partner in 1975, Iyengar already began to work on his own projects in collaboration with Graham and other architects. However, with Khan's demise, he was more directly involved in the process, and this collaboration continued. He pursued the concepts of superframes, mixed steel-concrete structures and other systems. Innovative superframe systems include the diagonal, the diarigid and composite typologies (Iyengar, 1986). In a 1983 study for an 85-story building in Houston, Texas, he used the basic vocabulary of a diarigid braced superframe consisting of ten columns in the building (Iyengar, 1986). Another example is the Columbus Circle project in New York. Two other buildings of technical feat that Iyengar engineered are the 1990 Broadgate Building in London, England and the 45-story Hotel Artes-Barcelona of 1992 at Spain's Olympic Village. Both are examples of structural art in steel. More recently, Iyengar and his SOM associates carried out the complex structural design of another masterpiece—the Guggenheim Museum, a sculptural building in Bilbao, Spain. He observed that Khan was responsible for realizing the different structural forms that are economically and structurally suitable for tall buildings with different heights (Iyengar, 1997). This was the beginning of a rapid evolution of tall structural systems that made subsequent innovations possible. Iyengar also made predictions for future tall buildings of the twenty-first century (Iyengar, 1997).

Several supertall buildings—not exceeding the height of the Sears Tower—have been built or conceived since Khan's death. A few supertall concrete or composite buildings have also been built. A recently built 1380-ft. (418-m) Jin Mao Building in Shanghai (1999) is a mixed system of steel and concrete that has a number of steel outrigger trusses tying the building's concrete tubular core to its exterior composite megacolumns. In all instances, the structural systems used have been derived from Khan's original ideas of rational design, either directly or in a modified manner.

There have been attempts at skyscrapers exceeding the height of the Sears Tower. Khan himself worked on the 168-story World Trade Center in Chicago that was never built. A few other mega-project concepts after his death are the 150-story, 1670-ft. (506-m) high Donald Trump's Television City in New York, the 210-story Chicago World Trade Center, the 125-story Miglin-Beitler Tower in Chicago, and the 1476-ft. (450-m) high Petronas Towers in Kuala Lumpur—the only one that has been built. The structure of the Petronas Towers primarily utilizes concrete for the frame of beams and columns, anchored to core walls. Steel-framed cantilevers were used to reach beyond the perimeter columns. The floor system used steel beams with metal deck and concrete topping. The structure thus fulfills Khan's prediction that concrete would become a very important material of the future and it applies the innovation by Khan of mixed construction combining steel and concrete.

Another project is the 1509-ft. (457m) high World Financial Center, in Shanghai, China, which is on hold at the time of this writing. An 1850-ft. (560m) high Grollo Tower was proposed at one time for the city of Melbourne, Australia. This $1.5 billion tower would have broken all previous height records.

Earlier, SOM completed the design of one other spectacular skyscraper in Chicago—the 108-story mixed-use 7 South Dearborn building, with a height of 1550 ft. (470m), topped out with two telecommunication antennas. Keeping up with the tradition of Khan at SOM, William Baker, a structural engineering partner of SOM, engineered this supertall building's structural system that employs a "stayed mast" concept with two stepbacks and three notches separating six distinctive groups of floors along the height of the building. The central 66-ft. (20m) square tubular concrete core acts as the "mast" and it links the perimeter structure ("stays") through steel outrigger trusses. (This project has become inactive as of this writing.)

Other proposed skyscrapers less than 2000 ft. (606 m.) tall at the time of this writing are: the Jakarta Tower, at 1830-ft. (555-m.); the Sao Paulo Tower, at 1624 ft. (492 m.); the Landmark Tower in Hong Kong, at 1883-ft. (571 m.); and the Citygate Ecotower in London at, 1509 ft. (457 m.). At this time, the realization of the Ecotower is a distinct possibility. If completed in 2008, as planned, this highly energy-efficient building will claim the title of the world's tallest building. In short, new innovations and socioeconomic realities are pushing building heights towards 2000 ft. (606 m.).

Buildings even taller than the dizzying 2000 ft. (606 m.) have been conceived. Some of these are the 2700 ft. (823 m.) Chicago World Center (never built); the 2222 ft. (674 m.) World Center for Vedic Learning in India (proposed); the 2755-ft. (835 m.) Millennium Tower in the Tokyo Bay (never built); and the proposed Bionic Tower rising 4,029 ft. (1221 m.) in Hong Kong. In the 1950s, Frank Lloyd Wright proposed the ultimate skyscraper—the well known "mile-high tower." In 1986, Colaco carried out an investigation on a hypothetical mile-high concrete building. He was assisted by a group of experts. He concluded that such a building was indeed technically feasible. Although steel, for such a building, would provide strength and ductility, Colaco favored concrete because of its stiffness, damping, and fire-proofing characteristics Of course, Eugene Tsui's dream of a two-mile high Ultima Tower piercing the clouds of the San Francisco sky tops the list. Leslie Robertson went even further and told me, "The only considerations are money and real estate. Otherwise, we could build to the moon." Whether such awe-inspiring heights are mere fantasies or practical possibilities at this time is another matter.

Khan demonstrated that the limit on the height of buildings is not necessarily determined by structural constraints alone. The practical limits on height are set by human physiology, environmental and aviation concerns, and the financial burden involved in building to the clouds. Some other barriers are the problems of moving a large population in and out, as well as supplying utilities and fire protection to the building. Despite these impediments, buildings have continued to grow taller, apparently not yet having reached their practical height limits. The concepts of superframes and mixed construction employing three-dimensional cantilever systems, explored by Khan in the 1960s and 1970s, constituted a significant leap forward in tall building design. The superframe idea presented a generic form of structural system with enormous potential that can be applied to tall and supertall buildings and that works well with architectural planning of internal spaces. Similarly, his vision of mega-structures and multi-use buildings is now a constant reality. Khan's influence continues.

Khan also left his legacy at IIT's School of Architecture. His role as a dedicated educator side-by-side with his professional career demonstrated that teaching was a very important part of his professional life. He worked closely with his students and he always felt that his frequent contact with them as their research adviser helped to stimulate new ideas and concepts and think them through. Students there continue to work on newer structural systems such as using hyperbolic paraboloid shape along the building height for high-rises while keeping the members straight. Sharpe observed, "We are still fulfilling Khan's wishes. He would probably experiment with such ideas, if he were alive today." Elnimeiri agreed: "IIT is continuing Khan's tradition by developing new systems and concepts. Visual modeling of structures, so much promoted by Khan, is still being actively done here."

Engineers continue their collaborations with architects on new projects using their vision, inventiveness and technical competence. As Petroski (1999) wrote, "Just as by standing on the shoulders of giants we can become even bigger giants, so it is that by climbing on the spires of skyscrapers, engineers can reach for ever taller skyscrapers." They may well reach much greater heights of buildings than what we can imagine. Khan laid down the path for them. He will always remain the guiding spirit. Future giants of skyscraper design will undoubtedly stand on his shoulders and look upon his work seriously. Students of tall building design will seriously study what Khan had accomplished, how he did it, and what he had to say on the subject. They will appreciate his constant search for structural logic and truth in architecture. They will be amazed to discover his untiring efforts to unite architecture and structural engineering—and his individuality—in facing the challenges of complex structural design. Sure future designers will be humbled by his insights relating to society and to humanity at large. Together, these will be Khan's lasting legacy. Meanwhile, his great structures will continue to soar into the sky and gleam in the sun.

EPILOGUE

The art of the modern-day skyscraper is the story of Fazlur R. Khan—a mild-mannered, introspective, and pragmatic engineer's engineer whose invigorating excitement for exploration and innovation was matched by his conviction that there is always a better way to design a building and improve the urban fabric.

Some of his beliefs and attributes of character were: success is not the end of the road; hard work brings unexpected reward; enthusiasm is contagious; striving for perfection brings quality and excellence; treating people with dignity and warmth wins them over. Embodiment of great structural artists, he gave much of himself to advancing the art and science of structural design. His influence as a grand skyscraper designer continues to be recognized by engineers and architects and can be felt far and wide.

He is one of those who in striding across the stage of life left the world and the history of urban civilization marked forever by their presence. Yet, sadly, he has not entered with the general culture to the same degree that star-architects, star-scientists and even star-academics have. This is the fate of many great heroes of engineering whose contributions to humanity go unrecognized by the general public. But certainly he was able to break the barriers of communication and establish for himself a superior image in the building profession as "one of the great structural engineers of our time."

Fazlur Khan looked up to the stars and with his supertall buildings reached for the sky but never forgot the earth under him.

Dr. Fazlur Rahman Khan

He fought the wind and the force of gravity
with elegance of vision and form.

But, beyond these professional goals,
well fulfilled, his concerns were the gravity of
the human condition and its amelioration.

The winds of war and evil, which he chose
to engage through beauty, tranquility, and love.

The elegance of life which he maintained,
by the elegance of his behavior toward all of us
he touched, by example of deeds and by
an open heart to all who sought his advice.

The form of cities which he so much understood,
proud towers, structures and spaces that
celebrate the human intellect, and, in the tradition
of great engineers, builders and architects,
maintain truth and integrity in all
the great many structures he conceived.

Vision which he now leaves
to all of us Lisl, Yasmin, Zillur, Martin, his family
around the globe, his friends, his partners,
students, and colleagues from east to west.

His is a clear spirit protected by a life
he dedicated with charity to all, with compassion
to the unenlightened, guidance to those who seek
enlightening, inspiration to engineers as well as
to architects, such as only a great engineer
and humanist could confer.

We will miss our good doctor, but we will
all live a more significant life because of the path
he marked with his life.

Bruce J. Graham (*Khan Tributes,* 1982)

"Whether a result of his abilities, his culture or his faith, Fazlur Khan in and through his life resolved the dilemmas of modernization and the conflicts of cultures. He presented a clear-eyed and inspired vision of what ought to be."

William L. Porter (*BAGC*, 1998)

Lynn Beedle seeking funds from President Ershad of Bangladesh
for the Fazlur Rahman Khan Chair (1989)
[Courtesy: Lynn S. Beedle]

John Zils, a Khan Associate, speaking at a reception on the
100th floor of the Sears Tower on the occasion of the inauguration
of Fazlur R. Khan Way in Chicago on June 16, 1998
[Photo by Mir M. Ali]

Commemorative postal stamp released in April, 1999 by the
Government of Bangladesh
[Courtesy: Aminul Karim]

27

৳ 4

বাংলাদেশ

Dr. FAZLUR RAHMAN KHAN   1929-1982

ডঃ ফজলুর রহমান খান   ১৯২৯-১৯৮২

BANGLADESH

৳ 8

REFERENCES/BIBLIOGRAPHY

ALI, M. M., 1983. "Are Engineers Happy People?", *Civil Engineering*, August, pp. 58-59.

ALI, M. M., 1990. "Integration of Structural Form and Esthetics in Tall Building Design: The Future Challenge," *Proceedings of the World Congress on Tall Buildings*, Hong Kong, November, pp. 3-12.

ARAMCO WORLD MAGAZINE, 1974. "The Hajj: A Special Issue," November-December.

ARCHITECTURAL RECORD, 1980. "Tent Structures: Are they Architecture?" May, pp. 127-134.

ASCE, 1972. "Structural Systems - Theme Report," *Proceedings of the International Conference of Planning and Design of Tall Buildings*, August 21-26, 1972, vol. 1a: *Tall Buildings Systems and Concepts*, American Society of Civil Engineers, New York, p. 405.

BAGC, 1998. *"Fazlur R. Khan Way" Dedication Ceremony*, Bangladesh Association of Greater Chicagoland, June 16.

BEEDLE, L. S., 1986. "Fazlur Khan . . . And Wholeness," *Technique and Aesthetics in the Design of Tall Buildings*, Institute for the Study of the High-Rise Habitat, Lehigh University, Bethlehem, PA, pp. 91-92.

BEEDLE, L. S., 1990. "Fazlur Rahman Khan Chair: A Progress Report, 1982-1989," May.

BEEDLE, L. S., 1992. "The Council on Tall Buildings and Urban Habitat," *Structural Engineering International*, March, p. 160.

BENNETT, David, 1995. *Skyscrapers - Form and Function*, Simon and Schuster, New York.

BILLINGTON, David P., 1983. *The Tower and the Bridge: The New Art of Structural Engineering*, Princeton University Press, Princeton, New Jersey.

BLASER, Werner, 1987. *Myron Goldsmith: Buildings and Concepts*, Rizzoli International Publications, New York.

BOYER, E. L. and Mitgang, L. D., 1996. *Building Community: A New Future for Architecture Education and Practice - A Special Report*, The Carnegie Foundation for the Advancement of Teaching; Princeton, New Jersey, p. 19.

CHANG, P. and Swenson, A., "A Study of an Ultra High-Rise Community," *Proceedings of the Symposium on Tall Buildings: Planning, Design and Construction*, Vanderbilt University, Nashville, TN, pp. 61-70.

CIVIL ENGINEERING, 1980. "Top Foreign-born Civil Engineers Speak Their Minds," October, pp. 115-116.

CTBUH, 1995. *Architecture of Tall Buildings*, Mir M. Ali and Paul Armstrong, Editors, Council on Tall Buildings and Urban Habitat Monograph 30, McGraw-Hill, Inc.

DEAN, Andrea O., 1980. "Evaluation: Trussed Tube Towering over Chicago," *AIA Journal*, October, pp. 68-73.

DEHAVEN, Anne S., 1995. "Fazlur Khan: Philosophical Engineer, Technical Genius," *Structural Engineering Forum Magazine*, March, pp. 22-27.

DIXON, J. M., 1970. "The Tall One," *Architectural Forum* 133, July/August, p. 44.

ENGEL, H., 1997. *Structure Systems*, Gerd Hatje Publishers, Germany (distributed in the USA by Distributed Art Publishers, New York), pp. 300-301.

ENR, 1971. "Fazlur Khan: Avant Garde Designs of High-Rise," *Engineering News-Record*, McGraw-Hill Publ., August 26, pp. 16-18.

ENR, 1972. "Construction's Man of the Year: Fazlur R. Khan," *Engineering News-Record*, McGraw-Hill Publ., February 10, pp. 20-25.

ENR, 1982. "Fazlur R. Khan," *Engineering News-Record*, McGraw-Hill Publ., April 1, pp. 12 and 72.

FABER, C., 1963. *Candela/The Shell Builder*, Reinhold Publishing Corporation, New York.

FINTEL, Mark, 1982. "Fazlur R. Khan (1929-1982)," *ACI Concrete International*, June, pp. 80-81.

FINTEL, Mark, 1986. "New Forms in Concrete," *Techniques and Aesthetics in the Design of Tall Buildings*, Institute for the Study of the High-Rise Habitat, Lehigh University, Bethlehem, PA, pp. 39-56.

GOLDBERGER, Paul, 1989. *The Skyscraper*, Alfred A. Knopf, New York, NY.

GOLDSMITH, Myron, 1986. "Fazlur Khan's Contribution to Education," *Techniques and Aesthetics in the Design of Tall Buildings*, Institute for the Study of High-Rise Habitat, Lehigh University, Bethlehem, PA, pp. 17-37.

GRAHAM, Bruce J., 1986. "Collaboration in Practice Between Architect and Engineer," *Technique and Aesthetics in the Design of Tall Buildings*, Institute for the Study of the High-Rise Habitat, Lehigh University, Bethlehem, PA, pp. 1-15.

GRAHAM, Bruce, 1989. *Bruce Graham of SOM*, Rizzoli International Publications, Inc., New York, NY.

HAYASHI, Alden M., 1999. "The Sky's the Limit," *Scientific American: Extreme Engineering*, vol. 10, No. 4, Winter, pp. 66-72.

HERBERT, G., 1999. "Architect-Engineer Relationships: Overlappings and Interactions," *Architectural Science Review*, Vol. 42, June, pp. 107-110.

HOYT, H., 1933. *One Hundred Years of Land Values in Chicago: The Relationship of the Growth of Chicago to the Rise of its Land Values 1830-1933*, University of Chicago Press, Chicago.

HUXTABLE, A. L., 1960. *Pier Luigi Nervi*, George Braziller, Inc., New York, NY.

IABSE, 1982. "IABSE Structures C-23/82," IABSE Periodica 4/1982, International Association of Bridge and Structural Engineers, Zurich, Switzerland, pp. 63-83.

IYENGAR, Hal, 1977. "State-of-the-Art Report on the Composite or Mixed Steel-Concrete Construction for Buildings," ASCE publication.

IYENGAR, Hal, 1984. "Recent Developments in Tall Buildings," Proceedings of International Conference on Tall Buildings, Singapore, October, pp. 25-36.

IYENGAR, Hal, 1986. "Structural and Steel Systems," *Techniques and Aesthetics in the Design of Tall Buildings*, Institute for the

Study of the High-Rise Habitat, Lehigh University, Bethlehem, PA, pp. 57-69.

IYENGAR, S. H., 1997. "Tall Building Systems for the New Century," *Structures in the New Millennium*, A. A. Balkema, Rotterdam, pp. 19-30.

IYENGAR, S. H. and F. R. Khan, 1973. "Structural Steel Design for Sears Tower," *Australian Conference on Steel Developments*, Austrian Institute of Steel Construction, Newcastle, Australia, May 21-25, pp. 11-18.

JENCKS, C., 1988. *Architecture Today*, Harry N. Abrams, New York, NY.

JOHNSON, Philip, 1978. *Mies van der Rohe*, The Museum of Modern Art, New York, NY, 3rd ed.

KHAN, A. R., 1996. *My Life* (in Bengali), Bangladesh Co-operative Book Society Ltd., Dhaka, Bangladesh (first published in 1964).

KHAN, F. R., 1955. "Analytical Study of the Relations among Various Design Criteria for Rectangular Prestressed Concrete Beams," Doctoral Thesis, Department of Civil Engineering, University of Illinois, Urbana, IL.

KHAN, F. R., 1967. "The John Hancock Center," *Civil Engineering*, October, pp. 38-42.

KHAN, F.R., 1969. "Recent Structural Systems in Steel for High-Rise Buildings," *Proceedings of the BCSA Conference on Steel in Architecture*, London, England, November 24-26.

KHAN, F. R., 1970. "Lightweight Concrete for Total Design of One Shell Plaza," *ACI Convention*, New York, April.

KHAN, F. R., 1972a. "Future of High Rise Structures," *Progressive Architecture*, October, pp. 78-85.

KHAN, F. R., 1972b. "A Philosophical Comparison Between Maillart's Bridges and Some Recent Concrete Buildings," *Background Papers*, 2nd National Conference on Civil Engineering: History, Heritage and the Humanities, Princeton University, Princeton, NJ, pp. 1-19.

KHAN, F. R., 1972c. "Influence of Design Criteria on Selection of Structural Systems for Tall Buildings," *Proceedings of the Canadian Structural Engineering Conference*, Montreal, Canada, March, pp. 1-15.

KHAN, F. R., 1973. "Evolution of Structural Systems for High-Rise Buildings in Steel and Concrete," *Proceedings of the Regional Conference on Tall Buildings*, Bratislava, Czechoslovakia.

KHAN, F. R., 1974a. "Tubular Structures for Tall Buildings," *Handbook of Concrete Engineering*, Mark Fintel, ed., Van Nostrand Reinhold, pp. 345-355.

KHAN, F. R., 1974b. "New Structural Systems for Tall Buildings and Their Scale Effects on Cities," Featured Paper, *Proceedings of the Symposium on Tall Buildings: Planning, Design & Construction*, Vanderbilt University, Nashville, TN, November, pp. 99-128.

KHAN, F. R., 1974c. "Changing Scale of the Cities," *Consulting Engineer*, April, pp. 69-73.

KHAN, F. R., 1976. "Precast Concrete for Tall Multiple Use Buildings - A Future Outlook," *CIBS41 Symposium III/Joint Committee Regional Conference*, Moscow, USSR, October.

KHAN, F. R., 1981. "Creative Teaching and its Influence on Innovative Concrete Structures," *Significant Developments in Engineering Practice and Research*, ACI Publ. SP-72, M. A. Sozen, ed., pp. 355-364.

KHAN, F. R., 1982a. "The Rise and Fall of Structural Logic in Architecture," *Chicago Architectural Journal*, Chicago Architectural Club, vol. 2, pp. 92-93.

KHAN, F. R., 1982b. "100 Story John Hancock Center in Chicago - A Case Study of the Design Process," *IABSE Journal*, J-16/82, August, 1982, pp. 27-34; *Engineering Structures*, January, 1983, pp. 10-14.

KHAN, F. R. and J. A. Sbarounis, 1964. "Interaction of Shear Walls and Frames in Concrete Structures under Lateral Loads," *Journal of the American Society of Civil Engineers*, 90 (ST3), June, pp. 285-335.

KHAN, F. R., S. H. Iyengar, and J. P. Colaco, 1966. "Computer Design of 100-story John Hancock Center," *ASCE Journal of he Structural Division*, ST6, December, pp. 55-73.

KHAN, F. R. and Mark Fintel, 1968a. "Effects of Column Temperature, Creep and Shrinkage in Tall Structures," *Final Report to the Eighth Congress of the International Association for Bridge and Structural Engineering*, New York, September, pp. 1015-1017.

KHAN, F. R. and Mark Fintel, 1968b. "Shock Absorbing Soft Story Concept for Multi-Story Earthquake Structures," *64th Annual ACI Convention*, Los Angeles, California, March; *ACI Journal*, May, 1969, pp. 381-389.

KHAN, F. R. and A. F. Nassetta, 1970. "Temperature Effects on Tall Steel Framed Buildings: Part 3 - Design Considerations," *Engineering Journal*, American Institute of Steel Construction, Chicago, Illinois, vol. 7, no. 4, October, p. 121-131.

KHAN, F. R., J. Zils, and M. Salem, 1980. "Five Million Square Foot Tent Roof," *Civil Engineering*, December, pp. 68-71.

KHAN TRIBUTES, 1982. Council on Tall Buildings and Urban Habitat, Lehigh University, Bethlehem, PA.

LIM, B. P., 1994. *Environmental Design Criteria of Tall Buildings*, Council on Tall Buildings and Urban Habitat, Lehigh University, Bethlehem, Pennsylvania.

MODERN STEEL CONSTRUCTION, 1972. "The Future of the Super Hi-Rise Building," First Quarter, pp. 3-9.

MODERN STEEL CONSTRUCTION, 1982. "Our Tribute…" 2nd Quarter.

NERVI, Pier L., 1956. *Structures*, McGraw-Hill, New York.

NERVI, Pier L., 1957. Nervi's Preface to *The Works of Pier Luigi Nervi*, Frederick A. Praeger, New York.

NEW YORK TIMES, 1996. "Malaysia Looks Down on World from 1,483 Feet," May 2.

NEWHOUSE, Elizabeth, ed., 1992. *The Builders: Marvels of Engineering*, Book Division of National Geographic Society, Washington, D.C., pp. 137-139.

NEWMAN, M. W., 1970. "Chicago: City of the Big Tombstones," *Chicago Daily News Panorama*, January 24, p. 4.

NEWSWEEK, 1973. "Spaces for our Time," December 24.

PECK, Ralph B., 1997. "Gaining Ground," *Civil Engineering*, December, pp. 54-56.

PETROSKI, Henry, 1982. *To Engineer is Human*, Vintage Books, New York.

PETROSKI, Henry, 1999. "Fazlur Khan," *American Scientist*, Vol. 86, January-February, pp. 16-20.

PETROSKI, Henry, 1999. "The Hubris of Extreme Engineering," *Scientific American: Extreme Engineering*, vol. 10, No. 4, Winter, pp. 94-104.

POST, Nadine M., 1989. "After Retirement: Raising Funds . . .," *ENR* Building Team Edition, October 12.

PROGRESSIVE ARCHITECTURE, 1982. "Invitation to the Haj," February, pp. 116-122.

PROGRESSIVE ARCHITECTURE, 1986. "Sears Resurrected," May, pp. 39-40.

RANDALL, F. A., 1949. *History of the Development of Building Construction in Chicago*, The University of Illinois Press, Urbana, Illinois (revised and expanded by John D. Randall, 1999).

RANKINE, John, 1997. *The World is your Client*, Engineers Australia Pty Limited, Crows Nest, Australia, pp. 45-46.

ROWLAND, C., 1965. *Frei Otto: Tension Structures*, Praeger Publishers, New York.

RUTHVEN, M., 1984. *Islam in the World*, Oxford University Press, New York and Oxford, p. 25.

SCHUELLER, Wolfgang, 1977. *High-Rise Building Structures*, John Wiley & Sons, New York.

SCHUELLER, Wolfgang, 1990. *The Vertical Structure*, Van Nostrand Reinhold, New York, NY.

SWENSON, A.T., 1971. "Technology: A Superframe Building," *Architectural Forum*, New York, September, pp. 58-60.

TARANATH, B. S., 1997. *Steel, Concrete and Composite Design of Tall Buildings*," Second Edition, McGraw-Hill Book Co., New York.

THE ECONOMIST, 1998. "Engineering: In Need of Heroes," May 16, pp. 115-117.

THE TIMES, 1984. "The Onteric Center Speaks," Council on Tall Buildings and Urban Habitat, Vol. 15, No. 1, May.

TIME, 1973. "Tallest Skyscraper," June 11.

TUCKER, Jonathan B., 1985. "Superskyscrapers: Aiming for 200 Stories," *High Technology*, January, pp. 50-63.

VIOLLET-LE-DUC, E. E., 1895. *Rational Building*; translated from an article on "Construction," in the Dictionnaire raisonné de l'architecture française, Macmillan and Company, New York and London.

VON ECKARDT, W., 1966. "New York's Trade Center: World's Tallest Fiasco," *Harpers 232*, May, p. 96.

WATSON, Donald, 1997. "Architecture, Technology, and Environment," *Journal of Architectural Education*, November, pp. 119-125.

ZILS, J. J. and R. S. Clark, 1986. "The Concrete Diagonal," *Civil Engineering*, October, pp. 48-50.

BIBLIOGRAPHY OF ARTICLES AND PAPERS

AUTHORED OR CO-AUTHORED
BY FAZLUR R. KHAN (1954-1982)

STUDY OF TESTS ON PRESTRESSED CONCRETE BEAMS, Third Progress Report on Investigation of Prestressed Concrete for Highway Bridges, Engineering Experiment Station, University of Illinois, June, 1954.

ANALYTICAL STUDIES OF RELATIONS AMONG VARIOUS DESIGN CRITERIA FOR PRESTRESSED CONCRETE BEAMS, (with N. Khachaturian and C. P. Siess), *Structural Engineering Research Series No. 105*, University of Illinois, October, 1955.

GANTRIES SET PRESTRESSED BRIDGE BEAMS (with A. J. Brown), *Engineering News Record*, January, 1958.

LOAD TEST OF 120 FOOT PRECAST, PRESTRESSED BRIDGE GIRDER (with A. J. Brown), *American Concrete Institute (ACI) Journal*, July, 1958.

USE OF ELECTRONIC COMPUTERS FOR ANALYSIS AND DESIGN OF MULTI-STORY BUILDINGS, *Proceedings of the Conference on Use of Computers for Analysis and Design of Structures*, I.I.T. Research Institute, June, 1963.

INTERACTION OF SHEAR WALLS AND FRAMES IN CONCRETE STRUCTURES UNDER LATERAL LOADS (with J. A. Sbarounis), *Journal of the American Society of Civil Engineers (ASCE)*, 90 (ST3), June, 1964.

METHODS OF BRACING AND STRUCTURE DEFLECTIONS, *Proceedings of the APIC 9*, ASCE, June, 1964.

DESIGN OF SHEAR WALLS, *Proceedings of the EPIC 9*, ASCE, St. Louis, MO, March, 1965.

DESIGN OF HIGH RISE BUILDINGS, *American Institute of Steel Construction (AISC) Symposium on Steel Structures*, Chicago, IL, Fall, 1965.

EFFECTS OF COLUMN EXPOSURE IN TALL STRUCTURES, PART A—TEMPERATURE VARIATIONS AND THEIR EFFECTS (with Mark Fintel), *ACI Journal*, December, 1965.

CURRENT TRENDS IN CONCRETE HIGH RISE BUILDINGS, *Proceedings of the Symposium on Tall Buildings*, University of Southampton, England, April, 1966.

ON SOME SPECIAL PROBLEMS OF ANALYSIS AND DESIGN OF SHEAR WALL STRUCTURES, *Proceedings of the Symposium on Tall Buildings*, University of Southampton, England, April, 1966.

OPTIMIZATION OF BUILDING STRUCTURES, *Proceedings of the Structural Engineering Conference*, University of Illinois, Chicago, IL, May 14, 1966.

EFFECT OF COLUMN EXPOSURE IN TALL STRUCTURES, PART B—ANALYSIS FOR LENGTH CHANGES OF EXPOSED COLUMNS (with Mark Fintel), *ACI Journal*, August, 1966.

THE BEARING WALL, *Architectural and Engineering News*, September, 1966.

COMPUTER DESIGN OF THE 100 STORY JOHN HANCOCK CENTER (with S. H. Iyengar and J. P. Colaco), *ASCE Journal of the Structural Division*, ST6, December, 1966.

VOIES NOUVELLES DANS LA CONCEPTION DES OSSATURES METALLIQUES DE BATIMENTS, Construction Metallique, Centre d'Etudes Superieures, *Journal Construction Metallique*, December, 1966.

TEMPERATURE EFFECTS OF COLUMN EXPOSURE IN HIGHRISE STRUCTURES (with Mark Fintel), *Proceedings of the Building Research Institute Conference*, Washington, DC, Spring, 1967; *Building Research*, September-October, 1967.

THE JOHN HANCOCK CENTER, *Civil Engineering*, October, 1967.

OPTIMUM DESIGN OF GLASS IN BUILDINGS, *Proceedings of the Building Research Institute Conference*, Washington, DC, May, 1967.

THE NATURE OF HIGH RISE BUILDINGS, *Indian Builder*, Journal of the Indian Builders' Association, Bombay, India, June, 1967; *Inland Architect Magazine*, July, 1967.

EFFECTS OF COLUMN EXPOSURE IN TALL STRUCTURES, PART C - DESIGN CONSIDERATIONS AND FIELD OBSERVATIONS OF BUILDINGS (with Mark Fintel), *ACI Journal*, February, 1968.

OFFICE TOWER DESIGN CUTS FRAMING COSTS, *Engineering News Record*, February 15, 1968.

SHOCK ABSORBING SOFT STORY CONCEPT FOR MULTI-STORY EARTHQUAKE STRUCTURES (with Mark Fintel), *64th Annual ACI Convention*, Los Angeles, CA, March, 1968; *ACI Journal*, May, 1969.

ANALYSIS AND DESIGN OF THE 100 STORY JOHN HANCOCK CENTER IN CHICAGO (U.S.A.) (with S. H. Iyengar and J. P. Colaco), *Acier Stahl Steel*, June, 1968.

EFFECTS OF COLUMN CREEP AND SHRINKAGE IN TALL STRUCTURES (with Mark Fintel), *ASCE Specialty Conference*, Chicago, IL, June, 1968.

COLUMN FREE BOX-TYPE FRAMING WITH AND WITHOUT RIGID CORES, *Eighth Congress of the International Association for Bridge and Structural Engineering (IABSE)*, New York, September, 1968.

EFFECTS OF COLUMN TEMPERATURE, CREEP AND SHRINKAGE IN TALL STRUCTURES (with Mark Fintel), *Final Report to the Eighth Congress*, IABSE, New York, September, 1968.

THE BEARING WALL COMES OF AGE, *Architectural and Engineering News*, October, 1968.

THE CHICAGO SCHOOL GROWS UP, *Architectural and Engineering News*, Annual Convention Supplement, June, 1969.

FRAMED TUBES AND INTERACTING FRAMED TUBES AND SHEAR WALLS," *Report to ACI Lateral Load Committee 421*, June, 1969.

CAISSON CONSTRUCTION PROBLEMS AND METHODS OF CORRECTION (with Clyde N. Baker), *ASCE Convention*, Chicago, IL, October, 1969.

RECENT STRUCTURAL SYSTEMS IN STEEL FOR HIGH-RISE BUILDINGS, *BCSA Conference on Steel in Architecture*, London, England, November, 1969.

EFFECTS OF COLUMN CREEP AND SHRINKAGE IN TALL STRUCTURES—PREDICTION OF INELASTIC COLUMN SHORTENING (with Mark Fintel), *ACI Journal*, December, 1969.

CONCEPTUAL DETAILS FOR CREEP, SHRINKAGE, AND TEMPERATURE IN ULTRA HIGH RISE BUILDINGS (with Mark Fintel), *ACI Annual Convention*, New York, April, 1970.

EFFECTS OF COLUMN CREEP AND SHRINKAGE IN TALL STRUCTURES: ANALYSIS FOR DIFFERENTIAL SHORTENING OF COLUMNS AND FIELD OBSERVATIONS OF STRUCTURES (with Mark Fintel), *ACI Annual Convention*, New York, April, 1970.

LIGHTWEIGHT CONCRETE FOR TOTAL DESIGN OF ONE SHELL PLAZA, *ACI Convention*, New York, April, 1970.

NEW STRUCTURAL SYSTEMS IN STEEL, *AISC Annual Convention*, Pittsburgh, PA, April, 1970; *ACI Special Publication*, Paper SP 29-1, 1971.

QUALITY CONTROL OF HIGH STRENGTH LIGHTWEIGHT CONCRETE FOR ONE SHELL PLAZA (with J. Stockbridge and E. Brown), *ACI Annual Convention*, Pittsburgh, PA, April, 1970.

RATIONAL METHOD FOR THE DESIGN OF CURTAIN WALLS, *Proceedings of the Conference on Wind Effects on High Rise Buildings*, Northwestern University, Chicago, IL, March, 1970.

NEW DESIGN APPROACH TO HIGH RISE CONSTRUCTION, *Proceedings of the Conference on Urban Environment*, ASCE, Rochester Section, May 15, 1970.

TEMPERATURE EFFECTS ON TALL STEEL FRAMED BUILDINGS (with A. F. Nassetta), *Engineering Journal*, AISC, October, 1970.

SURVEY OF PROCEDURES FOR ACCEPTANCE OF ELECTRONIC COMPUTER CALCULATIONS BY BUILDING OFFICIALS, (F. R. Khan, member), ACI Committee 118, *ACI Journal*, January, 1971.

RESPONSE OF BUILDINGS TO LATERAL FORCES, by ACI Committee 442 (F. R. Khan, member), *ACI Journal*, February, 1971.

INNOVATIONS IN STRUCTURAL STEEL SYSTEMS FOR TALL BUILDINGS, *Proceedings of the Canadian Institute of Structural Concrete*, May, 1971.

TENDANCES ACTUELLES DANS LA CONSTRUCTION DES IMMEUBLES DE GRANDE HAUTEUR A STRUCTURE EN BETON ARME ET EN ACIER," Anales de L'Institut Technique du Batiment et des Travaux Publics, Sepplement au No. 281, May, 1971.

"BUILDING DESIGN REDUCES STEEL WITH CONCRETE-TUBE WIND BRACING," *Engineering News Record*, June, 1971.

"CONCRETE - YEAR 2000," Report by ACI Ad Hoc Board Committee on Concrete (F. R. Khan member), *ACI Journal*, August, 1971.

"SERVICE CRITERIA FOR TALL BUILDINGS FOR WIND LOADING" (with R. A. Parmelee), *Proceedings of the Third International Conference on Wind Effects on Buildings and Structures*, Tokyo, Japan, September, 1971.

"BUILDINGS," *1972 McGraw-Hill Yearbook of Science and Technology*.

"A PHILOSOPHICAL COMPARISON BETWEEN MAILLART'S BRIDGES AND SOME RECENT CONCRETE BUILDINGS," *Civil Engineering: History, Heritage and the Humanities*, Princeton University, Princeton, NJ, 1972.

"NEW CONCEPTS IN HIGH RISE BUILDINGS," American Iron and Steel Institute Seminar for Journalists, New York, January, 1972.

"INFLUENCE OF DESIGN CRITERIA ON SELECTION OF STRUCTURAL SYSTEMS FOR TALL BUILDINGS," *Proceedings of the Canadian National Structural Engineering Conference*, Montreal, Canada, March, 1972.

"OPTIMIZATION APPROACH FOR CONCRETE HIGH-RISE STRUCTURES" (with S. H. Iyengar), *ACI Convention*, Dallas, TX, March, 1972; *Response to Multi-Story Concrete Structures to Lateral Forces*, ACI Symposium Volume SP36, 1973.

"DESIGN FOR PERCEPTION IN MOTION IN TALL BUILDINGS" (with R. Parmelee and S. H. Iyengar), *ASCE Annual and National Environmental Engineering Meeting*, Houston, TX, October, 1972.

"THE FUTURE OF HIGH RISE STRUCTURES," *Progressive Architecture*, Reinhold Publishing, Cleveland, Ohio, October, 1972.

"STRUCTURAL SYSTEMS FOR MULTI-STORY STEEL BUILDINGS," *Proceedings of the Swedish Institute of Steel Construction*, Stockholm, Sweden, October, 1972.

"RECENT DEVELOPMENT AND FUTURE OF HIGH RISE BUILDINGS," *Proceedings of the Tall Buildings Conference*, New Delhi, India, January, 1973.

"ANALYSIS AND DESIGN OF FRAMED TUBE STRUCTURES FOR TALL CONCRETE BUILDINGS" (with Navinchandra R. Amin), *The Structural Engineer*, March, 1973; Institution of Structural Engineers, London, England, April, 1973; *ACI Journal*, SP 36, 1973.

"EVOLUTION OF STRUCTURAL SYSTEMS FOR HIGH RISE BUILDINGS IN STEEL AND CONCRETE," *Proceedings of the Regional Conference on Tall Buildings*, Bratislava, Czechoslovakia, April, 1973.

"STRUCTURAL STEEL DESIGN FOR SEARS TOWER" (with S. H. Iyengar), *Australian Conference on Steel Developments*, Australian Institute of Steel Construction, Newcastle, Australia, May 21-25, 1973.

"SEARS TOWER (CHICAGO): WORLD'S TALLEST BUILDING" (with S. H. Iyengar and J. Zils), *Acier-Stahl Steel*, June-July, 1973.

"NEWER STRUCTURAL SYSTEMS AND THEIR EFFECT ON THE CHANGING SCALE OF THE CITIES," *Proceedings of the National Conference on Tall Buildings*, Zurich, Switzerland, October, 1973.

"BUILDINGS IN THE FUTURE," *Industrialized Building Exposition and Congress*, Louisville, KY, October-November, 1973.

"STRUCTURAL DESIGN INTEGRATED LOAD (HAZARD)," *IITRI Symposium: Designing to Survive Disaster*, Chicago, IL, November, 1973.

"TUBULAR STRUCTURES FOR TALL BUILDINGS," *Handbook of Concrete Engineering*, Mark Fintel, ed., Van Nostrand Reinhold, 1974.

"APPROACH TO TALL BUILDING STRUCTURAL SYSTEMS USING CONCRETE MASONRY BEARING WALL CONSTRUCTION," *National Concrete Masonry Association Convention*, Las Vegas, NV, January 16, 1974.

"CHANGING SCALE OF THE CITIES," *Consulting Engineer*, April, 1974.

"THE CHANGING URBAN SCALE—A SOCIAL TECHNOLOGICAL PHENOMENON, PARTS I & II," *67th Annual Meeting of the Building Owners and Managers Association International*, Portland, OR, June, 1974.

"NEW CONCEPTS—BY-PRODUCTS OF COMPUTER TECHNOLOGY," *ASCE Sixth Conference on Electronic Computation*, Atlanta, Georgia, August, 1974.

"NEW STRUCTURAL SYSTEMS FOR TALL BUILDINGS AND THEIR SCALE EFFECTS ON CITIES," *Proceedings of the Symposium on Tall Buildings: Planning, Design & Construction*, Vanderbilt University, Nashville, TN, November, 1974.

"A CRISIS IN DESIGN—THE NEW ROLE OF THE STRUCTURAL ENGINEER," *Proceedings of the National Conference on Tall Buildings*, Institution of Engineers, Malaysia, Kuala Lumpur, Malaysia, December, 1974.

"AMBIENT RESPONSE ANALYSIS OF SOME TALL STRUCTURES" (with George T. Taoka, Michael Hogan, and Robert Scanlon), *Proceedings ASCE Conference*, January, 1975.

"TALL BUILDINGS—RECENT DEVELOPMENTS IN STRUCTURAL SYSTEMS AND ARCHITECTURAL EXPRESSIONS," *Proceedings of the National Conference on Tall Buildings*, Athens, Greece, October, 1975.

"AMERICAN URBAN SKYLINE—PAST, PRESENT AND FUTURE," *ASCE Annual Convention*, Philadelphia, PA, September 1976.

"PRECAST CONCRETE FOR TALL MULTIPLE USE BUILDINGS - A FUTURE OUTLOOK," *CIBS41 Symposium III/Joint Committee Regional Conference*, Moscow, USSR, October, 1976.

"ARCHITECTURE IN DEVELOPING COUNTRIES," *Proceedings of the IABSE Symposium*, Munich, October, 1977.

"THE ROLE OF TALL BUILDINGS IN URBAN SPACE," *Proceedings of the Conference 2001*, UNESCO: Paris, France, November, 1977 (in English and French); *Urban Space for Life and Work*, 1978.

"PERFORMANCE OF ONE SHELL PLAZA DEEP MAT FOUNDATION" (with J. A. Focht and J. P. Gemeinhardt), *ASCE Journal of the Geotechnical Engineering Division*, May, 1978.

"DECISIONS FOR MAKING LIGHTWEIGHT STRUCTURES," the *International Symposium on Widespan Lightweight Structures*, May, 1979.

"SHEAR WALL STRUCTURES," *Hawaii Conference*, Maui, May 23-27, 1979.

"CREATIVE TEACHING AND ITS INFLUENCE ON INNOVATIVE CONCRETE STRUCTURES," `Three Sessions to Celebrate C. P. Seiss' Contributions to Research Education and Practice', *ACI Special Meeting*, Washington, DC, November, 1979; ACI Publ. SP-72, *Significant Developments in Engineering Practice and Design: A Tribute to Chester P. Siess*, 1981.

"WILL SOCIETY PERMIT THE MEGASTRUCTURE?" `The 50 Year Span', special feature of *New Civil Engineer*, August, 1980.

"STRUCTURAL AESTHETICS IN ARCHITECTURE AND ITS SOCIAL AND TECHNOLOGICAL RELEVANCE," *IABSE 11th Congress*, Vienna, Austria, August-September, 1980.

"STRUCTURAL SYSTEMS FOR MULTI-USE HIGHRISE BUILDINGS" (with M. M. El Nimeiri), *AISC Fall Convention*, Hollywood, FL, October 27-31, 1980; Council on Tall Buildings and Urban Habitat MONOGRAPH UPDATE, 1982; *Developments Tall Buildings*, van Nostrand Reinhold Co., New York, 1983.

"MASONRY BEARING STRUCTURES FOR TALL BUILDINGS - CAN THE FUTURE MATCH THE PAST," *First World Congress on Concrete Block*, Washington, DC, November, 1980.

"FIVE MILLION SQUARE FOOT TENT ROOF FOR THE HAJ TERMINAL" (with John Zils and Mohammed Salem), *Civil Engineering*, December, 1980.

"SAUDI ARABIA-IN SEARCH OF APPROPRIATE ARCHITECTURE," University of Petroleum and Minerals, Dhahran, Saudi Arabia, January, 1981.

"ARAB-ISLAMIC ARCHITECTURE AND ITS INFLUENCE ON NON-ARAB ARCHITECTURE," University of Petroleum and Minerals, Dhahran, Saudi Arabia, January, 1981.

"TRENDS IN HIGH-DENSITY LIVING AND WORKING SPACE IN URBAN CENTERS," University of Petroleum and Minerals, Dhahran, Saudi Arabia, January, 1981.

"APPLICATION OF TRADITIONAL MUSLIM PLANNING PRINCIPLES TO A CONTEMPORARY ARAB ENVIRONMENT: A CASE STUDY OF UMM AL-QURA UNIVERSITY, MAKKAH," *Symposium on the Arab City: Its Character and Islamic Cultural Heritage*, Medina, Saudi Arabia, February-March, 1981.

"STRUCTURAL THEORIES AND THEIR ARCHITECTURAL EXPRESSION—A REVIEW OF POSSIBILITIES," *Chicago Architectural Journal*, Chicago Architectural Club, April, 1981.

"EFFECTS OF STRUCTURAL REDUNDANCY AND IMPORTANCE ON DESIGN CRITERIA FOR STABILITY AND STRENGTH" (with M. M. El Nimeiri), *Annual Meeting of Structural Stability Research Council*, Chicago, IL, April 7, 1981; and Council on Tall Buildings and Urban Habitat MONOGRAPH UPDATE, 1981.

"100-STORY JOHN HANCOCK CENTER IN CHICAGO—A CASE STUDY OF THE DESIGN PROCESS," IABSE, Working Commission V Colloquium, London, England, September, 1981; *IABSE Journal*, J-16/82, August, 1982; *Engineering Structures*, January, 1983.

"THE RISE AND FALL OF STRUCTURAL LOGIC IN ARCHITECTURE," *Chicago Architectural Journal*, Chicago Architectural Club, vol. 2, 1982.

MAJOR PROJECTS

1958	Inland Steel Building, Chicago, Illinois
1962	60" Solar Telescope, Kitt Peak, Arizona
1962	United States Air Force Academy, Colorado Springs, Colorado
1963	Container Corporation of America, Corrugator Plant, Carol Stream, Illinois
1964	Business Men's Assurance Tower, Kansas City, Missouri
1965	Brunswick Office Building, Chicago, Illinois
1965	DeWitt-Chestnut Apartment Building, Chicago, Illinois
1965	Equitable Life Assurance Society of the United States, Office Building, Chicago, Illinois
1965	Illinois Central Air Rights, Master Plan, Chicago, Illinois
1965	University of Illinois, Circle Campus, Master Plan and Phases, I, II, III, IV, Chicago, Illinois
1967	Broken Hill Proprietary, Corporate Headquarters, Melbourne, Australia
1967	Spectrum Arena, Philadelphia, Pennsylvania
1969	Chicago Transit Authority, 13 Rapid Transit Stations, Chicago, Illinois
1970	John Hancock Center, Multi-Use Complex, Chicago, Illinois
1970	Marine Midland Bank, Rochester, New York
1971	Control Data Center, Corporate Headquarters, Houston, Texas
1971	One Shell Plaza, Office Building, Houston, Texas
1971	1010 Common Street, Office Building, New Orleans, Louisiana
1971	Hartford Fire Insurance Company, Office Building II, Hartford, Connecticut
1972	Crosstown Expressway, Multi-Disciplinary Comprehensive Transportation Corridor Plan, Chicago, Illinois
1972	Gateway Center, Office Building III, Chicago, Illinois
1972	One Shell Square, Office Building, New Orleans, Louisiana
1972	Two Shell Plaza, Houston, Texas
1973	First Wisconsin Center, Milwaukee, Wisconsin
1974	Bu Ali Sina University, Design Development, Hamadan, Iran
1974	Royal Gazette Ltd., Newspaper Plant and Office Building, Hamilton, Bermuda
1974	W. D. & H. O. Wills, Tobacco Processing Plant and Corporate Headquarters, Bristol, England
1974	Sears Tower, Corporate Headquarters, Chicago, Illinois
1975	Bandar Shahpour New Town, Development Plan, Master Plan, Management Program and Short-Term Housing, Bandar Shahpour, Iran
1975	Baxter Travenol Laboratories, Inc., Corporate Headquarters, Deerfield, Illinois
1975	Centre Sofil, Office Building, Beirut, Lebanon
1975	World Trade Center, Hong Kong
1976	Ohio National Bank, Columbus, Ohio
1976	Wolf Point Apparel Mart, Chicago, Illinois
1978	Hyatt International Hotels, Hotel and Cultural Center, Kuwait City, Kuwait
1978	King Abdul Aziz University, Makkah Campus Master Plan, Makkah, Kingdom of Saudi Arabia
1979	Europoint IV, Office Building, Rotterdam, The Netherlands
1980	Edmonton Center, Multi-Use Complex, Edmonton, Alberta, Canada
1980	King Abdul Aziz International Airport Facility, including the Haj Terminal, Jeddah, Kingdom of Saudi Arabia
1981	Universiti Kebangsaan Sabah Kampus, Master Plan, Kota Kinabalu, East Malaysia
1983	One Magnificent Mile, Chicago, Illinois
1984	National Commercial Bank, Jeddah, Saudi Arabia
1985	Onterie Center, Multi-Use Complex, Chicago, Illinois

BRIEF CHRONOLOGY

1929	Born April 3, Dhaka, Bangladesh
1950	Graduated in Civil Engineering from the University of Dhaka
1950-52	Taught Civil Engineering at the Ahsanullah Engineering College, Dhaka
1952	Left Dhaka for the University of Illinois at Urbana-Champaign, USA, for higher studies
1955	Obtained two Master of Science degrees in Civil Engineering and Theoretical and Applied Mechanics and a Doctor of Philosophy degree in Civil Engineering from the University of Illinois at Urbana-Champaign
1955-57	Worked at Skidmore, Owings and Merrill (SOM), Chicago
1957	Returned to Pakistan
1957-60	Worked as Executive Engineer with Karachi Development Authority in Pakistan
1960	Married Liselotte Anna Olga Turba, returned to the United States, joined SOM, Chicago
1960-82	Worked as Project Engineer, Associate Partner and Partner at SOM, Chicago
1962-82	Taught in the School of Architecture, Illinois Institute of Technology, Chicago
1976	Went on Haj to Mecca
1982	Died March 27, Jeddah, Saudi Arabia

232

HONORS/AWARDS/RECOGNITION

1952	Fulbright Scholar
1966	*Engineering News-Record*, Citation among the "Men Who Served the Best Interests of the Construction Industry"
1968	American Society of Civil Engineers, Texas Section, Award for Meritorious Technical Paper
1969	*Engineering News-Record*, Citation among the "Men Who Served the Best Interests of the Construction Industry"
1970	Chicago Chamber of Commerce, Chicagoan of the Year in Architecture and Engineering
1971	American Institute of Steel Construction, Special Citation
1971	American Concrete Institute, Wason Medal for Most Meritorious Paper
1971	*Engineering News-Record*, Citation among the "Men Who Served the Best Interests of the Construction Industry"
1972	American Society of Civil Engineers, Middlebrooks Award
1972	American Society of Civil Engineers, Illinois Section, Civil Engineer of the Year and Life Membership Award
1972	*Engineering News-Record*, Construction's Man of the Year
1972	University of Illinois, Urbana, Illinois, College of Engineering Alumni Honor Award
1973	American Concrete Institute, Alfred E. Lindau Award
1973	American Institute of Steel Construction, J. Lloyd Kimbrough Medal
1973	Institution of Structural Engineers, London, England, Oscar Faber Medal
1973	National Academy of Engineering, Admittance to Academy
1973	Northwestern University, Honorary Doctor of Science
1977	American Society of Civil Engineers, Ernest E. Howard Award
1977	Illinois Council of American Institute of Architects, State Service Award American Society of Civil Engineers, Cleveland Section, G. Brooks Earnest Award
1980	Die Eidgenossische Technische Hochschule (ETH), Zurich, Switzerland, Honorary Doktors Der Technischen Wissenschaften (Doctor of Technical Sciences)
1980	Lehigh University, Honorary Doctor of Engineering
1981	Progressive Architecture, 28th Award for Haj Terminal, King Abdul Aziz International Airport International Association for Bridge and Structural Engineering, International Award of Merit
1982	Skidmore, Owings and Merrill, Fazlur Khan International Fellowship Award
1982	University of Western Ontario, Canada, Fazlur Khan Award
1982	University of Illinois, Urbana, Illinois, College of Engineering Distinguished Civil Engineering Alumnus Award
1982	Lehigh University, Fazlur Rahman Khan Chair
1983	Agha Khan Medal for Architecture for Haj Terminal, King Abdul Aziz International Airport
1983	American Institute of Architects, Institute Honor Award
1993	Structural Engineers Association of Illinois, Installation of the Khan Sculpture in the Sears Tower
1998	City of Chicago, Street Named "Fazlur R. Khan Way" in Downtown Chicago
1999	Independence Day Award, Government of Bangladesh
1999	*Engineering News-Record*, One of the "Top People of the Past 125 Years"

STUDENT THESIS PROJECTS SUPERVISED AT IIT

	STUDENT	PROJECT
1962	David Sharpe	An Aircraft Hangar and Study of Long-Span Metal Structures
1962	Meiji Watanabe	Train Exhibition Hall
1963	Phyllis Lambert	A Study of Long-Span Roof Structures in Concrete
1964	Mikio Sasaki	A Tall Office Building
1964	Emmanuel Glyniadakis	A Sports Center
1964	M. L. von Broembsen	A Multi-Story Exposition Building
1965	Peter Doyle	A Sports Arena
1965	Christoph Sattler	City Hall in Germany
1966	A.G. Krishna Menon	A Ninety-story Apartment Building
1967	Dorman Anderson	An Urban University
1968	Lawrence Kenny	A Railway Station for Chicago
1968	Robin Hodgkison	An Ultra High-Rise Concrete Office Building
1969	Peter Pran	An Exhibition Hall with a Suspended Roof Structure
1970	Alfonso Rodriquez	A Form-Stiffened High-Rise Apartment Building
1971	Mahen Panchal	Concrete Library Building
1971	Heinz Sieber	Multi-purpose Building
1972	Michael Breitman	Study of Superframe
1973	Faramoz Shoai	High-Rise Concrete Masonry Building Structure
1974	Masami Hayashida	A Multi-use High-Rise Building
1974	Dick Ling	Consortium Hangar for B-747-S
1975	D. Kwong-Wah Lai	Pre-fabricated Concrete— 60-story Hotel/Office
1978	Mineo Tanaka	An Exhibition Hall with a Cable-Stayed Roof
1981	Wayne Petrie	43-story Office Building
1982	T. Bok	Multi-use Office and Apartment Building

PROFESSIONAL AFFILIATIONS

Adjunct Professor of Architecture,
    Illinois Institute of Technology
Advisory Committee for Aga Khan Program
    on Islamic Architecture at Harvard/M.I.T.
American Concrete Intitute, Fellow
American Institute of Steel Construction
American Society of Civil Engineers, Fellow
American Welding Society
Chicago Architectural Club
Chicago Committee on High-Rise Buildings
Council on Tall Buildings and Urban Habitat
International Association for Bridges and
    Structural Engineering
Chicago Mayor's Advisory Commission
    on Building Code Amendments
National Academy of Engineering
Prestressed Concrete Institute

PROFESSIONAL REGISTRATION

STRUCTURAL ENGINEER: Illinois; Hong Kong

PROFESSIONAL ENGINEER: Louisiana; Massachusetts;
New York; Ohio; Texas; Wisconsin; Washington, D.C.

ACKNOWLEDGEMENTS

I thank many individuals who have extended their help and encouragement in the realization of this project. I am indebted to Dr. Ashfaq Hossain for re-igniting the flickering flame of my desire to write a book on Fazlur Rahman Khan. I have been holding off this wish for many years hoping someone else would do it as I had been hearing rumors that several individuals were writing such books. The most powerful impulse occurred to me when Dr. Hossain, a Bengali friend of mine, urged me strongly to write a book on Khan when I visited him in New Jersey in November, 1997.

Of all people who helped me, I want to thank Dr. Lynn S. Beedle most for his continuous collaboration, kind advice, and guidance throughout the entire course of writing this book. I am equally grateful to Dr. Chester P. Siess, whom I met several times and who gave me information on the John Hancock Center and offered valuable advice and suggestions on this book. He and Dr. Narbey Khachaturian gave me most of the information that I included here concerning Khan's student life at the University of Illinois.

Special thanks are due also to Hal Iyengar—who knew Khan very well at a professional level—for giving me valuable insights into Khan's various projects, particularly the Sears Tower. Dr. Joseph Colaco gave me his enthusiastic support for the book and time out of his busy schedule to tell me the story of the John Hancock Center, on which he worked very closely with Khan.

I am especially indebted to John Zils, who gave me his utmost support and time throughout the project. Any time I was looking for some specific information about Khan's work at Skidmore, Owings and Merrill, I could always count on him.

I am deeply grateful to Bruce Graham for spending ninety minutes with me, on one occasion, at the Chicago Club—right after his arrival there from a long, delayed flight from Florida—and over three hours on another. Graham conveyed to me Khan's architectural notions and described his own relationship with Khan. My interview with him was of immense significance, because Khan and Graham had a long-lasting partnership at work. It also contributed to my understanding of Khan's philosophy of design.

To Mark Fintel, I owe my gratitude for providing information about his collaborative work with Khan and for giving me encouragement. Others who were helpful are Professors Ralph Peck and William Munse, Clyde Baker, Ray J. Clark, Mahjoub Elnimeiri, Hem C. Gupta, Nick Isyumov, Reginald Jackson, Hasan-Uddin Khan, Walter Lewis, Shankar Nair, William Porter, Leslie Robertson, David Sharpe, Jim Simon, Doug Stoker, and David Wickersheimer. David Sharpe gave me most of the pictures and sketches related to student thesis projects that Khan supervised at the Illinois Institute of Technology (IIT). Professor William Porter deserves thanks for help in getting information about Khan's involvement in the Aga Khan Islamic Architecture Program at MIT and Harvard University.

The archive of Khan's writings, letters, documents, and other materials preserved at the Ryerson and Burnham Library in the Chicago Art Institute greatly increased the book's scope. These were placed in the archive by Liselotte Khan. Mary Woolever at the Library was extremely cooperative in making all the archival boxes readily available to me. Jim Crouch gave me the information about Woolever and about the archive. Lisa Westerfield gave me the particulars of SOM's Fazlur Khan International Fellowship.

A special note of thanks is due to Chandra K. Jha, a close friend of Khan, for his help and advice. The information he gave me on Khan helped me in describing the Onterie Center project and in portraying the humanistic side of Khan. Prabhas Nag, another friend of Khan, was also very helpful in offering me his personal reflections on Khan. Khan's secretary, Jane Quinn, deserves special mention. She enabled me to take a glimpse of Khan's life at the office. She reviewed the chapter on Khan's death and offered constructive suggestions. I was struck by her unflinching loyalty to Khan even though many years have elapsed since his death.

It was my pleasure to know Robert Johnson—a long-time public relations chairman of the Structural Engineers Association of Illinois (SEAOI)—during the course of writing this book. He is a great admirer of Khan and was instrumental in the erection of the Khan Sculpture in the Sears Tower on behalf of SEAOI. He is a promoter of engineering as an important profession and a relentless champion of how engineers are viewed by the public and the media.

Thanks are due also to the following individuals in Bangladesh for their help: Jamilur Reza Choudhury, Bashirul Haq, Mosharaff Hossain, Zeaul Huq, Asif Iqbal, Abul Faraz Khan, Faizur Rahman Khan, A.K.M. Rafiquddin, Mahbubur Rahman, M. Mujibur Rahman, and Zillur Rahman Siddiqui. All of them gave me valuable information and helped me in many ways.

I would like to further express my gratitude to those individuals who knew Khan at a personal level and whose memories are still vivid even though they stretch back two decades or more—including Aminul Karim, Dawood Afzal, and Mahen Panchal. Khan's daughter, Yasmin, deserves my sincere appreciation for her cooperation.

I am deeply indebted to the following individuals who read several chapters of my manuscript at various stages: Kathryn Anthony, Paul Armstrong, Lynn Beedle, Bruce Graham, Hal Iyengar, Chandra Jha, Sam Lanford, Ingvar Schousboe, and Chester Siess. Their valuable suggestions, comments and criticisms have strengthened the contents of my book. Professors Beedle and Siess read the entire manuscript. Beedle edited the entire text while Professor Lanford did so very thoroughly for several major chapters. Both Beedle and Siess gave me valuable suggestions for the improvement of the book's content. Iyengar reviewed several chapters and offered his critical observations on the engineering aspects of the book. His comments were extremely useful to me. Graham read a few chapters and gave me his comments and suggestions on architectural issues as well as his reflections on the development of concepts for the Sears Tower, the John Hancock Center, the Brunswick Building, the Onterie Center and several other projects. Professor Schousboe, a former colleague and a dear friend of mine, has sadly passed away during the course of my writing this book. He had offered me much encouragement and many valuable ideas.

I also thank Christella Lai and Mahjabeen Quadri for their excellent work in preparing the sketches used throughout this book.

I am most grateful to Jane Cook for typing the entire manuscript and for taking the endless trouble on my behalf of making repeated changes to the text, cheerfully. Her unusual patience and cooperation in putting up with this work continually, deeply impressed me.

Finally, I thank my wife Morsheda for her sacrifice to let me spend the time away from her to do research and to interview people, occasionally by going out of town, and working on the manuscript for many long hours during weekends and nights.

POSTSCRIPT

There are two important questions to ask regarding this first definitive book on Fazlur Rahman Khan: Who was the man about whom this book is written? And, why is Mir Ali's book important?

In partial answer to the first question: Khan was one of the world's greatest structural engineers. Not only did he receive the highest awards for his engineering, but he was equally well-recognized for his architectural creativity. Vivid testimony of this is given in that just before his death, he was elected president of the Chicago Society of Architects.

Khan was a man of vision, of culture, and of compassion. He never forgot that he had an obligation to serve the people. He required that his designs meet local needs and respond to cultural expectations. He was dedicated to the team approach—an approach that extended beyond the usual professionals and, as the need arose, included cultural and social scholars as well.

In partial answer to the second question: Others will write books on Fazlur Khan—but few will possess all of Mir Ali's qualifications. As part of the Skidmore, Owings & Merrill team, Ali worked with Khan on some of his projects. He was close to him in later years. He knew Khan's friends. As a native Bangladeshi himself, he has a strong understanding of Khan's motivations and spirit.

This work will be of great value to those in the engineering and architectural professions, as well as to students. The general reader will find the book to be both informative and an inspiration.

In *Art of the Skyscraper: The Genius of Fazlur Khan* Mir Ali has presented to the world an ennobling tribute to Fazlur Rahman Khan.

Lynn S. Beedle

[Distinguished Professor, Lehigh University and Director Emeritus, Council on Tall Buildings and Urban Habitat]

Gravestone in Chicago's Graceland Cemetery, with Fazlur and Liselotte Khan's names and the Bengali lyric carved on it
[Courtesy: Michael Boles]

Fazlur Khan's gravesite at the Graceland Cemetery in Chicago. A Bengali lyric is carved on the gravestone.
[Courtesy: Michael Boles]

The technical man must not be lost in his own technology; he must be able to appreciate life, and life is art, drama, music, and most importantly, people.

DR. FAZLUR RAHMAN KHAN

INDEX

7 South Dearborn Building project, 222
500 North Michigan Building, 116
780 Third Avenue Building, 59, 103, 196
1010 Common Street Building, 91

Abdelrazaq, Ahmad, 75
Aga Khan, 207
Aga Khan Program on Islamic Architecture, 148, 179
Ahmed, Moudud, 204
Ahmed, Munir, 197
Ahsanullah Engineering College, 13, 20
Al-Rayes, Sabah, 183-84, 203
Aldrich, Eastman and Walch, 133
Ali, Mir M., 203
Allen, Roy, 139
American Bridge Company, 112, 117, 159
American Concrete Inst., 104, 178
American Inst. for Steel Construction, 104, 129, 178, 196-97, 199-200
American Inst. of Architects, 104, 121, 208
American Soc. of Civil Engineers, 104, 178, 207
Amin, Navin, 130
Amin, S. Y., 146
Ammann and Whitney, 113
Ammann, Othmar, 220
Amoco Building, 43, 211
Anderson, Dorman, 66
Arab International Bank, 98
architecture, structural engineering and, 9, 38, 49-53, 150-71
Aristotle, 40
Armas, Raul de, 147
Art Deco, 31, 220
Artigas, Juan Gardy, 104, 180
Arup, Ove, 169

Baker, Clyde, 116
Baker, William, 75, 222
Bangladesh, 11-13, 14, 16, 20-21, 185, 187-92, 197, 203-4, 207, 216-17
Bangladesh Assoc. of Chicago, 188-89
Bangladesh Defense League, 187
Bangladesh Emergency Welfare Appeal, 187, 193
Bank of China Building, 47, 211
Baum, Richard, 209
Baxter Laboratories Dining Hall, 96, 96-97, 136
Beeby, Thomas, 206
Beedle, Lynn S., 134, 173-76, 178, 182, 185, 186, 202-6, 209, 218, 226
belt trusses, 42, 94, 95, 98, 125
Bengal Engineering College, 13, 20, 21
Bey, Lee, 218
BHP Corporate Headquarters, 98
Biggs, Prof., 113
Billington, David, 118, 120, 121, 131, 162, 163-64, 170-71, 207
Bok, Derek C., 179
Bok, T., 74, 197
braced (trussed) tubes, 8, 47, 58, 59, 63, 65, 77, 99, 101-3, 106-21, 124
Breitman, Michael, 73, 77
Brenner, Daniel, 73
Breuer, Marcel, 155-56
bridges, 23, 39, 151
Broembsen, Melville Leopold von, 66

Brown, Andrew J., 33, 39
Brunel, Isambard, 98
Brunswick Building, 25, 39, 47, 58-59, 87, 87-88, 165, 216
BUET, 207, 217
bundled tubes, 8, 9, 47-48, 58, 59, 73-74, 99, 101, 122-35
Bunshaft, Gordon, 139, 147
Burkhardt, Titus, 196
Burnham, Daniel, 28, 30
Business Men's Assurance Tower, 39, 91-92, 92
cable-support roof systems, 96-97, 136-49

Calatrava, Santiago, 10, 38, 163, 167-69, 206
Calder, Alexander, 32-33
Candela, Felix, 10, 151, 163, 164, 167, 171
Carpenter, L., 130
Carson Pirie Scott Building, 31, 163
CDC Corporation, 127
Chang, Pao-Chi, 33
Chicago Architectural Club, 50, 179, 208
Chicago Building Code, 109-10, 127, 129, 179
Chicago Committee on High-Rise Buildings, 179
Chicago, high-rise architecture in, 28-32, 56, 59, 103, 118-19, 132, 134-35, 153, 157, 158, 163-64, 179, 214
Chicago World Trade Center project, 77-78, 195, 222
Choudhury, Abu Sayeed, 188
Choudhury, Jamilur Reza, 203, 205, 207, 217
Citicorp Center, 47, 63
Clark, Raymond J., 160
Cobb, Henry, 206
Colaco, Joseph, 9, 26, 97, 113, 116-17, 182, 184-85, 195, 213, 223
collaboration, idea of, 38, 54, 103, 120, 131, 152-58, 158, 197, 211
Columbia Presbyterian Hospital, 196
commemorative stamps, 217, 227
composite systems. See steel-concrete composite systems
computer analysis, 34-35, 39, 41, 46-47, 56, 62, 75, 103, 108-12, 116-17, 126-28, 144-45, 221
concrete buildings, 42-43, 43-44, 59, 78, 86-91, 98-104, 151, 164-65, 167, 170, 221, 222
concrete masonry, 74-75
concrete, research on, 20, 22-27, 33
Container Corp. Corrugator Plant, 39
Control Data Center, 49, 95
Coolidge, Charles A., 30
Council on Tall Buildings and Urban Habitat, 172-78, 196, 202
creep analysis, 89
Cross, Hardy, 20
curtain-wall construction, 32, 34, 44

Daley, Richard, 122, 134, 216, 218, 219-20
Danusso, A., 166
Davenport, A. G., 77, 113, 129, 144
DeWitt-Chestnut Apartments, 8-9, 35, 39, 42, 43-44, 49, 85, 86, 87
Diamant, Robert, 106
Dixon, Jeane, 116
Dober, Richard, 98
Doyle, Peter, 66, 66
Drake, Bill, 130, 198
Dulles Airport, 169-70
Dunlap, Bill, 122, 130

earthquake-resistant design, 61-62
Eiffel, Gustave, 151
Eiffel Tower, 45, 117-18, 120
Elnimeiri, Mahjoub, 64, 75, 157, 212, 224
Empire State Building, 31, 42, 43, 56, 106, 121, 125
energy conservation issues, 160-61
Engineering News Record, 104-5, 121, 200-201
engineering, structural, 10, 38-53, 150-71, 210-12
Ershad, Hussain Muhammad, 204, 226
Evren, K., 207
Eyerman, Tom, 198

Fathy, Hassan, 136, 196
Fayez, Zuhair, 203, 205
"Fazlur R. Khan Way," 181, 218-19
Fenves, Steven, 113
Fintel, Mark, 58-62, 88, 104, 199, 214
First Chicago School, 29, 30-31, 163-64
First Wisconsin Center, 92, 94, 94-95
floor design, 62
framed tubes, 8, 10, 35, 42, 43-49, 58, 86
Freyssinet, Eugene, 23, 24
Fuller, Buckminster, 32-33

Gaffney, Noelle, 134
Galilei, Galileo, 40-41, 44
Gapp, Paul, 104, 200, 207, 216
Gateway III Office Building, 49, 95
Gaudi, Antonio, 151, 163, 167, 168
Geiger-Berger, 146
Geiger, David, 146
Geyser, Richard P., 208
Glyniadakis, Emmanuel, 65, 65-66
Goldberg, Bertrand, 61
Goldberg, John, 113, 127
Goldberg, Paul, 50, 132, 200
Goldsmith, Myron, 55, 56, 164, 207; as IIT professor, 58, 63-66, 69, 75; influence on Khan, 156-57, 213; master's thesis of, 32, 40, 108-9; projects with Khan, 39, 97, 98
Graceland Cemetery, 198-99
Graham, Bruce, 82, 147, 154, 170, 198, 206, 221; aesthetics of, 156; influence on Khan, 157-59, 213; John Hancock Center, 106, 113, 117-20, 121; projects with Khan, 9, 32, 34, 39, 48, 51, 84, 86-89, 91-92, 95, 98, 99, 101-3, 152, 153, 164-65; Sears Tower, 123-24, 130, 131, 132, 135; tribute to Khan, 225
Gropius, Walter, 31
Guggenheim Museum (Bilbao), 222
Gujral, Perry, 147-48
Gulf University, 196
Gupta, Hem, 195

haj (pilgrimage), 137, 148
Haj Terminal, 96, 136-37, 136-49, 147, 149, 160, 179; award for, 105, 148, 207; construction of, 145-47; purpose of, 137-38, 148; roof material, 138-40; size of, 138; structural design for, 141-45; ventilation for, 147-48
Hanson, Holly and Biggs, 113
Haq, Bashirul, 189, 207
Hartman, Bill, 97-98, 113
Hasina, Sheikh, 204
Havers, Clopton, 44
Hayashida, Masami, 72, 73-74

high-tech movement, 156-57
Hines, Gerald, 89, 101
Hodgkison, Robin, 68, 69, 101
Hogan, Michael, 62
Holabird, William, 30
Holmes, Oliver Wendell, 41
Home Insurance Building, 30, 163
Hossain, Mosharraf, 191, 204
Hossain, Mukit, 189
Hua, Lo, 127
Huq, Zeaul, 14, 190, 191, 197, 203-4, 207
Huxtable, Ada Louise, 150

IIT, 31, 35, 53-54, 58, 63-66, 69, 73-75, 77,
    190, 197, 213, 223-24
Inland Steel Building, 34, 92, 93, 157
Inst. of Engineers of Bangladesh, 217
International Style, 31-36, 49, 50, 135, 156, 158
Iqbal, Mohammad, 62, 201
Islamic architecture, 98, 136-37, 140, 148, 179,
    196
Isler, Heinz, 10, 163, 164, 167
Ismail, Dr., 205
Isyumov, Nick, 62, 129
Iyengar, Hal, 9, 62, 78, 84, 86, 98, 102, 113, 152,
    153, 221-22; work on Sears Tower, 123,
    127, 128, 130, 132, 134, 213

Jackson, Reginald, 140
Jenney, William Le Baron, 28, 29, 33, 56, 121,
    135, 153, 163
Jha, Chandra, 101-3, 181, 187, 191, 194, 195,
    202, 218
Jin Mao Building, 222
John Hancock Center, 9, 106-21, 107, 114,
    134-35, 156, 215; award for, 104; as city
    symbol, 118-19, 214; construction of,
    112-13, 116, 159, 170; criticism of,
    17-18; Khan's fondness for, 117, 121;
    structural design for, 25, 26, 69, 106-13,
    213; tubular construction in, 10, 43,
    47, 59, 65, 99, 102; wind tunnel tests for,
    113, 115
Johnson, Gerald, 208

Karim, Aminul, 202, 203, 207, 218
Kenny, Lawrence, 66, 67
Khachaturian, Narbey, 22, 26-27
Khan, Abdur Rahman, 11-13, 14, 17, 18
Khan Chair (Lehigh U.), 202-6
Khan, Fazlur Rahman, 17, 19, 37, 80-83, 209;
    aesthetics of, 10, 36, 155-56, 157-58, 161,
    169; awards and honors of, 50, 104-5,
    121, 148, 149, 207, 233; Bengali political
    involvement, 187-92; Bengali projects of,
    189-90, 196; burial of, 198-99; business
    sense of, 159; career at SOM, 84-104;
    Chicago home of, 186; childhood home
    of, 16; concern for human issues, 105,
    133, 154-55, 160-61, 181-82, 186, 212;
    death of, 15, 194-201; doctoral thesis
    of, 22, 24; early life of, 11-13; early posi-
    tions of, 13-14; early SOM projects,
    33-35; education of, 12-13, 20-27; as
    Fulbright Scholar, 13; haj of, 149, 194-95;
    influence of, 210-24; interests of, 12, 21,
    185-86, 195; lectures and publications
    of, 25-26, 50-51, 56, 57, 79, 104, 191,
    195, 196-97, 213, 230-31; love for family,
    192; love of research, 78-79; love of
    travel, 185; as "master builder," 152-61;

memorial plaque for, 180; as mentor,
    160; personality of, 12-13, 27, 75, 159,
    182-85, 189, 191, 212; philanthropy of,
    191-92; posthumous recognition, 202-8;
    professional affiliations of, 172-79,
    196-97, 234; research and innovations
    of, 56-64, 75-79, 213; Saudi projects
    of, 136-49, 194-95; sculpture honoring,
    214-16; "structural empathy" of, 42;
    student theses supervised by, 54, 58,
    63-66, 69, 73-75, 77, 101, 136, 157, 197,
    234; as teacher, 75, 190-91, 197, 223;
    tributes to, 199-201; tubular concept of,
    9-10, 211
Khan, Hasan, 196
Khan, Khadija Khatun, 12, 17
Khan, Khalil, 197
Khan, Liselotte Turba, 14, 19, 23, 42, 184-85,
    192, 195, 197, 198
Khan, Mahbubur Rahman, 12, 17
Khan, Masuda "Leena," 12, 17, 198
Khan Prize, 202, 206, 217-18
Khan, Yasmin, 14, 19, 117, 192, 195, 198, 218
Khan, Zillur Rahman, 12, 17, 131, 188, 192,
    198, 218
Khondker, Sufian, 218
Kieler, Richard, 188
King Abdul Aziz U. project, 98, 160, 179, 194

Lai, D. Kwong-Wah, 74
Lambert, Phyllis, 64, 115
Latter and Meltzer Building, 97
Lavicka, Bill, 216
Le Corbusier, 31
Lehigh University, 173, 175-76, 202-6
LeMessurier, William J., 47, 63, 156-57
Lim, Bill P., 205
Lin, T. Y., 156
Ling, Dick, 74
load transfer, 25, 59-60, 88-91, 102-3, 108,
    109, 117, 126, 165
Lockett, Al, 116
Logcher, Robert, 113
long-span buildings, 64, 96-97, 139, 165-66
Lucky Goldstar Headquarters, 160, 196

Mahathir, Mohamad, 204
Maillart, Robert, 10, 91, 121, 151, 163, 164-65,
    168, 171
Makkah Univ. See King Abdul Aziz U.
Marinas, Carlos, 214-16
Marine Midland Bank, 60, 91, 165
Marvel, Thomas S., 208
master builders, 33, 150-54, 159
mat design, 89
McMaster, D. M., 115
membrane structures, 32-33, 149
Menn, Christian, 167
Menon, A. G. Krishna, 66
Merchandise Mart Building, 56
Merrill, John, 35, 121
Metcalf, Gordon, 122
Mies van der Rohe, Ludwig, 10-11, 21, 31-32,
    33, 38, 40, 51, 56, 63, 75, 86, 115, 132,
    153, 158, 164, 213
Miró, Joan, 216
Modernism, 31, 33, 49, 156, 158
Mokrin, Zamil A. R., 205
Monadnock Building, 30, 163-64, 165
Morley Builders, 140-41
motion perception research, 115

multi-use buildings, 106-8, 117-18, 223
Munse, William, 25, 117

Nag, Prabhas, 15, 195
Naguib, Hasan, 160
Nair, Shankar, 79
Nat. Academy of Engineering, 105, 178-79
Nat. Commercial Bank, 98
Nat. Life Building, 97
Nayyar, Sarv, 62-63, 197-98
Neo-Rationalism, 49
Nervi, Pier Luigi, 10, 38, 56, 121, 150, 151,
    156, 163-67, 169, 171, 213
Netsch, Walter, 39, 157
New York, high-rise architecture in, 28, 29,
    31, 43, 47, 56
Newmark, N. M., 20
Nicholas, Ralph, 187, 188
Noorani, Sadraddin, 218

Ohio National Bank Building, 99
One Magnificent Mile, 48, 59, 98-99, 99, 101, 196
One Shell Plaza, 26, 47, 78, 88-90, 89, 90, 165
One Shell Square, 49, 95-96, 96, 101
Onterie Center, 47, 59, 69, 98-99, 100, 101-4,
    156, 180, 196
Otto, Frei, 32-33, 149
outrigger trusses, 42-43, 95, 125, 222
Owens-Corning, 145-46
Owings, Nathaniel, 35

Pacific Plaza, 62-63, 94-95, 195
Pahlavian Treasures Building project, 98
Panchal, Mahen, 73, 75
Parikh, Himanshu, 206
Parque Central Towers, 77
Paxton, Joseph, 151
Peck, Ralph, 20, 21-22, 53
Petrie, Wayne, 74, 74, 191, 197
Petronas Towers, 134, 177, 211, 222
Petroski, Henry, 210, 215-16, 218, 224
Picardi, Al, 113
Picasso, Pablo, 97, 97-98
Post-Modernism, 36, 49-51, 153
Post, Nadine, 183
Pran, Peter, 69, 69, 190-91
Purdy, Corydon T., 30

Quinn, Jane, 183, 189, 192, 195, 198, 199

Rahman, M. Mujbur, 13, 190
Randall, F. A., 28-29
Rankine, John, 79
Rice, Peter, 10, 169
rigid-frame construction, 30, 42, 54
Robertson, Leslie, 43, 47, 174, 223
Rodriquez, Alfonso, 69, 70-71, 73
Roebling, John, 151
Root, John Wellborn, 28, 29, 30, 33, 121, 135,
    163-64, 165
Rosenwasser, Robert, 103
Rush, Richard, 147

Saarinen, Eero, 169-70
Salem, Mohammad, 139, 144, 146
Salleh, Muhammad Ridzuan, 202
Santayana, George, 155
Sarkar, Hubert Francis, 217
Sasaki, Mikio, 64, 65, 108
Sattler, Christoph J., 74
Schmidt, Louis, 115

Sears Tower, 9, 117, 121, 122-35, 123, 130, 156, 222; as city symbol, 118, 131, 132-33, 134, 214, 219-20; color of, 132; construction of, 124-26, 130, 159, 170; criticism of, 131-32; management of, 215, 216; minor problems of, 134; records held by, 134; renovation of, 133; roof antennas of, 128; shape of, 124; slenderness ratio of, 44-45; structural design for, 123-24, 126-30, 213; tubular construction in, 10, 43, 48, 59, 73
Second Chicago School, 32-36, 164, 179
Shah, M. H., 113
Sharpe, David, 40, 58, 64, 66, 75, 157, 224
shear lag effect, 45-47, 48, 102, 124-25
shear wall-frame interaction, 8, 40, 56-58, 87, 88, 94, 220
Shedd, Thomas, 20, 21-22
Shlemon, E., 130
Shoai, Faramoz, 74
Sieber, Heinz, 73, 75
Siess, Chester, 19, 22-26, 39, 116, 189, 219
Simon, James, 146
Simonds, O. C., 198
Skidmore, Louis, 35
Skidmore, Owings and Merrill, 13-14, 32, 38-39, 62, 153-60, 164, 182-83, 191, 195; Khan Fellowship, 206; Khan's posthumous influence, 221-22; Khan's projects for, 33-35, 84-104, 106-49, 213-14; management style of, 34, 38, 113
skyscrapers, design of structural systems for, 8-10, 40-51, 54-62, 75-79, 111-12, 168-69, 170-71, 220-24; four ages of, 30-36; market economy and, 33; optimum height of, 76; premium for height in, 40-41, 54-55; skeleton construction of, 30-31, 42; tallest, 121, 134, 177, 222-23; slenderness ratio, 44-45, 58, 103
Smith, James, 22
Snelson, Kenneth, 32-33
Sobek, Werner, 206
Solar Telescope (Kitt Peak), 39, 98
SOM. See Skidmore, Owings and Merrill
Spectrum Arena, 96
steel buildings, 29-30, 34, 42-43, 59, 91-104, 106-35, 159, 170, 221
steel-concrete composite systems, 8, 48-49, 60-61, 95-96, 220, 222
Steinman, David, 220
Stoker, Doug, 62, 128, 130, 184
structural analysis and research, 25, 34-35, 46-47, 52-63, 76-77, 89, 108-13, 117, 221. See also computer analysis
structural design, 8-10, 40-51; balanced concept, 41-42; charts for, 46-47, 57, 58; scale in, 40-41, 54-55, 64
Structural Engineering Research Laboratory (U. of Illinois), 20, 25, 34, 87
Structural Engineers Assoc. of Illinois, 214-16
structural model testing, 33, 34, 39, 87
"Suez Master Plan Study," 98
Sullivan, Louis, 28, 29, 30, 31, 52, 135, 163
superframes, 8, 32, 40, 51, 73, 76-77, 220, 221, 223
Swenson, Alfred, 33, 73, 77
synthetic materials, 75-76

Tagore, Rabindranath, 15, 185-86
Tanaka, Mineo, 73, 74
Telford, Thomas, 151

temperature concerns, 58-59, 87-89, 92, 103, 112, 129-30, 147-48, 154, 160
terrorist deterrence, 59
Tigerman, Stanley, 206
Timby, Elmer, 174
Tishman, John, 159
Torroja, Eduardo, 151, 167
Towery, Earl, 116
Trans Pacific Building, 196
TrizecHahn Office Properties, 133
trussed tubes. See braced tubes
Tsui, Eugene, 223
tube-in-tube, 8, 47, 58, 62, 87, 88, 95. See also framed tubes
tubular systems, 8-10, 35, 76, 220. See also specific types; concept of, 9-10, 39-40, 43-49, 54, 211; goal of, 46; mechanics of, 45-49
Tucker, Jonathan, 43
Two Shell Plaza, 60, 90-91, 91, 165

United Airlines Executive Office, 96
University Kebangsaan Sabah Kampus, 195
University of Dacca (Dhaka), 13
University of Illinois, 13, 20-27, 104. See also Structural Engineering Research Laboratory
urban planning and contexts, 87, 122, 133, 154-55, 158-59, 181-82, 212, 221
U.S. Air Force Academy bridges, 39, 98
U.S. National Bank, 196
U.S. Naval Training Center Dining Hall, 33-34, 39
U.S. Steel, 159

Valle, Gilberto do, 175
Viollet-le-Duc, Eugene, 151, 152-53

Wang, C. K., 20
Washington Monument, 120
Watanabe, Meiji, 74
Weidlinger, Paul, 113
Weyeneth, Eugene E., 81
Wickersheimer, David, 160, 182
Wiesner, Jerome B., 179
Wildermuth, Gordon, 139
Wills Tobacco Processing Plant and Headquarters, 98
wind bracing, 34-35, 40, 42, 63
wind-load resistance, 41, 42, 63, 89, 103, 109-10, 111-12, 113, 115-16, 124-25, 127, 129, 132, 144, 168-69
wind portals, 78-79
Wind Tunnel Laboratory (U. of Western Ontario), 77, 129, 144, 206-7
wind tunnel tests, 113, 115, 128-29, 160
Wiss, John, 115
Woelffer, Michael T., 180
Wolf Point Apparel Mart, 94
World Trade Center (Hong Kong), 98
World Trade Center (New York), 43, 56, 59, 121, 122, 211
World's Columbian Exposition, 30
Wright, Frank Lloyd, 223
Yunus, Muhammed, 192

Zasadney, A., 130
Zia, Khaleda, 204
Zils, John, 62-63, 118, 126-29, 133, 156, 212, 213-14, 226; and Haj Terminal, 139, 141-42, 145-46

DATE DUE